THE BITTERSWEET SCIENCE

THE BITTERSWEET SCIENCE

Racism, Racketeering, and the Political Economy of Boxing

Gerald Horne

INTERNATIONAL PUBLISHERS, New York

Gerald Horne is Moores Professor of History & African American Studies at the University of Houston. He has published more than three dozen books including "White Supremacy Confronted: US Imperialism & Anticommunism vs the Liberation of Southern Africa from Rhodes to Mandela", The Apocalypse of Settler Colonialism: The Roots of Slavery, and White Supremacy and Capitalism in 17th Century North America and the Caribbean.

International Publishers, NY 10011
Copyright © 2021 Gerald Horne

All rights reserved Printed in the United States
THIS PRINTING, 2021

All rights reserved. No part of this book may be reproduced or transmitted in any form or by any means, electronic or mechanical, including photo- copying, recording or any information storage retrieval system, without permission in writing from the publisher, except brief passages for review purposes.

Library of Congress Cataloging-in-Publication Data

Names: Horne, Gerald, author.
Title: The bittersweet science : racism, racketeering and the political economy of boxing / Gerald Horne.
Description: New York : International Publishers, [2021] | Includes index. | Summary: "Based upon exhaustive research in court records, memoirs, the files of the New York State Athletic Commission and related bodies from Nevada to New Jersey - not to mention the gangster venues from garish Las Vegas to venal South Philadelphia, this work tells the untold story of the grimy intersection of racism and racketeering in boxing"— Provided by publisher.
Identifiers: LCCN 2020041929 (print) | LCCN 2020041930 (ebook) | ISBN 9780717808298 (paperback) | ISBN 9780717808304 (mobi) | ISBN 9780717808311 (epub)
Subjects: LCSH: Boxing—History—United States. | Racism in sports—United
States. | Racketeering—United States. | Boxing—political aspects—United States. | Boxers (Sports)—United States.
Classification: LCC GV1125 .H68 2021 (print) | LCC GV1125 (ebook) | DDC 796.8309—dc23
LC record available at https://lccn.loc.gov/2020041929
LC ebook record available at https://lccn.loc.gov/2020041930

ISBN 10: 0-7178-0829-7   ISBN-13 978-07178-0829-8
Typeset by Amnet Systems, Chennai, India

Table of Contents

Abbreviations and Sources .... *vii*

Introduction 3
Chapter 1: Go West, Young Negro! 29
Chapter 2: Go East, Young Negro! 55
Chapter 3: The "Brown Bomber" Soars 81
Chapter 4: Fascism Floored/Black Boxers Rise 107
Chapter 5: Gangster's Paradise 133
Chapter 6: No "White Hope"? 161
Chapter 7: Truman Gibson & Joe Louis: Down for the Count? ... 185
Chapter 8: The Ali Regime 209
Chapter 9: Tales of Don & Bob 239
Chapter 10: The Return of the 'Great White Hope'? 261
Chapter 11: Corruption, Reform—and Beyond 283

Index *309*

Abbreviations and Sources

N.B. Only archival collections and books cited more than once are included in the following lists. As the reader is more likely to search out the full description of the source by the abbreviation provided, this list is in alphabetical order by abbreviation.

Archival collections

AASC-Emory: African Americans and Sports Collection, Emory University, Atlanta, Georgia
ASA-P: Arizona State Archives, Phoenix
Assembly-Pa: Records of the General Assembly, Pennsylvania State Archives, Harrisburg
CaSAC: State Athletic Commission, California State Archives, Sacramento
CHM: Chicago History Museum
DDEPL: Dwight D. Eisenhower Presidential Library, Abilene, Kansas
EIE-NJ: Governor Edward Irving Edwards, New Jersey State Archives, Trenton
Ellison-LC: Ralph Ellison Papers, Library of Congress, Washington, D.C.
Fisher-Pa: John Fisher Papers, Pennsylvania State Archives, Harrisburg
Fleischer-UND: Nat Fleischer Papers, University of Notre Dame, South Bend, Indiana
FlSA-T: Florida State Archives-Tallahassee
FT-UTnK: Fred Thompson Papers, University of Tennessee, Knoxville
Gibson-LC: Truman Gibson Papers, Library of Congress, Washington, D.C.
Gibson Trial File-NAR-Riv: U.S. District Court for the Central Court of California, Central Division (Los Angeles), Criminal Case Files, 27973, RG 21, National Archives and Records Administration-Riverside, California
HKBA: Hank Kaplan Boxing Archive, Brooklyn College, Brooklyn, New York
HSTPL: Harry S. Truman Presidential Library, Independence, Missouri
ISA-A: Indiana State Archives-Indianapolis
Johnson-SCH: Jack Johnson Scrapbook, Schomburg Center, New York Public Library, Harlem, New York City
Kefauver-UTn-K: Estes Kefauver Papers, University of Tennessee-Knoxville
LBJPL: Lyndon B. Johnson Presidential Library, Austin, Texas

Mann-LC: Arthur Mann Papers, Library of Congress, Washington, D.C.
McCarran-NHS-R: Pat McCarran Papers, Nevada Historical Society, Reno
Miller-SCH: Buster Miller Scrapbook, Schomburg Center, New York Public Library, Harlem, New York City
MinnHS-SP: Minnesota Historical Society, St. Paul
MoHS-SL: Missouri Historical Society, St. Louis
Moynihan-LC: Daniel Patrick Moynihan Papers, Library of Congress, Washington, D.C.
NAACP-LC: NAACP Papers, Library of Congress, Washington, D.C.
NAACPDC-Howard: NAACP-DC Papers, Howard University, Washington, D.C.
NAR-DC: National Archives and Records Administration, Washington, D.C.
NAR-Riv: National Archives and Records Administration, Riverside, California
Newfield-UT: Jack Newfield Papers, University of Texas, Austin
NHS-R: Nevada Historical Society, Reno
NJSL-T: New Jersey State Library-Trenton
NVSL-CC: Nevada State Library and Archives, Carson City
NYSAC: New York State Athletic Commission, New York State Archives, Albany
Oddie-UNV-R: Scrapbook of Governor Tasker Oddie, University of Nevada, Reno
Pfefer-UND: Jack Pfefer Collection, University of Notre Dame, South Bend, Indiana
Pinchot-LC: Gifford Pinchot Papers, Library of Congress, Washington, D.C.
Prosecutor's File: Records of U.S. Attorneys, Central Judicial District of California, Los Angeles, Selected Criminal Case Files, NA Identifier 38995426, RG 21, National Archives and Records Administration, Riverside, California
Ross-CHM: Barney Ross Scrapbook, Chicago History Museum
Runyon-NJ: Records of Acting Governor William Runyon, New Jersey State Archives, Trenton
SDHC: San Diego History Center
Sims-LC: William Sowden Sims Papers, Library of Congress, Washington, D.C.
Sirica-LC: John Sirica Papers, Library of Congress, Washington, D.C.
Tunney-UND: Gene Tunney Papers, University of Notre Dame, South Bend, Indiana
UND: University of Notre Dame, South Bend, Indiana
UNV-LV: University of Nevada, Las Vegas
Warren-LC: Earl Warren Papers, Library of Congress-Washington, D.C.
WDCPL: Public Library, Washington, D.C.
Wills-SCH: Harry Wills Scrapbook, Schomburg Center, New York Public Library, Harlem, New York City

Books

Assael, *Murder*: Shaun Assael, *The Murder of Sonny Liston: Las Vegas, Heroin and Heavyweights*, New York: Blue Rider, 2016

Aycock and Scott, *Joe Gans*: Colleen Aycock and Mark Scott, *Joe Gans: A Biography of the First African American World Boxing Champion*, Jefferson, N.C.: McFarland, 2008

Barrow and Munder, *Joe Louis*: Joe Louis Barrow, Jr. and Barbara Munder, *Joe Louis: 50 Years an American Hero*, New York: McGraw Hill, 1988

Benjaminson, *Story of Motown*: Peter Benjaminson, *The Story of Motown*, Los Angeles: Rare Bird, 2018

Benson, *Battling*: Peter Benson, *Battling Siki: A Tale of Ring Fixes, Race and Murder in the 1920s*, Fayetteville: University of Arkansas Press, 2006

Bodner, *When Boxing*: Allen Bodner, *When Boxing Was a Jewish Sport*, Westport, Conn.: Praeger, 1997

Brady, *Boxing Confidential*: Jim Brady, *Boxing Confidential: Power, Corruption and the Richest Prize in Sports*, Lytham, U.K.: Milo, 2002

Cohen, *Mickey Cohen*: Mickey Cohen, *Mickey Cohen, In My Own Words: The Underworld Autobiography of Michael Mickey Cohen, as Told to John Peer Nugent*, London: Prentice Hall, 1975

DeArment, *Gunfighter*: Robert K. DeArment, *Gunfighter in Gotham: Bat Masterson's New York City Years*, Norman: University of Oklahoma Press, 2013

DeStefano, *Top Hoodlum*: Anthony M. DeStefano, *Top Hoodlum: Frank Costello, Prime Minister of the Mafia*, New York: Kensington, 2018

Dettloff, *Ezzard Charles*: William Dettloff, *Ezzard Charles: A Boxing Life*, Jefferson, N.C.: McFarland, 2015

DiGirolamo, *Crying*: Vincent DiGirolamo, *Crying the News: A History of America's Newsboys*, New York: Oxford University Press, 2019

Dundee, *My View*: Angelo Dundee with Bert Randolph, *My View From the Corner: A Life in Boxing*, New York: McGraw Hill, 2008

Duran, *I Am Duran*: Roberto Duran, *I Am Duran: My Autobiography*, New York: Penguin, 2016

Fleischer, *Black Dynamite*: Nat Fleischer, *Black Dynamite: The Story of the Negro in the Prize Ring from 1782 to 1938*, Vol. I, New York: O'Brien, 1938

Fleischer, *50 Years*: Nat Fleischer, *50 Years at Ringside*, New York: Fleet, 1958

Forrett, *Slave*: Jeff Forrett, *Slave Against Slave: Plantation Violence in the Old South*, Baton Rouge: Louisiana State University Press, 2015

Gibson, *Knocking*: Truman Gibson, Jr., *Knocking Down Barriers: My Fight for Black America*, Evanston: Northwestern University Press, 2005

Gonzalez, *Inner Ring*: Rudy Gonzalez, *The Inner Ring*, Miami: RG, 1995

Heller, *In This Corner*: Peter Heller, *"In This Corner…!": Forty World Champions Tell Their Stories*, New York: Simon & Schuster, 1973

Horne, *Black and Brown*: Gerald Horne, *Black and Brown: African Americans and the Mexican Revolution, 1910-1920*, New York: New York University Press, 2005

Horne, *Black and Red*: Gerald Horne, *Black and Red: W.E.B. Du Bois and the Afro-American Response to the Cold War, 1944-1963*, Albany: State University of New York Press, 1986

Horne, *Black Revolutionary*: Gerald Horne, *Black Revolutionary: William Patterson and the Globalization of the African American Freedom Struggle*, Urbana: University of Illinois Press, 2013

Horne, *Counter-Revolution*: Gerald Horne, *The Counter-Revolution of 1776: Slave Resistance and the Origins of the United States of America*, New York: New York University Press, 2014

Horne, *Dawning*: Gerald Horne, *The Dawning of the Apocalypse: The Roots of Slavery, White Supremacy, Settler Colonialism and Capitalism in the Long 16th Century*, New York: Monthly Review Press, 2020

Horne, *Facing*: Gerald Horne, *Facing the Rising Sun: African-Americans, Japan and the Rise of Afro-Asian Solidarity*, New York: New York University Press, 2018

Horne, *Fire*: Gerald Horne, *Fire This Time: The Watts Uprising and the 1960s*, New York: Da Capo, 1997

Horne, *Negro Comrades*: Gerald Horne, *Negro Comrades of the Crown: African Americans and the British Empire Fight the U.S. Before Emancipation*, New York: New York University Press, 2012

Horne, *Race War!*: Gerald Horne, *Race War! White Supremacy and the Japanese Attack on the British Empire*, New York: New York University Press, 2003

Horne, *White Pacific*: Gerald Horne, *The White Pacific: U.S. Imperialism and Black Slavery in the South Seas After the Civil War*, Honolulu: University of Hawaii Press, 2007

Horne, *White Supremacy*: Gerald Horne, *White Supremacy Confronted: U.S. Imperialism and Anticommunism versus the Liberation of Southern Africa, from Rhodes to Mandela*, New York: International, 2018

Kessler, *Millionaire*: Harry Kessler, *The Millionaire Referee*, St. Louis: Harkess, 1982

Kram, *Smokin' Joe*: Mark Kram, Jr., *Smokin' Joe: The Life of Joe Frazier*, New York: HarperCollins, 2018

Lardner, *White Hopes*: John Lardner, *White Hopes and Other Tigers*, Philadelphia: Lippincott, 1951

Liebling, *Sweet Science and Other*: A.J. Liebling, *The Sweet Science and Other Writings*, New York: Library of America, 2009

Liebling, *Sweet Science: Boxing*: A.J. Liebling, *The Sweet Science: Boxing and the Boxiana*, New York: Viking, 1956

Lindsay, *Boxing*: Andrew Lindsay, *Boxing in Black and White: A Statistical Study of Race in the Ring, 1949-1983*, Jefferson, N.C.: McFarland, 2004

Lucas, *Original Gangster*: Frank Lucas with Aliya S. King, *Original Gangster: The Real Life Story of One of America's Most Notorious Drug Lords*, New York: St. Martin's, 2010

Mailer, *Fight*: Norman Mailer, *The Fight*, Boston: Little Brown, 1975

Mokhtefi, *Algiers*: Elaine Mokhtefi, *Algiers, Third World Capital: Freedom Fighters, Revolutionaries, Black Panthers*, London: Verso, 2018

Moore, *I Fight*: Louis Moore, *I Fight for a Living: Boxing and the Battle for Black Manhood*, Urbana: University of Illinois Press, 2017

Moyle, *Sam Langford*: Clay Moyle, *Sam Langford: Boxing's Greatest Uncrowned Champion*, Bennett & Hastings, 2006

Nagler, *James Norris*: Barney Nagler, *James Norris and the Decline of Boxing*, Indianapolis: Bobbs Merrill, 1964

Nurhussein, *Black Land*: Nadia Nurhussein, *Black Land: Imperial Ethiopianism and African America*, Princeton: Princeton University Press, 2019

Oates, *On Boxing*: Joyce Carol Oates, *On Boxing*, New York: Ecco, 2006

Obi, *Fighting for Honor*: T.J. Desch Obi, *Fighting for Honor: The History of African Martial Art Traditions in the Atlantic World*, Columbia: University of South Carolina Press, 2008

Pacheco, *Tales*: Ferdie Pacheco, *Tales from the 5th Street Gym: Ali, the Dundees and Miami's Golden Age of Boxing*, Tallahassee: University Press of Florida, 2010

Petersen, *Gentleman Bruiser*: Bob Petersen, *Gentleman Bruiser: A Life of the Boxer, Peter Jackson*, Sydney: Croydon, 2005

Reed, *Complete Muhammad Ali*: Ishmael Reed, *The Complete Muhammad Ali*, Montreal: Baraka, 2015

Rempel, *Gambler*: William C. Rempel, *The Gambler: How Penniless Dropout Kirk Kerkorian Became the Greatest Dealmaker in Capitalist History*, New York: Morrow, 2018

Rizzo, *Gangsters*: Michael F. Rizzo, *Gangsters and Organized Crime in Buffalo: History, Hits, and Headquarters*, Charleston: History Press, 2012

Rodriguez, *Regulation*: Robert Rodriguez, *The Regulation of Boxing: A History and Comparative Analysis of Policies Among American States*, Jefferson, N.C.: McFarland, 2009

Shropshire, *Being Sugar Ray*: Kenneth Shropshire, *Being Sugar Ray: The Life of Sugar Ray Robinson, America's Greatest Boxer and First Celebrity Athlete*, New York: Basic, 2007

Smith, *No Way*: Andrew R.M. Smith, *No Way But to Fight: George Foreman and the Business of Boxing*, Austin: University of Texas Press, 2020

Swanson, *Strenuous Life*: Ryan Swanson, *The Strenuous Life: Theodore Roosevelt and the Making of the American Athlete*, New York: Diversion, 2019

Tosches, *The Devil*: Nick Tosches, *The Devil and Sonny Liston*, Boston: Little Brown, 2000

Tunney, *A Man Must Fight*: Gene Tunney, *A Man Must Fight*, Boston: Houghton Mifflin, 1932

THE BITTERSWEET SCIENCE

Introduction

The boxer known as Beau Jack developed his skill as a fighter as a result of a brutal practice stemming from slavery in his native Georgia. Born in 1921, he became lightweight champion in no small measure because of his skilled participation in "battle royals" in Augusta, where for the enjoyment of affluent Euro-American members of the famed local golf club, he and other low-wage caddies and shoeshiners were blindfolded in a boxing ring and were compelled to slug one another until there was only one left. "Beau always won," said Bowman Milligan, who often witnessed these slugfests.[1] "Beau" was no "tomato can" or easily beaten opponent; as of 1955 he was adjudged to be "the greatest non-heavyweight draw in boxing history."[2]

Jack, born as Sidney Walker, and his fellow African-American combatants emerged from a culture that placed a premium on the ability to fight back. Interestingly, as the African slave trade accelerated in what was to become one of its major nodes—Madagascar—a vicious form of combat arose involving a violent dance or "fagnorolahy," which proceeds until a fighter is knocked

---

1. Clipping, no date, Odds and Ends on Boxing, Volume 10, University of Notre Dame–South Bend, Indiana (abbrev. UND). Joe Gans, an illustrious Negro boxer of the early 20th century, was also familiar with the "battle royal." His biographers painted a portrait of "up to ten young blacks... thrown into a ring (often blindfolded) and made to beat each other senseless until one remained standing"; purportedly, it was "outlawed in the Roman Empire"—"where feeding Christians to the lions was considered appropriate"—because of its abject brutality. See Colleen Aycock and Mark Scott, *Joe Gans: A Biography of the First African American World Boxing Champion*, Jefferson, N.C.: McFarland, 2008 (abbrev. Aycock and Scott, *Joe Gans*). See also Minutes, 6 December 1911, A1372-77, of New York State Athletic Commission, New York State Archives-Albany (abbrev. *NYSAC*): "Letter was received protesting vigorously against exhibitions known as 'battle royal' bouts...decided to forbid and abolish all such exhibitions...." But in the same collection, see Minutes, 3 January 1912: "ask permission to hold a battle royal at the Buffalo Foundrymen...."

2. *Argosy*, February 1955, Odds and Ending on Boxing, Vol. 35, UND.

out or the referee identifies a winner. Bouts are a blur of fists, elbows, knees and feet with bare knuckles crumpling bodies. Not limited to young men, increasingly young women have taken part as both combatants and managers; this tradition has spread to other slave trade nodes, such as the southeast coast of Africa, the Comoros Islands, Reunion, the Seychelles and Mauritius.[3] Across the continent, a similar process unfolded, with the development of capoeira, a form of choreographed combat with roots in Angola and Brazil.[4] Furthermore, stretching back centuries, hand-to-hand combat had attained a kind of popularity in vast regions of Africa itself.[5]

U.S. plantation slavery was notorious for the arranging of fighting contests among enslaved men in particular, where masculinity was honed.[6] The late 18th-century African writer Olaudah Equiano and his 19th-century counterpart, Frederick Douglass, both noticed the existence of fisticuffs on plantations, unsurprising given the brutal existence of exploitation and the supposition that fistic skill could win the admiration of women—relatives and admirers alike.[7] Slaveholders avidly promoted fighting among the enslaved, not only as an entertainment for themselves but also as a way to encourage division and rancor among captives. Hence, these fighters developed tactics, e.g., leg wrapping and head butting.[8]

Of course, women of African descent too were forced by circumstance to develop their own ability in self-defense.[9] In the 20th century, Gloria Thompson, referred to crudely as the "Chick Champ

---

3. *New York Times*, 5 November 2018.

4. Nestor Capoeira, *The Little Capoeira Book*, Berkeley: North Atlantic, 1995.

5. John V. Grombach, *The Saga of the Fist: The 9000 Year Story of Boxing*, New York: Barnes, 1977, 10.

6. Sergio Lussana, "To See Who was Best on the Plantation: Enslaved Fighting Contests and Masculinity in the Antebellum Plantation South," *Journal of Southern History*, 76 (No. 4, November 2010), 901-922. For more on assaults on Negro masculinity, see Gerald Horne, *Fire This Time: The Watts Uprising and the 1960s*, New York: Da Capo, 1997 (abbrev. Horne, *Fire*), 384.

7. T.J. Desch Obi, *Fighting for Honor: The History of African Martial Art Traditions in the Atlantic World*, Columbia: University of South Carolina Press, 2008 (abbrev. Obi, *Fighting for Honor*), 79, 95-96.

8. Jeff Forrett, *Slave Against Slave: Plantation Violence in the Old South*, Baton Rouge: Louisiana State University Press, 2015 (abbrev. Forrett: *Slave*), 167, 294.

9. Wendy Rouse, *Her Own Hero: The Origins of the Women's Self-Defense Movement*, New York: New York University Press, 2017.

of the World," was said to prefer men to women as opponents. She boasted, "I'll take on any man under 140 pounds...in the ring."[10]

Tellingly, the boxer formerly known as Cassius Marcellus Clay—later Muhammad Ali[11]—carries the name of the 19th-century Kentucky personality who bequeathed to the thumper his "slave" name. The elder Clay was not above engaging in duels and fights, and expressed respect for an enslaved woman who killed her "master"—part of his overall respect for the fighting fortitude of Africans, a trait to which he was an eyewitness.[12] In short, as his biographer put it, the elder Clay was a "fighting man," unsurprising given the culture of enslavement[13]—a culture that has bequeathed to the U.S. a raft of fighting metaphors.[14]

Actually, a factor that needs to be considered in contemplating both the compelled retreats of slavery and Jim Crow alike, is the often neglected point that the Africans were often talented fighters, quite willing to break the chains of iniquity—forcefully. It was hardly inevitable that white supremacy would triumph south of the Canadian border, and there was a competing fear that an alliance of Negroes, Indigenes, and a formidable foreign power might emerge triumphant.[15]

Truman Gibson, the highly educated Negro who somehow worked alongside mobsters in controlling boxing in the 1950s—the sportswriter Wendell Smith commented wondrously that he controlled the

---

10. Undated report on Gloria Thompson, Odds and Ends on Boxing, Vol. 15, UND.

11. See, e.g., Thomas Hauser, *Muhammad Ali: His Life and Times*, New York: Simon & Schuster, 1992; David Remnick, *King of the World: Muhammad Ali and the Rise of an American Hero*, New York: Random House, 1998; Muhammad Ali, *The Greatest, My Own Story*, New York: Ballantine, 1976. Cf. Randy Roberts, *Blood Brothers: The Fatal Friendship Between Muhammad Ali and Malcolm X*, New York: Basic, 2016.

12. C.M. Clay, *The Life of Cassius Marcellus Clay. Memoirs, Writings, Vol. I*, Cincinnati: Brennan, 1886.

13. H. Edward Richardson, *Cassius Marcellus Clay: Firebrand of Freedom*, Lexington: University Press of Kentucky, 1976, 36.

14. A partial list would include, e.g., low blow; body blow; down for the count; rope-a-dope; knockout blow; take off the gloves; pulling punches; bareknuckle brawl; roll with the punches; counterpunch; beat to the punch; throw in the towel, etc.

15. Gerald Horne, *Negro Comrades of the Crown: African Americans and the British Empire Fight the U.S. Before Emancipation*, New York: New York University Press, 2012 (abbrev. Horne, *Negro Comrades*).

"greatest fistic empire in history"[16]—argued subsequently that the sport being televised, often featuring men of ebony hue battering those not so endowed, was instrumental in the erosion of U.S. apartheid.[17] Assuredly, these repetitive images were inconsistent with the reigning philosophy of Negro submissiveness and subordination, not to mention that people like Gibson were in a position to garner lush fees, part of which could be siphoned into anti-Jim Crow measures and movements. Gibson was at the tip of the spear as Negroes—ably assisted by global allies—mounted their forceful challenge to Jim Crow. And it was not only boxing that was in play. Just after Gibson and Joe Louis partnered to seize a large size of the pugilistic pie, a U.S. Senate found that vis-à-vis "gambling activities in Chester [Pennsylvania],…the overall picture…is that the Jews and Italians are out to force the Negro policy operators into line," with the latter being led by "Julius Belcher, an active Negro Commie, during the heyday of the Sun Ship's Local Number 2" but who was "now a CPA [Certified Public Accountant]; the first Negro CPA in Pennsylvania."[18] But by then Belcher's comrades were compelled to stand back, opening the door for another force that could confront racketeers: the Fruit of Islam and the Nation of Islam which allied with Muhammad Ali.

On the other hand, 20th-century heavyweight Joe Frazier, whose name will ever be linked with that of Ali, given their punishing battles, represents, in a sad microcosm, the political economy of the sport. Born in 1944 in the former citadel of slavery that was Beaufort, South Carolina, his father lost his left arm, so the young Frazier dropped out of school in the 6th grade to help his family. After watching the "Brown Bomber," heavyweight champion Joe Louis, in action, he decided that he wanted to be a boxer. He filled a burlap sack with bricks, moss, corncobs and rags, hung it from a tree and pounded it daily for seven years. The exercise helped to form what became a devastating left hook used to pulverizing effect on opponents. Migrating to Philadelphia, Frazier worked in a slaughterhouse and would train by hitting sides of beef during his lunch

---

16. *Pittsburgh Courier*, 26 May 1951, Box 2, Truman Gibson Papers, Library of Congress, Washington, D.C. (abbrev. Gibson-LC).

17. Truman Gibson, Jr., *Knocking Down Barriers: My Fight for Black America*, Evanston: Northwestern University Press, 2005 (abbrev. Gibson, *Knocking*), 274.

18. J.N. McCormick to H.G. Robinson, 27 October 1950, Box 40, ad 12 and 13 (Memoranda and Meetings), in Records of Special Committee to Investigate Organized Crime in Interstate Commerce, CR9 [Rackets], CR10 [Juvenile Delinquency], U.S. Senate, 81st-82nd Congress, National Archives and Records Administration, Washington, D.C. (abbrev. NAR-DC).

break and after work.[19] So trained, he began a steady march to the pinnacle of the sport, generating millions of dollars in revenue in the process—before entering the grave in 2011 virtually penniless.[20]

* * *

African Americans were not the sole U.S. nationals forced to develop martial ability. Before the post-1945 dissipation of the crudest bigotry, a significant percentage of boxers were Jewish, and they too were driven to fight because of the harsh realities they faced. Jackie Fields, born in 1908, who grew up in a Jewish neighborhood in Chicago, charged that "being in the ghetto you had to fight."[21] Maxie Spoon, a 150-pound southpaw and the son of Russian-Jewish immigrants, started boxing in order to protect himself: "in those days," said this man, born in 1920, "every neighborhood had its gangs. If you walked into the wrong neighborhood, you'd get whacked."[22] One analyst said of Benny Leonard, the famed pugilist who did not lose a prizefight between 1912 and 1932, excepting a 1922 disqualification, that "he has done more to conquer anti-Semitism than a thousand textbooks"; Leonard himself argued that "you had to fight or stay in the house when the Italian and Irish kids came through."[23] In a process not unlike that which ensnared African Americans, Jewish Americans too were forced to run a toughening gauntlet.[24] (Intriguingly enough, just as enslaved Africans were forced to fight for the enjoyment of their captors, at the Auschwitz death camp, Salomo Arouch, a champion boxer of Greek Jewish ancestry, was forced to fight for the entertainment of his captors.)[25]

---

19. Funeral Program for Joe Frazier, 14 November 2011, African American and Sports Collection, Emory University, Atlanta, Georgia (abbrev. AASC-Emory).

20. Mark Kram, Jr., *Smokin' Joe: The Life of Joe Frazier*, New York: HarperCollins, 2018 (abbrev. Kram, *Smokin' Joe*), 8.

21. Questionnaire/Jackie Fields, no date, Box 28, Sub Group IX, Series 2, Hank Kaplan Boxing Archive, Brooklyn College, Brooklyn, New York (abbrev. HKBA).

22. Questionnaire/Maxie Spoon, no date, Box 24, Sub Group IX, Series 2, HKBA.

23. Questionnaire/Benny Leonard, no date, Box 28, Sub Group IX, Series 2, HKBA.

24. Rich Cohen, *Tough Jews*, New York: Simon & Schuster, 1988.

25. *New York Times*, 3 May 2009. See also Stanley Elkin, *Slavery: A Problem in American Institutional and Intellectual Life*, Chicago: University of Chicago Press, 1959.

African Americans were thus not the only group able to draw upon a historic reservoir of combativeness. Chinese Americans, likewise, not only had to confront bigotry in their homeland but could draw upon a reservoir of formal athletic contests that arose as early as 3000 BCE.[26]

Boxing as a sport was able to evade illegality—at least for a while—when it was popularized by Theodore Roosevelt. After he became president, his Harvard classmates did not remember much about him—except for his boxing exploits—and by 1904, he was boxing in the White House. But soon even TR was seemingly disdaining the sport, this after the rise of Jack Johnson, the bruising Negro heavyweight from Galveston, Texas, whose spectacular career contributed to a pressing crisis for white supremacy and male supremacy alike. For when Johnson rose, the president abruptly endorsed bans on boxing and especially films of same.[27] The analyst John Lardner may not be far wrong in arguing that the burly Johnson's "impact on popular feeling was sharper than William H. Taft's," just as his bellicose successor, Jack Dempsey, "overshadowed Calvin Coolidge."[28]

The roly-poly political boss—meaning TR—was responding to a gathering cry, enunciated as early as 1895 by Manhattan journalist Charles Dana, who railed against the "menace confronting the Caucasian race" presented by a proliferation of Negro boxers who, he believed, were a rising tide threatening to submerge white supremacy.[29] Such maladjusted thinking led to the search for a "White Hope," a heavyweight (in particular) who could initially defeat Jack Johnson, though their quest continued for a good deal of the 20th century. When the brawny Galvestonian bested Jim Jeffries in Reno in 1910, this was not just an expression of the sport moving westward toward a presumed racial fluidity in the west—a nostrum that did not prevent the scores of beatings and killings across racial

---

26. Stephen Acunto, *Champions' Boxing Guide*, no date, Box II: 863, Daniel Patrick Moynihan Papers, Library of Congress, Washington, D.C. (abbrev. Moynihan-LC).

27. Ryan Swanson, *The Strenuous Life: Theodore Roosevelt and the Making of the American Athlete*, New York: Diversion, 2019 (abbrev. Swanson, *Strenuous Life*), 61, 140, 248.

28. John Lardner, *White Hopes and Other Tigers*, Philadelphia: Lippincott, 1951 (abbrev. Lardner, *White Hopes*), 13.

29. Nat Fleischer, *Black Dynamite: The Story of the Negro in the Prize Ring from 1782 to 1938, Vol. I*, New York: O'Brien, 1938 (abbrev. Fleischer, *Black Dynamite*), 6.

lines that followed rapidly.³⁰ The absurdity of the quest was exposed when reportedly "the Japanese put forward a 'Brown Hope'" while "the Chinese put forward a 'Yellow Hope'" and a "Navajo Indian" also volunteered, all revealing that what was at stake, as much as anything else, was vanquishing the Negro, a mandate in a republic where this was a dire priority. Supposedly an "International White Hope Association" was formed, while mass ecstasy erupted among these devotees when amidst the mass bloodletting of World War I, Johnson was defeated in Havana by Jess Willard.³¹ By the late 20th century, boxer Jerry Quarry continued to insist that "Boxing needs a white champion to replace Cassius Clay," a barbed reference to the boxer then known as Muhammad Ali, who had stirred controversy by his antiwar stance, not to mention his Islamic religiosity.³²

Consequently, Negroes were incentivized to deny their actual ancestry, contributing to self-loathing, which was continuing retribution for having the gumption to be perceived as opposing the revolt against British rule that created the republic,³³ then the slaveholders' republic that resulted,³⁴ and the Jim Crow regime that quickly followed.³⁵ Hence it was, in 1939, that the California Athletic Commission took note of a report that indicated that in the Golden State "Filipinos and other dark skinned races are readily booked" for prizefights "but Negro boxers—My God, NO!" So, sly Negroes masqueraded: "Take the matter of Santiago Zorilla," a reputed "San Blas Indian, who was actually Negro [and] a fighter by the name of Gonzales, supposedly Mexican from El Paso but who was actually a Negro." At certain venues, there was "no evidence of any sort of discrimination except against Negroes;" thus "Mexican fighters have fought…time and again and many times have been the mainstay" of bookings.³⁶

---

30. Andrew Lindsay, *Boxing in Black and White: A Statistical Study of Race in the Ring, 1949-1983*, Jefferson, N.C.: McFarland, 2004 (Lindsay, *Boxing*), 10, 14.

31. Arly Allen, *Jess Willard: Heavyweight Champion of the World (1915-1919)*, Jefferson, N.C.: McFarland, 2017, 12, 32.

32. Kram, *Smokin' Joe*, 108.

33. Gerald Horne, *The Counter-Revolution of 1776: Slave Resistance and the Origins of the United States of America*, New York: New York University Press, 2014 (abbrev. Horne, *Counter-Revolution*).

34. Horne, *Negro Comrades*.

35. Gerald Horne, *Black Revolutionary: William Patterson and the Globalization of the African American Freedom Struggle*, Urbana: University of Illinois Press, 2013 (abbrev. Horne, *Black Revolutionary*).

36. *People's World*, 12 October 1939, F2219, Records of State Athletic Commission, California State Archives, Sacramento (abbrev. CaSAC).

(For reasons that remain unclear, there was a wrinkle: Negroes could be booked for fights taking place outside, but not in indoor arenas. Even a contemporaneous journalist could not figure out "the little intricacies of [the] mean little minds" of arena management.[37])

* * *

Thus, early on, when the well-known sociologist Robert Park (born in 1864), referred to Negroes—actually Negro men—as the "lady of the races,"[38] this dovetailed with pre-existing gendered theories about the purported reasons for mass enslavement, e.g., docility, and reassured those nervous about being in the midst of powerful men with two-fisted dynamism. Supposedly, the Negro—especially, in a gendered confabulation, the men—had a "yellow streak," i.e., they were cowards, afraid to fight, soft not hard, unworthy men, all part of their overall worthlessness. Paradoxically, this permeating mythos may have provided Negro sportsmen with even more impetus to prevail, contributing to their boxing successes.[39] (Moreover, this misconception often was accompanied by a contradictory companion, that the Negro man was a "brute," maybe a "beast," and thus had to be controlled by any means necessary. As the decades passed and Negroes gained more rights, this latter misconception became ever more useful.)

"Manliness" was part of this cockeyed equation, and unfortunately—but comprehensibly—homophobia was not absent from boxing. Typically, Roberto Duran repeatedly described his opponent in a multi-million dollar fight, "Sugar" Ray Leonard, as a *"maricón"* or "faggot."[40] When Benny Paret reportedly uttered similar slurs toward Emile Griffith, his opponent in 1962, the latter methodically executed him in the ring.[41]

---

37. *People's World*, 2 November 1939, F2219, CaSAC.

38. Jonathan Scott Holloway, *Confronting the Veil: Abram Harris, Jr., E. Franklin Frazier and Ralph Bunche, 1919-1941*, Chapel Hill: University of North Carolina Press, 2002, 136.

39. It is evident that a forcibly affixed conception of masculinity may have unleashed consequences yet to be grasped fully. See Anthony Stafford, *Homophobia in the Black Church: How Faith, Politics and Fear Divide the Black Community*, Santa Barbara: Praeger, 2013.

40. Roberto Duran, *I Am Duran: My Autobiography*, New York: Penguin, 2016 (abbrev. Duran, *I Am Duran*), 113.

41. *Guardian*, [London], 10 September 2015. See also *Gay City News* [Manhattan], 30 August-12 September 2018. The complicity of the state should not be ignored in assessing this tragedy. A report from the Federal Bureau

However, soon this curious thesis of Negro submissiveness and "softness" was co-existing uneasily with yet another oddity, the idea put forward by Nat Fleischer, an alleged boxing expert, who argued that Negroes—especially the men—were "less sensible to pain than most members of the more highly civilized white races." By then, it was Fleischer who was "sensible," to the point that there were a reported "1800 dark skinned boys" who were "participants in professional boxing in America in 1937," though the "total number of professional boxers does not exceed 8000"; however, some of the rising stars—Joe Louis, Henry Armstrong and John Lewis, for example—happened to be African American. This painful awareness of the influx of talented Negro boxers into the sport likely motivated his attempt to downplay the punishment in the ring they were able to absorb. His inexpertness in the etiology of pain notwithstanding, Fleischer had a point when he said, "my research has convinced me that not only was the ebony skinned athlete the founder of boxing in America but that without his presence in England, the sport never would have made the headway it did over there."[42]

The overriding bellicosity of U.S. culture also played a role in reproducing a culture of boxing. By 1915, Lieutenant Colonel Van C. Lucas, commander of the 22nd Corps of Engineers, asserted that boxing aided in "making of a good soldier" in that it "develops courage, self reliance, morality and physical condition."[43] As World War I was lurching to an inglorious close, Admiral William Sowden Sims was informed that "large numbers of soldiers and sailors—estimated at 20,000—have avowed their determination to adopt boxing for a livelihood on their return to civil life." Adam Empie of the Army, Navy and Civilian Board of Boxing Control in New York, found this to be an "appalling fact, as the fate of a large majority of professional boxers is to drift into a life of idleness."[44] Admiral Sims begged to differ. "Since my stay here in England of nearly two years," he said

---

of Investigation in 1968 identified Griffith as a "well known faggot" who frequented gay bars in Manhattan. See also Donald McRae, *A Man's World: The Double Life of Emile Griffith*, New York: Simon & Schuster, 2015. See also Rudy Gonzalez, *The Inner Ring*, Miami: RG, 1995 (abbrev. Gonzalez, *Inner Ring*), 7: Boxer Héctor Camacho "took a lot of shit from his compadres for being such a 'pretty boy.'"

42. Nat Fleischer, *Black Dynamite*, 4, 86.
43. Minutes, 13 December 1915, NYSAC.
44. Adam Empie to Admiral Sims, 13 February 1919, Box 50, William Sowden Sims Papers, Library of Congress, Washington, D.C. (abbrev. Sims-LC).

knowingly, "I have been particularly struck with the much higher plane that boxing and such like sports have attained in this country. They are patronized by many of the best people," and not just the hoi polloi, the impression often rendered stateside. It was "desirable," he concluded, that "similar conditions should be brought about in America," akin to what he experienced on the east bank of the Atlantic.[45] If, as was often said, the Battle of Waterloo was won on the "playing fields of Eton," it simply made good sense for the U.S., poised to surpass its former colonial master, to seek to emulate her, particularly given the resonance uniting pugilism and war-making.

Still, U.S. culture had difficulty in adjusting this "Etonian" approach to existing cultural norms, in that Jim Crow hampered the ability of certain boxers to polish their craft. Harry Wills, a top Negro heavyweight, had difficulty in convincing Euro-Americans to meet him in the ring, so he wound up battling fellow Negro Sam Langford an astonishing 22 times.[46] On 22 May 1923, a Wills representative was in a familiar position: conferring with the State Athletic Commission in Manhattan, "embodying protest," as the summary of the meeting suggested, "on the absence of real action in the plan for a proposed [fight] between [heavyweight] champion Jack Dempsey and Harry Wills."[47] A year earlier, on 13 June 1922, the same panel had met in Manhattan, also to hear a plaintive plea from representatives of the "bantam weight Danny Edwards" who, according to the record of this gathering, was "the best boy [meaning Negro] at his weight in this country but that he could get no chance to box for the championship because of the [adverse] feeling that existed against mixed bouts." Confirming the obvious, "there was discrimination being shown against the race of colored people." But the authorities seemed to object to the attempt to "force an issue on this one point" by dint of "partisan politics"; this conclusion was reached though Edwards's designees "were rather above the average colored people intellectually."[48] Evidence to the contrary notwithstanding, the authorities in the Empire State concluded with a flourish that "this Commission has done more for the colored people in various ways

---

45. William Sims to Army, Navy and Civilian Board of Boxing Control, 4 April 1919, Box 50, Sims-LC.

46. *St. Louis Globe Democrat*, 22 December 1958, Harry Wills Scrapbook, Schomburg Center, New York Public Library, Harlem, New York City (abbrev. Wills-SCH).

47. Minutes, 22 May 1923, NYSAC.

48. Minutes, 13 June 1922, NYSAC.

than has [ever been] done by boxing interests in this State."[49] (Given the dreadful records of their peers, the SAC may have had a point.)

South of the Mason-Dixon Line, there was little pretense of feigning anti-racism. In New Orleans, for example, there were the Docusen brothers—boxers including Bernard, a real puncher who once gave the eminent "Sugar" Ray Robinson a startling contest—who battled for years in court to show their ancestry was European and Filipino, not Negro, which was whispered. They were capitulating to Jim Crow laws that banned prizefights between Euro-Americans and African-Americans. So, like Jack Johnson previously, they fought in the west of the U.S.—congruent with the rise of Nevada—before seeking matches in the Pelican State.[50]

Ultimately—in a maneuver redolent of the corruption engendered by Jim Crow—the California Athletic Commission was stunned to ascertain that champion James Braddock, the Irish-American hero, agreed to fight Joe Louis on the basis that 10% of the latter's earnings thereafter be kicked back to Braddock and his manager.[51] Louis had to tread an obstacle-strewn path in his rise to the top of the sport: Since Jack Johnson's broad smiles after vanquishing various Euro-American foes were interpreted widely as a troubling sign of "Black Supremacy," Louis was instructed sternly to "keep a solemn expression in front of the cameras."[52] But even that concession in the hothouse climate that was racism could be easily interpreted as a funereal sign of white supremacy's imminent burial.

* * *

One of the reasons that so many boxers ended up penniless—even those like Joe Frazier who had generated gargantuan profits at the box office—was because the sport was dominated by mobsters and

---

49. Minutes, 5 September 1922, NYSAC.

50. Lloyd Glaudi, "New Orleans Puts Up Its 'Dukes,'" no date, Odds and Ends on Boxing, Vol. 19, UND. Henry Lanauze, City Recorder of Births, Deaths and Marriages for 64 years preceding his death in 1940, had ruled that "all Filipinos were Negros," compromising the boxers' case, though investigation revealed that the "great grandfather of Mrs. Viola Lytel Docusen, mother of the boxers, was Col. Jean Baptiste du Mole, commander of one of the Mississippi River forts for the Confederate army."

51. Special Meeting of State Athletic Commission, 17 January 1941, F2219, CaSAC.

52. Joe Louis Barrow, Jr. and Barbara Munder, *Joe Louis: 50 Years an American Hero*, New York: McGraw Hill, 1988 (abbrev. Barrow and Munder, *Joe Louis*), 43.

other characters of ill repute.[53] Ironically, as boxers like Joe Louis came to dominate boxing as the first half of the 20th century began to recede, this created an opening for the arrival on the scene of figures like Truman Gibson—and subsequently Don King beginning in the 1970s—who played a premier role in matchmaking. Gibson, generally viewed as a handsome man, with toffee brown complexion, *de rigueur* straight black hair, a slender nose and a sparsely drawn mouth, was slim and not too tall—in contrast with his bosses, Arthur Wirtz, a beefy man well over 200 pounds and more than six feet tall, and Jim Norris, about the same size. Gibson, said Norris, was "my number one man," which meant that Gibson was his liaison with the gangsters—such as "Blinky" Palermo and "Mr. Gray," or Frank Carbo[54]—with whom he was to stand trial and who often controlled the boxers themselves. It was a deviation from Jim Crow to have one like Gibson in such a key role in such a profitable sport: Ironically, he paved the way for the appearance of Don King, as the post-Jim Crow era allowed African Americans to operate corruptly without as many Euro-Americans acting effectively as puppeteers. Nevertheless, there was not a clean break between the eras symbolized by Gibson, then King, in that the latter—according to an inquiring journalist—"remained indebted to Palermo for years."[55]

Still, as to be expected, though much was made of King's sordid ties, his chief competitor, Bob Arum, often escaped similar attention. (Like King, he too was a boxing promoter, meaning he was akin to a movie producer: assembling all the elements for a contest was his mission, including arranging financing, securing the venue, publicizing the bout, etc.) For whatever reason, Arum was not viewed as negatively in the mainstream press as King—though his spouse candidly confessed all manner of connections to the likes of Tony Spilotro, a key vector of corruption in Las Vegas, and others such as Gus Greenbaum, with "mob associations…. I remember when Gus

---

53. From a structural viewpoint, mobsters need to be seen in a class context. See, e.g., Karl Marx, *The 18th Brumaire of Louis Bonaparte*, New York: International, 1968, 75: Here the lumpen are described as "vagabonds, discharged soldiers, discharged jailbirds, escaped galley slaves, swindlers, mountebanks…pickpockets, tricksters, gamblers…[procurers]…brothel keepers…." See also Horne, *Fire*: Here it is argued that as working-class movements declined, like a seesaw, lumpen movements—or organized crime families—increased in importance.

54. Barney Nagler, *James Norris and the Decline of Boxing*, Indianapolis: Bobbs Merrill, 1964 (abbrev. Nagler, *James Norris*), 4343, 62, 79.

55. *New York Post*, 26 May 1996, Box 54, Jack Newfield Papers, University of Texas, Austin (abbrev. Newfield-UT).

Greenbaum and his wife were killed," she recalled, "my father was so upset." She "remember[ed]" übergangster Moe Dalitz "very well" and was acquainted with a point that many had forgotten: The son of key mobster Lew Ferrell perished in the airplane crash that killed heavyweight champion, Rocky Marciano.[56]

For as the former boxer—and subsequent mobster—Mickey Cohen put it, "the Boxing World and the Racket World were almost one and the same. Most boxers were owned [sic] by rackets' people. And at one time six of the boxing titles," said this diminutive thug, born in 1913, "belonged to the guys in the so-called Racket World."[57]

This was a long-term trend. It was in 1922 that the New York State Athletic Commission railed against the "cheap gamblers who congregate around the [boxing] clubs" and demanded that they be "refuse[d] admission"; reference was made to the "wise gang" and "the Jimmy Kelly gang" as being particularly obnoxious.[58] Complicating the ability to ferret out the surplus of misdeeds in boxing was the fact that the U.S. press, the supposed watchdog, was often a toothless terrier when it came to monitoring the sport. Gene Tunney, a champion boxer, complained that he had "engaged two active newspaper men with daily columns to each of whom I agreed to pay five percent of my purses," and "in return for this they gave me sufficient mention in their columns to keep my name before the public and the big promoters." It was "customary to make monetary gifts to certain newspaper men after important matches."[59] Decades later, Muhammad Ali's trainer, Angelo Dundee, confirmed that sportswriters cooperated with the gray eminence of boxing, Frankie Carbo, underworld maven: "they would find fat envelopes stuffed with pictures of dead presidents," meaning U.S. currency. Nat Fleischer, the chronicler of the sport as a result of his leading the journalistic bible of the sports, was also accused by Dundee of being in the pocket of the mob, calling into question the very integrity of

---

56. Interview with Lovee Arum, 1 November 2016, University of Nevada, Las Vegas (abbrev. UNV-LV). See also Shaun Assael, *The Murder of Sonny Liston: Las Vegas, Heroin and Heavyweights*, New York: Blue Rider, 2016 (abbrev. Assael, *Murder*): Spilotro, says the author, was a "pathological killer" who "made the seventies the bloodiest decade on record when he was dispatched by the Chicago outfit [mob] to keep an eye on its Vegas interests.... [he] also led one of the most brazen burglary rings...."

57. Jim Brady, *Boxing Confidential: Power, Corruption and the Richest Prize in Sports*, Lytham, U.K.: Milo, 2002 (abbrev. Brady, *Boxing Confidential*), 27.

58. Minutes, 14 November 1922, NYSAC.

59. Gene Tunney, *A Man Must Fight*, Boston: Houghton Mifflin, 1932 (abbrev. Tunney, *A Man Must Fight*), 133.

The Ring.⁶⁰ Obviously, if the first draft of history is prepared by the ethically compromised, it complicates mightily the ability of subsequent historians to render an accurate story.

This culture of corruption was facilitated by the fact that boxing was a major sport without a regular schedule, strict regulation on a national scale (facilitating the arbitrage opportunities eased by scores of statewide regulatory bodies), reliable records, objective scoring, etc. It was a kind of "free enterprise" of deregulation or "neoliberalism" run amok; that is, it was a sport designed with raw capitalism in mind, which in turn lubricated the path for the arrival of gangsters who thrived in such an environment, especially when the bodies to be exploited were disproportionately those of an ebony hue. It was a "battle royal" updated for the 20th century.⁶¹

Indeed, boxing is in many ways the *ne plus ultra* of capitalism itself, the essence of its unavoidable accoutrements: white supremacy, masculinity, violence, profiteering, corruption.

Even Roy Wilkins, the otherwise staid NAACP leader, wagged his finger accusingly at the sport, while defending the boxer, soon to be known as Muhammad Ali, then under fire for his Islamic beliefs: "what could be done to the sport," he scoffed, "that others before him have done many times over and worse! This includes agreements, secret and otherwise, payoffs over and under the table, fixes, bribes, dope, et Cetera."⁶² Tellingly, perhaps the other sport that challenged boxing's pre-eminent role as a sink of corruption was a sport where non-humans were paramount: horse racing.⁶³

As closed-circuit viewing of prizefights at theaters, and pay-per-view of them at home, became more popular in the late 20th century, the sums involved were eye-watering. The admitted killer

---

60. Angelo Dundee with Bert Randolph, *My View From the Corner: A Life in Boxing*, New York: McGraw Hill, 2008 (abbrev. Dundee, *My View*), 36.

61. Undated article on Tim Witherspoon, circa 1990, Box 151, Newfield-UT.

62. Roy Wilkins to Edward Lassman, president of World Boxing Association, 24 March 1964, III: A35, NAACP Papers, Library of Congress, Washington, D.C. (abbrev. NAACP-LC).

63. See items, including clipping of unclear provenance, 5 May 1949, Carton 4, Records of Special Crime Study Commission on Organized Crime in California, University of California, Berkeley: Bookies wary of taking bets at certain horse races for fear of being rooked. See also *Washington Post*, 14 March 2020: "…federal indictment that charged more than two dozen people in or associated with horse racing in 'a widespread corrupt' doping scheme…arrests of 27 racehorse trainers, veterinarians and drug distributors…among those indicted were some big names of racing."

and mobster Salvatore "Sammy the Bull" Gravano addressed this in his riveting 1993 testimony before Congress. "Purses have gotten so big," he said, "that it doesn't make sense to fix a fight in order to collect a bet," the frequent praxis to that point. "While we would consider fixing a fight in order to set up for a big payday fight," he confessed ingenuously, "the money is in the purses not the betting." However, that only provided more reason for mobsters to dig their sharpened talons into the meaty flesh of boxers.[64]

Like flies to feces, the odoriferous sport attracted human scum effortlessly. Still seemingly dazzled by the sight, Bob Arum, Don King's chief competitor as a matchmaker, recalled dreamily a fight between middleweight bomb-throwers "Marvelous" Marvin Hagler and Thomas "Hitman" Hearns in 1980s Las Vegas. "They would come to the [gambling] tables, the pimps and the drug dealers, with suitcases filled with cash to bet. The weekend that we did those fights were the biggest weekends that not only Caesar's [Palace] had but [also] across the street at Barbary Coast, bigger than New Year's Eve."

Yet, as suggested by Gravano's appearance before Congress, it was understandable why pugilists often sought common cause with politicos—and vice versa. Arum was quite critical of those with whom he had to share frequently lucrative profits. This lengthy list included a former casino magnate who also staged prizefights—before moving to the White House. Days before the pivotal 2016 election, Arum venomously told an interviewer that Donald J. Trump was a "real crook, a bad, bad guy"; his fabled "golf courses were all built with Russian oligarch money, which means that [President Vladimir] Putin's a partner"; sputtering, he added, "if he God forbid ever got elected, Putin would turn us into like a puppet country." Speaking on an ethically questionable topic he knew well, he concluded dolorously that the hotelier and his partner, Dan Duva, "swindled us," to the tune of "two and a half million dollars."[65] Implicitly concurring, Alan Townsend, a former deputy mayor of New York City, quipped, "I wouldn't believe Donald Trump if he had his tongue notarized,"[66]

---

64. Testimony of Salvatore Gravano, 10 March and 1 April 1993, "Corruption in Professional Boxing, Part II, Hearings Before the Permanent Subcommittee on Investigations of the Committee on Governmental Affairs," U.S. Senate, 103rd Congress, First Session, Box 72, Fred Thompson Papers, University of Tennessee, Knoxville (abbrev. FT-UTnK).

65. Interview with Bob Arum, 20 October 2016, UNV-LV.

66. Brady, *Boxing Confidential*, 253.

an unethical trait that made him uniquely qualified to excel in the business of boxing.

But for Arum, it was hard to do business and avoid Trump, since by the time heavyweights Evander Holyfield and George Foreman exchanged blows in 1991, a publicist trumpeted that "Trump Plaza has played host to some of the greatest fights in history," with a "reputation" that was "unmatched."[67]

Trump was also known to consort with Don King, who in turn was not viewed benignly by Arum either. This African-American successor to Truman Gibson, was able to take advantage of the erosion of Jim Crow and profited handsomely as a result. One of his partners was the billionaire entertainment mogul Kerkor "Kirk" Kerkorian, who once had fought as a welterweight, along with his brother known as the "Armenian Assassin." Kerkorian cultivated ties to Mickey Cohen, L.A. mob boss, and placed bets with the notorious "Charlie the Blade" Tourine, a plug-ugly in cahoots with the boss of all bosses, Vito Genovese. Yet it was King who negotiated a deal with the celebrated Armenian-American capitalist, that made the loquacious former Clevelander the second largest stockholder in the MGM Grand Hotel, holding 600,000 shares worth $15 million in the 1990s.[68] But it was not only King who managed to benefit once Jim Crow was eroded: One analyst has maintained that Ali "made more fighting George Foreman in Zaire [today the Democratic Republic of the Congo] than Joe Louis made in his whole career."[69] That was in the 1970s. But by 2018, one boxing referee expressed the consensus when he contended that champion fighter, Floyd "Money" Mayweather, Jr., was then "the highest paid athlete in any sport."[70]

Still, despite these heady, eye-popping figures, more historically typical was the plight of Bob Lee, described in 1915 as a "colored heavyweight" who "complained" that he had been "promised…$50 for a six round bout and had [been] paid…$2."[71] Lee was lucky. Another fighter, the "Zulu Kid," boxed in a 1915 contest and

---

67. Publicity Material, 19 April 1991, Box 202, Stardust Resort and Casino Records, UNV-LV.

68. William C. Rempel, *The Gambler: How Penniless Dropout Kirk Kerkorian Became the Greatest Dealmaker in Capitalist History*, New York: Morrow, 2018 (abbrev. Rempel, *Gambler*), 17, 24, 80, 302.

69. Peter Benjaminson, *The Story of Motown*, Los Angeles: Rare Bird, 2018 (abbrev. Benjaminson, *Story of Motown*), 28.

70. Interview with Joe Cortez, 29 November 2018, UNL-LV.

71. Minutes, 20 December 1915, NYSAC.

"received no money for his services," contrary to what was agreed.[72] Sadly, most boxers were likely to be closer in experience to the "Zulu Kid" than Mayweather.

Nevertheless, what distinguished Negro boxers from others was the disparate impact of racism upon them, including their difficulty in attracting the post-boxing accomplishments that, for example, were accorded to Jewish-American boxers. Harry Kessler was undefeated in four years as a boxer while matriculating at the University of Missouri-Rolla, an institution that did not welcome Negroes. He became a metallurgical engineer, then served as a well-compensated referee for 27 years, including being the third man in the ring when Ali fought Cleveland Williams in Houston. By 1967 he was bidding to buy the pro-basketball franchise, the St. Louis Hawks.[73] Not only had he refereed the pivotal bout between Rocky Marciano and Archie Moore but also the Moore-Joey Maxim match. As an engineer he became wealthy when he helped develop several processes for improving steel. Emblematic of the experience of many Jewish Americans, he and his brothers, Sollie and Benny, became involved in boxing because, he said, "we [were] the only Jewish family…on the [St. Louis] North Side," a vicinity dominated by Irish Americans where, inexorably, fist-fighting became a popular diversion. Over his lengthy career, Kessler refereed 3500 amateur and professional fights, beginning in 1927, including 15 championship tiffs. "In the 20s," he recollected in the early 1980s, "boxing took the Irish out of the ghettos, in the 30s the Jews, in the 40s the Italians, in the 50s the Blacks and now the Latins." By then, he tooled around in a Rolls-Royce, motoring to his lavish home in Palm Springs (he also had a Park Avenue apartment in Manhattan). And there was his 50-foot-long boat.[74]

* * *

It was in 1964 that the heavyweight Sonny Liston, whose loss to Ali catapulted the former "Louisville Lip" into the ionosphere of fame, got into a heated confrontation with Las Vegas' top mobster, Moe Dalitz (who had roots in King's Cleveland), though the scalding words were exchanged at a posh Beverly Hills hideaway. "If you hit

---

72. Minutes, 27 December 1915, NYSAC.

73. *St. Louis Post-Dispatch*, 24 January 1967, Sub Group IX, Series I, Box 15, HKBA.

74. Undated clipping by *St. Louis Post-Dispatch*, Sub Group IX, Series I, Box 15, HKBA.

me," Dalitz growled menacingly to the barely literate boxer, "you'd better kill me, because if you don't, I'll make just one telephone call and you'll be dead in 24 hours."[75] Dalitz was no cipher: Former Nevada Governor Grant Sawyer said that the jowly and pugnacious battler "was probably as responsible for the successful gaming economy in Southern Nevada as any one person." Perhaps predictably, Liston died mysteriously at home a few years later in circumstances that remain opaque.[76] As shall be seen, Liston had questionable ties to various mobsters throughout his star-crossed career. One investigator charges that he agreed to take a "dive in his second fight with Ali," i.e., agreed to lose beforehand, thereby "making [Kirk] Kerkorian a lot of money," who then proceeded to give him a "sweet deal" on his Las Vegas abode.[77]

* * *

As suggested by the previous mentions of U.S. Presidents Roosevelt and Trump, the imbrication of boxing and politics has been a long-term trend. Since those poised to exploit often controlled more capital—financial and otherwise—than the boxers themselves, this tipped the scales in favor of the former, making it difficult to pass legislation to curb exploitation. Like Roosevelt, Trump, typically for many U.S. men, had an inordinate interest in the minutiae of boxing. In 1990, for example, in the midst of fighting off multiple bankruptcies, the brander and casino aficionado was said to "love boxing.... he'll talk hours about boxing.... he sees a reflection of himself in fighters."[78]

The same held true in spades for another man who aspired to occupy the White House. George Wallace, a former governor of Alabama and presidential aspirant in 1968, was a champion amateur boxer in the "Golden Gloves," foreshadowing his confrontational approach to maintaining Jim Crow.[79] John Sirica, the federal judge who helped to unravel the Watergate scandal that drove a president from office in 1974, bragged that as a young man, "I fought 175

---

75. Biographical File, Moe Dalitz, *Las Vegas Review Journal*, 3 September 1989, UNV-LV. For more on this troubling episode, see Rick Porcello, *The Rise and Fall of the Cleveland Mafia*, New York: Barricade, 1995, 204-205.

76. Biographical File, Moe Dalitz, *Las Vegas Review Journal*, 1 September 1989.

77. Assael, *Murder*, 14.

78. *USA Today*, 30 May 1990, Box 21, Sub Group X, Series I, HKBA.

79. Clipping, 2 January 1975, Box 22, Sub Group X, Series I, HKBA.

guys" in a year, "sometimes as many as four a night.... I was 37."[80] The former leader of the U.S. Senate, Harry Reid of Nevada, was boastful about his past as a boxer.[81]

An early business partner of Arum was Fred Hofheinz who, said Arum, "didn't think it was right to be a boxing promoter when he was mayor of...Houston."[82] Overseas, a founding father of modern Nigeria, Nnamdi Azikiwe, was a former welterweight puncher,[83] while Nelson Mandela was in a higher weight class.[84] The protagonist of the paradigmatic African novel, *Things Fall Apart*, was a local wrestling champion.[85] Berry Gordy was not an elected official but one of the pre-eminent African-American entrepreneurs of the 20th century and also a boxer. Arguably, the drive and forcefulness of this sport redounded to his benefit during his business career.[86] Something similar could be said for Bo Diddley, yet another former boxer who starred in popular music—and bluesman Willie Dixon too.[87]

It did not require an advanced degree to ascertain that qualities that inhered in adroit boxing—quick thinking, instinctively developing strategy and tactics for victory, tenacity, etc.—were fungible and adaptive to various environments, especially politics. This was particularly true of the political culture in the U.S., a nation which was created as a result of violent uprooting of Indigenes and of a pervasive brutality deployed to keep millions of the enslaved in line.[88]

Boxing reflected and refracted politics. Thus, when Primo Carnera boxed Joe Louis in the 1930s, this battle of the titans was constructed

---

80. *Washington Daily News*, 21 June 1960.

81. Harry Reid, *The Good Fight: Hard Lessons from Searchlight to Washington*, New York: Putnam's, 2008.

82. Interview with Bob Arum, 20 October 2016, UNV-LV.

83. Hogan Bassey, *Bassey on Boxing: Hogan Bassey's Own Story*, London: Nelson, 1963, iv: Foreword by Azikiwe.

84. Nelson Mandela, *Long Walk to Freedom: The Autobiography*, New York: Little, Brown, 2013.

85. Chinua Achebe, *Things Fall Apart*, New York: Anchor, 2010.

86. Benjaminson, *Story of Motown*, 25.

87. Nadine Cohodas, *Spinning Blues into Gold: The Chess Brothers and the Legendary Chess Records*, New York: St. Martins, 2000, 81.

88. See Gerald Horne, *The Dawning of the Apocalypse: The Roots of Slavery, White Supremacy, Settler Colonialism and Capitalism in the Long 16th Century*, New York: Monthly Review Press, 2020 (abbrev. Horne, *Dawning*). See also John Hope Franklin, *The Militant South, 1800-1861*, Cambridge: Harvard University Press, 1956.

as reflecting the then-ongoing Italian invasion of Ethiopia, providing momentum for African solidarity.[89]

Muhammad Ali's refusal to be conscripted into the U.S. military likely served as a spur for the movement opposing the war in Indo-China, just as it likely also energized supporters of that conflict. Decidedly in the latter category were the authorities in Minnesota, where a member of the state's Boxing Board, Fabian "Fay" Frawley, huffed in 1966, "I consider Clay [Ali] a discredit and disgrace to boxing...because of his unpatriotic remarks against wishing to serve his country in time of war."[90] His démarche was backed by his fellow panelists. President Lyndon Baines Johnson was deluged with anti-Ali mail, with Noble Chisman of Los Angeles summarizing the sentiment of many when he wondered with rebuking querulousness, "why are the likes of Cassius [Ali] and Stokely Carmichael," yet another antiwar African American, "allowed to defy the Selective Service Act?"[91] Ali's audacity revived fading memories of Jack Johnson who, while in London in 1911, asserted, "Fight for America?...I should say not. What has America ever done for my race?"[92]

And just as Ali became a lightning rod, absorbing the electric hostility of enraged conservatives, his chief opponent, Joe Frazier, took an opposing tack, asking waspishly, "What kind of man is this who don't want to fight for his country," adding, in the manner of a geo-political analyst, "if he was in Russia, or someplace else, they'd put him up against the wall." Frazier backed such stalwart Republicans as Presidents Richard M. Nixon, Ronald W. Reagan, and George H.W. Bush. He was friendly toward the Philadelphia police and their two-fisted, anti-Negro chief, later Mayor Frank Rizzo (Ali also spoke fondly of Rizzo, saying, "I like what I hear about him. I like his looks").[93] Contrary to these hosannas tossed at the feet of Republicans, when Archie Moore—whom Ali defeated per prediction in

---

89. Nadia Nurhussein, *Black Land: Imperial Ethiopianism and African America*, Princeton: Princeton University Press, 2019 (abbrev. Nurhussein, *Black Land*), 167.

90. Minutes, 17 March 1966, Boxing Board Records, Minnesota Historical Society, St. Paul (abbrev. MinnHS-SP).

91. Noble Chisman to President Johnson, 8 November 1966, Box 260, White House Central Files, Lyndon Johnson Presidential Library, Austin, Texas (abbrev. LBJPL).

92. Quoted in Joyce Carol Oates, *On Boxing*, New York: Ecco, 2006 (abbrev. Oates, *On Boxing*), 245.

93. Kram, *Smokin' Joe*, 130, 165.

Round 4—contemplated running for the state legislature in California in 1960, it was as a Democrat.[94]

Like his fellow premier heavyweights—Johnson and Ali—Joe Louis too was politically minded. In 1948, as his remarkable career headed toward eclipse, it was rumored that he was about "to enter politics...asked if his presence at Henry A. Wallace's speech in Harlem" was a sign of his leanings—referring to the Progressive Party, which did not exclude Communists and included Paul Robeson as a prime backer—the agile athlete hedged: "I have not made up my mind about this," he replied cagily, while adding, "Mr. Wallace made a wonderful speech [and] I liked it very much."[95] On the other hand, Gene Tunney, whose son went on to serve in the U.S. Senate—a post generally distant from the dreams of Negroes—cooperated with the neo-fascist Gerald L.K. Smith and became a fanatical anti-communist.[96]

Other boxers were similarly contradictory in their political stances. Roberto Duran, he of the "Hands of Stone," contemptuously and progressively termed the 1989 overthrow of his compatriot, Manuel Noriega, as paramount leader in Panama, the "biggest disgrace in the history of our country"; yet he stooped to wearing a flag of the disgraced so-called Confederate States of America into the ring. This latter display may shed light on why he lost his race for the Panamanian senate.[97]

Nonetheless, African-American boxers, particularly in the second half of the 20th century, were faced with a dilemma: On the one hand, golden doors were being opened as a result of the erosion of Jim Crow, which was to propel the likes of Don King to untold wealth; yet, as the case of Ali's anti-war posture indicated, there was a steep price to be paid for appearing to be too much in tune with the political left. Liston did not gain many fans among a generally conservative Euro-American majority, already beginning to grouse about the onset of desegregation when, upon returning to the U.S. from London in September 1963, he announced that he was "ashamed to be in America." According to an observant reporter, he was "upset over the Sunday bombing of a Negro church in

---

94. *San Diego Tribune*, 2 September 1960, Vertical File on Archie Moore, San Diego History Center (abbrev. SDHC).

95. Clipping, 20 February 1948, Sub Group X, Series I, Box 15, HKBA.

96. Gerald L.K. Smith to Gene Tunney, 8 July 1940, and Eleanor Roosevelt to Tunney, 14 May 1940, Box 1, Gene Tunney Papers, University of Notre Dame, South Bend, Indiana (abbrev. Tunney-UND).

97. Duran, *I Am Duran*, 231, 236, 244.

Birmingham."[98] This was not necessarily a sectional dispute, in that his boxing opponent, Floyd Patterson, felt compelled to sell his home in what was described as a "white area" of Yonkers, N. Y., since "no one wanted to play with my children"; in fact, "people have called my kids 'n-gg-r,' 'Sambo'" and worse. A notably malicious neighbor trained a dog to deface his property. "I tried," said the heavyweight of this experiment in desegregation, but "it just didn't work."[99] What was at play was a wider experiment to see if African Americans, now being buoyed by the tide crashing against Jim Crow, could be accepted as class comrades in more affluent areas, after long decades pointing in an opposing direction.

Pummeled mercilessly, often demonized as symbols of opposition to white supremacy, exploited shamelessly, African-American boxers understandably began to flee their homeland. It was Jack Johnson, while in London after his Copernican triumph over Jim Jeffries in Reno in 1910, who declared that he was predisposed to exile in such a site since overseas "I am treated like a human being,"[100] unlike the routine maltreatment to which he was exposed in the former slaveholders' republic. Over the years, he was emulated by his successors, including Archie "The Mongoose" Moore, a light heavyweight champion who held the distinction of battling both Ali and Rocky Marciano, two of the leading heavyweights. By the early 1950s he was in Argentina, where he was lionized. "I was perhaps the most popular man there besides [Juan] Perón," then national leader. There were many rumors at the time that Moore might exile permanently in Buenos Aires.[101]

* * *

Boxing involved battering and ultimately led to untold damage to the skulls, brains and bodies of contestants. The analyst Joyce Carol Oates has argued that 87% of boxers suffer brain damage during their lifetime, while from 1945 to 1985, 370 pugilists died from injuries

---

98. Clipping, ca. September 1963, Boxing Scrapbooks, Heavyweights, Vol. 17, UND.

99. Clipping, uncertain provenance, Boxing Scrapbooks, Heavyweights, Vol. 17, UND.

100. Oates, *On Boxing*, 245. On Johnson's lengthy sojourn abroad, including Russia, Barcelona and Mexico, see Gerald Horne, *Black and Brown: African Americans and the Mexican Revolution, 1910-1920*, New York: New York University Press, 2005 (abbrev. Horne, *Black and Brown*).

101. Clipping, no date, Vertical File on Archie Moore, SDHC.

directly attributable to the sport.[102] As early as 1928, one observer detected that the "early symptoms" of the condition known as being "punch drunk" typically "appear in the extremities" with a "very slight flopping of one foot or leg in walking...a peculiar tilting of the head...a staggering propulsive gait with the facial characteristics of the Parkinsonian [sic] Syndrome." Thus, said writer Arthur Mann, any "fighter who has fought 50 or 60 reasonably hard fights already is suffering from early degrees of [being] punch drunk."[103] By 1984, Ali—a reigning symbol of the sport, born in 1942—was adjudged by the eminent Dr. Stanley Fahn of the Medical Center at Columbia University to have "mild symptoms of Parkinson Syndrome." He had reason to know since, Dr. Fahn said, "I have been his primary physician."[104] Benny Leonard, arguably the premier Jewish-American boxer of his era, as early as 1924, when he was almost a decade away from retirement, was diagnosed as enduring "arthritis...of the right thumb with its resultant pain and disability"; perhaps worse was that this serious injury, which would destabilize a hard puncher like Leonard, may even have been worsened by medical practice: "it is our unanimous opinion," said an official body, "that inadequate treatment is responsible for the present condition."[105]

It was not just the pile-driving blows absorbed by boxers that contributed to these maladies. This was a manifestly unsanitary sport with the promiscuous spilling of tainted blood and other fluids, hacking coughs in the face of opponents, attendants blowing water

---

102. Oates, *On Boxing*, 93, 98. Cf., *Village Voice*, 3 May 1983, Box 20, Sub Group VIII, Series I, HKBA: Boxing analyst Bert Sugar has argued that according to a 1979 study by the American Medical Association, amateur and professional boxing was behind in fatalities with 0.13 deaths per thousand, compared to college football at 0.31. Still, for massive detail on the fatalities and injuries that have beset boxing, see Reports and Clippings, Sub Group XV, Series 6, Box 21, HKBA. See also Report, 11 April 1962, NYSAC: "Statistics show that professional boxing rates behind some ten sports in the number of fatalities. There was a tragic number of deaths (39) in the United States last fall in football in a period of ten weeks, including 28 high school students, whereas the record shows that in the entire year (1961) there were ten deaths covering the world including such important boxing areas as the United States, England, Japan, Philippines, Mexico and Chile."

103. Report, 1928, and Arthur Mann to Richard M. Johnson, ca. 1949, Box 4, Arthur Mann Papers, Library of Congress, Washington, D.C. (abbrev. Mann-LC).

104. Report by Dr. Stanley Fahn, 20 September 1984, Sub Group XIX, Series, 2, Box 3, HKBA.

105. Minutes, 6 September 1924, NYSAC.

in the face of fighters from their own mouths, all taking place in frequently smoke-filled venues.[106]

This was a real fear as Governor Edward Edwards of New Jersey was informed in 1922: A fan had just attended the stirring fight between Jack Dempsey and George Carpentier, and departed "scared to death" in that there was a palpable "danger to the ninety odd thousand" present "had there been a panic and especially a panic caused by fire."[107] To his credit, über-promoter Tex Rickard sought to stop smoking at boxing matches as early as 1922.[108] By 1928 Harlem's St. Nicholas Arena, a frequent site for prizefighting, was said to be "unsafe and is a fire hazard," though it was unclear if smoking was a contributing factor.[109] It is likely that smoking was a factor in this assessment since it was also in 1928 that Madison Square Garden was "advised to instruct all Garden employees, ushers, and special police in particular that the no-smoking rule...must be rigidly enforced at all boxing shows.[110] By 1961, welterweight contender Don Jordan was said to "smoke...all the time during training, that if they permitted him he would smoke in the corner." William Ming, a lawyer for Truman Gibson, commented that "a great many athletes, including fighters, smoke in training."[111]

Burning and choking smoke aside, venues for fights ranged from steaming hot to freezing cold. Contracting tuberculosis seemed to be an occupational hazard for boxers.[112] Joe Gans, Jack Johnson's precursor whom the heavyweight copied, became blind,[113] an occupational hazard given the incessant pounding in the head and face.

What needs to be explored further is whether the manifest struggle of certain boxers to qualify for a weight class, for example, a middleweight of a normal 160 pounds seeking to downscale under

---

106. Aycock and Scott, *Joe Gans*, 183.

107. Letter to Governor Edwards, 12 July 1922, Box 2, Governor Edward Irving Edwards, New Jersey State Archives, Trenton (abbrev. EIE-NJ).

108. Minutes, 24 October 1922, NYSAC.

109. Minutes, 19 January 1928, NYSAC.

110. Minutes, 24 February 1928, NYSAC. At the same site and source, see Minutes, 1 August 1933: Here "discussed [was] the advisability of abolishing the no-smoking rule."

111. Testimony and comment by William Ming, 13 April 1961, RG 21, U.S. District Court for the Central District of California, Central Division (Los Angeles), Criminal Case Files, 27973, Box 2486, National Archives and Records Administration, Riverside, California (abbrev. NAR-Riv).

112. Bob Petersen, *Gentleman Bruiser: A Life of the Boxer, Peter Jackson*, Sydney: Croydon, 2005 (abbrev. Petersen, *Gentleman Bruiser*), 154.

113. Aycock and Scott, *Joe Gans*, 58.

pressure to welterweight or lightweight, may have contributed to incipient anorexia or bulimia or other maladies.[114] Previous writers have argued that the "drying out process at the end of the training grind" which "denies [the boxer's] system liquid" in order to slip "under the required weight," can "deaden the gastric nerves of the stomach," meaning the fighter "can take body punishment without flinching," which is "what a manager wants." This too can lead to tuberculosis and can damage the kidneys, sweat glands and other excretory organs, producing a kind of temporary paralysis.[115]

* * *

This is a book that does not dwell heavily on the aspect of the sport that has been encapsulated in the term "The Sweet Science," i.e., the art of blocking blows, converting opponents into agents of their destruction, deftly dismantling an antagonist, etc. Instead, this book examines "The Bittersweet Science"—with an accent decidedly on the bitter.[116] This is a book that administers only a glancing blow in the direction of the sweetness of the mesmerizing counter-punching of Ronald "Winky" Wright or the brilliance of the "Ali Shuffle" or the smartness of the "windmill style" of Aaron "The Hawk" Pryor, whereby a left was launched followed in a seeming nanosecond by the right in the manner of an out-of-control windmill, or the

---

114. Minutes, 23 August 1927, NYSAC: "Tony Canzoneri, Pancho Dencio and Del Sanco, suspended indefinitely for reporting overweight for bouts." At the same site and collection, see Minutes, 25 February 1927: "Mike Durano…and Willie Smith…[suspended]…overweight…Sammy Vogel… [suspended indefinitely]…overweight…Jack Birns…suspended indefinitely…overweight…Joe Morro and Gerd Hohl…suspended indefinitely… overweight." At the same site see also Minutes, 3 September 1929: "Leo Podell. Boxer, license revoked because of mental incapacity." Whether as a result of punishing blows in the ring or an outgrowth of a pre-existing condition, "mental incapacity" deserves further exploration in the analysis of boxing. At the same site see also Report by Dr. Marvin A. Stevens on Tommy Dixon, boxer, and his discharge from the military because of "nervous condition…unpredictable rage spells, poor socialization, marked suspiciousness and hallucinatory experiences."
115. Arthur Mann, "Punch Drunk Fighters and Why," no date, Box 16, Mann-LC.
116. Cf., A.J. Liebling, *The Sweet Science and Other Writings*, New York: Library of America, 2009 (abbrev. Liebling, *Sweet Science and Other*). See also A.J. Liebling, *The Sweet Science: Boxing and the Boxiana*, New York: Viking, 1956 (abbrev. Liebling: *Sweet Science: Boxing*).

defensive astuteness of Jack Johnson whereby he could convert an opponent into the agent of his own unraveling. This is a book about the sweetness of victories—Jack Johnson knocking down the walls of bigotry[117] or Ali's anti-war triumph. This is most of all a book about racism and profiteering, exploitation and corruption in the sport that is boxing.[118] It covers a good deal of the 20th century, but I'm afraid the trends unspooled here have yet to disappear altogether.

---

117. Horne, *Black and Brown*.

118. See Graham Brooks, et al., eds., *Fraud, Corruption and Sport*, New York: Palgrave, 2013.

Chapter 1

Go West, Young Negro!

Boxing, it has been said, is as ancient as the urge to compete—or dominate. Along with running, it is one of the oldest sports: As early as 5000 years ago in China, there are reports of a form of this sport.[1] Another estimate suggests that the sport is 6000 years old.[2] During the Grecian era, Theseus, King of Athens, to guarantee pain and brutality in battles, obliged fighters to wear a pair of reinforced brass knuckles; warriors unable to withstand the rigor were tossed to the lions as fodder.[3] Wrestling, a close cousin of boxing, arose in ancient Egypt, perhaps 4900 years ago. For our purposes, however, boxing is associated with the early days of enslaving Africans in North America. There were forced matches to the death between bondsmen, organized by enslavers. This was creating a culture of fungible combat, the skills gleaned being applicable to fighting slavery itself—and enslavers, too. Reportedly, the first seven U.S. boxers to compete in England were Africans. Interestingly, Negro sailors confined to Dartmoor Prison during the War of 1812 between the U.S. and Britain ran a professional boxing school. Near that same time, stories were detailed concerning the presence of U.S. Negroes in the capoeira societies of Brazil, further evidence of the brawling ability that was developing.[4]

Just before then, late in the 18th century, Jack Broughton was among those who sought in the face of staunch opposition to introduce gloves into the sport: Bare knuckles remained in vogue for decades to come. From the arrival on the scene of Broughton and for more than 200 years thereafter, the bulk of prizefights were conducted in

---

1. Stephen Acunto, *Champions' Boxing Guide*, n.d. Box II: 863, Moynihan-LC.
2. Robert Rodriguez, *The Regulation of Boxing: A History and Comparative Analysis of Policies Among American States*, Jefferson, N.C.: McFarland, 2009 (abbrev. Rodriguez, *Regulation*), 23.
3. Arthur Mann, "Punch Drunk Boxers and Why," no date, Box 16, Mann-LC.
4. Obi, *Fighting for Honor*, 61, 202.

disreputable venues or pursuant to bribery of politicians and police, further adding to a culture of corruption on all sides.[5] The stalwart in this context was Thomas Molineaux (also spelled Molyneaux), born in the slave citadel that was Virginia in 1784, but who arrived in England in 1809, where he became a champion bare-knuckle heavyweight fighter. As was to be the pattern that accelerated with the ascendancy of Jack Johnson, his success collided with the doctrine of white supremacy. "In a long fight an African could not be beaten by a white man, if they were about equal to each other in size and strength and if the black knew something of fighting," it was said disconsolately. But why? "The Negro's skull was so thick that a blow on it would do no harm."[6] An account of a contest between "Tom Molyneaux" and Tom Cribb in England in December 1810 featured ringsiders carping that the Negro would prevail "unless something were done." Thus, "one of Cribb's seconds almost bit the Negro's thumb off."[7]

It was near that time that the British journalist Pierce Egan began declaiming about the "Sweet Science of Bruising," referring to a sport that early on seemed to carry "homoerotic overtones,"[8] though that apparently did not implicate the assailant.

Of the numerous examples of how a culture of combat had become ingrained among the enslaved, one stands out conspicuously: Bass Reeves was born enslaved in Paris, Texas, in 1838, but like so many in those harsh circumstances, he honed proficiency as a fighter—then knocked out his enslaver, fled to Indian Territory, today's Oklahoma, where he was renowned as a law enforcement officer notorious for his two-fisted prowess.[9] Reeves was able to capitalize on his skill, as did others, by fleeing, but those left behind were not so lucky. For across plantation borders enslavers habitually placed bets on the results of staged fights between enslaved men. Inexorably, flowing

---

5. Arthur Mann, "Punch Drunk Fighters and Why," Mann-LC.

6. Clipping of article by Bob Travers and George Baker, no date, Sub Group X, Series 1, Box 21, HKBA: "Molineaux was a ferocious looking Negro born in Virginia and there was some mystery about how he reached England. It is probable that he was a runaway slave." See also George MacDonald Fraser, *Black Ajax*, London: HarperCollins, 1997.

7. Account, no date, Sub Group X, Series I, Box 22, HKBA.

8. *Miami Herald*, 1 March 1987, Sub Group VIII, Series I, Box 16, HKBA.

9. John W. Ravage, *Black Pioneers: Images of the Black Experience on the North American Frontier*, Salt Lake City: University of Utah Press, 2008, 104. See also Art Burton, *Black Gun, Silver Star: The Life and Legend of Frontier Marshal Bass Reeves*, Lincoln: University of Nebraska Press, 2008.

from this evil was the point that these men—and they were mostly men—refined their competency when ensnared in altercations.[10]

Reeves's reputation continued rising in the post-bellum era. Yet just as he had fled to a technically separate jurisdiction—Indian Territory—Negro boxer Bobby Dobbs, born in 1869, went farther. The majority of this welterweight's career was spent in Europe, a tenure facilitated by his knowledge of German and Hungarian.[11] Other migrating Negroes were not being paid to crush skulls but were no less aggressive. Such a descriptor could easily be applied to Kid Gardener, who wound up in Cape Town in 1900: "you trying to class me with your Cape Town nigguhs?" he snarled, adding vociferously, "I'm from Texas and I ain't be tampered with."[12]

Other Negroes not as gifted linguistically as Dobbs, moved instead to Nevada, a state with a relatively small population then and still in the throes of seeking to subdue Indigenes, inducing a racial fluidity that often meant Negroes were not the main target of bile. Nonetheless, it was tempting fate for Negroes to bet that this fluidity could save them, since in some ways, lynching of Indigenes and other dissidents was essential to the creation of the state.[13] Moreover, early on the idea was afloat that both Indigenes and Negroes alike were barriers to civilization.[14] Yet Nevada provided opportunity in that as states farther east barred boxing, particularly across racial lines, the Silver State diverged in an opposing direction.[15]

It was not just a ban heading eastward. As late as 1910, a heavyweight championship fight was chased suddenly out of California by the governor. Perhaps influenced by the stout example of TR, things began to change.[16]

Nevertheless, by one account there were only 134 Negroes in the entire state of Nevada in 1900; in the early 21st century, one journalist observed that one of the "oldest surviving African American

---

10. Forrett, *Slave*, 294. See also Owen Swift, *Art of Self Defense or Boxing Without a Master*, Boston: Berry, 1851, Box 17, Marian Carson Papers, Library of Congress, Washington, D.C.

11. Louis Moore, *I Fight for a Living: Boxing and the Battle for Black Manhood*, Urbana: University of Illinois Press, 2017 (abbrev. Moore, *I Fight*), 66-67.

12. Nurhussein, *Black Land*, 101.

13. C.W. Bayer, "Profits, Plots & Lynching: The Creation of Nevada Territory," 1995, *University of Nevada, Reno*.

14. *Gold Hill News*, 17 April 1865, Vertical File-Boxing-Nevada, Nevada Historical Society, Reno (abbrev. NHS-R).

15. Lindsay, *Boxing*, 10.

16. Arthur Mann, "Punch Drunk Fighters and Why," Mann-LC.

institutions in Nevada," the Bethel African Methodist Episcopal church, was built in Reno in 1910.[17] This paucity of Negroes meant they were not perceived as threatening, easing the possibility for prizefighting involving them. Thus, as early as 1885 there were boxing matches involving men of African and European ancestry, something to be verboten in coming years.[18] By the early 20th century, this minuscule number of Negroes included Frank Backus of Reno, said to be 115 years old and born in the 1700s. He continued to drive a swill wagon,[19] a job that, caste-like, was often assigned to those of his ancestry.

However, being able to step into the ring to confront an opponent across racial lines did not necessarily guarantee a fair outcome. Such was the sad lesson learned by George Ellis, a Negro, and his opponent, Tom Mantor, an Irish miner, who squared off in Lincoln County, near the Utah border in 1905. The bout was ruled a draw, though Ellis was favored to win, a result which upset some men who had wagered on Ellis overcoming. Ellis had been residing in Fay, Nevada, and, it was said, was the "town's only representative of his race." In any case, a number of his neighbors decided that he was no longer welcome. He was robbed, then a concerted attempt was made to lynch him. After tying his hands, the assailants tossed the end of the rope over a branch and hoisted him upward by the neck, but lowered him before he was strangled. He had been accused of a number of local burglaries, besides disappointing the boxing audience. He denied the charges—then confessed in an attempt to save his life. Unrewarded, he was clubbed over the head with the butt end of a pistol, then ordered to skedaddle to Utah. Somehow he managed to spur a prosecution of the miscreants but, predictably, they were acquitted.[20]

Boxing was on a seesaw legally—outlawed, then legalized, then outlawed again. This created an opening for the likes of Nevada, which early on adopted forbidden practices barred due east, culminating with gambling and prostitution, all of which attracted men of ill-repute. But what, at least initially, helped to push the sport

---

17. *Reno Gazette Journal*, 18 February 2001, Vertical File: African-Americans, NHS-R.

18. *Reese River Reveille*, 7 February 1885, and 20 February 1885, Vertical File-Boxing: Nevada, NHS-R.

19. *Daily Silver State*, 23 December 1905, Vertical File: African-Americans, NHS-R.

20. *Nevada Appeal*, 28 March 1999, Vertical File: African-Americans, NHS-R.

into the charmed circle of legality was the shepherding of Theodore Roosevelt. The "Bull Moose" sought to exude a forward-leaning masculinity, appropriate for a nation busily subjugating Indigenes, forcibly segregating Negroes and colonizing Hawaii, the Philippines, Puerto Rico and Cuba. Coincidentally, as Roosevelt rose to prominence, sports too were rising in salience—and not just boxing. This was also the era of the accelerated popularity of basketball, particularly among Negroes.[21] For African Americans, sports had the advantage of stressing objective criteria for success: speed, jumping ability, reflexes, etc., thus partially circumventing the subjectivity of racist evaluation. As the historian Ryan Swanson put it, Jack Johnson "abruptly dethroned Roosevelt as America's most talked about boxer" in the first decade of the 20th century. This was occurring, perhaps not accidentally, as the politician "connected boxing with racial survival" and as Johnson critiqued TR's more odious policies, e.g., his unfairness toward Negro soldiers in Brownsville, Texas.[22] On the other hand, TR suffered one of the occupational hazards of the ring—de facto blindness in an eye—which may have been induced by his energetic boxing regime, and may have contributed to his souring on the macho sport.[23]

Complementarily, TR sparred with and was instructed by Otto Raphael, a Jewish American who had served as an official of the New York City Police Department, which TR had headed. At that juncture, many Jewish Americans—especially recent migrants with Eastern European roots—were bedeviled by bigotry, at times from their Irish-American and Italian-American neighbors. As matters evolved, Jewish Americans' increasingly close ties with certified members of the U.S. elite, along with their boxing acumen, aided mightily in this group's climbing the socio-economic ladder. By then a Jewish police official was a reigning symbol of purported equality in the republic, especially if the man was foreign-born and from Russia, the site of Raphael's roots. Thus, Raphael's closeness to TR allowed him to encourage the potent politician to speak out vigorously on a particularly destructive Russian pogrom in 1903—precursor of a

---

21. Bob Kuska, *Hot Potato: How Washington and New York Gave Birth to Black Basketball and Changed America's Game Forever*, Charlottesville: University of Virginia Press, 2004, 7.

22. Swanson, *Strenuous Life*, 228, 232. See also John Weaver, *The Brownsville Raid*, College Station: Texas A&M University Press, 1992.

23. Nat Fleischer on Sir Roy Welensky, *The Ring*, October 1962, Sub Group IX, Series II, Box 26, HKBA. On TR's loss of vision, see Arthur Mann, "Punch Drunk Fighters and Why," Mann-LC.

time when Washington was to style itself as a staunch defender of the Jewish community globally—this at a time when Jewish Americans were becoming influential and able to reward tribunes.[24]

But high level liaisons could not obscure the wider point that anti-Jewish fervor in the U.S. would not be easy to squelch. For it was in 1906, as Jewish boxers were beginning to make their mark, that featherweight Harry Tenny—otherwise known as Sam Tennenbaum—was killed in the ring: Relatives say that he had been drugged.[25] Faring better was "Young Jeff," born Meyer Ketchel in 1885 in Odessa, who, like many so situated, fought in the streets while reaching adolescence, sharpening his boxing skill. He went on to work as a sideman with yet another Ketchel—Stanley, one of Jack Johnson's early victims in the ring.[26] Sadly, Ketchel—the employer (born Stanislaw Kiecal of Polish descent)—was victimized once again, further padding the incredible mortality statistics of prizefighters: He was assassinated at the age of 24, shot in the back.[27]

Just as Joe Gans and Jack Johnson opened the gates of opportunity for Negroes, Raphael did the same for Jewish Americans. This long list came to include Harry "Champ" Segal, born in 1899, a welterweight whose heyday was 1914-1917; overall, in about 114 bouts, he attained 50 one-round knockouts. He was managed by Sam Fitzpatrick, who had managed Johnson, and according to one account, was related to the "famed Segal Lock Company," which amassed a significant market share in the U.S. This man of manicured fingernails was a friend of Ernest Hemingway, the writer and, as was common for those in his category, had comrades in the underworld, being on friendly terms with Frankie Carbo, the unelected Commissar of boxing subsequently. He was a colleague of Ben "Bugsy" Siegel, immortalized in Hollywood, and both—along with future boxing boss Frankie Carbo—were accused of slaying Harry Greenberg in San Francisco. He was also friendly with the boss of bosses: Al Capone. An aesthete, Segal was able to convert his boxing earnings

---

24. See *New York Times*, 3 September 1937; Undated clipping, Sub Group IX, Series 2, Boxing 20, HKBA. See also Mike Donovan, *The Roosevelt That I Know: Ten Years of Boxing with the President—and Other Memories of Famous Fighting Men*, New York: Dodge, 1909.

25. Clipping, 2 March 1906, Sub Group IX, Series II, Box 25, HKBA.

26. Undated article, Sub Group IX, Series II, Box 14, HKBA.

27. Nat Fleischer, *50 Years at Ringside*, New York: Fleet, 1958 (abbrev. Fleischer, *50 Years*), 45. See also Clay Moyle, *Sam Langford: Boxing's Greatest Uncrowned Champion*, Bennett & Hastings, 2006 (abbrev. Moyle, *Sam Langford*), 143.

into Renoir paintings and other symbols of wealth. His father, a lawyer, migrated to North America after a notably vicious pogrom. Unlike many Negro boxers, Segal had close relatives—e.g., Admiral Hyman Rickover, the father of the nuclear navy, on his mother's side, and his brother Herman, who worked alongside eminent jurist Louis Brandeis—who could aid him socially and financially, especially after anti-Semitism began its agonizing retreat, post-1945.[28] A similar socio-economic process attached to Albert Silverstein, also known as Al Turner: In 1910 he endured 13 prizefights, won New York State middleweight and heavyweight titles on the same night in 1917 (obviously weight classifications were elastic and Negroes were generally barred from competing, enhancing his success), and had his last fight in 1923. But by 1966, he was exposed to munificence as a chief of security for mega-millionaire J. Paul Getty.[29]

Like Segal, Barney Ross, who also happened to be Jewish, was a better boxer than Segal and Silverstein, and was also close to Capone, serving as one of his many messengers.[30] Like all too many Jewish men, he admitted, "it wasn't a question of whether or not you wanted to fight. You had to, in self-defense. The Jews and Italians were always at war. Many a night I would come home cut and bruised and get another lick at home, for fighting."[31] The pious Ross was studying to be a Hebrew teacher when his father was slain and the perpetrators freed, unsettling him mightily.[32] Born in 1909, Ross's toughness paid off for Washington when as a soldier during the Pacific War he singlehandedly slew 22 Japanese soldiers in one fiery night. He departed with aching wounds and was assuaged with morphine, which led to an addiction and his spending a sizable $250,000 on drugs in a scant four years.[33] Even before then, the great Negro pounder Henry Armstrong administered a fearsome beating on him, described as a "massacre" in 1938. Well before the war, he had become a fixture at race tracks and an obsessed gambler, blowing

---

28. Jimmy Breslin and Toney Betts, "Hoodlum," *True*, March 1961, Sub Group IX, Series II, Box 22, HKBA. On the Greenberg slaying, see Martin A. Gosch and Richard Hammer, *The Last Testament of Lucky Luciano*, Boston: Little, Brown, 1975, 249.

29. *Miami Beach Daily Sun*, 10 January 1966, Sub Group IX, Series II, Box 25, HKBA.

30. Undated note, Sub Group IX, Series II, Box 28, HKBA.

31. *Miami Herald*, 19 January 1967, Barney Ross Scrapbook, Chicago History Museum (abbrev. Ross-CHM).

32. *TIME*, 22 January 1967, Ross-CHM.

33. *Miami Herald*, 19 January 1967, Ross-CHM.

income sometimes even faster than he accumulated it,[34] making him more susceptible to the blandishments of those in Capone's circle.

Faring a mite better was Abe "The Little Hebrew" Attell, a featherweight champion at the beginning of the 20th century, who learned to fight in San Francisco by protecting himself from assault by Irish Americans. He attained further notoriety for his purported role in the 1919 so-called "Black Sox" scandal when baseball's World Series games involving the Chicago White Sox were fixed, i.e., certain players intentionally performed poorly in league with gamblers[35]—yet another suggestion of a growing trend, the fungus of corruption in boxing infecting other sports. By 1913 the New York State Athletic Commission was rebuking "Abe Attell for failure to box Phil Bloom, giving his reason that Attell refused to box because Blum [sic] would not lay down to him," meaning, lose on purpose.

In fact, just as it is difficult to discuss Black boxing in the 20th century absent a consideration of Johnson, Louis and Ali, the scholar Jeffrey Sussman has put Attell in a similar category—albeit for different reasons—arguing that "any history of boxing in the [U.S.] in the [20th] century would have to shadow the career of Abe Attell, for his presence unlocks the secrets of many fixed fights."[36]

The strength of Jewish boxers was no better revealed than when Joe Choynski beat the inimitable Jack Johnson in 1901. He was the son of Isidore Nathan Choynski with roots in Poland; the elder was a left-winger and friend of Mark Twain, and believed his son's victories complemented his own campaign against ant-Semitism. Following the bout with Johnson in Galveston, both were arrested for staging an illicit prizefight on a non-Jim Crow basis.[37] The strength of Jewish boxers was no better revealed than with the case of Johnny Green, who by 1912 was residing in Harlem. "Getting to school every day

---

34. *Boston Record American*, 19 January 1967, Ross-CHM.

35. Undated clipping on Attell, Sub Group IX, Series II, Box 28, HKBA. *New York Times*, 2 November 1920. For more on Attell and the baseball scandal, see *Reno Evening Gazette*, 2 October 1920. On Attell's gambling problems, see *Reno Evening Gazette*, 30 October 1920. See also on this point, Allen Bodner, *When Boxing Was a Jewish Sport*, Westport, Conn.: Praeger, 1997 (abbrev. Bodner, *When Boxing*), 8: Attell suspected of being "Bagman" for Arnold Rothstein, the purported mastermind of the fraud.

36. Jeffrey Sussman, *Boxing and the Mob: The Notorious History of the Sweet Society*, Lanham, Md.: Rowman & Littlefield, 2019, 23.

37. Undated clipping, Sub Group IX, Series II, Box 28, HKBA. In the same site but in Box 30 of this Sub Group and Series, see the informative photograph of Choynski and Johnson behind bars, guarded by grim-faced men with rifles and pistols.

was very nearly a matter of life and death," he confided later. It was "an Italian neighborhood" that he "had to pass through [and] an Irish neighborhood [and] a Polish neighborhood" too, converting him by necessity into a whirling dervish of flying fists: "I used to have to fight my way to school and fight my way home every day," said this ferocious bantamweight puncher.[38]

New York State consequently legalized prizefighting in 1896, and the examples of those like Raphael and Roosevelt stood as reasons why, billing the Empire State as—according to scholar Allen Bodner—"the first state to sanction the sport." Suggestive of the controversy involved, this measure was repealed in 1900, then reinstated in 1911, and repealed again in 1917—with the interregna providing an opening for Nevada.[39] Yet this may have been an example of capitalist supremacy clashing with white supremacy, in that this legalizing measure opened the door for ebony punchers to flatten their melanin-deficient opponents, thus igniting a perceived existential crisis for spokesmen of the latter. For this was an elongated era when the famous Negro leader Frederick Douglass could announce accurately that "to strike a white man [means] death by Lynch Law."[40] But how could this essential dictum withstand the sanctioned hammer blows of Negro bruisers? Something had to give.

* * *

Before Jack Johnson, there was Joe Gans. Widely considered to be the greatest lightweight champion of all time, he was born in Baltimore in 1874, though like Johnson he attained fame and fortune in Nevada; after all, boxing was banned in most U.S. states during his lifetime. And even where the sport was not banned, when bouts occurred in "private" clubs, often Negro spectators and fighters alike were barred. This form of segregation may have shaped one of Gans's more intriguing gambits: At times he would signal to his Negro friends the round of his knockout blow, so they could stealthily exit the venue to avoid being pummeled by Euro-American watchers who wanted a different result. The prospect of an unwanted skirmish had to be taken seriously, for as Negro boxers began to flex their muscles, white supremacists objected strenuously and sternly. Such was the case when the supremacists' favorite, Jack Skelly, lost his featherweight

---

38. *St. Petersburg Times*, 23 November 1972, Sub Group IX, Series II, Box 31, HKBA.
39. Bodner, *When Boxing*, 8.
40. Aycock and Scott, *Joe Gans*, 66, 86.

title to George "Little Chocolate" Dixon in New Orleans in 1892, the latter regarded as the first Negro (and Black Canadian) boxing title-holder in any weight class, leading to a furious crusade to bar interracial prizefighting. It was feared that Negroes would no longer accept the hocus-pocus of white supremacy as they were busily dismantling boxers of that persuasion in the ring. Barbados Joe Walcott (actually born in British Guiana in 1873, to be distinguished from the U.S. boxer of the same name) followed Dixon in being crowned welterweight champion in 1901, once having to lose a bout on purpose rather than risk his life. This was an inauspicious moment for Gans's arrival at center stage, especially since in some ways, Gans was the embodiment of the "Sweet Science" in that he argued that the key to all scientific boxing was placing one's feet always at 45 degree angles with weight centered so that one could smoothly move right to left or forward and back.[41]

The fact that Gans was U.S.-born attracted even more negative attention than that absorbed by the foreign-born Walcott and Dixon, since U.S. racists traditionally took a harder line against the U.S.-born Negroes.[42] Still, there is a further wrinkle: Peter Jackson was an African born in the Virgin Islands in 1869, though achieving fame as an Australian heavyweight. He journeyed to the U.S. and posed as a Jamaican and a Briton: His fluent French added to his cosmopolitan aura. Yet by the time he died distressed in 1901, he had found it difficult to secure bouts, perhaps because his weight class was viewed as the apex of masculinity, a Mount Everest that should not be scaled by Negroes so as not to puncture the aura of white supremacy.[43]

John L. Sullivan dominated the heavyweight ranks and, consequently, the sport itself. Per the dictates of white supremacy, he was unwilling to fight the redoubtable Jackson,[44] converting magically what may have been fear or cowardice into a manly defense of "the race." James J. Corbett was yet another Irish-American boxer who has been associated with the birth of the "sweet science" in that he jabbed and moved—as opposed to engaging in a pell-mell rush as if in a barroom brawl. Corbett deigned to fight Jackson, but after sixty-plus rounds leaving both men terribly battered, the referee stopped the fight, Corbett predictably crying, "I had been robbed,"

---

41. Aycock and Scott, 9, 41, 49. See also Rodriguez, *Regulation*, 29: Boxing was illegal in all 30 U.S. states in 1880.

42. Horne, *Counter-Revolution*.

43. Petersen, *Gentleman Bruiser*, 3, 6, 153, 154.

44. R.F. Dibble, *John L. Sullivan: An Intimate Narrative*, Boston: Little, Brown, 1925, 31.

while his father was braying, "you whipped the nigger." Market forces also intervened when most gamblers reputedly bet on the Negro prevailing; even Corbett confessed that Jackson "was the greatest fighter I have ever seen."[45]

The avoidance and denigration of Jackson was an aspect of a larger construction of a "White Pacific."[46] For as Jackson was being evaded, John Hergot (also spelled Herget), born in San Francisco in 1868, had migrated to Australia by 1887 and became a pioneer in successfully urging those from the "Lucky Country"—meaning Euro-Australians—to move to the republic. As a boxer, he fought as "Young Mitchell" (also spelled Mitchel); by 1910, he was a top political leader in the city of his birth.[47]

Thus it was in 1911 that Al Lippe, who had managed Gans, urged boxers to seek matches in Europe, where some were already making their mark in France.[48] Taking this advice was the welterweight known as the "Dixie Kid"—who happened to be a Negro, born in Fulton, Missouri, in 1883—along with Joe Jeannette and Sam McVey.[49] The "Kid," otherwise known as Aaron Brown, fought Walcott for the welterweight title, but the referee, not atypically, bet on Brown, disqualifying Walcott just as he seemed on the verge of triumphing.[50] (The repeated malfeasance of referees led to fracases often more energetic than prizefights; the New York State Athletic Commission in 1912 debated one case where a combatant was "accused of striking at the referee" and engaging in other "unsportsmanlike tactics.")[51] Still, the "Dixie Kid" dominated the welterweight ranks from about 1899 to 1914, though he was consigned ignominiously to a pauper's grave by about 1934.[52]

---

45. James J. Corbett, *The Roar of the Crowd*, New York: Putnam's, 1925, 109, 110, 141, 143.

46. Gerald Horne, *The White Pacific: U.S. Imperialism and Black Slavery in the South Seas After the Civil War*, Honolulu: University of Hawaii Press, 2007 (abbrev. Horne, *White Pacific*).

47. "The Referee and the Redhead," February 1943, MSS455, Conlon Scrapbooks on Boxing, California Historical Society, San Francisco.

48. Clipping, 1911, Sub Group VIII, Series I, Box 13, HKBA.

49. Clipping, no date, Sub Group VIII, Series I, Box 15, HKBA.

50. *San Francisco Chronicle*, 30 April 1984.

51. Minutes, 21 February 1912, NYSAC. See also Minutes, 21 November 1924, NYSAC: "Recommended...that the license of Richard Curley, as manager and second, be revoked for causing a disturbance, striking Referee Patsy Haley and attempting to kick Judge Charles Mathison."

52. Clipping, 1934, Sub Group X, Series, I, box 24, HKBA.

Such shenanigans (and the apparent success of Brown) did not dissuade the Negro teenager from Georgia, Eugene Bullard, who hopped aboard a ship and sailed to Scotland in 1912, where he qualified as a boxer, then aircraft pilot, then wartime hero in occupied France.[53] Like Bullard, another boxer, Sam Langford, too was exceedingly popular in France.[54]

This was the backdrop to Gans's pivotal 1906 bout with Danish-born Oscar "Battling" Nelson. Referred to affectionately as the "abysmal brute" by the paradigmatic racist socialist Jack London, Nelson boastfully proclaimed, before confronting Gans, "During my twelve busy years of fighting I have met just five different Negroes out of a string of nearly 100 battles. I feel proud of stating no colored man ever conquered me," though in a casual epithet he referred to one of these opponents as "a pretty tough coon." In his memoir this self-proclaimed "coon hunter" included a cartoon of "Battling Nelson's Colored Morgue" with stereotyped images of four recumbent Negroes. When he defeated one of his unfortunate Negro opponents, the band played, "All Coons Look Alike to Me."[55]

Unavoidably, but as was typical, when Nelson agreed to battle Gans, the Negro received less than half the fee paid to the former for this scheduled 42-round exertion.[56] Such lengthy bouts, testing the endurance of the most battle-hardened, were not abnormal. Across the border from San Diego in Tijuana, Mexico, in 1887, there was a 75-round match, for example, with the soon to be famed Wyatt Earp serving as referee. (As was also normal then, they had crossed the border for this spectacle since the purported "better element" in San Diego objected.)[57]

Gans faced a real dilemma: He was cited for the proposition that he could not make a living by fighting Negroes and would only fight men of European ancestry—but, Nelson notwithstanding, would

---

53. Phil Keith, *All Blood Runs Red: The Legendary Life of Eugene Bullard—Boxer, Pilot, Soldier, Spy*, Toronto: Hanover Square, 2019, 48-49.

54. Moyle, *Sam Langford*, 273.

55. Battling Nelson, *His Life, Battles and Career*, Hegewisch, Ill.: Nelson, 1909, 158-160. This book can be found at both the California Historical Society in San Francisco and the Huntington Library in San Marino. On London, see, e.g., Earle Labor, *Jack London: An American Life*, New York: Farrar, Straus and Giroux, 2013, and James L. Haley, *Wolf: The Lives of Jack London*, New York: Basic, 2010.

56. Clipping, uncertain provenance, Vertical File-Boxing, Nevada State Library and Archives, Carson City (abbrev. NVSL-CC).

57. Memo to File, 28 November 1957, Vertical File-Boxing, SDHC.

they fight him?[58] Yet despite the downside of fighting Nelson, it was understandable why he took the risk. With masculinity and who was to be deemed the emperor of same figuratively at issue, hundreds of Euro-American women flooded Goldfield, Nevada, on 3 September 1906 to witness this spectacle.[59] It was "the greatest glove contest for the lightweight championship ever held in America," or so said publicists. The "purse," it was said with conviction, "is the largest guaranteed sum ever offered for such an event," amounting to a sizable $30,000—though Nelson's share, consonant with racist dynamics, was to be $20,000 win or lose, with Gans taking the remainder, win or lose.[60]

Nelson proved true to his nickname, repeatedly butting his opponent—improperly—throughout the fight, as the referee turned a blind eye. Gans, likewise, was punched in the groin. Gans broke his hand in the 33rd round,[61] perhaps as a result of a rude encounter with Nelson's skull; yet, he prevailed, taking home a still hefty check for $11,500—making him automatically one of the more affluent U.S. Negroes—though he said he turned down a heftier $25,000 to lose and, presumably, repair the wounded indignity of white supremacy. A wounded Gans sported a tightly bandaged right hand after the fight, symbolic of the battle.[62]

Many of his Negro supporters also wound up bandaged—and worse. His victory, said one analysis, "caused the first serious outbreaks of racial violence against Blacks as a result of a boxing match." But it was hardly the last, as white supremacy had difficulty digesting the anomaly that "to strike a white man'" outside of the ring meant "Death by Lynch Law," but to do so inside the ring led to a handsome reward. As for Gans, he spread the wealth, sponsoring the pianist and fellow Marylander Eubie Blake back in his Baltimore hometown, who in turn wrote "Goldfield Rag" in honor of his patron, as the proceeds from fisticuffs began to provide bountiful dividends.[63]

---

58. *Nevada State Journal*, 2 August 1906, Vertical File-Gans-Nelson Fight, NHS-R.

59. *Nevada State Journal*, 8 August 1906, Vertical File-Gans-Nelson Fight, NHS-R.

60. Contract between Gans and Nelson and Program for Fight, Box 1, Collections on Goldfield, UNV-LV.

61. *Goldfield News*, 4 September 1906, Vertical File-Gans-Nelson Fight, NHS-R.

62. Clipping, 5 September 1906, Vertical File-Gans Nelson Fight, NHS-R.

63. Aycock and Scott, *Joe Gans*, 228.

Yet Blake's rousing chords were a kind of final dirge for Goldfield. From 1906 to 1910 it was the largest city in Nevada, boasting a population of 20,000 during this era of tumult, and became the leading political and economic power in the state.[64] But staging extravaganzas featuring the bashing of men of European ancestry was not the ideal route to prosperity in a white supremacist society, and after the Gans-Nelson bout, the city descended into vertiginous decline.

Not far from Gans and Blake's Baltimore hometown, in Washington, D.C., the seat of political power, Euro-Americans erupted in fury after the fight in 1906, randomly attacking African Americans. But two years later, when Nelson wreaked revenge by defeating Gans, Negroes returned the disfavor by beating Euro-Americans senseless. President Roosevelt would have had to be purblind to be oblivious to the dangerous implications of this retaliatory violence at the doorstep of political power and the frightening implications for same.[65]

Thus, moving prizefights hundreds of miles to the west did not forbid seismic eruptions, even at the seat of power. Seeking to capitalize on the illegality of the sport in states to the east, Nevada had moved in 1898 in the opposing direction, which would draw money to the state. Mining camps often sponsored fights as a means of drawing attention—and investors. However, when Negroes such as Gans began triumphing—for example, his defeat of "Kid" Herman near the same time as his victory over Nelson[66]—it was evident that there had been a miscalculation, in that capital was pouring in torrents into the pockets of those who were deemed unworthy, while inspiring fellow Negroes to mount the barricades. When Abe "The Little Hebrew" Attell was brought to Goldfield shortly thereafter to fight Freddie Weeks,[67] it was unclear if this was a signal that Jewish boxers were more acceptable than Negroes—or if this was mere coincidence.

* * *

Jack London's racist socialism was particularly dysfunctional in Nevada, where multiracial unity could have buoyed the bitter class

---

64. Undated pamphlet from Goldfield Historical Society, Vertical File-Goldfield, NHS-R.

65. Kenneth Robert Janken, *Rayford W. Logan and the Dilemma of the African American Intellectual*, Chapel Hill: University of North Carolina Press, 1993, 13.

66. Clipping, 26 January 1907, Vertical File-Boxing, NHS-R.

67. *Gateway Gazette*, 29 February 1996, Vertical File-Boxing, NHS-R.

struggles then unfolding; but it was difficult to overcome the hegemonic reality that the republic should be a "white man's country" and all not so designated should accommodate. A characteristic headline from this tempestuous era blared, "Tonopah Anarchists threaten to kill capitalists."[68] "Goldfield in Turmoil" was another headline, with the attendant story detailing the rampaging of the Industrial Workers of the World,[69] which had a firm foothold in the then flourishing mining industry. But months after Gans's victory, the news was about a setback: "IWW Rule is At an End," said the *Tonopah Daily Sun*. "[T]omorrow all stores and barbershops and saloons will refuse to employ any IWW men" was the gist.[70] The fact that paramount IWW leader "Big Bill" Haywood was able, temporarily, to escape conviction in 1907[71] did not erase the overriding point that the kind of racism to which Gans was subjected in Goldfield was infertile and hardly arable soil for the growth of working-class solidarity—nor victory.

Minimally, the raucous labor relations in Nevada were inhospitable to the idea of greeting warmly a Negro bent on mayhem. Months after Gans's victory, the IWW sought to "condemn" the Legislature for creating a state militia: "standing men at arms is a relic of *ante-diluvian, fossilized, fiendish* barbarism," the laborers insisted. In castigating a maneuver meant to squash themselves, they stressed, "the ONLY WEALTH PRODUCERS" were themselves.[72]

Gans may have known that Governor John Sparks of Nevada was born in Mississippi—not reassuring to any Negro—and continued moving westward, joining the Texas Rangers to fight the fearsome Comanches, before decamping to the Sagebrush State.[73] Sparks contacted President Roosevelt directly deploring the "domestic violence and unlawful combinations and conspiracies" involving "unlawful dynamiting of property, commission of felonies; threats" facilitated by "unlawful possession of arms and ammunition and the confiscation of dynamite." His recommendation? "Send" immediately, he

---

68. Clipping, 2 March 1907, Box 21, Pat McCarran Papers, *Nevada Historical Society, Reno* (abbrev. McCarran-NHS-R).
69. Clipping, 9 March 1907, Box 21, McCarran-NHS-R.
70. *Tonopah Daily Sun*, 2 March 1907, Box 21, McCarran-NHS-R.
71. *Tonopah Daily Sun*, 29 July 1907, Box 21, McCarran-NHS-R.
72. Tonopah Local 325 of IWW, Local 121 of Western Federation of Miners to Governor, 28 January 1907, Box 1, GOV 003 01020501, NVSL-CC.
73. James A. Young and B. Abbott Sparks, *Cattle in the Cold Desert*, Reno: University of Nevada Press, 1985.

said, "two companies of the troops of the Army."[74] In other words, the anti-labor climate being created would ultimately be detrimental to Negroes laboring in the quadrangular ring. "Immediately," Roosevelt, who coincidentally was souring on his earlier infatuation with the sport, moved to "direct" that "troops be sent to Nevada."[75] The governor was not assuaged, carping about the "constant state of war" between "two hostile camps" (not unlike two brawlers in the ring). The IWW had "three thousands" in their ranks with "fully one half…constantly armed," while the bosses controlled a "large number of watchmen and guards [who] were constantly armed." The former were "Communist and anarchist" in essence, necessitating the arrival of "Texas Rangers" in Nevada,[76] well practiced in perpetrating genocide against the once dominant Comanches, which the governor well knew.[77] Soon, martial law was imposed in Ely as copper miners went on strike.[78]

* * *

Into this highly charged climate arrived Jack Johnson, the ebony Texan with the finely chiseled physique. He was slated to fight Jim Jeffries in Reno, Nevada, once again walking in the footsteps of Gans. Also, like Gans, he was a "sweet scientist," a master of defensive strategy,[79] to the point where opponents not only became frustrated but an author of their own demise as a result. Indeed, the Marquess of Queensberry himself, whose name is associated with the elemental rules of the sport, termed him the "greatest *defensive* heavyweight of all time" [emphasis in original]. (However, he went too far when assaying that Johnson was "probably the most unpopular champion ever to hold the heavyweight title." Why? Because he was a Negro in a white supremacist society where the heavyweight champion was seen as the czar of masculinity? No, he said, it was because fans

---

74. Governor Sparks to President Roosevelt, 5 December 1907, Box 1, GOV 003 010120501, NVSL-CC.

75. President Roosevelt to Governor Sparks, 5 December 1907, Box 1, GOV 003 010120501, NVSL-CC.

76. Governor Sparks to President Roosevelt, 26 December 1907, Box 1, GOV 003 01010501, NVSL-CC.

77. Pekka Hamalainen, *The Comanche Empire*, New Haven, Conn.: Yale University Press, 2008.

78. *Carson City News,* 18 October 1912, Scrapbook of Governor Tasker Oddie, UNV-R (abbrev. Oddie-UNV-R).

79. Story on Negro boxer, no date, Box 1, Walter White Papers, SCH.

"pay to see action," meaning furious exchanges of blows, and with Johnson they received instead the blocking of blows or evading of same.)[80]

By consenting to fight Jeffries in Reno, Johnson was entering a lion's den. Gunslinger Bat Masterson, an avowed enemy of the Texas Titan, was proposed as a referee, which was akin to proposing the devil to be the judge of a battle between good and evil. Later, it was Masterson who beat the drums for a bout between Johnson and the towering Jess Willard in Havana—which the Galvestonian lost, supposedly restoring the status quo ante insofar as white supremacy was concerned.[81]

Meanwhile, when the *San Francisco Examiner* queried Governor D.S. Dickerson in Carson City as to the "rumor" as to whether he would cancel the upcoming bout between Johnson and Jim Jeffries,[82] the presumption was not that this drastic measure was being contemplated because of the Negro's skill in blocking blows. Cautiously, James Finch, the chief executive's secretary, replied that there was "no foundation" to this "rumor" and, besides, the governor "could not prevent [the] fight under law" and, in any case, was "not inclined to interfere."[83]

However, it was not just class struggle and racist tensions that were wracking Nevada at this fraught moment. The imminent arrival of boxers and their camp followers was bound to attract attention in a state already gaining a reputation for high-stakes gambling and a complement of prostitutes, especially Euro-Americans. The variable in the prelude to the rumble in Reno was the presence of a Negro star with a well-merited reputation for interracial coupling. Vaulting into action, Clyde Mann of the "Committee on Legislation for the Suppression…of the Predatory Traffic in Girls," or what he termed the "white slave traffic," railed vehemently against this noxious and "systematic" defiling, involving the "hunt, capture, sale and ruin of our girls," which was "ruthless, insidious and national—even international. Approximately 100,000 girls per year are recruited, more

---

80. Tenth Marquess of Queensberry, *The Sporting Queensberry's*, London: Hutchinson, 1915, 217.

81. Robert K. DeArment, *Gunfighter in Gotham: Bat Masterson's New York City Years*, Norman: University of Oklahoma Press, 2013 (abbrev. DeArment, *Gunfighter*), 111, 143.

82. Undated telegram to Governor D.S. Dickerson, GOV 004 01020502, Box 2, NVSL-CC.

83. James Finch to *San Francisco Examiner*, 20 June 1910, Box 2, GOV 004 01020502, Box 2, NVSL-CC.

from rural than urban homes." Anxiously, Mann, anticipating the arrival of Johnson and his crew, inquired if there were "adequate law or punishment in your state."[84] Finch, doubtlessly eyeing the bonanza to be delivered by a high-profile prizefight, again replied cautiously, asserting, "the evil is not practiced on a very large scale in Nevada"—then tied the matter up in process: "the subject will be taken up in the next session of the Legislature."[85] Mann pressed the matter, adding acidulously that "for horse stealing" Nevada provided draconian punishment but lagged on the matter of "stealing the daughters of your citizens."[86] As the time approached for Johnson's arrival, Mann observed that "50,000 girls per annum…are the prey of procurers" in this "army of prostitution."[87] Besieged, Finch sought to assure the governor, telling him, "we do not believe there is much of this traffic in Nevada. Of course, we have the usual proportion of lewd women but womanhood is so highly respected that even in the mining camps a woman is safer than on Broadway, New York, or State Street, Chicago."[88]

There are a number of ways to interpret this tawdry episode. As women's roles changed, with more entering the work force as a result of urbanization and technological advance (the typewriter, the automobile, electrification, mass transit via subways, increased immigration, etc.), this impacted the balance of forces between Euro-American men and women especially, creating anxiety among the former accustomed to the male supremacist status quo and fomenting anxiety manifesting in heightened fears about prostitution among Euro-American women.[89]

Then the arrival on the scene of Johnson—and Gans before him—Negro men often with wads of cash as an accoutrement, led to the supposition that, capitalist-style, their patriarchal privilege would be simply eroded by way of finance. Nevada in any event

---

84. Clyde Mann to Governor D.S. Dickerson, 22 March 1909, Box 1, GOV 0004 01020502, NVSL-CC.

85. James Finch to Clyde Mann, 20 April 1909, Box 1, GOV 004 01020502, NVSL-CC.

86. Clyde Mann to James Finch, 30 March 1909, Box 1, GOV 004 01020502, NVSL-CC.

87. Clyde Mann to James Finch, 16 June 1909, Box 1, GOV 004 01020502, NVSL-CC.

88. James Finch to Governor Dickerson, 25 June 1909, GOV 004 01020502, NVSL-CC.

89. See Ruth Rosen, *The Lost Sisterhood: Prostitution in America, 1900-1918*, Baltimore: Johns Hopkins University Press, 1982.

was engaged in arbitrage, attracting desperados of various sorts,[90] including pimps from other states, and even other prizefights and their accompanying wastrels, such as James J. Corbett versus Bob Fitzsimmons in the seat of power itself, Carson City, in 1897.[91] The baggage delivered by these boxing titans often included disreputable elements. John L. Sullivan, a heavyweight champion of this era, was said to be "sponsored" by gangsters in Chicago[92]—a future home of Jack Johnson, which early on was rightly regarded as a haven for mobsters.[93] Even Gans was said to associate with Chicago's leading Negro gambler—John "Mushmouth" Johnson—who was accused of seeking to arrange preordained results in some of his more contested bouts.[94]

* * *

Johnson's stunning defeat of Jeffries in 1910 was more than just a turning point in boxing, which it certainly was. It upended musty stereotypes about the alleged "yellow streak," purported cowardice and supposed "softness" of Negro men, as the dark-skinned Johnson became de facto king of masculinity. It inspired racist attacks—and counterattacks. In the future birthplace of Muhammad Ali, Euro-Americans attacked Negroes for their outward enthusiasm hailing Johnson's triumph, and in response Negroes struck back with vigor in Louisville.[95] A Carson City periodical captured the tensions of the time as it reported breathlessly on the "general movement in most of the large cities to suppress the showing of the fight films," meaning the unassailable triumphs on celluloid of Johnson and Gans, among others: In "many of the big cities, especially in the South, where the Negro population ranks high in numbers, the

---

90. Clifford Alpheus Shaw, *The Last Days of the Daly Gang at Aurora, Nevada*, 2017, UNV-R.

91. Clippings, 1897, Republican State Central Committee Scrapbook, UNV-R.

92. Ishmael Reed, *The Complete Muhammad Ali*, Montreal: Baraka, 2015 (abbrev. Reed, *Complete Muhammad Ali*), 107.

93. John J. Binder, *The Chicago Outfit*, Chicago: Arcadia, 2003, 7, 9, 119.

94. Moore, *I Fight*, 45.

95. Vincent DiGirolamo, *Crying the News: A History of America's Newsboys*, New York: Oxford University Press, 2019 (abbrev. DiGirolamo, *Crying*), 268, 370.

authorities are putting the ban on the fight pictures fearing that [said images] further swell the chests of the colored men."[96]

Nevada's venture into federal arbitrage backfired when technology emerged that allowed prizefights that might be banned elsewhere to be captured on film, then broadcast widely. On the other hand, this was not a backfire in that ultimately it led to multi-million-dollar prizefights in the desert, pushing untold riches into the purses of Nevadans (and non-Nevadans too). In the short term, just after the Johnson win, many cameras were confiscated and not returned,[97] but that could only create a secondary market for these "used" cameras purloined from behind closed doors by the unscrupulous or a ramping up of production to replace these new-fangled devices. Nonetheless, San Francisco, even then proud of its supposed sophistication, was one of the first jurisdictions to bar screening of the Johnson triumph.[98] That was in September 1910; by December there were huge crowds for screenings of the film in Reno.[99] Yet confiscating cameras and barring film showings could not erase the memories of what one local journal described as the "several hundred colored people" who came to the fight.[100]

The response in Carson City was emphatic. By 1912 legislation was passed that banned "miscegenation," i.e., "fornication between certain races prohibited.... if any white person shall live and cohabit with any black person, mulatto, Indian or any person of the Malay or brown race or of the Mongolian or yellow race, in a state of fornication," said person would be fined $500 or imprisoned "not less than six months or more than one year, or both."[101] Then the other shoe dropped when the legislature mandated that an "exhibition with gloves" should be "between white men."[102] One possible interpretation of this tortured skein of events is that once labor was bludgeoned,

---

96. *Carson City Daily Appeal*, 7 July 1910, Vertical File-Johnson-Jeffries Fight, NHR-R.
97. *Reno Evening Gazette*, 12 July 1910, Vertical File-Johnson-Jeffries Fight, NHR-R.
98. *Reno Evening Gazette*, 9 September 1910, Vertical File-Boxing-Nevada, NHR-R.
99. *Reno Evening Gazette*, 16 December 1910, Vertical File-Boxing-Nevada, NHR-R.
100. *Reno Evening Gazette*, 27 June 1910, Vertical File-Johnson-Jeffries Fight, NHR-R.
101. "Revised Laws of Nevada," Volume I, 1912, Box 1, Elmer Rusco Papers, NHR-R.
102. "Laws of Nevada, 29th Session, Chapter 58, p. 69, 1919, Box 1, Elmer Rusco Papers, NHR-R.

just as Negroes were battering their alleged "betters" for pay, a chain reaction was created seeking to erect sexual barriers as an adjunct of disrupting nascent multiracial unity—while strangling the ability of Negro men to gain financial leverage by dint of brawn and brain. Or to put it another way, the strains on white supremacy were exposed when in order to preserve the legerdemain of bigotry, men of European ancestry were barred by law to fight Negro men and run the risk of jeopardizing the racial project by losing—just as Nevada had jeopardized the project in the first instance by sanctioning the Johnson-Jeffries battle.[103] A telling indicator was glimpsed in 1912 when Nevada's Governor Tasker Oddie was sitting beside South Carolina's Governor Cole Blease, who said he was itching to "lynch Jack Johnson," a threat that had to be taken seriously, and the Carson City man did not object.[104] But it was too late: The genie was out of the bottle, and despite the racist to and fro in coming years, boxing was now unleashed as yet another weapon against white supremacy.

Neighboring Arizona had to confront a similar specter. The authorities were assured that boxing "will not fall into the hands of unscrupulous promoters and gamblers," a futile hope as matters evolved. But what seemed to sway opinion was the descriptor affixed to boxing: "the manly art."[105] Stridently, an objector warned that "the effect of prize fighting can be only brutalizing—particularly in respect to the youth of our state"; thus, "repeal" of laws allowing boxing was demanded.[106] The governor agreed, as he fretted in 1919 about the effect of such a move on "returned soldiers," but finally concurred that the sport should be "abolished" as it was akin to "bullfighting"—it "falls within the same class."[107]

Yet even if the sport were to be outlawed, the images captured on celluloid were harder to ban. White supremacists may have wanted to seize and destroy the film footage of Johnson's triumphant visit to Manhattan shortly after the turning point in Reno. Already, the

---

103. *Sparks Tribune* [Nevada], 25 July 1923, Vertical File-Johnson-Jeffries, NHR-R: More discussion here of segregation in the boxing ring. For more on this praxis in Nevada, see "Clipping, 21 February 1919, Sub Group XV, Series XIII, Box 46, HKBA.

104. Clipping, December 1912, Oddie-UNV-R.

105. S.F. Fraser to Hon. Harry Jennings, House of Representatives, 18 February 1919, RG 1, SG Series, 1.1.4 Box 002, Arizona State Archives, Phoenix (abbrev. ASA-P).

106. H.P. Cory to Governor Thomas Campbell, 20 November 1919, RG 1, SG Series, 1.1.4, Box 002, ASA-P.

107. Governor Thomas Campbell to H.P. Cory, 21 November 1919, RG 1, SG Series, 1.1.4, Box 002, ASA-P.

northern neighborhood known as Harlem was becoming a wellspring of Negro activism, and this perception was bolstered when thousands from this besieged minority crowded the streets, seeking a peek at this latest hero. Some were shooting off fireworks, others were simply shouting. In Herald Square in midtown, a number of the so-called "colored sports folk" gathered at their favorite watering hole, the Baron Wilkes' Hotel, to confer and carouse with Johnson while thousands more blocked the major thoroughfare.[108]

Frantically, white supremacy then launched a global search for a "Great White Hope" who could not only defeat Johnson but, more than this, restore what was perceived to be the natural order of things: a man of European ancestry as the reigning symbol of masculinity. Actually, the search itself revealed that more than that was at stake: Part of the purpose of this hunt was as much to undermine Negroes, as it was to elevate Euro-Americans. How else to explain what struck the writer John Lardner as the picaresque journey of "one talent scout, Walter (Good Time Charlie) Friedman," who "went to China to look for a white hope among the Chinese peasants."[109] Perhaps more in line with the lineaments of white supremacy was the "'White Hope' Heavyweight Championship," that was won by "Gunboat" Smith in 1914."[110]

The Negro writer Ralph Ellison found it necessary to file away one report by Lardner who wondered why the search for a "White Hope" rarely applied beyond the heavyweight ranks (speculatively, the man at this level could be more easily seen as the emperor of masculinity, as opposed to any below). It remained wondrous, however, why this search led to China and inspection of the combative skills of Chinese peasants.[111]

This search for a "White Hope" was taken quite seriously by numerous Euro-Americans. As one analyst put it, "the white race felt itself under fire" and acted accordingly. Eagle eyes were scrutinizing mining camps, farmlands, factories and docks. Any beefy man of a certain height and weight was putatively eligible. As one fretful writer put it, "Jack Johnson was the biggest single issue in the white

---

108. Fleischer, *50 Years*, 74.

109. Lardner, *White Hopes*, 20.

110. Peter Heller, *"In This Corner...!": Forty World Champions Tell Their Stories*, New York: Simon & Schuster, 1973 (abbrev. Heller, *In This Corner*), 31.

111. Report by John Lardner, 25 June 1949, Box 209, Ralph Ellison Papers, Library of Congress, Washington, D.C. (abbrev. Ellison-LC).

man's world."¹¹² In fact, the search for a "White Hope" was so serious that it arguably contributed to a decline of anti-Semitism, in that an impressive array of Jewish boxers were invited to participate—to their immediate benefit—in a continuation of a long-term trend.¹¹³ As Joe Louis was climbing the ladder of pugilistic success, a rung or three behind him was Izzy Singer, described as "New York's young Jewish heavyweight" and a "finalist in the Chicago Stadium's 'White Hope' tourney."¹¹⁴ Even more ironically—or bizarrely—by 1950, a Miami periodical quoted one observer for the notion that Moscow centered in the most populous region of Europe, was best positioned to crown the newest "Great White Hope"¹¹⁵ though in this instance the demands of anticommunism seemed to override the requisites of white supremacy.

More traditionally, after Johnson was chased from the continent, the beefy Nebraskan Luther McCarthy earned the dubious title of being the sturdiest of the "White Hopes." Known variously as "The Fighting Cowboy" or "Big Brutus" or simply "Luck," the stolid Irish-American slugger was celebrated—among some. Alas, his luck ran out in Alberta, Calgary, in May 1913, when he collapsed after fistic exchanges in the first round of a bout with Arthur Pelkey—and died.¹¹⁶

As evidenced by the "white slave traffic" scare and resultant anti-miscegenation law in Nevada, Johnson had lit an explosively flammable fuse when he publicly consorted with Euro-American women, a "blunder" that led to his prosecution and subsequent flight into exile.¹¹⁷ Apparently, his sojourn in Europe led to his knowledge of French and Spanish. By July 1914 he was in Russia, where he communed with George Thomas, a Negro from Georgia who, said Johnson, "amassed a fortune" there, and the two affluent African Americans "became close friends." Evidently, this "confidential agent of Czar Nicholas" was "taking part in military councils and other phases of the war preparations" as the lights were on the verge of being doused in Europe. He "had been in Russia more than twenty

---

112. George Lemmer, "'White Hope', Fight Stories," November 1931, Box 2, Dempsey-Tunney Fight Collection, CHM.

113. Horne, *Dawning*.

114. Clipping, 7 April 1937, Sub Group IX, Series II, Box 23, HKBA.

115. *Miami Daily News*, 13 April 1950, Sub Group X, Series I, Box 9, HKBA.

116. *New York Times*, 27 May 1913; *Miami Herald*, 26 June 1947, Sub Group X, Series 1, Box 6, HKBA; *Salt Lake Tribune*, 25 May 1913.

117. Jack Johnson, *Jack Johnson is a Dandy: An Autobiography*, New York: New American Library, 1970.

years." Luckily, Johnson was able to dodge the revolutionary flames then lapping at the doors of St. Petersburg and Moscow and fled to Barcelona, a favorite city of his where he considered residing. He claimed that while in Spain he toiled on behalf of Washington, scanning the waters for German submarines. Still, despite his service to the state, Johnson was not viewed warmly in his homeland, because of his flouting and flaunting of imposed sexual norms—and his penchant for administering devastating blows to outmatched opponents of a lighter hue. "I have never been able to agree with the point of view of [Booker T.] Washington," he confessed,[118] a militant path he exemplified when he moved to revolutionary Mexico and sought to establish a beachhead against Jim Crow.[119] Johnson, said boxing aficionado Nat Fleischer, was "one of the brainiest fighters I have ever known"[120]—an opinion that is not easy to dispute.

The upset ignited by the brawny slugger was evidenced even after he had left the ring, as if he could never be forgiven for so audaciously challenging the status quo. In 1930 his proposal to regulators in New York to "engage in three two-minute round exhibitions with Philadelphia Jack O'Brien at a local club" was peremptorily "denied."[121] In 1938 he was again in the Empire State and appealed to the authorities to allow him to conduct boxing and wrestling shows at 68th Avenue and 65th Place in Long Island City, and desired, as it was said, "licensing of same." Stiffly and coldly, the Athletic Commission replied that they "could not give consideration" to his application.[122]

* * *

Johnson's exultant tour of Manhattan was a prelude to a crackdown on interracial slugfests in the Empire State. By 1913, this issue was debated at the State Athletic Commission; there was a "thorough discussion of the matter" and it was "unanimously decided that the present rule of the Commission which prohibits any licensed club in the State from holding mixed bouts should be sustained." Thus, the "proposed bout between [Sam] Langford [Negro] and Gunboat Smith would be withdrawn."[123] Why? "The rule of the Commission

---

118. Jack Johnson, *Jack Johnson in the Ring—and Out*, Chicago: National Sports Publishing Authority, 1927, 5, 92-93, 104, 239.
119. Horne, *Black and Brown*, passim.
120. Fleischer, *50 Years*, 77.
121. Minutes, 19 June 1930, NYSAC.
122. Minutes, 17 May 1938, NYSAC.
123. Minutes, 24 September 1913, NYSAC.

forbids mixed bouts," it was said brusquely, though one Commissioner dissented.[124] Still, pressure was on New York to change course, not only because a growing Negro population was objecting, but also because entrepreneurs may have noticed that such bouts were often winners at the box office: Various audiences resonated to the idea of a symbolic "race battle."[125] By late 1915 John Reisler appeared before the Commission and requested that the "ban on mixed be lifted."[126]

Though he may not have recognized it then, historical momentum was with Reisler, as the examples of Gans and Johnson and their Nevada triumphs had aided in unleashing forces that would not be denied.

---

124. Minutes, 10 September 1913, NYSAC.

125. Gerald Horne, *Race War! White Supremacy and the Japanese Attack on the British Empire*, New York: New York University Press, 2003 (abbrev. Horne, *Race War!*).

126. Minutes, 29 November 1915, NYSAC.

Chapter 2

Go East, Young Negro!

Sparsely populated Nevada stole a march on fellow states by legalizing prizefighting when competitors like New York were swaying back and forth on this prickly matter. But Nevada had a tiny Negro population, and that factor and the attendant focus on subduing Indigenes—especially the Paiutes—along with an expectation that bouts across the racial line would simply reinforce prevailing racial and gender norms, may have lulled Carson City into assuming that a victorious Joe Gans or Jack Johnson was not possible. But they did triumph, and when technology allowed for the filming of these victories and transmission nationally, if not globally, there was a mad scramble to revert to the status quo ante, culminating in a number of states—including but not limited to Nevada—seeking to bar interracial contests. It appeared, however, that there was a national appetite for such matches, and this market force then allowed in following years for the ascendancy of those like Battling Siki and other two-fisted African competitors.

But the path toward such ascendancy was hardly smooth, not least because of the proliferation of organized crime forces tied to various ethnic and ethno-religious groupings—Italian Americans and Jewish Americans principally—who were hardly equal opportunity contractors. In some ways, the latter were buoyed by a renewed interest in the sport by the U.S. ruling elite, who thought—akin to London—that boxing was useful in the development of a dominating ethos seen as essential to imperialist hegemony. So the sport began to spread east from Nevada, especially to the U.S. Northeast, where the forces unleashed by the recently concluded world war had deposited hundreds of thousands of Negroes from Dixie and the Caribbean, who then had the right to vote and therefore influence a sport subject to government regulation.

This new departure for the sport motored ahead on a white supremacist basis, with hardly a consideration of an alternative. Thus, on Friday, 9 November 1923, under the auspices of the New

York State Athletic Commission, which had oversight of boxing, a large meeting was convened of commissioners, boxers, managers and sportswriters. Among the luminaries present were Gene Tunney, heavyweight contender, along with sportswriters from the major daily newspapers, including the *New York Times* and wire services such as the Associated Press—but nary a Negro or anyone else not defined as "white."[1] This gathering was an emblem of the growing importance and respectability of the sport, as Nevada was shoved aside. Indicative of this trend was the move from the west to Gotham by the infamously gallivanting gunfighter, Bat Masterson, who too had a decided interest in boxing—and was a sworn antagonist of Jack Johnson.[2]

Despite the enhanced scrutiny of the sport, as evidenced by the above gathering, a mountain of corpses continued to be a distinguishing characteristic of boxing. One of the more graphically reported was the death in the ring of Frankie Jerome. He fought Bud Taylor at Madison Square Garden on Friday evening, 11 January 1924—but in the 11th round of a contest scheduled for 15 rounds, he collapsed and shortly died at Bellevue Hospital. The day of the contest a group of doctors deemed him to be "physically fit." After the blows that led to his collapse, he was taken to his dressing room and "appeared to revive." But by Sunday he was dead, a "direct cause… was a ruptured blood vessel in the head," doubtlessly a result of one of Taylor's sledgehammer blows.[3]

* * *

In the highly charged atmosphere following World War I—revolutionary upsurge in Eastern Europe, hysteria about the recrudescence of radicalism in the U.S. and elsewhere—Nevada executed a reversal, seeking to ban prizefighting across racial lines, upset with the perceived Frankenstein's monster created in the form of ebony battlers like Gans and Johnson. However, impressed with the apparent value of prizefighting in toughening men for battle, not unlike the insight realized by TR—before Johnson's prevalence—certain U.S. elite elements, moved by the London old saw about the athletic fields of Eton contributing to victory on the battlefields of Waterloo, began yet another reversal, moving to legalize prizefighting.

---

1. Minutes, 9 November 1923, NYSAC.
2. DeArment, *Gunfighter*, 110.
3. Minutes, 14 January 1924, NYSAC.

This was an uphill climb, however, given the specter of Johnson and the understandable pre-existing animus toward the sport in light of the obvious detrimental health consequences. "After a great amount of work in an endeavor to get our Boxing Bill passed," said Adam Empie of the Army, Navy and Civilian Board of Boxing Control in New York in 1919, "we were not successful.... the bill went through the Judiciary Committee of the Senate and was passed through that body by an overwhelming majority." The subordinate body, the state "Assembly has always shown itself to be more in favor of Boxing than the Senate," but bureaucratic maneuvering by opponents proved successful.[4]

However, the tides of change were not in favor of these opponents. At that pivotal postwar moment, Washington was in the process of supplanting London as the premier global power, and was straining to learn from this nation in decline. Thus, said Empie, the "superior condition of Boxing in that country"—meaning Britain—"was the inspiration" for his effort to implant the sport in the U.S. military in the first instance, i.e., the aforementioned ANCBC. The "lines on which" he was "proceeding are the same as have produced such beneficial results in Great Britain. Boxing in that country was at one time in an even worse condition than that which exists in America today and it was only when men of social prominence, such as the Earl of Lonsdale, Sir Claude de Crespigny, Lord Charles Beresford, the late Admiral, the Hon. Victor Montague and others of social eminence took up the sport, that Boxing took a leap forward and has never looked back."[5] TR was a likeminded man of "social eminence" who in some ways anticipated the London turn.

By June 1919, Empie was elated to report that Washington was now marching in the large footprints of London. "In six months we have succeeded in getting 100 prominent men, including a Secretary of State, Presidents of universities, Generals, Admirals, Governors of states, U.S. Senators and distinguished clergymen to publicly identify themselves with a sport hitherto no self-respecting man could allow his name to be associated." A little arm-twisting was deployed since "many were in the first instance, timid and reluctant to permit their names to be publicly recorded." Now that Johnson had been pushed aside—to exile, then U.S. prison—this eminent body "succeeded after much effort in compelling [Jess] Willard," who had bested Johnson in Havana, and "[Jack] Dempsey," accused of being

---

4. Adam Empie to William Sowden Sims, 5 May 1919, Box 50, Sims-LC.
5. Adam Empie to William Sowden Sims, 16 April 1919, Box 50, Sims-LC.

a draft dodger, "to compete for a [heavyweight boxing] Belt," or title, "presented by this Board."[6]

William Sowden Sims, an admiral once in charge of all U.S. naval operations in Europe, was instrumental in this process of delivering boxing into the realm of respectability. He was well connected. In December 1918, President Woodrow Wilson, not in the best of health, still took time to write to "My Dear Admiral Sims" from Grosvenor Gardens, London, to inform him that "my inclination jumps with yours. I should be very glad to have a conference with you," he said brightly: "come over to Paris for a conversation," he insisted, taking time from protracted peace talks and League of Nation designs.[7] Admiral Sims joined with Franklin K. Lane, a former U.S. Secretary of Interior, a scion of the DuPont fortune, and Justice Bartow Sumter Weeks of the Supreme Court of the State of New York in this campaign. "We have purchased a site within a few blocks of the Grand Central Terminal" in the heart of Manhattan, Sims was told, "and our excavation has been completed at a cost of $110,000." They were bent on building an athletic palace with "nearly three times the annual income of the National Sporting Club of London" slated to host "boxing matches between the champions of the British army and navy and the champions of the army and navy of the United States."[8] In other words, rather than the racial ruckuses that had ignited so much controversy, now there would be battles between nations, as a prelude to less racially sensitive bouts between the likes of Willard and Dempsey.

The New York State Athletic Commission snapped into acquiescence, ruling in 1922 that "all soldiers and sailors who are members" of the military with "a record of at least 90% active duty and continuous service be eligible to compete in the Armories of the State of New York for the promotion of boxing, wrestling and other manly sports." The latter two words signaled that what was at stake was masculinity.[9] A decade earlier, leaders of the NYSAC told Baron Pierre de Coubertin of the International Olympic Committee that the "Games" over which he presided "are now being held at Stockholm," yet "nearly every sport [is] represented except boxing. Boxing is one of the most popular sports in the world," it was said, two years after Johnson's victory in Reno, and thus "this manly sport" should

---

6. Letter to William Sowden Sims, 10 June 1919, Box 50, Sims-LC.

7. Woodrow Wilson to Admiral Sims, 27 December 1918, Box 50, Sims-LC.

8. G. Borglum, International Sporting Club of New York City, to William Sowden Sims, 4 November 1920, Box 50, Sims-LC.

9. Minutes, 6 June 1922, NYSAC.

be included in the spectacle.¹⁰ Yet the Commission's sympathies toward Negroes only extended so far, as they refused adamantly to exert pressure to make sure that Negro battlers could compete for champion. Unsurprisingly, a "colored delegation" were accorded an ice-cold greeting.¹¹

In time, the postwar push of the U.S. elite for boxing created some successes, among which was heavyweight Gene Tunney, who styled himself as an intellectual and whose son later was elected to the US. Senate. In 1926 he informed James Farley, chairman of the New York State Athletic Commission, that he had been a "soldier in France"; there, he recounted, "I won the [boxing] championship of the AEF [American Expeditionary Force]." Since then, he said, "I have had one hope and desire [:] to become the heavyweight championship of the world," a dream soon realized.¹² His purported urbane cosmopolitanism aside, Tunney too upheld the renewed consensus on the sport, when it was reported that he "published a statement in the daily press that if he won the heavyweight championship boxing contest...he would never box with a colored man for the title."¹³ Tunney also was not above coming dangerously close to unethicalness: He subsequently confided that "in the first contest with Jack Dempsey," even "before I landed the first blow, I actually felt a hole in the padding of the ring with the ball of my right foot which I kn[e]w would add leverage and accordingly increase the power at the time of impact."¹⁴

Perhaps appropriately, the debut of this new era of fisticuffs, featuring Willard and Dempsey in 1919, was one of the most brutal to date. As late as 1964, federal judge John Sirica, who was to expose the Watergate shenanigans less than a decade later, compelling the resignation of a president, was musing to his comrade, Dempsey, that "undoubtedly Willard is still suffering from the effects of the beating he got that night."¹⁵ Also appropriately, there were charges that

---

10. John Dixon, Chair of NYSAC, and Frank O'Neill, Commissioner to Baron Pierre de Coubertin, A1372-77, NYSAC.

11. Minutes, 13 June 1922, New York State Athletic Commission, NYSAC.

12. Gene Tunney to James Farley, 1 August 1926, Box 1, James Farley Papers, Library of Congress, Washington, D.C.

13. Edward Carter to Gifford Pinchot, 8 September 1926, Box 1483, Gifford Pinchot Papers, Library of Congress, Washington, D.C. (abbrev. Pinchot-LC).

14. Gene Tunney to "Dear Peg," 10 February 1947, Sub Group VIIII, Series 1, Box 17, HKBA.

15. John Sirica to Jack Dempsey, 10 January 1964, Box 118, John Sirica Papers, Library of Congress, Washington, D.C. (abbrev. Sirica-LC).

hanky-panky was involved in that the battered loser, Willard, agreed with the allegation that the victor's gloves were loaded with plaster, a contention backed by "Doc" Kearns, Dempsey's top aide. The wily Kearns was said to have engaged in this beastliness to insure a 10-1 bet of $10,000 that his man would win.[16] That Kearns would later boast that "I know more about...Capone...than any movie could show me"[17] hardly quelled suspicions. Dempsey waved away lingering doubts since he professed to have "no friendship with Big Jess [Willard]" since "he always resented me"[18] and was little more than a sore loser, a fixture in the contentious sport. As for Willard, by 1944 he was 60 and described by an observer as "pitiful" serving as an "exhibit in [a] freak show."[19]

No matter. Dempsey was well on his way to supplanting Johnson as the star of the ring, heavyweight champion, the newly crowned czar of masculinity, though controversy continued to dog his every step. Just before deposing of Willard, he faced Fred Fulton and decked him quickly in the first round.[20] Months later, a leader of the recently formed National Boxing Association asserted that the vanquished fighter "confessed that he agreed to go through a fake with Jack Dempsey at Harrison Field" in New Jersey but the "Manassa Mauler" then "double crossed him" and administered a staggering "knockout."[21] By 1923 a crowd of 90,000 amassed in the Polo Grounds in Harlem, ordinarily a shrine to baseball. Reportedly, 25,000 more battled the police seeking to get inside to watch the unfolding spectacle. An "Abridged Version of the Social Register" was present: That was the accurate claim decades later, as squeezing into seats were Archie and Kermit Roosevelt, Elihu Root, a dean of the U.S. diplomatic corps, William K. Vanderbilt, scion of a major fortune and, of course, the sultan of swat himself, baseball's Babe Ruth. Dempsey limped away with a nifty $500,000.[22] He limped because his less than intimidated opponent, Luis Firpo, the Argentine "Wild Bull of the Pampas," knocked him out of the ring and he landed awkwardly on his hip. Subsequently, Dempsey developed a "real bad" case of

---

16. *Miami Herald*, 9 January 1964, Sub Group VIII, Series I, Box 24, HKBA.
17. *Miami Herald*, 22 May 1959, Sub Group VIII, Series I, Box 24, HKBA.
18. *New York Daily News*, 24 December 1978, Box 118, Sirica-LC.
19. Clipping, 1944, Volume X, Odds and Ends on Boxing, UND.
20. *New York Times*, 28 July 1918.
21. Roy F. Schoonmaker to "Sir," 3 January 1920, Box 1, CORRESP. 1919-1920, Records of Acting Governor William Runyon, New Jersey State Archives, Trenton (abbrev. Runyon-NJ).
22. *New York Times*, 14 September 1973, Box 118, Sirica-LC.

arthritis.²³ This bout was a kind of coming-out party for the sport, "the first heavyweight championship bout held in this state," said the New York authorities. Still, the Athletic Commission was "anxious" since the promoter, Tex Rickard, "had no written agreement with anyone" but a "verbal agreement with Dempsey" guaranteeing him "37½ percent" of the revenue garnered, and Firpo, "12½ per cent with both boxers sharing in the profits of the pictures in addition,"²⁴ referring to filming, a growing revenue stream despite the barring of Jack Johnson's explosive movies—and, thus, a growing source of contention.²⁵

According to his detractors, Dempsey also had a "real bad" case of corruption. Gene Tunney, who battled him manfully in 1926, recalled later the "many rumors…intimating that Jack [Dempsey] had tossed the Philadelphia fight because of a huge betting coup. Supposedly, Dempsey had been offered a $125,000 bribe. Some people identified me with it," which he disdainfully denied, while in their similarly controversial Chicago bout, he watched suspiciously as the "underworld, its politicians and the boxing elements" all "fraternized." Of course, Tunney had reason to despise his opponent since after one of their matches, he recalled, "for three days I could not recall the names of my most intimate acquaintances" as he sustained a severe "concussion" and "all seemed queer."²⁶ Dempsey seemingly had a deficit in cognizance too, for as he admitted decades later, "when I talk to someone who is really intelligent and well read, I feel uncomfortable that I didn't have a proper education." He then tended to solidify his self-assessment when he added, "I'm inclined to believe in reincarnation…. I'll come back…as a lion." Dempsey, who consorted with gangsters, had by 1929 lost the still stunning sum of $3 million and "had to borrow $100 to come to New York from

---

23. *New York Daily News*, 24 December 1978, Box 118, Sirica-LC. Argentina was then developing an ever closer relationship with its boxing counterparts in the U.S. See Minutes, 8 September 1924, NYSAC: Conferring with their peers were representatives of the Argentine press: "they requested permission to obtain the forms of our files in our procedure for enforcing and regulating boxing"—and vice versa, deposited were the "rules and regulations of the Buenos Aires Boxing Commission."

24. Minutes, 7 August 1923, NYSAC.

25. Minutes, 4 November 1927, NYSAC: "The Motion Picture Operators Union" demanded more money "for work, labor and services in connection with the exhibition of the Dempsey-Tunney pictures…. The Commission informed all hands it was a matter for the courts to decide."

26. Tunney, *A Man Must Fight*, 243, 246, 249.

Chicago"[27]—all of which made him eminently susceptible to bribes and corruption.

The dazed Tunney still represented a hope harbored in certain quarters in being a puncher who could credibly aspire to be mistaken for a patrician. On cue, just as Tunney was mounting his class ascension by way of the boxing ring, the elite Georgetown University started a boxing team. It was December 1926 and 70 recruits reported. By January the first contest took place—not with battlers from nearby (and predominantly Negro) Howard University but, instead, the U.S. Naval Academy in relatively distant Annapolis. Five thousand spectators turned out, and for the next four decades boxing became one of the favorite sports; admittedly, there was a hiatus, but the point remained that, symbolically at least, future State Department diplomats were battling future naval officers,[28] toughening both to confront the battles that Washington inexorably must face if it were to replace London, as the elite postwar adoption of boxing intended.

Nevertheless, it would be an error to assume that the entire U.S. population was endorsing this turn toward boxing, for this supposition would not account for the barrage of protests pelting Yale man, premature environmentalist and Pennsylvania Governor Gifford Pinchot. On the one hand, a sportswriter rebuked him after the politico was said to have "termed Jack Dempsey [a] cad and brute" as he stumbled from the ring in "blinded condition" en route to his dressing room: his elbow is alleged to have bumped into [a] Philadelphia woman and knocked her out of [her] seat for which she is suing for fifty thousand dollars."[29] On the other hand, Pinchot was being bombarded with protest after what boxing opponent C.H. Kimball of Brooklyn called contemptuously "that bloody spectacle—Tunney beating up Dempsey," praying that it "not [be] permitted again in your state again." Like others, he sought to distinguish elite support for the sport and what was now unfolding. "The way Teddy Roosevelt" and others "put on the gloves for a little exercise is totally different," he insisted, in contrast to "commercial beat up contests," the new norm. Seemingly sputtering, he castigated the "rotten, dirty, miserable…beastly exhibitions" and declared that he had "met many

---

27. *New York Daily News*, 24 December 1978, Box 118, Sirica-LC.

28. Article, 17 June 1988, Boxing File, Special Collections, Georgetown University, Washington, D.C.

29. Frank Menke to Gifford Pinchot, 1 October 1926, Box 1483, Pinchot-LC.

men in [those] few days and they all say it was a veritable disgrace for the City of supposedly Brotherly Love to tolerate this stench."[30]

It was not just a Brooklynite who was upset. From faraway Independence, Iowa, P.C. Heege told the beleaguered governor that "prize fighting gathers today criminals and spreads disease" and, besides, it "provide[s] profits for political crooks." With a final expression of disgust, he uttered, "God have mercy on us."[31] F.M. Fishbaugh of York, Pennsylvania, lamented that "not many years ago, there was only one state in the Union (Nevada) where a prize fight could be staged. Now the governor of Pennsylvania has let down the bars" to the detriment of the state, he suggested.[32] (This enhanced popularity of boxing was also a change in the Keystone State, since the sport had been banned there previously as early as 1867.[33])

Closer to home, Dr. Lewis Haupt of Philadelphia wondered why the nation "condemned bull-baiting" and "cock-fighting," while approving "diabolical and demoralizing" boxing.[34]

Pinchot's indirect response was to write a check for a grand $385 for 14 tickets to the Tunney-Dempsey battle, "near the ringside" was his stated preference,[35] putting him within range of splattering blood. As the situation evolved, Pinchot's implicit endorsement of the sport represented the gathering consensus among the U.S. ruling elite generally, which was to win out.

The writer Arthur Mann was among the many stunned by the turnabout on boxing that Dempsey symbolized. "Boxing was suddenly heralded as a boon to mankind after being outlawed," he said with wonder; "hundreds of books" were rushed to market, "purporting to justify boxing's claim to a place in the realm of beneficial sports activities." Tossed aside cavalierly were concerns about health. "Repetitious black eyes are…harmful," he warned, as "the tissue around the eyes is broken down. Circulation is impaired. Optic nerves weaken. Bad eyesight follows," up to and including

---

30. C.H. Kimball to Gifford Pinchot, 26 September 1926, Box 1483, Pinchot-LC.

31. P.C. Heege to Gifford Pinchot, 23 September 1926, Box 1483, Pinchot-LC.

32. F.M. Fishbaugh to Gifford Pinchot, 27 August 1926, Box 1483, Pinchot-LC.

33. Report of Task Force on Boxing, Joint State Commission, April 1990, RG 7, N, Carton 11, Records of the General Assembly, Pennsylvania State Archives, Harrisburg (abbrev. Assembly-Pa).

34. Dr. Lewis Haupt to Gifford Pinchot, 19 August 1926, Box 1483, Pinchot-LC.

35. Gifford Pinchot to Frank Wiener, 25 August 1926, Box 1483, Pinchot-LC.

"blindness," the "same with a blow to the head or to the heart or to the kidneys," at times adding to the ranks of the "insane"—and the dead. "Symptoms of [the] punch drunk are quite the same as those of encephalitis, paralysis and other forms of brain injury...fifty percent of prize fighters show these symptoms sooner or later," he advised, referring mostly to the first half of the 20th century. However, part of the attraction of this sport was not only its role in hardening future troops for battlefields but also the captivating scent of profit thereby generated. "2,000,000 was taken in by the boxing clubs in New York state during 1932. New York is the center of the business. About $1,500,000 of this went to 945 licensed boxers. This makes an average of $1,500 per boxer in New York state for the year. But he didn't make that much in New York state because 100 headliners of the ring divided $1,000,000," leaving "$500,000 to be divided among the 845 or less than ten dollars per week" for the sorry remainder. It may have been worse than this since even this paltriness had to be shared: "should the fighter attempt to go it alone," without management, "he would soon find himself hornswoggled by contract phraseology." In any event, "most of the big clubs have a staff of spoilers. They are brutal, mauling battlers who can make the most skilled boxer look bad in even victory," driving downward the ability to negotiate for larger purses of those fighters who managed to win.

But again and again Mann returned to the stiff price boxers paid for the entertainment of some. The "early symptoms" of what came to be called being "punch drunk" did not necessarily "seriously interfere with fighting. In fact, many who have only these early symptoms fight extremely well and the slight staggering may be noticed only as they walk to their corners." But ever present are "periods of slight mental confusion," often accompanied by a "staggering propulsive gait" along with distinct "facial characteristics."[36]

Gene Tunney, who was able to get the best of Jack Dempsey and then became a prominent public figure, illustrated how and why professional batterers were at such risk. "I went into a clinch with my head down," he said, then "I plunged forward and my partner's head came up and butted me over the left eye, cutting and dazing me badly"; his opposite number then "stepped back and swung his [fist] against my jaw with every bit of his power. It landed flush and stiffened me where I stood...that is the last thing I remembered for two days. They tell me that I finished the round, knocking the man out." It would be 48 hours before he began to regain what remained

---

36. Arthur Mann, "Punch Drunk Fighters and Why," undated, Box 16, Mann-LC.

of his senses. "From that incident," Tunney asserted, "was born my desire to quit the ring forever...I wanted to leave the game that had threatened my sanity before I met with an accident in a real fight with six-ounce gloves that would permanently hurt my brain."[37] Yet, despite his admonition, Dr. Harry Kaplan maintained that being "punch drunk" was not acquired in the ring but was a hereditary condition not caused by blows to the skull.[38]

Despite the mounting evidence that boxing was not conducive to good health, regulators mesmerized by the tax revenue that was generated for state coffers and the profits accruing to their cronies, instead tended to focus on something else altogether. Cackling over the good fortune of the sport in 1930, Albany regulators found boxing to be in "a healthy condition despite the wave of general depression sweeping the country," in part because "it is a pleasant, enjoyable red-blooded man's sport." Thus, rather than fret over the morbidities that accompanied this supposedly bright picture, instead the regulators warned darkly about the "faker in the boxing ring [who] knows now that the practice of groveling on the floor pretending injury" was delivering results but was actually a "disgusting spectacle."[39] This was not how a "red-blooded man" was expected to perform.

Tunney also proclaimed that a "fair percentage of the manager's profession is a mere racket for [the] parasite." Tim Mara, part of a family that was to control the professional football franchise, the New York Giants—worth hundreds of millions of dollars today—demanded, said Tunney, a quarter of "all my earnings" in the prelude to the Dempsey fight, an "awful holdup." An irked Tunney asked querulously, "what profession has left as many derelicts in its wake?"[40] Interestingly, it was in November 1924 that Tunney's manager, William Gibson, appeared before the New York State Athletic Commission. Tunney was accused of "refusing to box" for a purse he

---

37. *New York Daily News*, 3 August 1928; Report, 1928, Box 4, Mann-LC.
38. Arthur Mann to Richard M. Johnston, ca. 1949-50, Box 4, Mann-LC.
39. Athletic Commission to Secretary of State Ed Flynn, 1 January 1931, NYSAC.
40. Tunney, *A Man Must Fight*, 243. The Maras are not the only family invested in professional football that got an initial boost from boxing. See also Clipping, 22 August 2000, Sub Group VIII, Series I, Box 18, HKBA. Art Rooney, late patriarch of the Pittsburgh Steelers, qualified for the Olympics as a boxer, then became an active promoter in the Steel City, including promoting the important match between Ezzard Charles and Jersey Joe Walcott on 18 July 1951 at Forbes Field in Pittsburgh.

deemed inadequate. There was no reference to the boxer's objection to the manager's share of the purse.[41]

This rampant corruption was an essential element of the rebirth of the sport, and New Jersey was in the vanguard. Early in 1920 the chief executive of the Garden State refused to accede to the demand that a bout be canceled though he knew of the distinct possibility that the outcome was predetermined—or "fixed."[42] As boxing gained popularity, it tended to attract ill-intentioned profiteers seeking to benefit from "fixed" matches. Similarly, if a fighter needed cash, then was matched against a brutal bruiser, he might be predisposed to participating in a "fixed" match. This may have been the case for Ray Bennett, who was "disqualified for 'laying down'" in a bout on 4 July 1929. "Bennett stated he boxed the best he could," which may have been accurate, but he faced a "30 day suspension" nonetheless.[43]

Then there was the 1920s fight slated for the Newark Armory, which was "oversold." The governor was told that 10,000 were "clamoring for admission" amidst "confusion and disorder," a chaotic scene worsened by the "scarcity of police officers," as the "mob was in control." Incentivized, "every spectator from the lower priced seats had crowded over into the more expensive ones" in a "disgraceful scene."[44] Contributing to the image of a sport descending into corrupt disarray, the charge was made that the result of the light heavyweight championship bout between Georges Carpentier and Barney Lebrowitz—known as "Battling Levinsky"—was "fixed."[45] The possibility that gambling interests were pre-determining boxing outcomes arose again when a New Jersey state boxing inspector at ringside stopped a fight because of an alleged injury—for the second time in a week—leading a journalist to lambaste this "joke of boxing."[46]

Of course, in a society wracked with bigotry, it became difficult to ascertain the validity of these charges. Thus, when a petition was

---

41. Minutes, 14 November 1924, NYSAC.
42. William Runyon to Roy Schoonmaker, 6 January 1920, Box 1, CORRESP. 1919-1920, Runyon-NJ.
43. Minutes, 9 July 1924, NYSAC.
44. John Smith to Governor Edward Irving Edwards, ca. 1920, Box 2, EIE-NJ.
45. Clipping, no date, Box 2, EIE-NJ.
46. *Newark Evening News*, 24 June 1929, Box 3, CORRESP. 1929-1931, Records of Governor Morgan Foster Larson, New Jersey State Archives, Trenton.

circulated by the "Anti Prizefight Committee of the State Council of Churches" in New Jersey, objecting to a bout between Benny Leonard and Lew Tendler, it was hard to separate objection to a match between two Jewish boxers from the pervasiveness of anti-Semitism.[47] Was it coincidental that a similar objection was made to a bout between the Negro battler Harry Wills and the Argentine bruiser Luis Firpo, in the wake of the repeal of an anti-boxing law?[48] That is, was the objection more to the boxers than to boxing?

There is suggestive evidence. Jack Bernstein, a lightweight champion, claimed that he was "swindled out of many a victory by judges who 'fixed' his decisions" since he was "a Jew from Yonkers"; it was "only 'natural,'" it was said, "that the Gentile fans would come out in droves to see him get knocked out." Besides, on 17 December 1923 at a contest at Madison Square Garden, he was reportedly "approached by the underworld to 'throw' the fight," and his failure to comply apparently backfired against him.[49] Hy Godfrey knew precisely what a backfire could entail. Born in the early years of the 20th century, by 1923 he was a boxer in Indiana. The Ku Klux Klan, he recalled later, "was at its height," especially in Terre Haute. Thus, he said chillingly, "when I disrobed and the Star of David was plainly visible on my trunks...[the audience] started to boo and holler and I could hear them screaming 'Kill the Jew'.... I will never forget that night." Godfrey was "especially afraid that the crowd would not let me out of the arena." This was not a unique event: "the same thing happened to me a few months later when I was fighting Cotton Nelson in Nashville." He was sufficiently intimidated that eventually he changed his name back to Gottfried since many promoters thought he was a Negro fighter because of the looming presence of George Godfrey, a prominent ebony heavyweight of his era.[50]

---

47. Undated petition, Box 2, EIE-NJ. See also James R. Fair, *Give Him to the Angels: The Story of Harry Greb*, New York: Smith and Durrell, 1946.

48. Undated petition, Box 9, CORRESP. 1922-1926, Records of George Sebastian Silzer, New Jersey State Archives, Trenton.

49. Undated analysis, Sub Group IX, Series I, Box 3, HKBA.

50. *Richmond Jewish News*, 1 February 1980, Sub Group X, Series I, Box 9, HKBA. Jewish Americans were not the only group so victimized. See undated column by Westbrook Pegler, ca. 1923, Sub Group VIII, Series I, Box 11, HKBA: Michael McTigue "won the light heavyweight title from Battling Siki, an authentic, blue gum jungle Negro.... the unwisdom of a colored man with a title at stake in accepting a match with an Irishman named Michael McTigue in Dublin on St. Patrick's night was obvious and the result was merely the confirmation of the obvious."

Then there were the stressors that Godfrey—or Gottfried—endured that may have undermined others. Thus, Harry Gordon, an active bantamweight in the 1920s, especially in Philadelphia, by 1954 had committed suicide.[51] The man known as Lou Stillman, who operated an eponymous boxing gym, recalled a time in 1919 when Billy Grupp would get drunk and rant, "the Jews are responsible for this war. All the German people got killed because of the Jews." This was at Grupp's gym at 116th Street and 8th Avenue in Harlem, where numerous Jewish fighters trained—but such ranting caused them to abandon the facility,[52] perhaps hampering their boxing ability.

Repeatedly, Jewish-American boxers claimed that the environment which dictated sheer survival drove them into the ring. There was Abraham Hollandersky, born in Russia, who fled pogroms for New London, Connecticut, by 1894. "Abe the Newsboy" (like many of that era, he honed his mettle by battling for a prime commercial corner on which to sell his wares) was termed the "toughest little man who ever lived"; cross-eyed, he "never stopped attacking and never seemed to tire" when fighting distressed opponents. He fought bears and wrestled kangaroos in Australia too.[53] The aptly named Jake "Soldier" Bartfield, was born in 1892 in Austria, but in North America rose quickly as a fighter, once giving the talented Harry Greb all he could handle. How did he choose boxing? Boxing chose him was the essence of his response: "Someone tried to beat me up in the U.S. Army so I came back to him and almost knocked him cold." and thus was launched his career as a heavy hitter.[54]

* * *

As the foregoing suggests, by the 1920s, Jewish Americans were, according to one source, the "dominant nationality in professional prizefighting, followed by the Italians and the Irish. Ten years later Jews sank to third place, preceded by the Italians and the Irish," then fell further after 1945 with the anti-fascist revulsion targeting bigotry and as more opportunities arose, especially as a result of benefits for military veterans, meaning that by 1950, participation of Jewish Americans in this brutal sport was "miniscule." As noted, and unfortunately, the diminutive Abraham Attell may have been the symbol of Jewish-American combativeness for many (Benny Leonard aside)

---

51. *The Ring*, June 1954, Sub Group X, Series I, Box 11, HKBA.
52. File on Lou Stillman, no date, Sub Group IX, Series II, Box 28, HKBA.
53. Report, 8 February 2002, Sub Group IX, Series 1, Box 1, HKBA.
54. Undated report, Sub Group IX, Series 1, Box 1, HKBA.

though he was accused credibly of "fixing" fights. This was an adjunct of a kind of primitive accumulation of capital—and influence—by which a hard corps of Jewish Americans successfully sought income, class elevation and privilege, thereby eroding to a degree ethno-religious bias against themselves. Thus, throughout this tumultuous decade, Jewish Americans were instrumental in the industries which ultimately were to propel Nevada, including prostitution, gambling, rackets generally (including labor racketeering), and bootlegging. As scholar Allen Bodner put it, "Dutch Schultz, Waxey Gordon, Bugsy Siegel, Arnold Rothstein, and Lepke Buchalter [also known as Louis Lepke, among other monikers] were all Jewish. The gamblers who did business in the rear of each fighting club were Jewish, as were many of the managers and promoters."[55]

Among those who benefited was Harry Kessler, a former newsboy at the busy intersection of Jefferson and Olive streets in St. Louis, where each hawker occupied a corner, creating proximity that inevitably eventuated in fists flying. By 1920, the battle-tested young Jewish man was enrolled at the University of Missouri-Rolla, where those of his background were few and far between. "An aura... seemed to indicate that we wore black capes and had horns growing out of our foreheads," he groused later. Yet boxing was racially segregated, meaning "white fighters fought whites; black fighters fought blacks," and he was grouped in the former category, meaning that despite anti-Semitism, he was well on his way to converting his boxing talent into a related field, becoming the self-proclaimed "Millionaire Referee."[56]

Kessler was not unique in having to fight his way out of his neighborhood. The boxer known as as Cupie Gordon (also known as Kewpie), born in 1905, came to maturity in New York City and quickly concluded, "I just was raised in a neighborhood where you had to fight to be one of the boys, so I thought I might as well get paid."[57] Eddie "Newsboy" Curley was born Isaac Morochnik in

---

55. Allen Bodner, *When Boxing Was a Jewish Sport*, Westport, Conn., Praeger, 1997 (abbrev. Bodner, *When Boxing*), 129-130. See also undated clipping, Sub Group X, Series I, Box 35, HKBA: "It is not...by coincidence that Jews became conspicuous in boxing during a time when they were equally conspicuous in bootlegging, crime, prostitution, and gambling.... by the late 1920s, perhaps one third of all professional boxers in this country were Jewish."

56. Harry Kessler, *The Millionaire Referee*, St. Louis: Harkess, 1982 (abbrev. Kessler, *Millionaire*), 19, 49.

57. Undated file on Gordon, Sub Group X, Series I, Box 11, HKBA.

Russia and arrived in the U.S. at the age of five in the early 20th century. Passing away in 1992 at the age of 87, his obituary recalled that he "learned to fight to protect himself as an immigrant Jewish boy in a mostly established and mostly Italian neighborhood."[58] Eddie Fletcher—born Edward Fleischer—was a boxer in the early 1920s, before transmuting his fistic skill into organized crime, becoming a leader in the notorious "Purple Gang" in Detroit, before being shot to death.[59] Sailor Friedman, also known as Solly Friedman and William Friedman, merged the fates of Curley and Fletcher when just before a bout in Milwaukee, he was beaten insensible by thugs who kidnapped him, falling victim to a feud between competing Chicago gunmen who had varying interest in his survival.[60] The pugnaciousness bred in Jewish neighborhoods did not always lead to criminality. Leo Fried fought as Bobby Harris in the 1920s before becoming an attorney, then labor leader in Oakland.[61] David Fine was born in Poland but arrived in the U.S. by 1893, where he boxed as "Kid Manning," then sang opera and played semi-professional baseball before becoming owner and founder of the Boston Royal Petticoat Company.[62]

* * *

Of course, these preceding accounts may exaggerate somewhat the domination of Jewish Americans, to the detriment of Italian Americans, among others. But what is hard to avoid is that barring Negroes facilitated this overall ascendancy of those defined as "white" who theretofore had been languishing at the bottom of the class ladder, which sheds light on how and why this began to change decades later. Still, there was no unanimity of opinion among Euro-Americans generally. To a degree, it was thought that the contents of the pot of gold were finite: When men like Truman Gibson and Don King began to seek a share, pre-existing white supremacy mandated that the reaction would not be mild.

One advantage held by Jewish Americans generally denied to their African-American counterparts was that they could vote, which created all manner of plusses. Thus, by 1922, attorney Thomas Brown of Perth Amboy, New Jersey, informed the governor's top aide that

---

58. *Boston Globe*, 6 November 1992, Sub Group X, Series I, Box 6, HKBA.
59. File on Eddie Fletcher, no date, Sub Group X, Series I, Box 8, HKBA.
60. Clipping, 27 October 1923, Sub Group X, Series I, Box 9, HKBA.
61. File on Leo Fried, no date, Sub Group X, Series I, Box 8, HKBA.
62. Report, 12 January 1978, Sub Group IX, Series 1, Box 16, HKBA.

"Middlesex County has a large number of Jewish boys who vote the ticket regularly," thus entitling them to "patronage"—the numerous jobs encircling boxing, such as inspectors, referees, ushers, concessionaires, etc.—since they were such "great boxing fans."[63] In a likeminded vein, Joseph di Benedetti of South Orange, who was pressing similarly, was told bluntly that he was "misinformed as to the lack of representation of Italian-Americans" in "state positions" of the type that attorney Brown had been inquiring about.[64]

Deprivation of the right to vote generally obtained for Negroes in Dixie, but such was not the case in Pennsylvania, underscoring why by the 1960s, so much blood was shed in seeking to secure the electoral franchise. By 1926, a Negro attorney in Philadelphia was bidding to be installed on the Boxing Commission, an influential post that could also mean garnering what was colloquially termed "legal graft." Thus, George Carry argued, "since the colored people are interested in the matter of boxing I feel that their interests would receive more attention by having on the board the right representative of that group," meaning himself.[65] James Williams of Pittsburgh was also interested in the "position of Boxing Commissioner" and informed a man with clout that "I have heard…that you are favorable to a Colored Man holding one of the three positions."[66] J.G. Robinson of the periodical published by the African Methodist Episcopal church, unctuously conceded that "[I am a] Negro admirer of yours" who hailed the governor's dismissal of a previous boxing commissioner—"one of the finest things you have done since your election." Now he wanted Governor Pinchot to "find another man of our group…to appoint" to this potent post.[67] Suggestive of how important this position was is the point that Robert Vann, publisher of the nationally influential *Pittsburgh Courier*, and possibly the most influential Negro statewide, put in his own bid to be appointed boxing commissioner.[68]

---

63. Attorney Thomas Brown to Secretary to Governor, 6 April 1922, Box 2, EIE-NJ.

64. Secretary of Governor to Joseph di Benedetti, 6 April 1922, EIE-NJ.

65. George Carry to Harold Beitler, 16 December 1926, MSS Group 156, Box 4, John Fisher Papers, Pennsylvania State Archives, Harrisburg (abbrev. Fisher-Pa).

66. Letter from James Williams, 27 December 1926, MSS Group 156, Box 4, Fisher-Pa.

67. J.G. Robinson of "A.M.E. Church Review" to Gifford Pinchot, Box 1517, Pinchot-LC.

68. Robert Vann to Gifford Pinchot, 25 August 1926, Box 1517, Pinchot-LC.

There were a finite number of such plums, leading to a scramble. Many Italian Americans felt particularly aggrieved. Chris Dundee was a top boxing promoter in Miami in the second half of the 20th century and was the brother of the better known Angelo Dundee, a prime trainer, working alongside Muhammad Ali for years. "Nobody would give an Italian a break in boxing," he groused, "so we thought we'd make ourselves sound like Irish,"[69] meaning a surname change: He was born Cristofo Mirena.[70]

Similarly hard to avoid is the point that revenue from boxing was sufficiently attractive to turn heads. The *Everlast Boxing Record and Blue Book*, thought to be authoritative, indicated that by the early 1920s, fans were paying millions to watch boxing matches, and state coffers were being filled in turn to the tune of hundreds of thousands of dollars.[71] In California, the State Athletic Commission was seemingly ecstatic by the mid-1920s: It was "almost unbelievable to think," it was said, "that during the year 1925, 1,605,644 fans witnessed the exhibitions of the fistic sport and paid into the clubs," including the American Legion, "a sum in excess of two and one half million dollars"; at that point the sport represented "nearly a three million dollar business annually." Perhaps overoptimistically, their conclusion was that a "very conservative estimate is that at least 60 percent of the gross receipts of a show is immediately paid to the boxers." Despite this positive glow, the body was sufficiently skeptical to note that the name of the referee was "not announced until he entered the ring" which—again overoptimistically—"makes it practically impossible for anyone to influence the referee in any way." Thus, "sham or collusive contests are no longer perpetrated upon the public in this state" and, moreover, there was the "wonderful success of the Hollywood [American] Legion" and their contests, which involved "exempting the Legion from the 5 percent state tax," a boon to this conservative group.[72]

Like a boxing match, there was a contest between profit and maintenance of racist norms. By 1919 in the soon-to-be rapidly growing state of Arizona, state representative Harry Jennings was instructed

---

69. Ferdie Pacheco, *Tales from the 5th Street Gym: Ali, the Dundees and Miami's Golden Age of Boxing*, Tallahassee: University Press of Florida, 2010) abbrev. Pacheco, *Tales*), 16.

70. Nick Tosches, *Night Train: The Sonny Liston Story*, London: Hamilton, 2000, 120.

71. *Everlast Boxing Record and Blue Book*, ca. 1921, Wills-SCH.

72. Annual Report "For the Period Commencing December 1, 1925 to November 30, 1926," F2190, D039855, CaSAC.

to vote for a "bill that will promote the manly art of boxing"[73] (though apparently there was no consideration of the wider point that Negroes could subvert masculinity by becoming the masters, stirring repressed memories of who would prevail during the early days of settler colonialism).[74] State regulation was seen as the way out since that would stymie "unscrupulous promoters and gamblers"[75] of the kind that had brought Gans and Johnson to neighboring Nevada, for example. Correspondingly, the state's governor was told that "the effect of prize fighting can be only brutalizing—particularly in respect to the youth of our state," thus a "repeal" legalization was demanded.[76] The coy governor responded that legalization was meant to appeal to "returned soldiers" who supposedly yearned to strap on the gloves and start punching; he, in fact, thought the sport should be "abolished," like "bull fighting," which "falls within the same class."[77]

There is a continuing debate as to how Jack Dempsey, the heavyweight whose brutal style in some ways defined the "Roaring Twenties," sought to avoid boxing Negroes. After he administered a vicious whipping, victimizing Jess Willard—who in turn had been lionized after defeating Jack Johnson in Havana, restoring temporarily the presumed racial norm—Dempsey supposedly asserted that like John L. Sullivan decades earlier, he was "'drawing the color line'" and refusing to sully his gloves by boxing Negroes.[78] One has to tread carefully here, given how misquotation—or mal-quotation—has been an occupational hazard in the sport. For example, decades later, when Jim Crow was thought to be beyond the pale, the prominent journalist Jonathan Yardley observed that Dempsey and his successor, Rocky Marciano, "both were widely thought of as Great White Hopes," though the former "seems not to have been comfortable with the Great White Hope label, while Marciano seems to have been something of a racist."[79]

---

73. S.F. Fraser to Honorable Harry Jennings, 18 February 1919, RG1 S.G. Series, 1.1.4. Box 002, ASA-P.

74. See Horne, *Counter-Revolution*, passim.

75. S.F. Fraser to Honorable Harry Jennings, 18 February 1919 , RG1 S.G. Series, 1.1.4. Box 002, ASA-P.

76. H.P. Cory to Governor Thomas Campbell, 20 November 1919, RG1, SG Series, 1.1.4, Box 002, ASA-P.

77. Governor Thomas Campbell to H.P. Cory, 21 November 1919, RG1, SG Series, 1.1.4, Box 002, ASA-P.

78. Brady, *Boxing Confidential*, 25.

79. *Los Angeles Times Book Review*, 22 May 1977, Box 118, Sirica-LC.

Whatever the case, the historical record does not necessarily vindicate Yardley's viewpoint. One of Dempsey's Negro peers was Harry Wills—whom fellow boxer Gene Tunney termed the "dark menace."[80] Wills claimed that he was awarded $50,000 for not fighting Dempsey and that this was a racist transaction fundamentally based on the premise he might prevail, recreating the Jack Johnson controversy. Thus, said Wills, he was forced to fight Sam Langford, yet another Negro battler, 22 times out of his 100 bouts all told.[81] "The four best fighters of [Jack] Johnson's time as champion," said analyst John Lardner, were "Sam Langford, Joe Jeannette, Sam McVey and Harry Wills. They were all Negroes" and all were blocked in their attempt to succeed Johnson. In a cynical display of allotting boxing contracts in a manner that putatively violated antitrust regulation, these Negro contractors were barred. Instead, promoted in their place, was Dempsey, who, said Lardner, was "formally acquitted of draft evasion in 1920."[82] Meanwhile, one unscrupulous essayist suggested that four of the five Negroes—Wills was excluded curiously—should be jammed "into a ring for a battle royal,"[83] inevitably maiming most.

Wills, the "Black Panther of New Orleans,"[84] as he was known—or the "Brown Panther" in other instances[85]—was born in 1893. The relatively tall, 6'2" puncher[86] was entering his prime as a fighter when his adamant challenge to Dempsey arose. By 1960 a Negro journalist argued forcefully that "race dethroned Wills fight." Dempsey replied that "one reason that I never fought Harry Wills was that he was a Negro," offloading responsibility to others higher in the class and political hierarchy, who were deathly afraid of rioting—e.g., what followed Reno 1910. The leading promoter Tex Rickard was still smarting over the criticism leveled at him for arranging the Johnson-Jeffries brawl: "when Johnson won," said this same journalist, "Tex was accused of humiliating the white race."[87] Another observer blamed Mayor Jimmy Walker of New York City who, it was reported, would not allow a mixed bout in his bailiwick, while (according to this same source), potent politico James Farley insisted

---

80. Tunney, *A Man Must Fight*, 133.
81. *St. Louis Globe-Democrat*, 22 December 1958, Wills-SCH.
82. Lardner, *White Hopes*, 29.
83. Undated essay, Sub Group X, Series I, Box 26, HKBA.
84. Brochure, no date, Wills-SCH.
85. Undated clipping, Wills-SCH.
86. Mexican Identification Card, no date, Wills-SCH.
87. *Jet*, 11 February 1960, Wills-SCH.

that Dempsey box Wills in New York—or not at all.[88] Yet another journalist wrote contemporaneously in 1925 that Dempsey, instead of being known as a draft dodger, avoiding the turbulence of World War I, should be termed an "African Dodger" for avoiding Wills, a comment sufficiently telling to be retained by a leading activist of that time.[89]

Whatever the case, like Johnson before him, by 1925 Wills was seeking succor south of the border in Mexico,[90] as did yet another frustrated Negro heavyweight, Sam Langford. Though effectively blind, he won the heavyweight crown there in 1922 in a one-round knockout.[91] However, by May 1924, allies were seeking "to hold a benefit boxing show" for him, since he was "in need of funds." That a skilled battler like Langford would be in dire straits led the New York State Athletic Commission to propose a "general fund to take care of all boxers in need of assistance," an initiative long overdue.[92] Earlier, Langford, Wills and McVey had moved to Panama, because fighters in the alleged democratic republic headquartered in Washington refused to fight them.[93] The fact that he had to fight disabled was indicative of his future: By the age of 64, the man referred to with a dearth of kindness as "Tar Baby" was not only blind but bankrupt.[94]

Langford, as much as Gans and Johnson, needs to be seen as a symbol of a twisted era. His ancestors had fled New Jersey in the 1770s for Nova Scotia. He had to fight Joe Jeannette 17 times because so many were reluctant to enter the ring with him—even Johnson did not want to fight him.[95] Just as his ancestors fleeing the incipient republic for Canada was indicative of the republic's unfriendliness as far as Negroes were concerned, it was the International Boxing Union in Paris which refused to recognize Jess Willard as the champion until he met and defeated Langford, underlining once again that Negro allies often were to be found abroad.[96]

---

88. Undated clipping, Wills-SCH.

89. *Washington Daily American*, 25 March 1925, Box 1, Eugene Davidson Papers, Howard University, Washington, D.C.

90. Mexican Travel Document, ca. 1925, Wills-SCH.

91. Undated clipping, Volume XVIII, Odds and Ends on Boxing, UND.

92. Minutes, 2 May 1924, NYSAC.

93. Clipping, 25 March 1918, Sub Group XV, Series XIII, Box 46, HKBA.

94. Undated clipping on Langford, Volume IX, Odds and Ends on Boxing, UND.

95. Steve Laffoley, *Pulling No Punches: The Sam Langford Story*, Lawrencetown Beach, Nova Scotia: Pottersfield Press, 2013, 20, 158.

96. Moyle, *Sam Langford*, 289.

A striking moment took place in this ongoing saga on 4 September 1923. "Paddy Mullins (manager of Harry Wills)" and the boxer himself "appeared" before the New York State Commission "in reference to Wills' challenge to Jack Dempsey." Conclusion? "It was up to the promoters"—meaning Rickard—to organize the bout.[97] There was a replay on 10 August 1926. It was then that the New York State Athletic Commission "reserved" a "decision" on Tunney's "application" for a "boxer's license." Then Dempsey "appeared requesting a license" and "submitted a contract in which he signed to box Wills… this antedates an option on his services which he gave to Tex Rickard to meet an opponent selected by Rickard." Then "Harry Wills… appeared relative" to the Dempsey contract and "informed" the NYSAC "that his manager received $55,000 for signing" this document "of which he received his share." A license for Dempsey was then "deferred."[98] Retrospectively, it is not easy to ascertain the upshot of this mini-drama, except that it appears to vindicate at least an initial willingness of Dempsey to cross the color line.

Jack Hay, who claimed to be Dempsey's unacknowledged son out of wedlock, by 1986 pooh-poohed the notion put forward by boxing buff Hank Kaplan that "'with the title belt in hand Dempsey wouldn't risk fighting [Jack] Johnson in an alley brawl.' I don't agree," Hay said. "It was Rickard alone," the promoter, "that by then had received verbal orders from the Governor of New York state as well as the President of the United States to NOT [emphasis in original] stage a mixed race HW [heavyweight] title bout. This secret, then, had to be kept." So it was "contemplated first to stage the [proposed] bout in Mexico and this having failed…Canada"[99]—far beyond U.S. jurisdiction.

As Hay's comment suggests, there was extreme concern in elite circles as to who held the heavyweight crown. Hence, in 1926 the Negro Tiger Flowers fought Harry Greb for the middleweight crown, without a major eruption. Flowers, the "Georgia Deacon," a fast and elusive southpaw, won without the angst induced by Johnson beating Jeffries (was it because Greb was Jewish, or was it because it was a battle in a lesser weight class? The latter, I think). So, it was said, the purported Johnson-Dempsey bout was staged for private gamblers, a fairly common occurrence then, and not just in Saskatoon. Still, one analyst calls this alleged dustup the "Roaring Twenties' version of

---

97. Minutes, 4 September 1923, NYSAC.
98. Minutes, 10 August 1926, NYSAC.
99. Jack Hay to Hank Kaplan, 12 May 1986, Sub Group VIII, Series 1, Box 10, HKBA.

the Hitler diaries"—meaning, a fraud.[100] Yet another source asserts pointedly that, yes, it was Rickard who blocked Dempsey from fighting Wills or any other Negro, since he "feared boxing would suffer if [Harry] Wills won," besting the Manassa Mauler, foiling the fabulously lucrative Tunney fight.[101]

As for Dempsey, he did not do badly after hanging up his gloves, becoming a fixture in fashionable Manhattan watering holes, including his own. He also exemplified the increasing retreat from blatant anti-Semitism, which accelerated post-1945, when he took on, as his trainer, Theodore Weinstein (also known as Teddy Hayes), who boxed between 1915-23, then quit to work for the champion. This was also part of the centuries-long evolution of "whiteness" which portended an eventual retreat of bigotry directed against fellow Europeans. Thus, by the 1960s, Weinstein—or Hayes—was an affluent oilman residing in Midland, Texas, once home of the Bush family of presidential fame. Before that he was associated closely with Ed Flynn, the former political boss of the Bronx, an Irishman, thus representing at least in microcosm a kind of reconciliation between Jewish Americans and Irishmen, a relationship that had bedeviled the former for decades in the U.S.[102]

Perhaps because of his wise decision to stage many of his fights-south of the border, Wills left an estate in 1958 of a relatively sizable $100,000, placing him in the stratosphere of Negro earners.[103] For as Negroes accumulated more capital, like Jewish Americans, they were destabilizing traditional hierarchies and upsetting normative stereotypes, which could only roil society. After leaving the swatting sport, Wills resided comfortably at 76 St. Nicholas Place in Harlem, though his other holdings included a 20-family building at 465 West 148th Street, a huge, sprawling farm in Dinwiddie County, Virginia, where a neighbor of his was one of the few Negro Congressmen of that time, Arthur Mitchell; then there was his estate in Dutchess County, New York.[104] Ultimately, as Jim Crow was forced into a helter-skelter retreat, even more African Americans were able to accumulate more wealth and by example contradict the nostrum that Negroes were fated to be the mudsill of society, which in turn served to disturb and trouble the rancid status quo.

---

100. "Fight Beat," December 1983, Sub Group VIII, Series I, Box 10, HKBA.
101. *Boston Evening American*, 1939, Volume XII, Boxing Notes, UND.
102. File on Theodore Weinstein/Teddy Hayes, 1966, Sub Group IX, Series I, Box 12, HKBA.
103. Undated clipping, Wills-SCH.
104. Clipping, no date, Wills-SCH.

Wills was not the only ebony pugilist capturing attention in the 1920s. There was the Senegalese pounder known as Battling Siki, otherwise known as Louis Mbarick Fall.[105] Like Johnson, he too produced startling headlines, e.g., "Singular Senegalese Slows Southerner," the latter being a flummoxed Euro-American named appropriately, "Joe White." The latter, said an observer, "was on the canvas so many times in the early rounds that Siki thought he was trying to start a crap game."[106] Like other ebony pounders, Siki was subjected to racist denigration, with the wildly popular columnist Westbrook Pegler lamenting that the boxer "tried hard to understand civilization but never quite got the idea."[107] Decades after he had expired, Siki was still being flayed for his purported "Simian Arms" that meant victories which "shocked the civilized world" and this was "no exaggeration"; Europeans and Euro-Americans in the ring with him were like a "Christian thrown to the lions," which was "unthinkable." Siki was like "something out of a zoo"; yes, "the jungle came out in Siki."[108]

Like many boxers, Siki's management was questionable. By September 1923, his "American representative...Gene Sennett" was "questioned as to why Siki was matched to box George Godfrey in Philadelphia on October 8 when he was already under contract to box Kid Norfolk in Madison Square Garden on October 12, which match was made prior to the Godfrey one."[109] By August 1924, he was hauled again before the New York State Athletic Commission, along with his manager Robert Levy, since, it was said, "Siki had engaged to box at Albany contrary" to a rule forbidding fighters from scheduling matches close together without a decent interval.[110] Though allegedly illiterate, Siki could speak English, French, Spanish, Dutch and German, among other languages, including his mother tongue. A Muslim, he fought during the war, then arrived in Manhattan in 1923. Up to his tragic and still unsolved murder in 1925, he earned tens of thousands of dollars, once again upsetting the idea that those like himself should be the dregs of society. A lavish tipper—at times leaving ten times the amount of the check—there

---

105. See Minutes, 20 November 1923, NYSAC: Fall petitions to have his "Ring Name" recognized—Battling Siki.
106. Clipping, 9 February 1924, Sub Group X, Series II, Box 43, HKBA.
107. Column by Westbrook Pegler, 1925, Sub Group VIII, Series I, Box 17, HKBA.
108. Clipping, 15 August 1951, Sub Group VIII, Series I, Box 13, HKBA.
109. Minutes. 23 September 1923, NYSAC.
110. Minutes, 15 August 1924, NYSAC.

was sincere mourning in Harlem upon his passing, with the Reverend Adam Clayton Powell, Sr. providing a heartfelt eulogy.[111]

The West African champion was viewed as a successor to Jack Johnson—though he was not a heavyweight. The U.S. press leapt upon, and inflated, every negative allegation about him. It wasn't just in North America that he was hounded, for when he defeated Georges Carpentier in Paris, predictably riots erupted—"between elated blacks and American sailors," as a subsequent analyst put it. As was their wont globally, Euro-Americans began to pressure Parisian officialdom to impose a putrid Jim Crow, presumably on the premise that this latticework of iniquity required global emulation in order to survive domestically. He was termed variously the "French Jack Johnson" and the "Wild Man of Borneo," neither sobriquet intended as complimentary. Like Johnson, he married a woman of European descent, which also heightened apprehensions that the tables of masculinity were being turned and that the dark-skinned men would be the masters of the ring, taking home big payouts, followed by becoming attractive to "their" women and perhaps, down the road, becoming the masters generally. The boxer's very name did not reassure, in that he chose his *nom de guerre* in homage to a famed battler from the former German East Africa—now Tanzania—who fought the Germans in the 1890s. Did a gangster slay him after he failed to "fix" a fight? Such was the scuttlebutt.[112]

Another ebony champion, the aforementioned Tiger Flowers, fared little better. An exceedingly religious middleweight, after defeating Greb he took on "Slapsie" Maxie Rosenbloom on 9 November 1927 in Detroit and managed a 10-round draw. Three days later he knocked out Leo Gates in four rounds in New York. It was his final fight. Of course, he carried his Bible into the operating room and had a prayer on his lips as the ether took effect, but he never recovered consciousness. He died on the operating table.[113]

* * *

By 1926 the sport had endured a stunning turnabout, moving rapidly from being outlawed to being embraced by the U.S. ruling elite, which in turn created opportunities for numerous Jewish Americans and Italian Americans in particular. As for Negroes, below the

---

111. Undated article by John Lardner, Box 209, Ellison-LC.

112. Peter Benson, *Battling Siki: A Tale of Ring Fixes, Race and Murder in the 1920s*, Fayetteville: University of Arkansas Press, 2006, 11-13, 34, 93.

113. Undated clipping, Volume XII, Odds and Ends on Boxing, UND.

heavyweight ranks—still seen as sacrosanct—they too were climbing upward, a journey that the premature deaths of Battling Siki and Tiger Flowers could not arrest. Hence, in New York, now the new epicenter of the sport, replacing Nevada, there was a sense of self-satisfaction. The NYSAC annual report for 1926 concluded elatedly that "boxing and wrestling today is (sic) in as healthy and sound a condition as it ever was," though this was not saying that much given the sport's previous outlaw status. "The greatest evil of all," it was announced gravely, was "betting"—though, prematurely it was blared, that wagering had "been reduced to practically a minimum by the enactment of a rule prohibiting certain known undesirable characters admission to club premises and holding licensed clubs to strict accountability for a rigid enforcement of same." Still, in the preceding period, 233 boxers had been suspended, along with 27 managers.[114] This did not bode well, sunny optimism aside.

---

114. Minutes, Annual Report, 1926, NYSAC.

Chapter 3

The "Brown Bomber" Soars

Boxing had received the firm imprimatur of the ruling elite, which saw it as a way to better emulate London—on the verge of being supplanted by U.S. imperialism—while generating wealth for some. It had been a neck-snapping reversal, driven by the exigencies delivered by world war. It had been not so long ago that the sport was viewed as barbaric and cruel, encouraging gambling and attracting bottom-feeders besides. The clergy were in the vanguard of opposition, but as so often happened, when their paymasters changed course, so did they.[1]

Jim Crow had retreated to the fortification that allowed Negro boxers to challenge European and Euro-American fighters—so long as they were not heavyweights, as that weight class still clung unsteadily to the slowly eroding ledge of white supremacy. But before the decade of the 1930s ended, the Negro battler known as Joe "The Brown Bomber" Louis was to implode that last bastion into smithereens, reigning as heavyweight champion roughly from 1937-1949, coterminous with the New Deal, the Fair Deal, and an era when white supremacy was thought to be back on its heels. Still, the blockade of Negro heavyweights had lasted for more than two decades, before Louis was to burst through this wall of inequality.[2] That is, Jack Johnson's bruising fists had left a deep imprint on the consciousness of the U.S. elite. Yet, Louis's popularity was such that even subsequent leaders, e.g., Dr. Martin Luther King, Jr., told a story—possibly apocryphal—dramatizing his influence: A Negro was in the gas chamber and as poisonous fumes invaded his lungs he cried out, "Save me, Joe Louis, save me."[3]

Louis, who styled himself as a kind of anti-Johnson, still emerged as a kind of folk-hero, a one-man gang vindicating Negro humanity

---

1. *Kentucky Post*, 22 April 2002, Sub Group IX, Series 2, Box 21, HKBA.
2. Moyle, *Sam Langford*, 289.
3. Oates, *On Boxing*, 62.

as he pummeled into submission one European or Euro-American after another. Charles Duncan was a child of the Negro middle class in Washington, D.C., and went on to prominence as a Dartmouth- and Harvard-trained attorney. Class credentials aside, he represented the sentiments of a wider Negro community when he confessed to being stirred emotionally by Louis's triumphs. "The minute he would win," he subsequently reminisced, "the street would erupt...in glee and jubilation"; a stone's throw from the White House and Capitol, "from 7th to 14th Sreet" there were "wall-to-wall people" cheering and ululating. After all, he said, at that juncture, there was "very, very little to be proud about...we used to count progress in terms of whether there had been a decrease in the number of lynchings from the years before.... 'well, there were only 13 this year, last year there were 40, so we're really making progress.'"[4] Though dimly recognized then, Louis's triumph, as revenue streams increased, opened the door subsequently for Truman Gibson and other Negroes to claim downstream wealth and influence, then parlay that into overall civil rights victories.

Still, as Louis was poised on the brink of earth-shattering success, the sport's regulators in Albany were pointing "with pride to the increased interest in boxing and wrestling over previous years in that the amount of taxes collected exceeds the estimated earnings of the department.... the year just ended," speaking of 1935, "is the best we have had since 1931 and the amount of taxes will exceed 1934 by at least 40%"—though the figures contemplated were merely in the hundreds of thousands of dollars.[5] As for 1934, regulators were preening since "interest in the sport has increased over the last year in that the amount of taxes collected exceeds the estimated earnings" of the Commission. But even that rosy horizon was challenged by "so-called bootleg boxing and wrestling shows" able to escape regulation—and taxation.[6] Nonetheless, the trend line was upward. The next year regulators lamented the "reduction in taxes collected for the year 1936 over the previous year," while adding quickly that this was "in no means indicative of a lessening of interest in the sport of boxing and wrestling" since "no heavyweight championship bout was held this year" and this bell cow "usually earns...about $25,000 to $35,000 in taxes," a figure that would increase exponentially

---

4. Oral History, Charles T. Duncan, 11 May 2002 and 23 April 2003, Historical Society of Washington, D.C.

5. Report to Secretary of State Ed Flynn, 31 December 1935, NYSAC.

6. Minutes, 31 December 1934, NYSAC.

in coming years, delivering a bouquet of profits to cronies.[7] By 1937 the Commission was "gratified to report that it [had] exceeded the estimated earnings" which reflected "the increased interest in boxing" owing to "the greater attendance due to the admission prices… being scaled lower than in previous years." Again, there was a protest against Chicago seeking to attract "heavyweight championship" bouts, as if Manhattan should rightfully possess a stranglehold over this bounty.[8]

The Great Depression was still biting in 1939, so there was another unwanted "reduction in taxes collected" then, but again this was because the "important heavyweight championship bout which is generally staged in New York City was held in Detroit," reinforcing the ability of promoters to play upon the inbred competition generated by federalism, by inducing jurisdictions to engage in a race to the bottom as they tossed out even more tax breaks to attract these contests.[9] Thus, at the end of the decade regulators were straining to increase revenue by "increasing attendance and income of wrestling clubs"; not only "permit the use of women wrestlers," but also "four men 'battle royal' wrestling in one ring…to create the proper publicity and 'ballyhoo' would be a great help."[10]

The ominous gathering clouds of war in Europe increased the impact of the Selective Service Act, which meant, it was said without glee, "a great number of our licensees…have failed to renew." The reduction of talent and participants led to a reduction of "prices of admission…to meet public [decreased] demand."[11]

However, a new situation—the ascendancy of Louis and other Negro batterers—created a new problem. "Bouts between two Negro fighters are not good draws at the gate," said one commentator. "White fight fans are more or less convinced that Negro fighters do not try their best against each other." And, as Muhammad Ali was able to figure out decades later to his monetary benefit, "75 percent of the white customers go to a mixed fight with the hope of

---

7. Report to Secretary of State Ed Flynn, 31 December 1936, NYSAC.

8. Report to Secretary of State Edward J. Flynn, 31 December 1937, NYSAC.

9. Report to Secretary of State Michael F. Walsh, 31 December 1939, NYSAC.

10. Minutes, 22 October 1940, New York State Athletic Commission, NYSAC.

11. Minutes, 31 December 1940, New York State Athletic Commission, NYSAC.

seeing the white fighter...'emerge victorious,'" especially at Madison Square Garden.[12]

As things turned out, Gans and Johnson—or Peter Jackson for that matter—were not (pardon the expression) "black swans." Instead they were harbingers, upsetting the consensus that Negroes (men, that is) were "yellow," "soft" and all the rest. Pivoting in a way to preserve the racist vitriol, Negro men were reconstructed as bestial "brutes" to the point that a few decades later, Chris Dundee, Miami promoter and brother of Angelo, Ali's trainer, opined, "Kid, everything being equal, there has never been in the history of boxing a white boxer who can beat an equal black boxer."[13]

More revenues can at times produce disorientation too. One of those streams of revenue was produced by radio, an item that soon became ubiquitous in households—providing a boost to the consumer electronics business—and helped to propel Louis's popularity, as his fights often were accompanied by groups of Negroes assembled around this electricity-powered device awaiting yet another triumph for their hero. It was on 16 July 1929—weeks before the stock market collapse—that the New York State Athletic Commission entertained the "application of Station WABC to broadcast the bouts from Ebbets Field," Brooklyn.[14] The man known as Goldie Ahearn helped to pioneer the broadcasting of big-time boxing over national radio networks. Born Isidore Goldstein in Russia on Christmas Day in 1898, he lived for 75 years, becoming the first promoter licensed when boxing was legalized in Washington, D.C. Louis and Ahearn were two sides of a coin, benefiting themselves and the communities from which they sprung.[15]

Louis proceeded carefully, conscious of sensitivities. The man Louis had to beat in order to advance was James Braddock, whose devolution ideologically represented an ironic advance. "I don't draw the color line," he said, feinting left, "but the championship of the world should stay in the hands of the white race," he concluded, pounding right. Again, reviving the question of the integrity of Dempsey, it was reported similarly, that the "Mauler" was "volunteering to train any well recommended White Hope, to stop Louis before he could get to the championship." The Negro journalist

---

12. Clipping, 12 November 1938, Buster Miller Scrapbook, Schomburg Center, New York Public Library, Harlem, New York City (abbrev. Miller-SCH).
13. Pacheco, *Tales*, 55.
14. Minutes, 18 July 1929, NYSAC.
15. Undated clipping, Sub Group IX, Series I, Box 1, HKBA.

William Pickens, who wrote these words, added with a nod to Louis: "they trapped Jack Johnson by the woman route."[16] Though Louis consorted frequently with lighter-skinned Negro women, his son recollected that he pursued an anti-Johnson path: "never have your picture taken alone with a white woman" was his guiding light, lest he unnecessarily inflame the cockles of those who took white [male] supremacy much too seriously.[17]

By 1935 Louis was a headliner at Yankee Stadium, exchanging blows with the overmatched Max Baer. The box office was overflowing, according to an observer: "there is hardly a spot in the civilized world," he said, "which is not represented at the ringside.... no boxing match, in all its history, has attracted such a wide range of interest." They had arrived from "Paris, from London, from Milan... from South America...from Cuba"—and "no less than four Japanese newspapers have men at the ringside."[18]

As for Johnson, he was well past his prime as a puncher, but still flexing his political muscles. By 1933, a journalist wrote, "Hitler is a dangerous man; even Jack Johnson thinks so"; this was his conclusion after a "long trip" to the "[old] continent"; with prescience, the battler observed, "There are too many ruffians among his storm troopers. They'll bear watching."[19] A report in late 1932 from Hamburg referred derisively to "Der Schwarze" champion.[20] Nonplussed, Johnson vowed to open a "gym" in Germany.[21] Validating the nascent notion that fattening the purses of Negro boxers could lead to political impact, an article from Barcelona—his favorite city—indicated that Johnson had "purchased an interest in a periodical published weekly in Spanish and devoted to socialism and sports."[22] Anticipating the massive shift of Negro voters from the GOP to the Democratic Party, earlier he had formed "Negro [Al] Smith Clubs" boosting the fortunes of the precursor to Franklin D. Roosevelt as New York State governor.[23]

---

16. Abe Feldman File, circa 1930s, Sub Group IX, Series I, Box 8, HKBA. In applying for his boxing license in California in 1935, Braddock listed his "race" as "Irish American." See Boxing License and Renewal Applications, F2214, D3986, California State Archives, Sacramento.

17. Barrow and Munder, *Joe Louis*, 43.

18. Program for Louis-Baer bout, 24 September 1935, Box 1, AASC-Emory.

19. Clipping, ca. 1933, Jack Johnson Scrapbook, Schomburg Center, New York Public Library, Harlem, New York City (abbrev. Johnson-SCH).

20. Clipping, 26 November 1932, Johnson-SCH.

21. Clipping, no date, Johnson-SCH.

22. Clipping, ca. 1933, Johnson-SCH.

23. Undated clipping, Johnson-SCH.

Nonetheless, in a premature burst of progressivism, Johnson put forward an idea for cleaning up the sport that it would take decades to engage and even today has yet to be implemented, sadly enough; for at the end of this decade of turmoil, he announced portentously, "Certainly I'm in favor of federal boxing control," thereby eroding the corrupt fiefdoms of narrow-minded state agencies. Why? "Present conditions are terrible," he said dolorously. "The sooner the government takes over—and cracks one-man control—the better."[24] Such outspoken views may serve to explain why the heavyweight chose exile from his homeland. Early on the New York State Athletic Commission was monitoring his multifaceted activities, once extending surveillance to his "boxing act in...a Brooklyn theatre" as they were seeking to "ascertain...if Johnson is really boxing or hippodroming [sic] with a real comedian or actor in the company."[25]

More than most, Johnson realized that boxing continued to be a dangerous outing, a reality which was discovered by the audience at an unlicensed contest in Cortland, New York, in early 1929. For there a boxer was killed in the ring, an event that was becoming so routine, it seemed to be numbing and undermining outrage.[26] Nate Siegel met a similar—and different—fate. In 1934 a shotgun was fired through the window of his home in Revere, Massachusetts, slaying this Boston-born former New England welterweight champion.[27]

As the revenues streaming into boxing increased in velocity, so did the arrival of novices with dreams of getting rich—or at least prosperous—quick, by any means necessary. Max Baer, who was to exchange blows with Joe Louis, killed Frankie Campbell in the ring in 1930; some fans' outrage may have been heightened since the victorious Baer, like many Jewish boxers of that era, sported the Star of David on his trunks (Baer's father was Jewish).[28] This display of ethno-religious pride was not just a quirk of Baer. Sammy "Kid" Meadows also had the emblem on his trunks.[29] Predictably, an Albany legislator then pressed regulators to bar "the wearing of any emblem or insignia on trunks" and the like that carried a "particular

---

24. *Minneapolis Star Journal*, 16 December 1939, Johnson-SCH.
25. Minutes, 27 September 1921, NYSAC.
26. Minutes, 5 March 1929, NYSASC.
27. Clipping, ca. 1934, Sub Group IX, Series II, Box 23, HKBA.
28. *San Francisco Chronicle*, 25 August 2005, Vertical File-Boxing, San Francisco Public Library.
29. Undated report, Sub Group IX, Series 1, Box 16, HKBA.

appeal to racial or religious groups"—and, just as predictably, the Commission complied.³⁰

But this did not stanch the flow of this minority into the ring. Among the Jewish Americans driven into the sport was Georgie Abrams, born in 1918 in Roanoke, Virginia, and an active middleweight by the 1930s. "How did you happen to choose boxing," he was asked, and he answered forthrightly: "actually to defend myself…a tough mob of 18 & 19 year olds called 'The Wharf Rats'…delighted in picking on me."³¹

* * *

"The Brown Bomber" was not the only Negro thumper who entered the spotlight in the 1930s.³² There were others, and their very presence was a solvent applied to traditional notions of masculinity, then white supremacy; this also delivered more income into the pockets of Negro families reeling from the ravages of the Great Depression. Among these stellar fighters was Henry Armstrong, born as Henry Jackson on the twelfth day of the twelfth month in 1912 in Columbus, Mississippi. Like many from that part of the Magnolia State (including my parents), he migrated to St. Louis and attended the elementary school named after the man who led the Haitian Revolution (Toussaint L'Ouverture) then Vashon High School (the alma mater of my older brother and sister), where he graduated in three and a half years, garlanded with the honor of being designated Poet Laureate of his graduating class. Yet he quickly found that society was hardly interested in literary talent, so he became a boxer and then became the only champion to hold three titles simultaneously, all sub-heavyweight, of course. Yet, like Louis, who had to fork over future earnings in order to get a shot at the title, Armstrong had his managerial contract sold slave style to Hollywood personalities George Raft (who had strong gangster ties) and Al Jolson. Naturally, he had no veto over this transaction that governed his future.³³

Armstrong's mother was reputed to be of Iroquois descent, meaning he had two streams of combativeness flowing figuratively in

---

30. Minutes, 22 November 1940, NYSAC.

31. Undated report, Sub Group IX, Series 1, Box 1, HKBA.

32. See David A. Wiggins and Ryan A. Swanson, eds., *Separate Games: African American Sports Behind the Walls of Segregation*, Fayetteville: University of Arkansas Press, 2016.

33. Clipping, 24 September 1961, Negro Scrapbook, Missouri Historical Society, St. Louis (abbrev. MoHS-SL).

his veins. This came in handy since his St. Louis neighborhood was dangerously close to an enclave of Euro-Americans, meaning he often had to fight two opponents simultaneously. Purportedly, his heart was a third larger than average with, said one analyst, "one of the lowest beats," which did little to curtail his endurance. His fury inside the ring had to be accompanied with steeliness outside since he had to rub shoulders frequently with mobsters. Before entering the ring to fight Ceferino Garcia he was accosted by comrades of the infamous gangster Ben "Bugsy" Siegel who offered him a hefty $75,000 to lose the fight intentionally—which ended in a draw, with even the referee saying he feared for his life. Apparently, his manager, Eddie Mead, was not above corruption either. Perhaps understandably, after retiring as a boxer—and like the heavyweight George Foreman decades later—Armstrong dedicated himself to saving souls, becoming a pastor of a flock at Mount Olivet Baptist Church, at 2912 St. Louis Avenue in the heart of the Mound City.[34]

When shaping his sermons, Armstrong had a rich experience to draw upon, as he kept returning to the bribery episode. "I had one bribe offer," he said, referring to the incident above. "It was right in Los Angeles at the Main Street gym. The fight was Ceferino Garcia for the middleweight championship.... He was the Filipino with the terrific bolo punch," a kind of upper-cut or a punch designed to do maximum damage to the jaw or chin, often delivered via a wind-up from the hip. There was a "meeting of some sort at the gym" and "I was led to the back room" where "everybody was smoking cigars." Then one of the smokers "put all this money on the table, just stretched it out like a deck of cards. It looked like about $15,000 in bills," maybe more, then "one of them said...'that money means they want you to take a dive in three rounds.'" Insulted, "I walked out of the room." Yet, he continued, "when I was champion and running up that sensational victory string," meaning multiple victories, "I'm sure some men I fought against took a dive.... I know my manager made at least one [attempt], probably more."[35] Though he may have been biased toward a fellow St. Louisan, the self-proclaimed "Millionaire Referee" Harry Kessler claims Armstrong was the "most underrated" boxer of his era[36]—and his ethical compass may have been as underrated as his pugilistic prowess.

---

34. Kevin Madden, "Henry Armstrong," *Missouri Life*, 7 (No. 6, January-February 1980): 45, 47, 49-51, 53, 55-56, 58, MoHS-SL.

35. Undated account by Henry Armstrong, Odds and Ends on Boxing, Vol. 35, UND.

36. Undated column by Bob Broeg, Sub Group IX, Series I, Box 15, HKBA.

The third man in the ring had a clear vantage point from which to evaluate those he was watching. Referees were also in a position to tip the balance, in a scandalously corrupt sport, toward one battler or another. Hence, they were subjected to justifiable scrutiny by the authorities. Thus, what was announced in Pennsylvania in 1936 was not the first time this was said: The "appointments" of referees and judges "should not be announced or made until immediately before the fight was to take place and thereby prevent the gambling element from having any previous knowledge of the officials. Under the old condition, appointments were announced two days before a fight was to take place which enabled the gamblers and the managers of the fighters to approach the said officials many times fixing the fights in advance."[37] Thus, a topflight boxer like Armstrong had to battle his opponent and bribers, and occasionally referees too.

Armstrong was not unique in his estimate of referees and judges. Arthur Donavan was a leading referee beginning in the 1930s, though it was claimed that he was not neutral but a partisan and had acted thusly repeatedly. When manager James J. Johnston, Jr. appeared before regulators in the Empire State in order to reproach this compromised evaluator, he was so dissatisfied with the response that, in the Athletic Commission's words, he "increased the volume of his voice" then "arose from his chair…in a surly manner" as if he were going to emulate the boxer he supervised. For his troubles, he was "suspend[ed]" and Donavan continued on his merry way.[38] A few months later, both Donavan and a boxing judge were accused similarly. The referee was said to have "deliberately stood behind" a contestant "throughout the whole fight watching every movement that [Henry "Homicide Hank" Armstrong] made, which put him in a position where he [the referee] could not see punches delivered by Armstrong." Also queried was why the Negro battler, a top-shelf boxer, "was not permitted to punch Lou Ambers [his opponent] when he put him against the rope" and why "five rounds were taken away from Armstrong"; "ninety percent of the newspaper men at the ringside gave the fight to Armstrong. There were pictures taken of the fight which was positive proof that Henry Armstrong was an easy winner," though Donavan disagreed adamantly: "he is incompetent," was the fiery accusation directed at the referee, and "his license should be taken away from him." He was accused of "being prejudiced against Armstrong" as, once more, corruption tended to

---

37. John S. Fine to P.S. Stahlnecker, Secretary to the Governor, 23 August 1936, Box 1517, Pinchot-LC.
38. Minutes, 14 March 1939, NYSAC.

operate against the material interests of the Negro who generally did not have the connections—and certainly not the complexion—to act similarly.[39]

For at this juncture, the regulators treated staunch anti-racists as if they were extraterrestrial invaders. Such was the experience of journalist Dan Burley of Harlem's *Amsterdam News* when he came to protest: "it was explained to Mr. Burley," it was said condescendingly, "that the question of the color line was never thought of or considered by this Commission"—a damning self-indictment in retrospect, given the apartheid society in which they were operating.[40] For the regulators knew all too well that matchmakers frequently were "showing preference to managers of boxers and boxers in certain cases are managed by matchmakers or their relatives." These were garden-variety conflicts of interest especially since "payments to boxers in certain cases are not being made promptly,"[41] suggesting that non-favored fighters could sweat through ten rounds, then wait interminably to be paid, sweating even more profusely.

This inglorious state of affairs was driven in part because the Commission itself may have been compromised. Just before this conflicted episode, Nat Fleischer, the unofficial recorder of the sport, charged (as the regulator itself put it), "Louis Beck, Chief Inspector of this Commission was associated with the gambling element, using his official position with the Commission to peer over the shoulders of the judges assigned to various bouts to thus gain knowledge as to how the votes of these judges were likely to go, then join a group of gamblers in the rear of the boxing club, pass on his information and participate in the betting."[42]

It is clear that Armstrong had a talent that could have benefited his peers—corrupt officialdom aside—not only being able to duck punches but (with some difficulty) also to escape the unprincipled clutches of management. The analyst Arthur Mann was among those who complained about "parasitical management," meaning that even when a fighter was entitled to two thirds of the purse from a bout, he rarely walked away with more than half, "if that much." And it was not just Negro boxers, though they were more vulnerable. Primo "The Ambling Alp" Carnera ascended to the apex as heavyweight champion by 1933, yet he was an exemplar of what could be "likened to a whale with a species of small sucker fish attached to

---

39. Minutes, 29 August 1939, NYSAC.
40. Minutes, 12 September 1939, NYSAC.
41. Minutes, 20 February 1931, NYSAC.
42. Minutes, 14 January 1936, NYSAC.

his side as he swims along"; for "attached to Carnera" were "seven men who receive a percentage," seizing "sixty five cents of every dollar that Carnera earns." Another prime-time fighter, Max Baer, was "hardly better off." Such parasitism accelerated as managers on a wider scale were propelled into the business by the like entrance of politicos and racketeers—whom the managers often accompanied.[43]

Mann may have had in mind Philadelphia's Max "Boo Boo" Hoff, born in 1892 to poor Russian Jewish immigrants, who became a boxer, then a manager of boxers. By the late 1920s he controlled the largest stable of prizefighters nationally, to the point where they were incorporated—under his name, of course. He had dealings with other boxers, including Tunney, and other mobsters too, including Capone. The exertions of boxers and bootlegging meant that for a while he was one of the richest gangsters—and men—in the U.S.[44] Another Capone torpedo who migrated into boxing was Nessie Blumenthal. One of his jobs was to keep Chicago cabbies in line for his boss. He also had been accused of murder. His boss, as should be apparent, loved boxing and dreamed of "owning" a champion, and Blumenthal became one of his scouts, wandering through gyms seeking Italian talent particularly. Later Truman Gibson, the Negro liaison with mobsters, hired him to manage a gym at Madison and Hamlin in Chicago.[45]

Carnera also played a role in illustrating how white supremacy operated in the ring. This occurred when he battled the Negro heavyweight George Godfrey, born in Mobile in 1900 as Feab S. Williams. He took the name of the elder George "Old Chocolate" Godfrey, a throwback from the John L. Sullivan era, who held the title of "Negro Heavyweight Champion"—or "World Colored Heavyweight Champion"—a title then garnered by the younger. The latter was once told that if he won a particular bout, the Ku Klux Klan would kidnap and lynch him. His opportunities limited, he served as Dempsey's sparring partner and reportedly made him look foolish; then he became an actor. Still, by 1928 he was ranked second as a contender. Signed to fight Carnera, he lost on a "foul" in a bout that was viewed widely as predetermined by the gangster handlers of the "Ambling Alp."[46]

When Carnera fought Louis, this was not—according to conservative pundit Westbrook Pegler—just a battle between two fighters,

---

43. Arthur Mann, "Punch Drunk Fighters and Why," no date, Box 16, Mann-LC.
44. Undated clipping, Sub Group VIII, Series I, Box 10, HKBA.
45. Clipping, 26 October 1974, Sub Group VIII, Series I, Box 3, HKBA.
46. Article, 20 July 1988, Sub Group VIII, Series I, Box 6, HKBA.

but between crime families, with the "Alp" tied to New York City and the "Brown Bomber" tied to the Midwest; but Louis's prime handler, the Michigan bookmaker John Roxborough, as a Negro was hardly competitive in the realm of illicitness. More to the point, this bout was seen by many as a proxy for the ongoing tensions between Italy and Ethiopia, that culminated in the invasion and occupation of the latter.[47] This contest may have been more than symbolism, for it was not unusual when the consul general of Italy appeared on behalf of Carnera when he encountered choppy waters in New York, and this intervention proved to be successful.[48] The "Ambling Alp" needed help, it was thought, since it was claimed that when the "Brown Bomber" dropped explosives upon the mountaintop that was his head, Carnera was unable to fight back effectively since he had been drugged beforehand.[49]

Part of Louis's popularity rested on his becoming a geopolitical symbol, a representation exemplified by his multiple bouts in the 1930s with the German, Max Schmeling, at a time when Berlin-sponsored fascism was on the march. Ironically, despite the rancid anti-Semitism of Germany then, Schmeling's manager was Joe Jacobs, of Hungarian Jewish descent, taking home a significant percentage of the boxer's earnings.[50] In return, the pliable Jacobs even went as far as giving the Nazi salute when Schmeling made an appearance back home.[51] Schmeling, a foreigner, may have fared better than his Negro peers in that he was said to receive two thirds of his purses—Jacobs received "only" 7-1/3%—with the rest divvied up between and among various parasites.[52] The New York authorities were quite solicitous to the German's requests, e.g., the time in 1929 when he "informed the Commission that he is leaving for Germany...and will be gone for at least two months" in the midst of a managerial dispute. It was then that Jacobs was said to be "not a fit person to hold a license to conduct the business of managing licensed boxers," though "the boxer indicated a desire to retain Jacobs as an adviser."[53]

---

47. Undated column, Sub Group VIII, Series I, Box 17, HKBA.
48. Minutes, 16 April 1931, A1372-09, NYSAC.
49. Minutes, 4 October 1935, NYSAC.
50. Minutes, 22 January 1928, NYSAC.
51. David Margolick, *Beyond Glory: Joe Louis vs. Max Schmeling and a World on the Brink*, New York: Knopf, 2005.
52. Minutes, 15 January 1929, NYSAC.
53. Minutes, 13 February 1929, NYSAC.

The authorities had reason to think that the German slugger was hardly beyond reproach, suspected Nazi ties aside. He was accused of participating in bouts with preordained outcomes, a bonanza for gamblers in on the fix.[54] Yet he continued to enjoy entree into elevated circles. Thus, in 1933 Timothy Mara, whose family was to control the fabulously profitable New York Giants football team, joined with Dempsey to promote his bout with Max Baer: "The House of Calvary, Cancer Hospital, Bronx, will participate in the profits of the show," it was announced self-righteously in an attempt at sanitizing and laundering.[55] Especially after the coming to power of Adolf Hitler as chancellor, Berlin was protective of this slugger. In April 1933 a "cable from the German Boxing Commission deploring the treatment accorded Max Schmeling in this country because of the recent political unrest" was received.[56]

This cesspool of unethicality was not just limited to profiteering. Billy Delaney once managed champions Corbett and Jeffries, before managing Jack Brady, who was fighting a Negro heavyweight and was getting shellacked. So Delaney instructed his charge, "the next time he knocks you down, swear at him. Call him a big blanket-blank!" The boxer did so, and his enraged opponent landed a solid punch on Brady's jaw before he could even get up off the floor and, promptly, the prone fighter was awarded the victory and the winner's share of the purse—because of the alleged "foul."[57]

Anti-fascist activists in the U.S. were hardly solicitous toward Schmeling. The Non-Sectarian Anti-Nazi League of New York City produced a broadside featuring an intimate portrait of the boxer alongside Adolf Hitler, with the admonition, "Don't be taken in by Nazi ballyhoo.... Weaken Hitler by Boycotting the Louis-Schmeling Fight." They warned that "Berlin will send a 'Cheering Squad' of 1000 storm troopers," making for "the largest Nazi Ego-Builder of 1938."[58] Revealingly, Louis's posture as the anti-Johnson may have inspired the Galvestonian to help train Schmeling earlier in the decade.[59]

It was not just the Galvestonian who was placed in an odd position. This bout even split family and comrades down the middle.

---

54. Minutes, 8 December 1939, NYSAC.
55. Minutes, 14 March 1933, NYSAC.
56. Minutes, 21 April 1933, NYSAC.
57. Clipping, May 1936, Sub Group VIII, Series 1, Box 6, HKBA.
58. Broadside for Louis-Schmeling Fight, 1938, New-York Historical Society, Manhattan.
59. *Indianapolis Recorder*, 18 July 1931, Johnson-SCH.

"We all picked Schmeling to beat Louis," confessed Charles B. Garabedian, attorney and intimate of the powerful Kennedy family in Boston; but one member of the clan "said that Louis would knock Schmeling out in the first round and we all laughed at him"[60]—with nervousness no doubt.

* * *

The rise of boxing was also a time for a recrudescence of fascism and other forms of bigotry. It was in this fiery crucible that many Jewish Americans came to maturity. By the 1980s, Matthew Feldman was a respected state senator in New Jersey but he had not forgotten a time when he "had to fight his way in and out of his Jersey City Talmud Torah, then joined friends to break up meetings of the pro-Nazi Bund. 'I always felt that my non-Jewish peers respected Jewish power,'" which in turn bolstered the profile of Benny Leonard and other punchers. "The Jewish fighter or ballplayer were [sic] held in higher esteem than the Jewish scholars" then, he said, not unlike what was occurring among Negroes.[61]

However, a cardinal difference between the two was that often a Jewish-American fighter could change his name, dispense with wearing the Star of David on his trunks, and could then possibly elude the harsh edge of anti-Semitism. Melanin-rich Negroes by and large did not have this option. After the revenues for boxing rose, name changing became endemic, which in a sense was a guidepost on the centuries-long road to "whiteness" or acceptance of ostensible European outliers into the wider family of "white America." To be sure, Italian-American prizefighters and others who faced the sting of bigotry also had available such an escape hatch: In one meeting the New York State Athletic Commission entertained the petition from Abraham Lieberman to adopt the "ring name" of Arty O'Leary, and J. William Genzardi became Johnny Williams.[62] Leading the way was Benjamin Leiner who became Benny Leonard, then Joseph Kanasola became Canastota Bob.[63] Joseph Leonardi became Joe Leonard.[64] Julius Goldman became Young Goldie, and Fred

---

60. Oral History, Charles B. Garabedian, 19 June 1964, John F. Kennedy Presidential Library, Boston.
61. Matthew Feldman, "The Jewish Veteran," July-August 1986, Sub Group IX, Series I, Box 8, HKBA.
62. Minutes, 30 January 1923, NYSAC.
63. Minutes, 24 July 1923, NYSAC.
64. Minutes, 16 January 1923, NYSAC.

Rosenberg became Johnny Rose.[65] (Jack Rosen also became Johnny Rose.) Similarly abbreviated was Benny Greenblatt who became Benny Green,[66] and Sammy Greenspan became Sammy Green.[67] Morris Fishbein became Moe Fisher.[68] James Kleinschmidt became Jimmy Klein.[69] Harry Kremelhein became Harry Howard.[70] Then Michael Colonnese became Mike Collins (note the preference for Irish-sounding names, despite the reality that this group also was unable to evade bias altogether). Leo Kolekowsky became Leo Kole and Michael Consulmano became Mickey Taylor.[71] Mike Posateri became Mike Dundee[72] and another presumed Italian became Dickie Dundee.[73] Florian Hardner became "Allentown Dundee."[74]

Having said that, it is similarly striking how certain boxers sought to appropriate the identity of famed Negro punchers: Anthony Camperlango became "Italian Joe Gans"[75] and Cyril Quinton became "Panama Joe Gans."[76] (Then there was "Baby Joe Gans.")[77] When Florine Petta became "Battling Johnson," was this a nod to the Galvestonian?[78] Another way to view this is as a tacit acknowledgment that the old idea of Negro masculinity—"soft," "yellow," "coward"—was evolving under the hammer blows of Negro boxers. More simply, Peter Kohleman became Pete Coleman,[79] a move toward Anglicization which was also a trend. Thus, Pete Carfagna became Peter Carr, and Armand Di Pasquale became Eddie Dempsey.[80] Joseph Cuffori became Henry Smith.[81] Mike Credico

---

65. Minutes, 26 June 1923, NYSAC.
66. Minutes, 2 January 1923, NYSAC.
67. Minutes, 6 February 1923, NYSAC.
68. Minutes, 15 May 1928, NYSAC.
69. Minutes, 30 October 1923, NYSAC.
70. Minutes, 9 January 1923, NYSAC.
71. Minutes, 30 August 1927, NYSAC.
72. Minutes, 17 April 1923, NYSAC.
73. Minutes, 28 May 1923, NYSAC.
74. Minutes, 9 October 1923, NYSAC.
75. Minutes, 10 August 1926, NYSAC.
76. Minutes, 16 October 1923, NYSAC. I am not certain how to analyze how and why Michael Flamier became the "Zulu Kid." See Minutes, 24 July 1923, NYSAC. Remarkably, my listing of name changes is only a small percentage of those executed.
77. Minutes, 5 March 1929, NYSAC.
78. Minutes, 20 February 1923, NYSAC.
79. Minutes, 13 March 1923, NYSAC.
80. Minutes, 11 January 1927, NYSAC.
81. Minutes, 16 January 1923, NYSAC.

became Danny Brown.[82] In one fell swoop in one meeting, Olaf Jorgensen became Al Johnson, Florian Strozewski became Larry Dayton, and Ludwig Soreca became Lew Hurley.[83] Edward Sacerdote became Edward Priest, simply translating his surname into a presumably more acceptable English.[84]

An accomplice of this renaming practice took place when there arose the Milwaukee lightweight pounder Jack O'Toole, who was said to be "definitely Jewish" but who married an Irish woman and "took her name for boxing purposes." (It is unclear if a similar route led to Jacob Buxbaum becoming Jack O'Keefe.)[85] Sammy Ford junked the surname "Abrams" because, he said, Jewish and Italian fighters did not sell tickets.[86]

Al "Bummy" Davis may have been the most infamous of fighters of this type, in that he was born Albert Abraham Davidoff and, unlike some of the previously noted boxers, was a serious contender as both a lightweight and welterweight. With roots in the Brownsville neighborhood of Brooklyn, he too was Jewish and for a time fought under the name of Giovanni Pasconi. He was said to have once challenged Ben "Bugsy" Siegel to a fight, and fought and lost to both Beau Jack and Henry Armstrong.[87]

At least for a while, ensconced in this charmed circle was the boxer known as Mickey Cohen, who went on to become a leading mobster, this after starting off as a newsboy—and there hangs a tale. As suggested by the aforesaid case of Harry Kessler—and others—starting life as a newsboy was part of the creation story, a rite of passage, especially for Jewish boxers. Lew Tendler, born in 1898 in Philadelphia, is another example: He used his fists to gain and keep the most lucrative newspaper selling corner in the City of Brotherly Love. Battling mostly successfully in the lower weight classes, from bantamweight to welterweight, he earned almost a million dollars in the ring, which was then poured into restaurant ownership in his hometown and Atlantic City. "In those days they hardly taxed you," he said of the Internal Revenue Service—a sentiment which might come as a surprise to the heirs of Joe Louis, who was famously

---

82. Minutes. 23 January 1923, NYSAC.
83. Minutes, 23 August 1927, NYSAC.
84. Minutes, 20 September 1927, NYSAC.
85. Undated clippings, Sub Group IX, Series II, Box 18, HKBA.
86. *Boston Globe*, August 1983, Sub Group IX, Series II, Box 24, HKBA.
87. See Allen Bodner, *When Boxing Was Jewish*, 82-87; Undated clipping, Sub Group IX, Series II, Box 28, HKBA.

hounded by the taxman. Tendler's scrapes as a newsboy prepared him well for the ring and thereafter.[88]

Violence inhered in working-class life in any case and certainly was part of a newsboy's job; he had to brawl to protect the corner on which he sold his wares, which was tied to protecting his revenue, his honor, even his newspapers. With a surplus of dishonor, newspapers—often part of chains owned by plutocrats like William Randolph Hearst—often induced brawling as a kind of entertainment to promote more sales. This was an adjunct of the corporate press promoting boxing itself. Arguably, Jack Johnson learned the rudiments of press promotion, even the value of boxing itself, from his days as a youthful newsboy on the turbulent streets of Galveston.[89]

The same holds true for Meyer "Mickey" Cohen, born to an Orthodox Jewish family in Brooklyn with roots in Kiev: By the age of six he was hawking newspapers on the tumultuous streets of Los Angeles, the city to which his family had moved and where he made his mark. There he could be found in Boyle Heights, aggressively occupying the busy corner of Soto and Brooklyn streets. Eugene Biscailuz, who became the top law enforcement official in Los Angeles County, was from the same neighborhood, and this tie became quite useful to Cohen after he became the region's top mobster. "He was close to me," said the diminutive thug, "but we couldn't be so close openly because of public opinion. But he was my father confessor." As a teenager Cohen became a prizefighter. "Boxing was illegal then so I started out boxing in bootleg clubs...for three two-minute rounds," a rite of passage for many a brawler. "I boxed for the American Legion in Compton, Watts, East Los Angeles...I boxed almost every night...I lost very few fights," he boasted. "I got completely involved in the boxing world and it and the racket world were almost one and the same. Most boxers were owned by racket people. And at one time six boxing titles belonged to guys in the so-called racket world." He worked closely with Benny Greenberg, a "fight promoter" who had a connection with topflight boxer John Henry Lewis. Cohen was "like Benny's arm, Benny's muscle," which brought him into contact with the "black fight promoter by the name of Fred Irwin."

Idle boasts aside, by his early twenties, Cohen had done a tour of duty on the mean streets of Cleveland—which produced both future Las Vegas bigfoot Moe Dalitz and promoter Don King. After losing a bout, not a common occurrence, he became a bouncer at nightclubs,

---

88. Undated article from "The Boxing Register," and Obituary of Tendler, 7 November 1970, Sub Group IX, Series I, Box 34, HKBA.

89. DiGirolamo, *Crying*, 59, 368, 370, 492.

then a bodyguard for more affluent mobsters, then a kind of "hitman" or paid assassin. Impressing those higher in the food chain, this underling rose to become boss of the outfit out west and, more particularly, in the growing metropolis that was Los Angeles.[90]

Exemplifying the rightward tilt of those of his class, as late as 1974 Cohen was claiming that "Cassius Clay [Muhammad Ali] is a rotten example for kids," an apparent reference to his antiwar stance. As for Cohen, he fought 79 fights professionally, which included five champions, but his most serious injury came in prison, where he was partially paralyzed after a lead pipe was applied professionally to his skull.[91] Despite his travails, Cohen did quite well financially—if his wardrobe is a guide. He owned 1500 pairs of socks, 300 suits and 60 pairs of shoes. He was obsessive, often washing his hands a hundred times a day. He was frequently seen with Hollywood stars, including Sammy Davis, Jr.[92] He was also ethnocentric, once referring to his "enemy" as "the Sicilians," i.e., his comrades in corruption. "The people of Los Angeles ought to get down on their knees and thank God for Mickey Cohen," he rasped, "because if it wasn't for me the Wops would have this town tied up."[93]

Obviously, these illicit forces were not necessarily pursuing equal opportunity policies. The man called the "Hollywood Godfather"—Billy Wilkerson—who, like others of his ilk, incinerated much of his paperwork, making it difficult to trace his untoward activities, still left evidence that he employed Golden Gloves fighters as busboys so they could act as bouncers in his clubs, yet his son argues that "Black employees were nowhere to be found" in his varied businesses.[94]

As Cohen's presence suggested, sunny Southern California was also becoming a magnet for prizefighters. Icons of the film industry often felt the need for bodyguards, and who better to serve in this role than a man who had demonstrated his mettle publicly for pay? Mae West, the oft-described "blonde bombshell," chose Johhny Indrisano, a boxer, as her muscle. She had a fondness for men of

---

90. Mickey Cohen, *Mickey Cohen, In My Own Words: The Underworld Autobiography of Michael Mickey Cohen, as Told to John Peer Nugent*, London: Prentice Hall, 1975 (abbrev. Cohen, *Mickey Cohen*), 2, 8, 12, 23.

91. *Los Angeles Times*, 13 November 1974.

92. *Saturday Evening Post*, 27 September 1958, Sub Group IX, Series II, Box 30, HKBA.

93. *Saturday Evening Post*, 4 October 1958, Sub Group IX, Series II, Box 30, HKBA.

94. W.R. Wilkerson, *Hollywood Godfather: The Life and Crimes of Billy Wilkerson*, Chicago: Chicago Review Press, 2018, 9, 90, 176, 186.

this category, becoming quite friendly with William "Gorilla" Jones, a high caliber Negro middleweight, and when strident objection arose to his presence—not least from her own circle—she bought a building that housed him and hired his parents. They had met in 1934 and she served as his manager, becoming one of a number of Euro-American women playing a central role in the careers of Negro boxers. Jones was a kind of reincarnation of Battling Siki in his flashiness: He had a pet lion that sported a diamond-studded collar. They would remain friends until his death. West also claimed that her influence on Owney Madden, a top mobster, led to the bout between Joe Louis and James Braddock in 1937, which transformed the sport. This was consistent with her bias toward Negro boxers, including featherweight "Chalky" Wright, whom she hired as her driver; he also packed a pistol, which proved to be of little avail when he died under suspicious circumstances. It was murder, said West.[95]

Sadly, what befell Wright may have been a function of West's unsavory ties. The platinum blonde entertainer was known to consort with Madden, who occupied the pinnacle of the gangster life and covertly managed a number of boxers reportedly including Carnera, Braddock, and Maxie Rosenbloom—an all-star lineup. Madden also exerted outsized influence on top management, including Joe Jacobs, and was said to have "pulled the strings" for the increasingly prominent Tunney.[96]

Wright's demise was quite a loss. A correspondent of boxing maven Hank Kaplan described him as a "Negro born in Mexico" who "could speak Spanish well" and whose "parents were United States citizens." And he was said to be "Mae's bed partner." His bilingualism positioned him to be a natural bridge between the Negroes and the population of Mexican origin.[97]

West, however, was not the only woman who became a booster of boxers. There was the woman known as "Madam Bey" who was born in Turkey in 1881 to French and Armenian parents and known early on as Hranoush Agaganian. She attended the American College in Constantinople, where she met her spouse, who was posted to the legation in Washington, D.C. She spoke English and six other languages and became close to President William McKinley; she was

---

95. Jill Watts, *Mae West: An Icon in Black and White*, New York: Oxford University Press, 2001, 207-208, 276.

96. Benson, *Battling*, 57. For an early exploration of mobsters and boxing, see *Detroit News*, 9 October 1930, Sub Group VIII, Series I, Box 13, HKBA.

97. Bill Mahoney to Hank Kaplan, 12 January 1981, Sub Group VIII, Series I, Box 13, HKBA.

standing near him when he was assassinated in 1901. By the onset of World War I, the couple had become U.S. nationals and became rug merchants, which allowed them to buy a 30-acre spread near 516 River Road in Chatham Township, New Jersey. There this enthusiast of U.S. culture opened a training camp, hosting Armstrong, Carnera, Siki (she would not expel him from her circle despite pressure), Kid Chocolate, Sandy Saddler, and many more.[98]

Madam Bey's attraction to boxing was not hers alone. The enhanced popularity of the sport also meant that a growing corps of actors, accustomed to adoring fans and klieg lights, also were attracted to boxing—either before their stardom or afterward.[99] An actor, Victor McLaglen, once battled Jack Johnson in the ring.[100]

A man who excelled inside the ring and on the stage as well was the Negro actor known as Canada Lee. Born in Harlem in 1907, he was a musical virtuoso as a pianist and violinist, making his debut at the prestigious Aeolian Hall in New York City at the age of 11; by 13 he had become a successful jockey and a professional boxer of note by his teens. By his twenties he was a contender for the welterweight title, but a blow to the head deprived him of sight in his right eye, driving him from the ring permanently. He then migrated to stage and screen, working alongside such auteurs as Orson Welles and Alfred Hitchcock. He was to run aground as the New Deal and Fair Deal morphed into the Red Scare, as Lee was targeted for being insufficiently hostile to the Communist Party.[101]

Lee saw concord between boxing and music, two of his chief passions, since both involved intelligence, rhythm and artistry, not to mention mental agility, toughness, dedication and discipline. Lee was an exemplar of the sport as "sweetness." "Fighting is beautiful...brutality doesn't appeal to me," he explained. "That's for the

---

98. Article by Robert Hageman, 18 April 2005, Sub Group VIII, Series I, Box 2, HKBA.

99. See Philip Paul to Hank Kaplan, no date, Sub Group VIII, Series I, Box 16, HKBA. The actor/boxing axis includes Lou Costello, Broderick Crawford, Hume Cronyn, Reginald Denny, Richard Dix, Errol Flynn, Scott Brady, Bob Hope, Victory Jury, Edgar Kennedy, Bruce Cabot, Robert Warwick, Hobart Bosworth, Robert Mitchum, George O'Brien, Jack Palance, John Payne, Anthony Quinn, Dale Robertson, George Raft, Robert Ryan, Frank Sinatra, Dean Martin, Stuart Whitman, Richard Boone, Tom Tyler and others.

100. Lee Kerr, "Boxing Trivia," December 1968, Sub Group VIII, Series I, Box 12, HKBA.

101. Mona Z. Smith, *Becoming Something: The Story of Canada Lee*, New York: Faber & Faber, 2004.

maulers. But boxing, that's like hot music. You have to think. You feint to make the other guy do what you want him to do. That's the fun, not nailing him": The fun was not necessarily in unfrocking one's opponent.[102]

Even as a boxer, Lee—born as Leonard Canegata—was encountering difficulties in the ring well before his transformative eye injury. He was disqualified by the referee during a bout with Tommy White in 1928.[103] By February 1929 he was "reprimanded" by the authorities after a match.[104] Then in October 1929 he was dragged into the dock once again, this time for failure to fulfill a contract to box at the "Jamaica Club" and thus was "suspended."[105] By 1930, his manager sought to pressure regulators to force Lee to fork over a hefty $363—and they were not averse to complying.[106] By July 1931 Lee faced off again with his manager, Jim Buckley, who claimed that his client owed him a sizable amount of money after this parasite agreed to release the fighter from their contract. The result? The authorities decided to "deduct 1/3 of Lee's future ring purses and turn the same over to Buckley until such time as the above amount is paid."[107]

"Chalky" Wright's demise was simply the most extreme example of the uncertain fates of Negro boxers. Joe Louis was able to parachute into fame, as noted, only by pledging a percentage of his future earnings to his opponent, Braddock. Also gnawing at Louis's earnings, according to the State Athletic Commission in California, were the usual suspects, e.g., the promoter Mike Jacobs, but also the raconteur Damon Runyan, who "had an interest, four per cent...in the earnings of Joe Louis."[108]

While Louis was being systematically looted, Tunney was expanding his horizons. He visited the Soviet Union in 1931 and, predictably, was unimpressed. There was "wretchedness" at "nightmare" proportions. As for the American Youth Congress, thought to be close to Moscow at the top level, it was little more than a "mess of termites" and "Un-American, unpatriotic, subversive and seditious"

---

102. Ibid., 29.
103. Minutes, 1 August 1928, NYSAC.
104. Minutes, 13 February 1929, NYSAC.
105. Minutes, 8 October 1929, NYSAC.
106. Minutes, 27 June 1930, NYSAC.
107. Minutes, 22 July 1931, A1372-09, NYSAC.
108. Transcript of Hearing of State Athletic Commission, 17 January 1941, 9:30 A.M., Whitcomb Hotel, San Francisco, F2219-2221, CaSAC.

besides.[109] This verbal fusillade was the prelude to Tunney strapping on his gloves, this time to lead a drive to purge the AYC of Communist Party members.[110] By 1935 he was in China, refereeing a match featuring Chinese boxers and expanding his range of contacts in the bargain.[111]

* * *

Professional wrestling was a funhouse mirror version of boxing, exaggerating farcically the more absurd and onerous aspects of the latter, including contests with preordained outcomes, bloodshed real and imagined, raucous fans, crass exploitation of those in the ring, etc. A commonplace incident occurred in San Diego in late 1939 when George Koverly was grappling with Karl Davis, but left the ring and "kicked a spectator. The spectator, enforced by others, took Koverly on," leading to a "ringside riot," just one in a series of cases where "tactics....liable to incite riot" were deployed.[112]

Just as there was a symbolic representation in the Louis-Carnera bout—think Ethiopia vs. Italy—this tendency was exaggerated in wrestling: As tensions rose between Washington and Tokyo, more Japanese wrestlers were licensed in California.[113]

There were a few Negroes too, who would be useful as foils, not unlike Jack Johnson. For example, Jack Claybourn, born in Minneapolis and living in Marysville, California, adopted the ring name "Black Panther."[114] (Reversing field, the boxer once known as "Marcus Garvey McCray" decided to reduce his name simply to "Marcus McCray.")[115] There were Native Americans also, useful as foils, reminding some in the audience of the spoils of settler

---

109. Gene Tunney, "Youth Congress and the Communistic Blight," reprinted from *Liberty*, 31 August 1940, Box 7, GT-UND.

110. Press Release, 19 June 1940, Box 7, GT-UND.

111. United Press International Dispatch, 9 April 1935, Box 1, Francis McCracken Fisher Papers, Arizona State University, Tempe.

112. Chief Inspector, Northern District to Athletic Commission, 3 November 1939, F2191, CaSAC.

113. See License and Renewal, D3986, F2220, CaSAC: 27 September 1935, Tsutao Hin igami (asked his "color," a question typical of the era, his response was "Japanese"; 1936, Mitsugu Hamanaka; 7 January 1936, Kaimo Kudo, born in San Francisco; Tetsuro Sato, born in Japan.

114. See License and Renewal, D3986, F2220, CaSAC: Jack Claybourn, 10 October 1936.

115. Minutes, 22 April 1946, NYSAC.

colonialism.[116] (Native Americans were likewise prominent in boxing in Oklahoma; by the 1930s there was reference to a "crew of all-state leather pushers fighting under the banner of the Pond Creek" which, in martial language, "meets an invading Indian squad from the United Pueblo boarding schools of Santa Fe and Albuquerque.... bouts will be broadcast.")[117]

However, at least in what came to be called Silicon Valley, Louis Lopes, the local American Legion leader, acknowledged that "while popular support of wrestling in San Jose has steadily increased under the sponsorship of [the AL], the fact is outstanding that this community will not support profitably more than one wrestling show per week."[118]

The militaristic American Legion was also conservative and a staunch defender of the status quo—which included Jim Crow. The progressive State Senator Robert Kenny quickly complained about bias in league with Daniel Shaw, the Pacific Coast representative of the premier Negro periodical, the *Chicago Defender*. Both men informed Governor Culbert Olson that Hollywood Legion Post 43 sought to bar "Negro boxers." They were "not allowed to compete," though there was a "parade of whites, Orientals, Europeans and all others from the four corners of the earth...[including] Filipinos...and Italians" entering the ring, all "save the American born Negro...were made welcome. We ask 'why'?" An elaborate answer would have involved an elaborate exploration of the Negro's fraught history in the U.S., including firm opposition to the founding of a slaveholders' republic,[119] a question then hardly contemplated. Still, Shaw and Senator Kenny went on to remind the state authorities that these same malign forces had "ever shown willingness to call upon Bill [Bojangles] Robinson to execute dance routines," a safe performance; some even "graciously entered the spotlight beam" when it was shone "upon Joe Louis and Henry Armstrong." Yet the fact remained that "this stadium is the only place in the state where Negroes dare not box nor apply for boxing licenses." This was "increasing tension" at a time when, once again, Negroes would be expected to make the ultimate sacrifice during a prospective "World War which

---

116. License and Renewal, D3986, F2220, CaSAC: Ben Tenario, also known as "Chief Little Wolf," born in 1912 in Colorado.

117. Announcement, ca. 1930s, Box 4, Folder 32, Milton Garber Collection, University of Oklahoma, Norman.

118. Louis Lopes, Commander Memory Post # 399 of American Legion, San Jose, to John R. Quinn, 28 November 1936, F2219-2221, CaSAC.

119. Horne, *Counter-Revolution*, passim.

is developing." Chairman Jerry Geisler expressed sympathy, since Negroes "supply some of the best participants and contestants in sporting events in this day and age,"[120] a factor that in the long run would change the policy of the American Legion as it transformed the trajectory of sports and the U.S. as a whole.

However, this epochal transformation did not occur automatically or spontaneously. It required quite a bit of punching, inside and outside the ring. The latter occurred once more in downtown Los Angeles on 16 November 1939 when the State Athletic Commission convened again to probe bias at the Hollywood Legion Stadium. "I don't want to stir up any bad feelings," said this self-described "colored American citizen" as Europe plunged into the flames of war; "but," he continued, "there are not only forty thousand Negroes in Los Angeles but twenty million" nationally that were "complaining" vociferously about the corrosiveness of bigotry.[121]

Backed by the local, and multiracial Communist Party, a growing number of influential Negroes became ever more clamorous in protesting racism in boxing. The coalition included prominent attorney Loren Miller, future Congressman Augustus Hawkins, future City Councilman Gil Lindsay, and attorney Hugh McBeth, described by the Communist press (in an article retained by the Athletic Commission) as being of "portly frame" with a "deep bass voice" and—quite strategically—"present Liberian Consul for Los Angeles," delivering important global ties.[122] Matt Crawford, a leader of this "popular front" in Oakland-Berkeley, representing the National Negro Congress, saluted Henry Armstrong for "cancelling his fight under sponsorship of the Hollywood Legion."[123] Joe Louis too, said Lou Seligson, the Communist journalist, was expected to "raise his modest soft spoken voice," adding that Armstrong "has never been allowed to fight for the Legion Stadium on its regular Friday night cards" but was instead offered less lucrative spots.[124]

This was a bold move by Armstrong, for a major problem was a dearth of venues to host the massive audiences who wished to see

---

120. Transcript, 15 September 1939, F2219, CaSAC.

121. Transcript, 16 November 1939, F2219, CaSAC.

122. *People's World*, 10 October 1939, and Transcript 14 November 1939, F2219, CaSAC.

123. Matt Crawford to State Athletic Commission, 18 November 1940, F2219, CaSAC.

124. *People's World*, 14 October 1939; State Athletic Commission, F2219, CaSAC.

him perform his handiwork. The Athletic Commission knew that the centrally sited Olympic Auditorium was unsafe, in "that in case of a panic" induced by "fire or earthquake," "tremendous hazards" would ensue, exacerbated since "management admits more people than can be safely seated in spite of numerous warnings." This was not peculiar to this site since at the normatively bigoted Hollywood Legion stadium, "overcrowding" was a "habit" too.[125]

The Communist press was quite harsh in assessing Seth Strenlinger, the first chairman of the State Athletic Commission, denoted as "the Father of Hollywood Jim Crow" and also, coincidentally enough, "a member of the Board of Directors of [Legion] Post No. 43." It was "rumored" that he was "exceptionally hard on Negro fighters" and "fined them at the slightest provocation," not unusual, as the case of Canada Lee suggested. There were wrinkles in that "Negro managers and handlers" were "allowed to scamper all over the ring but Negro boxers—My God, NO!" This local "Czar of Boxing" was also quite close to "big motion picture money."[126]

The problem for the SAC was that a number of Negro boxers were unleashed in the Golden State, many of them fleeing the terror of Jim Crow Dixie and the desert of opportunity that was the Rocky Mountain West. They were driven, no doubt, by the golden examples of the likes of Armstrong and Louis—the Gans and Johnson of the subsequent generation—and wished to duplicate their success and apparent wealth. Their presence was at odds with an ethos determined to maintain the Negro as the mudsill of society, which contributed to ructions of various sorts. Among the applicants for a license was John Louis Brantford, born in Corpus Christi and previously a valet. The footloose Negro boxer was once convicted of "conspiracy to burglary" in Pocatello, Idaho, but advised the Commission that this was a minor detail of "no importance." Sidney Brent, previously a bootblack, born due north in Washington, may have caused more concern when he advised that his "manager" was "SELF," forestalling, if only temporarily, parasites.[127]

---

125. Jim Genshlea, Chair of Athletic Commission, to Jack Kipper, 5 April 1934, F2219, CaSAC.

126. *People's World*, 12 October 1939; State Athletic Commission, F2219, CaSAC.

127. See file on John Louis Brantford, 5'10½", 1935, and Sidney Brent, 5'11", 147 pounds, born 8 May 1911. See also file on Sam Brown, Negro, 5 January 1934, Fresno residence, 5'5", 134 pounds, born in South Carolina, 15 November 1914; Frankie Butler, Negro, 1934, 5'6", 140 pounds, born in Miami, 15 May 1912; James Best, Negro, 1934, born in Sheridan, Wyoming,

* * *

As a new decade, the 1940s, commenced, prizefighting had established a foothold in U.S. culture and society, symbolized by the popularity of Armstrong, Louis and a bevy of battlers. The antifascist war was to witness, at least for a while, a stinging setback for white supremacy, which seemed to bear too close a resemblance to the bloodthirsty foe in Berlin. This was to open the door for Negroes to enter other sports, especially the pastime of baseball, which would further erode the formidable walls of Jim Crow.

---

22 April 1913; William M. Britt, 1934, 5'5", born in Newark, New Jersey, 22 November 1909, F2214, D3986, CaSAC.

Chapter 4

Fascism Floored/Black Boxers Rise

California was to experience enormous growth during the war, driven by tremendous government expenditure, becoming an exemplar of the so-called "arsenal of democracy."[1] Negroes became a reliable pillar of antifascism, which was all the more important, for in certain urban nodes, such as Newark, where they came to predominate, fascism was rife. Often the target of these vipers was the sprawling Jewish community which, according to writer Alex Portnoff, incurred "the hatred of a sizable pro-Nazi movement." There were tens of thousands of Jewish Americans in this New Jersey town where, said Portnoff, they confronted "the only place in America where Hitler sympathizers maintained a formidable presence." According to his account, the mobster Abner "Longie" Zwillman[2] "bankrolled a loosely organized gang to break up the Nazi rallies" there and "appointed one of his enforcers Nat Arno (né Sidney Abramowitz) a former lightweight boxer" to organize a band of "criminals" and "prizefighters" to do this dirty work.[3] Unsurprisingly, it was later that the analyst Lou Halper concluded that Newark "produced a record number of topflight Jewish boxers," and he included Benny Leonard, the "great idol of our time." Consistent with other analyses, Halper said "that Leonard did as much with his fistic prowess to gain respect of the Jews" as "did the Anti-Defamation League," a famed civil rights group. It was in

---

1. Roger W. Lotchin, *The Bad City in the Good War: San Francisco, Los Angeles, Oakland and San Diego*, Bloomington: Indiana University Press, 2003; Roger W. Lotchin, *The Way We Really Were: The Golden State in the Second Great War*, Urbana: University of Illinois Press, 2000; Roger W. Lotchin, *Fortress California, 1910-1961: From Warfare to Welfare*, New York: Oxford University Press, 1992.

2. Zillman was also sometimes referred to as Longey

3. Alex Portnoff, *New Jersey Monthly*, 2 July 2005, Sub Group IX, Series 1, Box 1, HKBA.

the city's Third Ward that "forces of aggression were generated and honed."[4]

Such an enterprise could only impress upon other beleaguered groupings, e.g., Negroes, the value of having within the ranks both gangsters and fighters. Assuredly, the onset of world war impacted the foregoing—and more. New York regulators were raking in less revenue, since in 1944, for example, there were only two championship bouts. Besides, "champions of all classes...with the exception of the featherweight" were all in the military. In turn, this helped to instigate sniping at supposed rivals for talent, e.g., the Amateur Athletic Union: Empire State regulators thought they should swallow whole the AAU.[5]

Because of the decline in revenue, Albany regulators felt compelled—even after the war—to press boxers to fight, even when they were not ready to do so. By 1952, for example, "Sugar" Ray Robinson was being pressed to fight though, he said, he had just endured a "severe case of heat prostration," along with "scarred tissues removed from my eyes." "I beg of you," said the besieged boxer, "to go along with my doctor's advice" to rest for a while[6]—but regulators pressed him nonetheless to fight. Later, referee Joe Cortez captured the consensus when he said that Robinson was the "greatest of all time...the master of all," an opinion he said was shared by both Muhammad Ali and "Sugar" Ray Leonard, both aspirants for this lofty descriptor. But regulators were willing to jeopardize his career, and possibly his life, for revenue.[7]

---

4. Lou Halper, *Jewish News* [New Jersey], 20 October 1977, Sub Group IX, Series I, Box 12, HKBA. See also *Boston Herald*, 18 April 1997: Chaim Herzog, an Israeli president, born in Belfast, was Ireland's bantamweight king before migrating to Palestine in 1935. In 1947, Leonard was refereeing a bout when he fell and hit his forehead, perishing from "either a cerebral accident or a coronary thrombosis." See Report by Dr. Vincent A. Nardiello, 22 April 1947, NYSAC.

5. Report to Secretary of State Thomas J. Curran, 30 December 1944, NYSAC.

6. "Ray Robinson" to Commissioner R.K. Christenberry, 29 September 1952, NYSAC. See also Will Haygood, *Sweet Thunder: The Life and Times of Sugar Ray Robinson*, New York: Knopf, 2009; Herb Boyd, *Pound for Pound: A Biography of Sugar Ray Robinson*, New York: Amistad, 2005; Kenneth Shropshire, *Being Sugar Ray: The Life of Sugar Ray Robinson, America's Greatest Boxer and First Celebrity Athlete*, New York: Basic, 2007 (abbrev. Shropshire, *Being Sugar Ray*).

7. Oral History, Joe Cortez, 29 November 2018, UNV-LA.

Negroes streamed into Sacramento too, during this era, embodied for our purposes when on 20 January 1941, Archie Moore—listed as born 13 December 1917 (though this has been disputed) in Collinsville, Illinois (also disputed)—registered for his boxing license from his new home in San Diego. Then listed as 5'11" and 160 pounds,[8] Moore was to go on to claim the title of light heavyweight champion and to battle the best heavyweights. "My hero was Kid Chocolate," he said later, referring to a Cuban virtuoso who was dominating the ranks as early as the 1930s. "I read everything about him I could find. I worshipped him." He was an apt pupil since, as one journalist put, for "long years the good fighters avoided him" especially since—quite atypically—"nobody...ever persuaded him to take a dive."[9]

Moore—"The Mongoose"—was appropriately nicknamed since the sport remained infested by snakes of various sorts. Typically, in 1943 the authorities were investigating a bout between Charles Burley and Holman Williams: The referee, Abe Roth, was suspected of "collusion affecting the results."[10] As the war wrapped up in 1945, the authorities denounced a "so-called fight between Speedy Cannon and Jimmy Hayden. Neither man even tried to inflict punishment upon the other" in what amounted to a "debacle."[11] No, it was a "farce," said another observer, since the two were "pulling their punches" in "pre-arranged" choreography. "I gave no decision and held up their money," said a ringside authority.[12] This was hardly unusual. A "Chicago Negro," a welterweight, was charged with being party to a "phoney fight." Ray Carlen, the former manager of his opponent, remarked "there is no place in boxing for safety-first kids," suggesting perhaps that fake fights saved lives.[13]

It was not just Carlen who was raising eyebrows since a recent "probe" placed "Oakland pugilism in a bad light." Then there was Bobby Andrews, the referee described as "obese" and who, besides, "obviously doesn't know much about the refereeing end of the fight game...is the individual who a few months ago was escorted from the ring to the dressing room by a corps of gendarmes. Andrews, on that occasion, gave Tyree White, an undeserved decision over Alex Vega." In yet another fight, a promoter carped that "guys just

---

8. File on Archie Moore, 20 January 1941, F2214, D3986, Boxing License and Renewal, CaSAC.
9. Vertical File, Archie Moore, clipping from *San Diego Union*, SDHC.
10. Transcript, 17 May 1943, F2191, CaSAC.
11. C.G. McKnight to Dave Stevenson, 24 December 1945, F2219, CaSAC.
12. Frank Manfredo to Donn Shields, 24 December 1945, F2219, CaSAC.
13. *Oakland Tribune*, 31 August 1943, F2191, D3985, CaSAC.

fall down," not even bothering to engage in sincere fakery. Worse, he groused, was that "every other person" present in the audience was a "colored person and those [that] were not colored, outside of some Hollywood people, were Mexicans with babies in arms." Meanwhile, Mike Jacobs was seeking to set up a match in Los Angeles with Joe Louis, and even the Athletic Commission was surprised to find that not only were the "Brown Bomber's" "earnings...cut about five ways, ten percent of which goes to Jimmy Braddock and his manager"—part of the deal that led to the Irishman's agreeing to fight in the 1930s—but even Damon Runyan, the raffish writer, "had an interest...."[14] In other words, Negroes could take titles but could not profit to the same degree as others, as white supremacy once again sought to claim a victory while in retreat. The fact that overwhelmingly the managers of fighters in California were of European ancestry created a structural platform for white supremacy.[15] There was also a paucity of Negro judges, referees and timekeepers—and promoters and members of the Athletic Commission.[16]

The exploitation did not just include a boxer's purse being carved up like a Thanksgiving turkey by various rapacious sharks and barracudas. It was also a matter that their ability to earn purses was blunted by devious manipulation. Take Beau Jack, for example, the lightweight boxer who was marinated in the cruelty of the "battle royal": In 1942 he got a further taste of his brutal background in Augusta, Georgia, when he beat Allie Stolz, which was supposed to determine the challenger to fight Sammy Angott—who then quit the sport. But rather than make Jack the champion, it was determined he must then fight Tippy Larkin; but even beating him would not allot him the crown. Instead, he had to enter a new labyrinth, a tournament whereby he had to defeat other fighters, most of whom he had already beaten, including Chester Rico, Maxie Shapiro and Joe Peralta. Jack was backed initially by the almost two dozen members of the prestigious Augusta National Golf Club, but that did not spare him from being derailed.[17]

For as a once desperately poor Negro, his life chances were limited. By 1943 he was having trouble making the weight to fight as a lightweight, having a swollen knee besides, which did not bode well

---

14. Transcript of Special Meeting of Athletic Commission, 17 January 1941, F2219, CaSAC.

15. Boxing License and Renewal Applications, F222-2223 D 3986, CaSAC. (Pictures are attached.)

16. Clipping, 5 December 1942, Miller-SCH.

17. Clipping, 5 December 1942, Miller-SCH.

for his fighting future.¹⁸ By 1947 he was raging about "how I was cheated out of $500,000...by shysters and leeches." He recounted the battle royals, when at times 10 men could be found in a small ring raring for combat but, he lamented, "at 27 I'm disgusted and disillusioned."¹⁹ By 1952, even his manager, Charles Wergeles, urged regulators to deny him a license "for the good of boxing and mostly his own personal health," given the "punishment" he had been absorbing in the ring—"a pitiful thing to watch." Wergeles said, "on account of his leg condition which he broke a few years ago, he is handicapped when he has to back up and is helpless on these occasions."²⁰ By 1952 he had returned to the beginning, back in Augusta at the age of 31, en route to, again, shining shoes for a living.²¹

The travails of Jack notwithstanding, Joe Louis was better positioned to grab bulging purses—and thus in better position to be exploited. As Louis entered the stratospheric realm of folk hero, buoyed by his defeats of Carnera of fascist Italy and Schmeling of fascist Germany (later accused of being a "Nazi paratrooper during the war")²², John Roxborough, his manager who guided his career and happened to be a Negro and "numbers runner," along with his comrade and fellow Negro and manager Everett Watson, were convicted of various offenses relating to this illicit multi-million-dollar business.²³ This prefigured the clipping of the wings of Truman Gibson, who became Louis's partner at the tail end of the latter's career—before he too was convicted for various offenses in the early 1960s, contributing to Negro suspicions that this was hardly coincidence but rather part of a larger diabolical scheme to make sure that this besieged minority would not rise from the bottom rungs of society.

With Roxborough destabilized, more opportunities arose for the promoter Mike Jacobs,²⁴ a former newsboy and close colleague of Tex Rickard, who became associated with Louis at the onset of his

---

18. Minutes, 8 October 1943, NYSAC.

19. Report, ca. 1947, Box 131, Jack Pfefer Collection, University of Notre Dame, South Bend (abbrev. Pfefer-UND).

20. Report by Charles Wergeles, 6 November 1952, NYSAC.

21. Minutes, 31 October 1952, NYSAC.

22. Column, 1948, Odds and Ends on Boxing, Vol. XVIII, UND. Louis's son wrote that Schmeling became a fascist hero after beating his father, and was embraced by Hitler. See Barrow and Munder, *Joe Louis*, 72.

23. Undated clipping, Boxing Notes on Joe Louis, Vol. IV, UND.

24. *New York Times*, 27 January 1953. (This obituary provides basic information on his life and career.)

career's upward trajectory. From this perch he came to control virtually every weight class championship. By 1946, according to one investigation, he was said to "monopolize" the "$16,000,000 a year boxing industry" in a manner "dedicated almost solely to his personal enrichment." This man, born to Jewish immigrant parents in Manhattan, was also present at the inflection point when the reign of Jewish boxers began to recede, but this group remained well positioned beyond ringside. "All the champions and virtually all the top U.S. boxers" were said to be under his thumb; his "control" of the "New York fight market" and his preferential ties to Madison Square Garden assisted immeasurably this entire trend. Moreover, "many of the fight reporters are on his payroll" (this trait of journalists being tied to promoters was nothing new, as Gene Tunney had observed; in this instance, Jacobs often supplied complimentary tickets to journalists, who could then sell them for a royal ransom). The end result was Jacobs had become Louis's "real manager," especially after Roxborough was sidelined,[25] making him the "boxing dictator,"[26] according to a related report. In the end, according to Louis's son, Jacobs also cheated his father monumentally.[27]

Hence, "Uncle Mike" Jacobs was crowned as the "Supreme Ruler" of the sport—and "its many shady" ancillaries, according to one observer. He controlled not only Madison Square Garden but had a "monopoly on the use of the big baseball stadiums for fights," which emboldened him further. But just as Louis balked at following the path of Johnson, the middleweight "Sugar" Ray Robinson, the legendary puncher who was said by many to be the best "pound-for-pound" of all time,[28] was also said by this commentator to be "proud and independent" and unwilling to kiss Jacobs's ring. "He had fought on his own terms" and was "understandably bitter" about his jousting with Jacobs. "You don't earn the championship on merit any more," he was said to have asserted. "You buy it," a reference to the estimate that "at least one third of the nation's professional fighters still are owned or controlled by crooked managers, who fix fights in order to pull off gambling coups." Singled out was Frankie Carbo, who came to supplant Jacobs as being regarded as the de facto "Czar" of the sport (ultimately in a kind of partnership with Truman Gibson, Louis's man), except that his ties to organized

---

25. Report by John Field and Earl Brown, 1946, Odds and Ends on Boxing, Vol. XIII, UND.
26. Undated report, Odds and Ends on Boxing, Vol. XI, UND.
27. Barrow and Munder, *Joe Louis*, 150.
28. Shropshire, *Being Sugar Ray*.

crime families were more overt and obvious. "Mr. Gray," as he was called—often found in the shadows—coincidentally was in constant attendance at Stillman's Gym in Manhattan, where many of Jacobs's fighters trained.[29]

Though Louis was styled as the anti-Johnson, Jacobs made sure that—like the Galvestonian—the "Brown Bomber" assiduously avoided other Negro boxers, including Leroy Haynes, Lorenzo Pack, Jack Trammel, Curtis "Hatchetman" Sheppard, Tiger Jack Fox and Lee Q. Murray, who, like Wills, Langford, McVey, et al., then proceeded to bludgeon each other into indignity. While Jacobs ran Madison Square Garden, such sterling Negro fighters as Archie Moore, Charley Burley, Ezzard Charles and Lloyd Marshall were generally excluded.[30] Unfortunately, Jacobs's nonfeasance was not his alone. When he was near the apex of his popularity, an analyst of the 1936 Olympics noticed that Negroes were about 10% of the U.S. population but, by his count, won half the medals, a result not necessarily embraced at home for fear it might reinforce Negro confidence and self-esteem—not necessarily congruent with white supremacy.[31] Likewise, when Jacobs was not arranging rich purses enriching a handful, he was denuding Negroes not only of funds and pride but, in turn, boosting non-Negro pounders. (As for Jack Johnson, he continued to poke jabs at Louis, at least indirectly: When the "Brown Bomber" was at the summit of his renown, the Galvestonian termed "Joe Gans and [Barbados] Joe Walcott [as] the greatest there ever was…. they were masters"—this at a moment when Louis was being touted as most deserving of such glowing appraisal.[32])

Yet it was not as if Louis—a bold attacker on Jim Crow—was a simple dupe or even the consistent antipode of Johnson, as he was imagined. Despite his posing as the anti-Johnson, Louis (according to Ishmael Reed) spoke progressively, even radically, at a gathering of the Southern Conference of Human Welfare (derided by antagonists as little more than a "Communist Front"), in a manner reminiscent of the Galvestonian: He denounced Jim Crow and its companion, the poll tax, limiting the Negro franchise.[33] Louis was terribly

---

29. Undated report on "The Boxing Racket," Sub Group VIII, Series I, Box 11, HKBA.

30. Report, January 1970, Sub Group XV, Series XIII, Box 46, HKBA.

31. Report by Curt Reiss, September 1941, Odds and Ends on Boxing, Vol. V, UND.

32. Interview with Jack Johnson, 16 March 1941, Odds and Ends on Boxing, Vol. III, UND.

33. Reed, *Complete Muhammad Ali*, 382.

upset by the maltreatment of Negro soldiers, willing to make the conclusive sacrifice of giving one's life, yet pummeled by Jim Crow barriers nonetheless. Louis's attorney, Truman Gibson, recalled later that "every bus driver in the South was deputized and armed" to force Negro soldiers to the back of the bus, leading to more than one violent confrontation. As Louis's son suggested, exaggerating for dramatic effect, more Negro soldiers were killed by these vigilante drivers than by Nazis.[34]

Louis was flirting with danger by embracing such positions and, in the process, polishing a global profile. When Archie Moore found himself in faraway Fiji in the early 1940s, he encountered numerous and "ardent Joe Louis fans," especially when he was enjoying their music, which resembled the U.S.-born form known as "jazz," perhaps a bridge across the Pacific.[35]

Yet Louis was facing immense structural barriers. It was in the 1940s, as his popularity continued to grow, that Frank Barbaro decided to hold a "White Hope Boxing Tournament" in order to develop a man of European ancestry who could shoot down the "Brown Bomber."[36] No credible candidates for this dubious title arose, but the point remained that there remained those who were gunning for Louis. (Still, Louis's son said that Billy Conn, the man who "could run" but couldn't "hide" in the ring, was styled as a "white hope" slated to put the champion in his place.)[37]

Though ostensibly Louis did not cross the red lines of supposed propriety as had Johnson, the demented search for a "Great White Hope" saw no surcease—despite the vertiginous rise of antifascism, the purported antidote. Even before Conn, one commentator noticed a "tour of Central and South America" with "the hope that somewhere in those regions, unheralded and unknown to the fistic fraternity in these parts, there might be some husky white fighter who could answer to the general measures of a 'white hope.'"[38]

The sidelining of Louis's man, Roxborough, notwithstanding, the antifascist wave ironically did create an opening for another kind of equal opportunity, thus benefiting Negro organized crime. Ellsworth "Bumpy" Johnson, born in South Carolina in 1905 and

---

34. Barrow and Munder, *Joe Louis*, 143.

35. Archie Moore and Leonard B. Pearl, *Any Boy Can: The Archie Moore Story*, Englewood Cliffs, N.J.: Prentice Hall, 1971, 162.

36. Report by Charles P. Ward, 2 August 1941, Odds and Ends on Boxing, Vol. V, UND.

37. Barrow and Munder, *Joe Louis*, 119.

38. Clipping, 1936, Sub Group XV, Series 18, Box 76, HKBA.

making his mark in Harlem, where he passed away in 1968, was tied to Italian-American gangsters, such as Charles "Lucky" Luciano. But, not unlike Truman Gibson, Johnson also tended his own illicit garden, involving, inter alia, bookmaking, smuggling, bootlegging, numbers, prostitution, gambling, extortion and general, roughhouse tactics and mayhem. Described by his prime Harlem successor as "five foot nine, looked to be about 160 pounds..., he had a round, brown skinned face and a receding hairline" and, said Frank Lucas, was "refined and classy." Once Lucas espied Joe Louis "headed... to pay respects to Bumpy. 'Always good to see you Mr. Johnson,' he said removing his hat." Louis, said Lucas, "was an all around good guy...I ended up becoming friendly with Joe. When he was in town, we might have a drink together or just hang out at a club for a minute. I wasn't big on having a whole lot of personal friends. But Joe quickly became one of the few...he was a good friend. He'd known me for so long I could just relax and be myself around him. I'm sure Joe knew what I did for a living," especially since he provided the boxer with "fifty grand" to settle a tax claim.[39]

Retrospectively, it is easy to comprehend why Louis may have wanted to cultivate ties to the disreputable, given the shark-filled waters in which he was swimming. Gus Dorazio, who could easily be included in the "bum of the month club" that provided pliable opponents for Louis to mow through—he had his time in the spotlight in 1941—was convicted of murder by the end of the decade.[40] The number of predators surrounding Louis increased exponentially when he was in the process of stepping down from the ring and entering a partnership with Truman Gibson in league with the fabulously wealthy Jim Norris and Arthur Wirtz to follow Rickard, then Jacobs, as the titans of the sport. Their combine was not strong in Los Angeles and San Francisco but certainly was in New York City, Chicago, Cleveland and Detroit, all mob-infested sites.[41] Even Norris, his ostensible partner—a man out of Colgate University and the posh prep school in Lawrenceville, New Jersey—said of Louis,

---

39. Frank Lucas with Aliya S. King, *Original Gangster: The Real Life Story of One of America's Most Notorious Drug Lords*, New York: St. Martin's, 2010 (abbrev. Lucas, *Original Gangster*), 67, 74, 78, 87, 217. Lucas adds, "I saw the actor Sidney Poitier in the sitting room one afternoon talking with Bumpy.... I saw people like Billy Daniels and Billy Eckstine in the formal dining room for dinner." He also espied "Detroit Red," who in the following decade was to be known as Malcolm X.

40. Clipping, ca. 19 May 1949, Sub Group X, Series I, Box 23, HKBA.

41. Clipping, July 1949, Sub Group VIII, Series I, Box 16, HKBA.

apparently without scorn, "he atrophied competition. He was a one-man combine in restraint of boxing trade."[42]

This apparent munificence directed from Johnson to Louis was a reflection of the latter's luminescence, which in turn was driven in no small part by the factor that ever had driven Negro advance domestically: international attention. Roxborough, the champion's manager, recalled his client's visit to Mexico City and Havana and points southward in early 1947. "Joe has never been received anywhere so hysterically," he said with wonder, as "thousands and thousands of people would be at the various airports," including Bogotá, where "the crowd got so completely out of hand that the police could do nothing...they just wanted to touch him," presumably hoping whatever magic Louis possessed could be transferred as if by osmosis.[43] It was also in 1947 that Governor Alfred Driscoll of New Jersey was importuned by L.H. Tompkins, who reminded him of his role in bringing "45,000" to the "Joe Louis exhibition at Bari Stadium, Bari Italy, August 27, 1944," and now this association, he argued, merited a patronage job in the Garden State.[44]

"Boxing was and is international in scope," said Louis's comrade Truman Gibson quite wisely: "the only reason for his camp appearance[s]," speaking of his wartime tour of U.S. military facilities abroad, "was to show white soldiers, a side of Blacks that they did not know or appreciate. Joe at every camp at his own expense, bought a steak dinner for every soldier. This, of course, caused him problems later on with the IRS [Internal Revenue Service]"—and likely too with short-sighted Euro-American corpsmen.[45] For all were not pleased when Louis, in Salisbury, Great Britain, objected strenuously to the Jim Crow standards insisted upon by the U.S. elite and soldiers. The barriers fell, and many of the latter were unhappy as a result. Soon, Louis was battling with another opponent: the taxman.[46]

But this crass exploitation of those like Louis was endemic at the lower levels too. By 1944 the "Cocoa Kid"—otherwise known as Luis Harwick—was slated to touch gloves in center ring with Billy Smith.

---

42. Clipping, October 1949, Sub Group VIII, Series I, Box 16, HKBA.

43. *Detroit Times*, 23 March 1947, Boxing Notes on Joe Louis, Vol. VII, UND.

44. L.H. Tompkins to Governor Driscoll, 19 June 1947, Box 16, Item Book 162, Governor Alfred Driscoll Papers, New Jersey State Archives, Trenton.

45. Oral History, Truman Gibson, 27 July 2001, Harry S. Truman Presidential Library, Independence, Mo. (abbrev. HSTPL).

46. Gibson, *Knocking*, 238, 242-243.

The referee, Frankie Brown, was idling in the dressing room, "changing my clothes," he said. Then bolting into the confined space was "Chief Inspector [who] came into the room and told me that he had heard some bad rumors about the main event and that they were to the effect that it was to be a 'bag' fight with Billie [sic] Smith on the winning end." The two were "fighting about a minute and half when Cocoa Kid was hit by Smith [with] a very light blow on his left side, followed by a right across the chin and he rolled with the punch," a "very light punch" at that. But the Kid crumpled like a cheap suit: "he went down and wanted to take a count." This was the first round. It happened again in the third round. When it happened again, the referee finally rendered a "no decision"—and ordered that both purses not be dispersed pending an investigation—though Brown was certain that the "Cocoa Kid was trying to take the easy way out and lose the fight to Billy Smith." Brown was struck by the "fluctuation of odds being peddled around the Auditorium." The Kid was seen as the "better fighter" but, alas, he had "personal difficulties...serious illness of his mother...difficulties with his wife, his former wife"—and others. The referee was no novice: "I have been in and out of the game for twenty years," he said. Al Sandell of the Commission was present that night and knew of "heavy betting that night that was being made on the outcome of the contest"—even the "Cocoa Kid had bet on his opponent," at least that was the scuttlebutt. There were "large sized wagers" by his opponent, not boding well for an honestly competitive bout. Sensing something awry, there was "general murmur and howling" by the audience throughout. The Kid, who was questioned at the hearing, was distraught. His unfortunate mother "can't eat...her intestines are closing on her. They feed her in a vein," plus she endured a "couple of transfusions every week," and he was "the only support of the family"—and "I have quite a lot of family. There are a lot of small kids." Besides, he was not faking in the ring. "My eye was cut," he cried. "I was dazed."[47] The Commission was mildly sympathetic. There was a unanimous vote to suspend him for six months, while his purse of over $500 was deposited as a fine in the state's coffers.[48] In other words, a man on

---

47. Record of Hearing, 5 December 1944, San Francisco, F2191 D3985, CaSAC.

48. Minutes, 16 December 1944, F2191 D3985, CaSAC. Family matters often cropped up as a consideration for the authorities to ponder. See Minutes, 24 January 1928, NYSAC: "Andy Divodi, boxer and Jerry Pelton, manager, appeared. Divodi was informed of a complaint lodged here by his

the brink of economic collapse sought a rescue and, for his labor, was pushed further into the abyss. At least he was not banned for life.

Even if this draconian penalty had not been exacted, the objective circumstance—desperate financial problems among the universe of boxers combined with ever rippling revenue streams generated by the sport—virtually guaranteed a culture of corruption. By October 1945, Henry Christian and V.P. Watson squared off but, as was reported, they were "thrown out of the ring for faking a fight" after being "warned at least six or seven times by the referee and he finally tossed them out in the third round." Supposedly, both accused said they were "guilty." Fans were "stamping and booing." This was after Watson admitted, "I…fought two nights, Wednesday and Thursday" just before the Christian match.[49] In early 1946 a referee reported that the bout between Bill Kingsland and Buddy Thomas was illegitimate. The crowd booed and the referee shouted, "You guys are going to have to punch harder"—though Kingsland said his swollen thumb was hampering his combativeness.[50] Yet this raised a number of other factors. Bouts with phonily predetermined outcomes were the equivalent of killing the goose that produces golden eggs, for that would lead to alienation of the fan base, chasing them into other arenas—baseball and football and, then, basketball games. But secondly, forcing a boxer to fight aggressively when injured was morally reprehensible and bound to reduce the number of young men willing to fall on their swords for the overall sake of the sport—even given financial desperation.

The overall climate was not conducive to ethical perfection. In 1946 a run-of-the-mill beef erupted between Ray Brown, an ebony puncher and his manager, James Boyd Brown, who also maintained a gambling business on the side, including a crap table on Central Avenue in Los Angeles, rapidly becoming the heart of the African-American community in the Southland.[51] A gambler managing a boxer then was akin to Dracula guarding the blood bank. But as long as there were 17-year-old youth, like Fred German, who was willing to claim that he was 18 so he could try his luck for $4 per fight, there would be openings for the unscrupulous to exploit.[52]

---

wife on January 19 and was urged to effect an immediate settlement with her. Divodi denied that he was married to the woman in question."
   49. Transcript, 29 October 1945, F2191 D3985, CaSAC.
   50. Transcript, 24 January 1946, F3920, 190-209, CaSAC.
   51. Transcript, 24 January 1946, F3920, 190-209, CaSAC.
   52. Transcript, 23 May 1946, F3920, 190-209, CaSAC.

Or they could end up like light heavyweight battler John Henry Lewis, who like so many boxers was subjected to a beating about the eyes, resulting in irreparable damage, meaning, said trainer Ray Arcel, "he never saw the punches that knocked him out."[53] Or they could tempt fate by double-crossing those with experience in such ugliness. Thus, Henry Armstrong, when he was "offered close to seventy five thousand dollars to take a dive" or a "bribe" to lose, could have instead "bet back of myself and get rich," in other words, either take the "dive" and bet against his heavily favored self or, alternatively, knock out the opponent, and wagering via a third party with bookies who expected him to lose, thus turning the tables and "get rich," or "get killed" in the bargain.[54] Armstrong was skating on ever more fragile ice. Just before this bribe attempt, he upset the powerful promoter, Mike Jacobs, when he left his aegis for the embrace of another, who then staged a welterweight championship bout in Britain with the deft puncher and Ernie Roderick.[55] Armstrong was a valuable "property" because of his ability to compete in three weight classes, opening more possibilities for matches and opponents—and revenue.

Armstrong may have been bold, but he was not singular in his audacity, nor in the attempt to influence his boxing behavior. In 1947 Rocky Graziano's license to box in New York was revoked because of his failure to report an offer of a bribe of $100,000.[56] "Sugar" Ray Robinson was offered a bribe in 1946. Then residing in Harlem at 207 St. Nicholas Avenue, the competitor admitted, "I have been approached many times...by gamblers who wanted me to throw a fight." His license was suspended for 30 days and he was assessed a $500 penalty.[57] Robinson had a reputation, unusual among boxers, of being scrupulous concerning contracts and business, which may have been influenced by his similarly oriented manager, George Gainford, a sharp operator: In 1948 a boxer he managed, George Gaskin, hauled him before regulators on the charge that Gainsford was "not paying him his share of the purses."[58]

---

53. *Sunday News*, 9 August 1942, Sub Group VIII, Series I, Box 24, HKBA. See also Minutes, 24 October 1952, NYSAC: Coley Wallace, an actor and heavyweight, who once outpointed Rocky Marciano, was said in 1952 to have endured "staining of both corneas...likely due to thumbing."
54. Heller, *In This Corner*, 216.
55. Clipping, March 1952, Sub Group VIII, Series I, Box 23, HKBA.
56. Minutes, 7 February 1947, NYSAC.
57. Minutes, 14 February 1947, NYSAC. See also *New York Post*, 30 January 1947.
58. Minutes, 27 February 1948, NYSAC.

Thus, there were reasons why gamblers thought that even topflight boxers could be seduced. Bill Poland was a heavyweight who fought with the Star of David on his trunks and was managed by "Doc" Kearns, who had handled Dempsey. He was slated to receive for a bout less than what he had agreed upon and out of frustration, he admitted, "I confess I took a dive." This was in 1941 in a contest with Harry Bobo; still alienated, he fought Eddie Blunt in Washington, D.C., and cheated again, then took another "dive" with Bobo: "I just plain stuck my chin out,'" a "'helluva act," he conceded, though he added somewhat disingenuously, "[I] never bet on fights."[59]

Again, what was at play was that as the revenue streams of the sport increased, the degradation of those who produced this wealth became ever more pronounced, which also tended to attract the vultures and carrion feeders of society, in a circle devoid of virtue. William Haughton, chairman of the California Athletics Commission, admitted in April 1945 as the war was lurching to a close that "there has been considerable doubt as to whether the boxing game is honest...there has been so much talk these days about the throwing of fights that one wonders whether there isn't some fire where there is so much smoke as there is.... I have been reading in altogether too many newspapers talk about the fixing of fights" and, yes, there were "fights that were thrown." And, yes, "gamblers are behind it," a trend that was reaching warp speed as gambling in nearby Nevada was about to accelerate. "We know what it [gambling] did to baseball," he said, a reference to the 1919 so-called "Black Sox" scandal, which implicated the boxer Abe Attell and which devastated the game. A fellow commissioner, A.P. Entenza, a tad optimistically, announced that "we are today the most athletically honest state in the union... we are way ahead of New York, Pennsylvania, Ohio, Illinois"— possibly accurate but irrelevant in light of the endemic corruption in those states. But even this Pangloss as administrator, who said he had "all the data at my finger tips," acknowledged, "we have only had four of record in three years," meaning "fixed" fights. "There is a lot of talk of course," about what he saw as an overblown problem. Governor Earl Warren, whose presence at this gathering underscored its importance, seemed to diverge from the Pollyanna-type thinking, when he admitted, "I don't pick up a sporting page these days except I read something about a fight that doesn't have a good odor to it." He should have paid closer attention to Entenza when he asserted, "we have no police power and receive no salary...we are the scum of the appointive commissions of the state," an admission

---

59. Clipping, January 1995. Sub Group IX, Series 2, Box 19, HKBA.

pointing to why they might be subject to corruption more than other members of "appointive commissions." This was especially the case since Chairman Haughton conceded that "since racing has closed down" this had left "boxing [as] the only outlet for the gamblers"[60]—another explanation for enhanced corruption. A report was to reveal that Robert Chase confessed, "in my years as manager, matchmaker and promoter I've fixed…fights…all kinds," which was hardly a revelation in general terms but no less striking.[61] Then again, with the companion sport of wrestling descending into stark farce, how could boxing resist? Indeed, by 1946 in New York, wrestling was attracting more and more spectators.[62] Despite this good news, the wider point was that by 1947 income from boxing and wrestling had decreased by 28%, attributable to "no open-air Heavyweight Championship contest" (in 1946 the Louis-Billy Conn contest "had a gross income of $1,900,000" and "accounted for approximately forty percent of the gross income" that year).[63]

It is not clear if Chase was involved in San Diego in 1944 when Jack Coggins was said to have come out of his corner "in a very peculiar way making no effort to protect himself" and "deliberately took many blows in the stomach that he could have avoided" as "people were hollering 'fake'"; there was a "lot of money bet on the fight," said George Thompson, a commission inspector, "more money than the contest warranted." Ned Bryan, another inspector, noted that fans did not react circumspectly and "kicked the panels in the office door" nearby, then "went outside and broke several windows." Maybe they knew, as subsequent investigation revealed, that "there was money supposedly being bet around town," meaning "lots of money being on this fight." There was "heavy gambling…on the outcome of the contest" as there was "pitching" by Coggins's opponent and "catching" by Coggins. "Everybody in the house sensed the affair" and "showed their displeasure by booing."[64]

The opportunities for corruption were not just limited to the decline of horse racing and the hunger of gamblers. Thus, Ernest Simmons, described as a "licensed boxer…slugged the for[e]man of the plant while at work," opening the door to his exerting undue

---

60. Minutes, 24 April 1945, F2191 D3985, CaSAC.
61. Undated report, Odds and Ends on Boxing, Vol. XXX, UND.
62. Report to Secretary of State Thomas J. Curran, 31 December 1946, Minutes, NYSAC.
63. Report to Thomas J. Curran, 31 December 1947, Minutes, NYSAC.
64. "In the Matter of…Coggins-Nisbert Boxing…Meeting of the SAC," San Diego, 4 April 1944, F2219-2221, CaSAC.

influence on a commissioner in order to avoid suspension and a dent in his livelihood.[65] The opportunities for growth in boxing also meant more boxers entering the ring—meaning more boxers subject to paying the ultimate price. According to one report, the number of deaths in the ring amounted to 4 in 1943, 6 in 1945, and 11 in 1946.[66] Yet this was likely an undercount for it is unclear if the tally included Albert Morales Silva, who perished in the ring in October 1945 at the hands of Felix Miramontes. Silva was a Mexican national, and both were making their debut.[67]

By 1949, a "shocking increase in the number of deaths in the ring" was reported—"Sam Baroudi in a headliner fight with Ezzard Charles...following only a months the death of Jimmy Doyle...in a fight with [Sugar] Ray Robinson." This was leading to the nightmare scenario envisioned by some when Gans, Johnson and Jackson first began to flex their muscles: Negroes not only beating Euro-Americans in the ring but killing them, a symbolic reversal of the horror of lynching.[68]

The gushing revenue streams produced by the sport also attracted more willing to fish in these murky waters. For example, the 1940s witnessed the arrival into prominence of the British boxer of African ancestry, Randy Turpin: He gave U.S. stalwarts, e.g., "Sugar" Ray Robinson, quite a bit to handle. Turpin's brother, Dick, was an ex-middleweight champion of Britain and the first man of his ancestry allowed to fight for a British title. However, just like the pounders on the west bank of the Atlantic, Turpin developed his skill as a young boy since "fights with other boys occurred often" then.[69] As in the U.S., the postwar climate globally—at least initially—was conducive to democratic advance, because of the antifascist upsurge, which tended to crest in 1945 and the following months. By 1947 the British Board of Boxing Control removed the so-called color bar,

---

65. Jim Genshlea, Secretary of Commission to Jerry Geisler, 10 July 1941, CaSAC.

66. Undated clipping, Odds and Ends on Boxing, Vol. 18, UND.

67. Minutes, 18 October 1945, Minutes and Hearings, F2191 F3985, CaSAC.

68. Clipping, 1949, Sub Group VIII, Series I, Box 9, HKBA. In April 1947, Doyle testified that he was in "very satisfactory" condition after suffering a concussion, and a medical examination revealed no "evidence of fracture or other bone pathology...of the skull." Minutes, 11 April 1947, NYSAC.

69. Randy Turpin, "Why I Became a Fighter," 1947, Odds and Ends on Boxing, Vol. XXIX, UND.

making Negro pounders eligible for the first time to compete for national championships.[70]

Turpin's meritorious presence led to unusual conclusions; hence, it was said, "were it not for Randy's fighting ability, the probability that the color line in British championship bouts might still be on"—perversely, this "had often been mentioned."[71] However, the supposition seemed to be that the "color line" turned on the desire to exclude the inferior when actually it was precisely the opposite. This reflected the problem when the "color line" began to erode and presumably rational explanations were put forward for its existence—and erosion. Yet this battling proved to no avail when he was shot to death in 1966 in his home in England, further ratifying the spectacularly high rates of mortality of prizefighters, who made a living by dint of a kind of violence—that often boomeranged and waylaid them in turn.[72]

The general problem was that the pestilential white supremacy had yet to yield, despite the pressure exerted by a gathering antifascist—and global—movement. This resistance often was aided by boxers. Gene Tunney, for example, was in close touch with neofascist Gerald L.K. Smith. By the summer of 1940, Smith's "Committee of 1,000,000" had joined with Tunney and "pledged its complete cooperation in your attempt to lead the patriotic young people of America into the organization of a youth movement free from subversive and communistic influence." Like Tunney, Smith too had "frequently condemned the Red [Communist] leadership within the American Youth Congress," adding with a twist, "you can count on our committee for full cooperation with your most worthy effort."[73] Eleanor Roosevelt begged to differ. A patron of the AYC,[74] she felt compelled to reprimand Tunney, instructing him that she objected to "your proof that the American Youth Congress is Communist because they were congratulated by [Soviet leader] Molotov"—that, she replied sternly, "is pretty slim proof."[75] Undaunted, Tunney countered with a right cross, telling the First Lady that "Communist

---

70. Report, 1947, Odds and Ends on Boxing, Vol. XIV, UND.

71. Undated material on Turpin, Box 5, Folder 88, Nat Fleischer Papers, UND.

72. *Free Press*, 18 May 1966, Odds and Ends on Boxing, Vol. XLVI, UND.

73. Gerald L.K. Smith to Gene Tunney, 8 July 1940, Box 1, Tunney-UND.

74. See Robert Cohen, *When the Old Left Was Young: Student Radicals and America's First Mass Student Movement, 1929-1941*, New York: Oxford University Press, 1993.

75. Eleanor Roosevelt to Gene Tunney, 14 May 1940, Box 1, Tunney-UND.

influence in the American Youth Congress is entirely out of proportion to its membership."[76] Undeterred, Tunney went on to become a vector of anticommunist rebuke,[77] thereby strengthening the forces of reaction who, understandably, did not count many Negroes within their ranks.

Then there was the related matter of boxing being able to advance while other sports were mired in the quicksand of bigotry. This was notably the case for football, also boosted into increased popularity during the reign of President Theodore Roosevelt. By 1940, Marion Motley, one of the best running backs to play the game, was enrolled at the University of Nevada-Reno—all 6'1" and 240 pounds of him.[78] (He was also a punishing boxer.) However, this bull of a back faced the same barriers as Jack Johnson did three decades earlier when the University of Idaho squad was reluctant to compete on the gridiron with the Wolfpack, supposedly because of racism, though it was hard to rule out the possibility that they simply did not want to endure his hammer blows. Later Motley recalled a Nevada-Idaho game where "the stands were roaring" with demented cries of "Get that Nigger! Kill that nigger! Kill that alligator bait!" At Brigham Young University in Provo, Utah, "Kids used to follow us around on the street...asking me, 'Where's your tail? You're supposed to have a tail.'" Perhaps worse, he found subsequently that referees refused to sanction opposing players when they mauled him illicitly on the field.[79] This was not just an expression of racism, it was a manifestation of the revulsion at the idea that sanctuaries for those defined as "white" were now being opened to competition from those previously thought to be the mudsill of society. Thus, this was also an expression of fear at the prospect of debilitating competition by those thought to be the enemies of the [white supremacist] state. It was a complex and compounded form of hysteria.

The Hollywood Legion continued to be a problem. By June 1940 Dr. Herbert Smith, representing the "County Ministers Association," instructed disdainfully and condescendingly that "if our colored gentlemen feel that they should have a larger representation in the boxing field, their request should be for a permit to conduct boxing

---

76. Gene Tunney to Eleanor Roosevelt, 16 May 1940, Box 1, Tunney-UND.
77. Press Release, 19 June 1940, Box 1, Tunney-UND.
78. "The Total Pack Edge" on Marion Motley, 25 August 1997, Wolfpack Edge Collection, University of Nevada, Reno.
79. File on Marion Motley, Box 22, UNR Biographical Files, UNV-R. On Motley as a boxer, see *Nevada State Journal*, 17 April 1941, Vertical File-Boxing, NHS-R.

in their own colored section, rather than to attempt to force their demands upon the Hollywood Legion Post."[80] By mid-1942 the State Athletic Commission was complaining because the Legion's fights were exempted from state taxation, meaning—said Willie Ritchie of the SAC—"many boxers earn better average purses when they appear at the Hollywood Legion Club than they can anywhere else in the United States...due to the fact that the Hollywood Legion Club enjoys a fine clientele."[81] In other words, Jim Crow bans on Negro boxers were redounding to the benefit of non-Negro punchers, giving them a stake in a reactionary status quo.

Negro boxers were primed to be plucked since they were becoming leading contenders, guaranteeing sizable purses, while Jim Crow meant, even with one as elevated as Joe Louis, that they could be cheated rather easily. Thus, even with low-ranked punchers there were raging disputes. By the Spring of 1940, the Athletic Commission was wrangling about "disputed contracts on a colored boxer, named Leo Turner who had contracts on him, one being Joe Silveria of Hollister and other being Alfred Tex Salkeld of Portland."[82]

Nothing new there. But what was new—and this point and counterpoint was to characterize the sport for decades to come, especially as white supremacy made an agonizing retreat, signaling democratic advance—was that ushers, doormen, ticket sellers and box office employees were "joining a union," with the authorities proclaiming boldly, "that is a constitutional right."[83] What was happening in part was that the private sector was being impinged upon by the state, and though Negroes were not shareholders in the former, they were stakeholders—or voters—in the latter, providing leverage. Days after the attack on Pearl Harbor, Jerry Geisler of the State Athletic Commission informed President Roosevelt that as chairman of the State Athletic Commission "as well the Horse Racing Board...I have been directed to offer the properties, facilities,

---

80. Dr. Herbert Smith to Hollywood American Legion, 2 June 1940, F2191, CaSAC.

81. Willie Ritchie, Athletic Commission to Jerry Geisler, 28 July 1942, F2219, CaSAC.

82. Archie Closson to Jerry Geisler of Athletic Commission, 25 April 1940, F2191, D3985, Minutes and Hearings, CaSAC.

83. Transcript, 17 April 1942, F2191, CaSAC. See also Transcript, F2191, D3985, CaSAC, Minutes and Hearings: "In re: Labor Unions at 501 Hall of Records...in the Matter of the Necessity of Ushers, Doormen, Ticket Sellers and Box Office Employees Joining a Labor Union," Los Angeles, 17 April 1942, 10 A.M.

assets, personnel and manpower of our horse racing, boxing and wrestling interests" to Washington—"for the duration of the war." Negroes as part of the FDR coalition—albeit as second-class members due to the competing leverage of Dixiecrats—could weigh in to their benefit.[84] As the war progressed, Governor Earl Warren, soon to be deified because of his role as U.S. Supreme Court Chief Justice in 1954 in invalidating Jim Crow juridically, was said to be "interested" in this proposal since, it was reported, he "realizes that the funds the state derives from boxing and wrestling [goes] to the Yountville Home for Veterans" and, in any case, the majority of the commission's appointees were made by him.[85] (Unfortunately, in the immediate term this meant that Santa Anita Race Track was used as a detention center for interned Japanese Americans while, in some cases, Negroes migrating from Texas and Louisiana moved into their abandoned homes in Los Angeles, as "Little Tokyo" became "Bronzeville.")[86]

For various reasons the sport required the jolt of energy delivered by punchers like Archie Moore. Maybe it was because actual battles with bullets whizzing were more engaging than gloved men exchanging blows. By early 1943, as the ordinarily popular Henry Armstrong was facing off at the Olympic Auditorium in Los Angeles, a "house of approximately $20,000" was "expected"; however, "during the past few years," the secretary to the Athletic Commission continued, "houses have been so poor at the Olympic and the scale of prices so low," the Armstrong fight was seen as a step forward. "Boxing is picking up," it was reported eagerly, in that "Olympic has already drawn over $13,000 this year; specifically with [Armstrong] and Jimmie McDaniels on January 5, 1943."[87]

Armstrong was a useful barometer of the health of the sport. He was not only a multiply crowned champion, he also was candid about the seamier side of the sport. The entertainer "[Al] Jolson wanted Eddie Mead to handle me," but "Mead had always been in with gangsters down through the years—Owney Maddon [sic], Bugsy Siegel, Frankie Carbo," a murderers' row of mobsters. In fact,

---

84. Jerry Geisler to President Roosevelt, 11 December 1941, CaSAC.

85. Remarks of Governor Earl Warren, 24 April 1945, Minutes and Hearings, F2191 D3985, CaSAC.

86. Horne, *Fire*, and Horne, *Facing the Rising Sun: African-Americans, Japan and the Rise of Afro-Asian Solidarity*, New York: New York University Press, 2018 (abbrev. Horne, *Facing*).

87. Secretary of Athletic Commission to A.P. Entenza, 18 February 1943, F2219, CaSAC.

the man proposed as his manager was at "what one time was called the 'knockout man' for the gangsters. If you don't pay up something they'd put a bomb under you. He used to do that all the time. He made a lot of money" perpetrating such dirty deeds. Thus, he "had three managers" ultimately, "George Raft" (actor *cum* gangster comrade), Jolson (gangster toady), and Mead (actual gangster).[88] Raft was prototypical: A close comrade of Siegel and Madden, he too was a former newsboy, who became a boxer at the tender age of 14—a logical transition—then a baseball outfielder and dancer, before migrating to the silver screen, then using those connections to muscle in on boxers.[89]

Armstrong was a complement to Louis but, like any slugger, he could not resist the ravishes of time. It was in August 1943 that the torch was passed, when he fought "Sugar" Ray Robinson, then ascending. New York regulators found Armstrong's "showing" to be "poor," though this was "due to Robinson's unquestioned superiority." However, it was concerning that the St. Louisan even managed to lose to Beau Jack,[90] a devastating blow for both since the Augustan saw "Henry Armstrong as my great idol."[91]

And then there was Ralph Gambina, who boasted later, "I had the biggest stable in California from about 1940 to 1954.... I must've had around 200 fighters, including amateurs." His two top fighters were welterweight Jimmy McDaniels and lightweight Cisco Andrade, both of whom might have been champions—had Gambina bent to pressure from the underworld. Gambina himself, born around 1907 with roots in Williamsburg, Brooklyn, boxed as a professional bantamweight to middleweight and, completing the circuit, played a tough guy in the movies—a combination of Raft and Mead, in other words.[92] Gambina appeared in scores of movies, but the plot involving the murder of his client, boxer Phil Kim, was likely beyond any script he ever scanned.[93] Despite the evident income delivered by his thespianism, his California license as a manager was suspended

---

88. Heller, *In This Corner*, 209.
89. *Los Angeles Times*, 27 November 1980, Sub Group VIII, Series I, Box 18, HKBA.
90. Minutes, 1 June 1944, NYSAC.
91. Report, 1947, Box 131, Pfefer-UND.
92. Clipping, July 1969, and undated, Sub Group VIII, Series I, Box 8, HKBA.
93. Undated from Hank Kaplan's "Boxing Digest," Sub Group VIII, Series I, Box 8, HKBA.

in 1961 for taking 50% of the purse earned by heavyweight Reuben Vargas, when the law said he should take no more than a third.[94]

Part of the problem was that it was not easy for the sport to attain liftoff in California when bars still remained forbidding boxers squaring off across racial lines. There was ever a tug here with some lusting for metaphorical racial battles—especially African versus European—as a way to stir primordial sentiment or even stoke discord and disunity. There were others who feared the emergence of another Jack Johnson—whose skill as a bullfighter during his exile in Spain may have proved useful in subduing animal-like racists[95]—with the related and purported untoward consequences. And, yes, there were those who for simple democratic and progressive reasons wanted these barriers to fall post-haste.

The latter grouping faced a notably formidable barrier in that Washington, D.C., the pacesetter in formulating national policy, was not necessarily on their side. In fact, in 1937, the Boxing Commission there refused to sanction bouts across the color line.[96] In 1941 the local chapter of the NAACP discussed a virulent complaint from Senator John Overton of Jim Crow Louisiana, who objected to Negroes boxing as he was "very much concerned about the percentage of crimes committed by colored people in the District," which could be worsened by bringing these putative criminals into crowded arenas. Moreover, it was reported, "Joe Turner, the boxing promoter and Gabe Menendez, his match maker, have been instructed not to put more than two mixed bouts on any of their boxing shows"—meaning "an additional restriction on opportunities of colored boys to earn a livelihood," theoretically driving them to the life of crime to which Senator Overton objected.[97] But it was not just prizefighting that meant barriers. Walter White, leader of the NAACP (National Association for the Advancement of Colored People), was told in early 1941 of the "failure of the AAU [Amateur Athletic Union] and the boxing tournament management to give Negro boxers from the South, representation in the National Golden Gloves tournament."[98]

---

94. Clipping, 19 December 1961, Sub Group VIII, Series I, Box 8, HKBA.

95. *Nevada State Journal*, 19 March 1918, Vertical File-Boxing, NHS-R.

96. *Washington Tribune*, 3 July 1937, Vertical File-Boxing Commission, Special Collections, Public Library, Washington, D.C. (abbrev. WDCPL).

97. Louis Lautier to Major Ernest Brown, 7 July 1941, Box 44, NAACP-DC Papers, Howard University, Washington, D.C.

98. E.B. Henderson, Public Schools of Washington, to Walter White, 17 January 1941, Box 44, NAACP-DC Papers, Howard University, Washington, D.C. (abbrev. NAACPDC-Howard).

Thus, NAACP leaders were informed that "entries for colored boxers in the District AAU Boxing Championship were rejected, although all regulations [were] fulfilled except as to color of skin."[99] The response was blunt: the AAU "will not sanction mixed racial competition between Negroes and whites."[100]

Being blocked from the amateur ranks meant being deprived of competition and being subjected to yet another obstacle on the path to lucrative matches. It also blocked an important rung of upward mobility—for Negroes. Thus, Ed Gersh was a Golden Gloves champion in the 1940s, but by the 1980s, after a not particularly distinguished career as a boxer, this Euro-American had become, according to an observer, a "sportsman millionaire" and "one of the most respected managers," having under contract the highly touted Olympian, Howard Davis, Jr. He controlled property in the Dominican Republic and, naturally, was included within the ranks of the increasingly conservative Republican Party.[101]

Gersh illustrated a repetitive trend: Those who were not Negroes often had more advantages than those who were. Leon Shub, for example, started boxing in Washington, D.C., in 1930 at the age of 17 at the Jewish Community Center, when all boxing, professional and amateur, was illegal there. Amateurs boxed in Alexandria, Virginia, and Rockville, Maryland. Then on 11 May 1934, Congressman Fred Hartley of New Jersey, later infamous as an anti-labor crusader, introduced a bill to legalize boxing in D.C. "I, Leon Shub," he later said, "received the first amateur license (#1),"[102] then was inducted into the District's Boxing Hall of Fame in 1995 after a prosperous life.

The capital of capital also suffered what California endured: It was in late 1943 that the boxer John Garner, then a military man, appeared before the commission in the District of Columbia to announce that he took a "dive" against Tee Hubert for $300—and untold gain for gamblers.[103] Arguably, preservation of the color line enabled a moral lassitude that in turn destabilized the sturdy rigor required to confront corruption: What stouter form of corruption pertained in the

---

99. Arthur A. Greene, YMCA Director of Health and Physical Education, to Thomas Kenalym, Tourament Director, Boston, Box 44, NAACPDC-Howard.

100. Letter from E. Joseph Aronoff, NAACPDC-Howard.

101. *New York Times*, 31 May 1987, and Press Release, 6 May 1983, Sub Group IX, Series I, Box 9, HKBA.

102. Clipping, Circa 1995, Sub Group IX, Series II, Box 23, HKBA.

103. *Washington Post*, 2 November 1943, Vertical File-Boxing Commission, WDCPL.

nation besides white supremacy? At least, maintaining a color line allowed for the untrammeled presence in the sport of unqualified men who would prefer to agree to going down for the count beforehand for a fee, rather than run the risk of injury against a brawler in an honest competition.

Washington was under unremitting pressure to erode if not abolish the color line. There was the blowback of gusts propelled by the antifascist war requiring the indictment of racist Berlin, not to mention undermining Tokyo's posture as the "Champion of the Colored Races": Indeed, the latter claim struck a chord among African Americans particularly, thereby jeopardizing national security.[104] Then there were the gains made domestically by Negro Communists tied to Moscow during the war. Ben Davis, Jr., for example, was elected to the New York City Council from Harlem in 1943 and re-elected in the premature postwar bloom in 1945[105]; he was backed by Negro celebrity par excellence Paul Robeson[106] and another talented Negro Communist, the defense attorney William Patterson,[107] along with the leading Negro woman intellectual of that era, Shirley Graham[108] (soon to wed W.E.B. Du Bois and nudge him into the ranks of the Communists to whom she had sworn allegiance previously).[109] Part of the charge made by these radicals and their multitudes of global allies was that U.S. imperialism was a fraud in claiming to be a paragon of human rights virtue in the battle of ideas with Moscow. This charge resonated in the Caribbean[110] and Africa particularly,[111] sites

---

104. Horne, *Race War!*.

105. Gerald Horne, *Black Liberation/Red Scare: Ben Davis and the Communist Party*, Newark: University of Delaware Press, 1994.

106. Gerald Horne, *Paul Robeson: The Artist as Revolutionary*, London: Pluto, 2016. Cf., Andrew M. Kaye, *The Pussycat of Prizefighting: Tiger Flowers and the Politics of Black Celebrity*, Athens: University of Georgia Press, 2004.

107. Horne, *Black Revolutionary*.

108. Gerald Horne, *Race Woman: The Lives of Shirley Graham Du Bois*, New York: New York University Press, 2001.

109. Gerald Horne, *Black and Red: W.E.B. Du Bois and the Afro-American Response to the Cold War, 1944-1963*, Albany: State University of New York Press, 1986 (abbrev. Horne, *Black and Red*).

110. Gerald Horne, *Cold War in a Hot Zone: The U.S. Confronts Labor and Independence Struggles in the British West Indies*, Philadelphia: Temple University Press, 2007.

111. Gerald Horne, *White Supremacy Confronted: U.S. Imperialism and Anticommunism versus the Liberation of Southern Africa, from Rhodes to Mandela*, New York: International, 2018 (abbrev. Horne, *White Supremacy*).

of cheap labor and vast raw materials alike, necessitating an erosion of the color line at home in order to preserve these assets.

It was only a matter of time before these factors landed in Washington, and the U.S. as a whole, with the force of a bolo punch.

But the opponent to which this blow was directed was no stiff or "tomato can" just waiting to recline supine. Instead, this opponent was shifty—a "cutie" in the parlance of the trade—and an adept and bruising counter-puncher at that. Davis was jailed by 1950; Robeson's passport was snatched, reducing his income from the six figures to the low four figures; Patterson was jailed; Du Bois was indicted. And with those stalwarts safely muzzled and muffled, then hesitant steps were made to erode Jim Crow, under the aegis of Earl Warren, leaving Negroes without the insight to figure out what was happening—or what was to come.

Thus, by late 1946, the amateur bouts in Washington known as the "Golden Gloves" continued to be a "lily-white affair," with "the local AAU [Amateur Athletic Union] steadfastly refusing admittance to amateur boxers of all races," according to a Negro journalist in a position to know. But an important straw in the wind was that the powerful Eugene Meyer, proprietor of the *Washington Post*, chose to withdraw support from the spectacle "until the color ban had been removed,"[112] signaling that the U.S. elite found this praxis no longer sustainable.

However, the pro-Jim Crow forces were not willing to go down without a fight. A few weeks later, in apparent rebuke, a congressman from Michigan, one Frederick Van Ness Bradley, introduced a bill to "prohibit mixed bouts in the District of Columbia," adding sinew to the muscle of the Boxing Commission's edict; it was deemed to be "unlawful for any individual of a race other than the Caucasian to engage" in the District in "any boxing contest with an individual of the Caucasian race."[113] Then the congressman introduced a bill to ban boxing altogether, perhaps as a way to eliminate the distinct possibility of a latter-day Gans or Johnson arising to inflict mighty blows on the ideology of white supremacy.[114]

---

112. *Washington Afro-American*, 23 November 1946, Vertical File-Boxing Commission, WDCPL.

113. Proposed Legislation, 80th Congress, 1st Session, House of Representatives, 3 January 1947, Vertical File-Boxing Commission, WDCPL.

114. HR 213, 80th Congress, 1st Session, House of Representatives, Introduced by Mr. Bradley of Michigan, Vertical File-Boxing Commission, WDCPL.

But the domestic forces were buoyed by global gusts—a condition precedent for domestic advance historically[115]—and the pro-Jim Crow forces were in a defensive crouch. By 1948 there was a campaign to install a Negro on the Boxing Commission in what was, after all, a majority Negro city,[116] a crusade that rapidly gained traction,[117] as the forces of reaction embarked on a long march of retreat.

---

115. Horne, *Negro Comrades*.

116. *Washington Afro-American*, 16 October 1948, Vertical File-Boxing Commission, WDCPL.

117. Clipping, 17 September 1949, Vertical File-Boxing Commission, WDCPL.

Chapter 5

Gangster's Paradise

Contrary to the prognostications of the wizened, the antifascist triumph did not mean a rosy dawn of progressivism, which would continue to level Jim Crow barriers, thereby uplifting Negro boxers, continuing a trend inaugurated a half-century earlier by Gans and Johnson. Yes, the decade following 1945 did witness a number of victories, culminating in 1954 with the U.S. Supreme Court led by Earl Warren invalidating Jim Crow in principle. However, the pushback against this momentous move was like that of a cornered but still dangerous bruiser, with Jim Crow fighting back furiously, refusing to go quietly into the gloomy night of defeat and desuetude. This pushback also created fertile conditions for the continuing, then spectacular, ascension of the power behind the throne of boxing: organized crime.

One trend that did continue, arguably initiated when radio made its debut in the 1920s, was the continuing flow of new revenue streams, both benefiting some Negro boxers while it attracted the most blighted of the underworld. The 1950s also saw the advent of television as a household appliance, providing instant access to a vast audience of millions, willing to be subjected to advertising in order to gain access to fights. At one juncture there were five weekly televised boxing shows. This was occurring as Jim Crow was finding it difficult to survive—particularly after radicals like Robeson had been safely tucked away in the margins of society, making it difficult for the actor-activist and his comrades to wield the mass influence he once did. Simultaneously, this directed more dollars into the pockets of these athletes and those like Truman Gibson, who was orchestrating this new departure. Indeed, as Gibson has suggested, the process he directed was a silent partner in the retreat of Jim Crow, insofar as it helped to erode the color line in boxing, normalizing what was previously verboten—Negro boxers battering into incoherence those once thought to be the "ruling race." Ironically, this put the latter "in his place," not above the rest but just like any other, which of itself destabilized white supremacy. The dollars directed into the coffers of Negroes at the same time uplifted them on the class ladder, providing more funds for human rights campaigns and a boost for consumer spending, which then, at least theoretically, could provide endorsement of more of the same by those elites profiting from the consumer items produced. Hence, a turning point occurred in 1951 when word emerged that the contest of two of the main aspirants for Louis's crown, Ezzard Charles and "Jersey" Joe Walcott would not be televised: Panic ensued as fans protested and certain elites, not uninterested in providing "bread and circus" diversions in the midst of a shooting war on the Korean peninsula that was not going well, were disgruntled. So television makers forked over a cool $100,000 to promoters, and the fight was televised, except in Pittsburgh where it was held (which incentivized locals to attend in person). Also in 1951, "Sugar" Ray Robinson fought Randy Turpin of Great Britain, providing the largest amount to date ever taken in for a title match below the heavyweight level.[1] Turpin's presence opened the door to a wider European audience too. Manhattan was not faring badly either, in that for their bout at the Polo Grounds in Harlem in September 1951, they drew a crowd of 61,000 who delivered $767,000 at the gate.[2]

It was also in 1951 that the first closed-circuit broadcast in the history of boxing took place, featuring Louis returning from retirement, as he fought various claims on his dwindling wealth. At this match, 22,000 fans in eight cities paid 50 cents to $1.30 each, and yet another revenue stream for the sport was created.[3] Near that same time, Robinson battled Turpin, and the fact that fans could watch the match beyond New York City helped to propel the former's already skyrocketing popularity even higher as fans stormed the theaters showing the contest. Riots erupted in Chicago as crowds amassed. Bursting through police lines, 1500 boxing fans smashed heavy glass doors at the theater where the match was to be seen, fearing they would not gain entrance otherwise because of intense demand. If they had planned ahead, perhaps they could have travelled to Albany, Pittsburgh, Baltimore, Washington, D.C., and other sites where the contest was shown.[4]

---

1. Report, January 1970, Sub Group XV, Series XIII, Box 46, HKBA.
2. Minutes, 5 December 1952, NYSAC.
3. Assael, *Murder*, 168.
4. Undated Report, Odds and Ends on Boxing, Vol. XVII, UND.

Such battles outside the ring were nothing new. To a degree it was inevitable that the audience would begin to imitate the battlers they sought to see, especially as U.S. soldiers were battling furiously on the Korean peninsula, creating an overall climate of unleashed bellicosity. Thus, again, in August 1951 a reporter described a "near riot" in Madison Square Garden, as Kid Gavilan took on Billy Graham, and an upset fan "tried to hit [referee Mark] Conn with a stool," leading to "special police" being summoned.[5]

Increasingly, referees were targeted. That same year, boxer Rocky Compitello was accused of punching the third man in the ring, then "wrestled" him and finally, with a flourish, "kicked" him "in the lower groin."[6] The racketeering manager Thomas "Tommy Ryan" Eboli was accused of attacking a referee in the ring in order to express dissatisfaction with his judgments.[7]

Did enhanced revenue contribute to more determined battlers less likely to tolerate perceived errors by referees, jeopardizing rich payouts, leading to the battering of the third man in the ring? Maybe, maybe not. For it is similarly reasonable to infer that enhanced revenue would attract more hungry fighters. But at least in the Empire State by 1956, it was found by regulators that "the number of participants in professional boxing has decreased," an outgrowth of many factors, including the "drying up of small boxing clubs which must rely upon gate receipts solely for survival," which in turn had led to monopolization at Madison Square Garden.[8] Another possible factor was the post-1954 opening, theoretically creating opportunity in other sports and other walks of life, for Negroes especially. In the late 1950s, the St. Nicholas Arena in Harlem, the site of many a bout, closed down, meaning, said regulators, a "decrease in boxing shows which numbered 74 in 1959" and "98 in 1958."[9]

For it was in 1950 that the head of the Syracuse Wrestling Club was grousing about the negative impact of televised boxing, which "caused many of our potential customers to stay home...rather than attend our shows" which "cuts down the State Tax collected."[10] Part

---

5. Clipping, 29 August 1951, Sub Group X, Series I, Box 23, HKBA.
6. Patrick J. Callahan, Deputy Commissioner, to R.K. Christenberry, 16 November 1951, NYSAC.
7. Hearing Transcript, 11 January 1952, New York State Athletic Commission, NYSAC.
8. Report to Carmine De Sapio, Secretary of State, 31 December 1956, NYSAC.
9. Minutes, 7 January 1960, NYSAC.
10. B.V. Mangin to Daniel Dowd, 15 September 1950, NYSAC.

of the problem faced by wrestling was that many fight fans did not take the "sport" seriously—even regulators termed it "an acrobatic vaudeville act" that supplanted "legitimate wrestling," which was "ordinarily quite dull."[11] With televised boxing gobbling audiences that otherwise might flock to wrestling exhibitions, the latter found it necessary to become even more outrageous to attract attention. "We don't like boxing and they don't like us," said one wrestling promoter: "We sell entertainment...costume has a place in our business.... in any business you need a villain and the villain winning is good for business"[12]—which Muhammad Ali was to demonstrate as the erstwhile competitors began to overlap. Eventually, fans might have appreciated more the original than the copycat, for in a few years Albany regulators ascertained there were "1538 professional wrestling exhibitions and 616 professional boxing contests" during the calendar year.[13]

Nevertheless, as of 1951, Albany was marking a "larger income" from boxing "than any of the two preceding years." The downstream consequence was that it attracted visitors who fattened the purses of restaurants and hotels alike.[14] This was occurring though the mecca of the sport—Madison Square Garden—initiated "Ladies' Night" with tickets at "half price"; there was an added bonus in that "there is no rowdiness at a show when women are there"[15]—perhaps a surprise to embattled referees.

Truman Gibson, Louis's partner, could be considered the Chief Operating Officer of this vast enterprise, though his modest salary seemed a throwback to Jim Crow rather than an acknowledgment that his presence represented a step away from this atavistic praxis. Earl Dickerson, a leader of Black Chicago,[16] testified on his behalf at the 1961 federal trial where his theretofore bright career came to a screeching halt. "I have known [him] since he was in his late teens," said this lawyer and entrepreneur, who, like Gibson, was friendly toward the Communist Party. "I met him at his home," speaking of Columbus, Ohio, "to confer with his father about the merger of his

---

11. Report to Thomas J. Curran, 31 December 1954, Minutes, NYSAC.

12. Minutes, 6 June 1952, NYSAC.

13. Report to Caroline Simon, Secretary of State, 31 December 1960, NYSAC.

14. Report to Thomas J. Curran, Secretary of State, 31 December 1951, NYSAC.

15. Minutes, 20 November 1952, NYSAC.

16. Robert J. Blakely, *Earl B. Dickerson: A Voice for Freedom and Equality*, Evanston: Northwestern University Press, 2006.

company with ours in Illinois." He also reacquainted himself with Gibson when he "was on the football team" at the University of Chicago and often would drop by Dickerson's office to read law books and discuss knotty legal questions. Gibson was his "understudy" in the trailblazing high court case, "Hansberry v. Lee," a tie solidified by their mutual membership in the elite Negro fraternity, Kappa Alpha Psi. "He lives in Chicago just about a half block from me," said Dickerson. "His family and my family are very close associates."[17]

Providing a deposition in late 1955 when, as ever, he was enmeshed in a legal imbroglio, requiring disgorging of details of his life, Gibson revealed further detail. "In 1943 and 1944 when I was the civilian aide to the Secretary of War," bringing him closer to William Hastie, another top Negro lawyer and later a federal judge, "I organized a troop of professional boxers that visited army camps.... I had worked in a law office that represented Joe Louis in Chicago," whom he had "known since 1937." Since he already knew that "there is always more interest in a heavyweight fight than any other division," it was only natural that Louis, upon his first retirement in 1949, would ally with the shrewd attorney, Gibson;[18] at least by 1960, when he was dragged for the umpteenth time before a congressional committee investigating the sport, he mentioned nonchalantly that "we were putting on over hundred fights a year,"[19] many of them televised.

Involved in yet another legal quagmire in 1961, he informed a federal court, "I would like to take sole credit for conceiving of it," meaning the tie-up between Joe Louis and the International Boxing Club, backed by James Norris and Arthur Wirtz. He went to the "Hearst Group" first, however. This was occurring as it became clear that Mike Jacobs was in decline, felled by a "disability," and there was a "promotional vacuum" that he was determined to occupy. The recently minted Columbia Broadcast System (CBS) en route to television dominance after establishing itself formidably in radio, sought to organize a "tournament of champions," but quickly got

---

17. Testimony of Earl Dickerson, 2 May 1961, Box 2487, RG21, District Court for the Central District of California, Central Division (Los Angeles), Criminal Case Files, 27973, NAR-Riv.

18. Deposition of Truman Gibson, 7 November 1955, New York City, Box 131, District Court for the Central District of California, c-21-2015-0013/021-2016-0735, CR 27973, NAR-Riv.

19. Testimony of Truman Gibson, 5-9 and 12-14 December 1960, Hearings Before the Subcommittee on Antitrust and Monopoly, Committee on the Judiciary, U.S. Senate, 86th Congress, 2nd Session, Part II, Estes Kefauver Papers, University of Tennessee-Knoxville (abbrev. Kefauver-UTn-K).

cold feet and "was anxious to get out of the business"[20]—and Gibson was eager to enter.

Described as a "strikingly handsome man, whose light brown complexion and straight black hair set off alert eyes, a slender nose and a delicately drawn mouth," Gibson could well be considered (along with Dickerson, an attorney and insurance industry mogul himself) the most potent Negro business executive nationally. He was slender and of medium height, in contrast with the prime stockholders in this lucrative business, Arthur Wirtz, who was more than six feet tall and a beefy 225 pounds, and Jim Norris, also large—six feet tall and 210 pounds, viewed as "graceful" with thick black hair and magnetic dark eyes. Gibson was Norris's right-hand man, which was not a minor position to be in since Norris conceded that "my family is worth three hundred million [dollars]," a considerable sum even today, and certainly in 1950. Despite this wealth, or perhaps because of it, Norris was accused of involvement in "fixing" of fights. Undeniable was that the Gibson-Wirtz-Norris operation had promoted 80% of all world championship bouts from June 1949, when Joe Louis was in the process of (temporarily) retreating from the ring, and sparking into being what became the International Boxing Club, quickly reaping millions. But there were unsilent partners, too, exemplified when Norris got sick and received a handsome floral arrangement from Albert Anastasia, a bona fide mobster. Norris admitted to a lengthy friendship with Sam Hunt, a fellow Chicagoan whose nickname was "Golfbag," since he carried his machine gun in a case that resembled how one might lug around a favorite putter and driver. Anastasia's right-hand man was Frankie Carbo, whose unprepossessing size—5'8" tall and 180 pounds—belied his justified reputation as a natural born killer: The same was true for his style of neat dressing, since one might have imagined his outfits splashed with blood. His soft brown eyes and rapidly receding gray hair seemed to fit well his sallow complexion.

There had been advance on the racial front, as noted, in the 1950s, but still, what befell Gibson in particular was not unexpected insofar as his very class position belied the nostrum that Negroes should be forevermore the mudsill of society. Thus, all of a sudden, there was a banging on his front door, followed by the shouted but insistent cry, "We're from the FBI!" Upon granted entrance to his abode, they

---

20. Testimony of Truman Gibson, 26 April 1961, RG 21, District Court for the Central District of California, Central Division (Los Angeles), Criminal Case Files, 27973, Box 2487, NAR-Riv.

manhandled him, slapped handcuffs on him and marched him to a small jail cell.[21]

Norris graciously agreed to testify at Gibson's trial, though even impartial commentators might have wondered why he was not in the dock beside him, especially since the self-proclaimed "Millionaire Referee" Harry Kessler admitted subsequently that "whenever I stepped into the Garden on a Friday night" (meaning Madison Square Garden), "there sat Jim Norris ringside with some of the [most] nefarious looking persons I have ever seen…real life hoods!" Kessler implied that when the boxing trainer Ray Arcel was bludgeoned in the streets for reasons that still remain not altogether clear, Norris's "nefarious" comrades carried out what amounted to a "mob hit."[22] Certainly, Gibson by this point was closely related to some of the more ethically challenged figures in the sport, including Jack "Doc" Kearns, whose antics stretched back to Dempsey. By 1952 Gibson was acting as his attorney.[23]

Norris was compelled to admit that he had a "certain relationship" with Carbo and "paid" his spouse a cool $40,000. Norris was spotted with Carbo in public venues though "Mr. Gray" was a "master gunman…gangland's top pistol for hire," said a commentator. "Bugsy Siegel had personally selected Carbo to blast a highly dangerous stoolpigeon who'd threatened to betray Louis 'Lepke' Buchalter," another noted mobster. Those who negotiated with Norris, who had vast connections in industry, journalism and politics, were likely impressed, if not intimidated, by such an association.[24]

A dangerous nexus linked sports and gambling, an intersection that undergirded the so-called "Black Sox Scandal" marring baseball in the wake of World War I, and Carbo embodied this tendency. Senator Estes Kefauver of Tennessee, who styled himself as a kind of crime-fighter in Washington, had his eyes on the man also known as Paul John Carbo, born in New York City in 1904, early on. He was aware of his 17 arrests for vagrancy, felonious assault, grand larceny, robbery and "five for murder." He was also indicted in 1939, along with Bugsy Siegel, for the murder of Harry Schacter, alias Greenberg,

---

21. Nagler, *James Norris*, 21, 43, 62, 79, 119, 142, 167, 223, 246.

22. Kessler, *Millionaire*, 308-309. On gangsters and boxing, see *New York World Telegram*, 14 January 1952, Box 5, Fleischer-UND.

23. Minutes, 21 August 1952, NYSAC.

24. Walter Wager, "The Man Who Smashed Frankie Carbo," 1962 Edition Boxing Yearbook, published by *TRUE, The Man's Magazine*, 46-49, 61, Box 209, Ellison-LC.

known colloquially as "Big Greeney."[25] Others said that Carbo's rap sheet began when he was 11 years old; his first murder rap came in 1924, when he was indicted for killing a taxi driver in the Bronx.[26] Just as one did not have to use a weapon in order to intimidate, it was enough to wield it flagrantly, and Carbo's fearsome reputation alone often was enough to deliver fruitful results. As one journalist put it, "it was like the old days when even doctors wouldn't say 'cancer' just as if the word itself would kill." His adversaries and peers alike "hated" and "dreaded" him but were reluctant to even mention his name, let alone blab to the authorities about him. His liaisons were similarly viewed, including that with Hymie "The Mink" Wallman, who managed several top boxers for Carbo and was a link between the latter and Jim Norris, Truman Gibson's supervisor. This rotund Manhattan furrier happened to control a shocking number of fighters who appeared on nationally televised contests. His own ugly reputation was useful in seeking to intimidate a labor force he confronted that included a corps of Communists.[27] Testifying before Senator Kefauver as "Herman" Wallman, he acknowledged that his boxers dominated television, and that he knew Carbo and Gibson well, while sprinkling his remarks with references to "Jimmy the Wop."[28] "The Mink" was accused of paying bribes to Bertram Grant, a boxing judge, "on at least five occasions."[29]

The man known as Frank "Blinky" Palermo was a key player in this plot. "When I was three years old," he told a federal court, "I had typhoid fever and it left my eyes like that"—seemingly blinking uncontrollably—"and ever since then they started calling me Blinky.... I used to blink more than I do now," he said, speaking of his "granulated eyelids." By the time of this 1961 trial, he was 57, but "I had to go to work when I was 12 years old. I went to the fifth grade"—then departed school. "My father had a farm," which meant he was not left destitute, but "boxing was my business"; "I never boxed," he conceded. He entered the repugnant sport of

---

25. Hearings Before the Subcommittee on Antitrust and Monopoly, Committee of the Judiciary, U.S. Senate, 86th Congress, 2nd Session, Part II, 5-9 December, 12-14, 1960, Box 490, Kefauver-UTn-K.

26. Nick Tosches, *The Devil and Sonny Liston*, Boston: Little Brown, 2000 (abbrev. Tosches, *The Devil*), 76.

27. Walter Wager, op. cit., 46-49, 61, Box 209, Ellison-LC.

28. Testimony of Herman Wallman, 5-9 and 12-14 December 1960, Hearings Before the Subcommittee on Antitrust and Monopoly Committee on Judiciary, U.S. Senate, 86th Congress, 2nd Session, Box 490, Kefauver-UTn-K.

29. Minutes, 3 July 1958, NYSAC.

boxing in 1936. A mere 5'4" tall and rarely above 150 pounds, he once "used the name of Shapiro. I used to play baseball with a [semi-pro] Jewish team." The elusive Palermo—who had a cousin with the same name—also used the alias George Tobias, further complicating attempts to track him down.[30]

* * *

Also testifying before Senate Kefauver was the Negro pounder Ike Williams, who said that "Palermo came to my training camp in 1949 when I was training for the second [Kid] Gavilan fight. He said fellows offered him a hundred thousand for me to lose the fight. I had to be crazy [to refuse]" but then "he just robbed the hell out of me from my money." Already "he borrowed ten thousand from me." Then, said, the put-upon pounder, "I received thirty-three thousand four hundred fighting Beau Jack in Philadelphia. I never saw a penny of that. And thirty-three thousand five hundred. Jesse Flores in New York. I never saw a penny of that. The [boxing] commission doesn't care, they don't care. I fought those two fights for nothing, and paid taxes on them!... Palermo stopped by and picked the money up...he started crying about he's broke and he's going to get his brains blown out. If he didn't pay some people he said he needed my purse to pay off some old debts." Then, continued Williams, "I purposely lost the fight to Billy Fox because they promised me that I would get a shot to fight for the title if I did." The insistent Palermo came to him once again, and he signed another contract "for this fight with Jimmy Carter. No one knew I was injured. Blinky says, 'Ike they want to give you fifty thousand dollars to lose the fight. Six months' time he'll fight you back again and lose it back to you.' I said no. I should have done it"—perhaps the most revelatory aspect of his unburdening, for it exposed that the material incentive pushed boxers toward corruption. His failure to accept this deal, he said, was "one of the reasons why I'm broke now."[31] Williams was a punching bag for gangsters. Mickey Cohen admitted that "during

---

30. Testimony of "Blinky" Palermo, 10 May 1961, Box 2487, RG 21, District Court for the Central District of California (Los Angeles), Criminal Case Files (Transcripts), 27951-27973, NAR-R.

31. Heller, *In This Corner*, 269-272, 297. As horrific as Williams's experience was, it seemed to pale in comparison to what boxers experienced postwar: "Between rounds Dow had applied burning matches to Walker's kidneys in an effort to 'pep up' the Philadelphian...not entirely unknown in the trade." Report, August 1948, Sub Group IX, Series I, Box 16, HKBA.

the war and when I was still in the boxing world, I made a match for Ike Williams" while the insultingly nicknamed "Nig" Rosen "was managing Ike and was in Philadelphia."[32] However, it was Palermo who was his chief exploiter, instructing investigators at one point that, yes, he was "abusive" toward the fighter because "sometimes he would eat more than he should—like eat bread."[33]

Thus, Gibson was not in ideal company when he testified before Senator Kefauver and was forced to acknowledge his intimate knowledge of sordid events. Worst of all was his admission of association with Carbo, the prematurely gray killer who spoke in a guttural hoodlum growl, straight out of a gangster movie.[34] "I would say that Jake La Motta," the man later glorified as the "Raging Bull" of middleweights, "was very close to Carbo…. I know that Carbo knows [Chris] Dundee and has known him for many years." Gibson also limned the obvious: "[the] majority of the money is in the heavier weight category," and that "boxing over the years has been essentially a monopoly type operation from the days of Tex Rickard to Mike Jacobs to ourselves." But he should have recognized that in a land officially disfigured still by apartheid, his conspicuous presence was no minor detail. And although Jacobs officially was fading from the scene, Gibson knew that "[Sugar] Ray Robinson was a frequent borrower from Mike Jacobs," just as his man, "Joe Louis, during the war, borrowed from Jacobs $220,000" and continued to owe him in various ways.[35]

Louis was no innocent, but instead was apparently making the miscalculation that his ties to the left—Southern Conference for Human Welfare, former Vice President Henry Wallace, et al.—could allow him to swim in murky waters, just as others did. It was not just his relationship to Negro mobster "Bumpy" Johnson: As early as 1940 he was photographed with gangster Mickey Cohen at a testimonial dinner at the Beverly Hills Hotel.[36] This was a gross misestimate. On the other hand, "Sugar" Ray took a different route and did not necessarily end well either. By late 1950 as the war in Korea was heating up, he was to be found in Paris denouncing Communists,[37] then took

---

32. Cohen, *Mickey Cohen*, 68-69.
33. Minutes, 27 April 1951, NYSAC.
34. Walter Wager, op. cit., Ellison-LC.
35. Testimony of Truman Gibson, 5-9 and 12-14 December 1960, Hearings Before the Subcommittee on Antitrust and Monopoly, Committee on the Judiciary, U.S. Senate, 86th Congress, 2nd Session, Part II, Kefauver-UTn-K.
36. Cohen, *Mickey Cohen*, 88.
37. *Miami Herald*, 22 December 1950, Sub Group X, Series I, Box 4, HKBA.

what was described as a "verbal poke" at Paul Robeson, the lodestar of the left.[38] But "Sugar" was to find that life could be unsweet for those of his hue, which he might have recognized after defeating German boxer Gerhart Hecht in West Berlin, recently rescued from Communist encirclement by a massive U.S. airlift: A riot ensued, bottles and stones rained down on the ring, and he was forced to hide under it.[39] Evidently, the spectators were unimpressed with his anti-communism, delineating the limitations of Negro "integration" into the U.S. consensus.

Jack "Doc" Kearns by the 1950s was managing another boxing star, Archie "The Mongoose" Moore, rapidly gaining attention as a light heavyweight. Recall that he used to manage Dempsey: His roots in the sport reached back decades, when as a teen he travelled to Alaska with Jack London, the writer and socialist *cum* "white supremacist." Speaking before Senator Estes Kefauver and his bird-dogs in Washington, he spun elaborate tales about how "Tex Rickard and Wyatt Earp and all those fellows came in the same year up there." Back then he was known as "Young Kid Kearns," and "Wyatt Earp was my manager for a while around San Francisco." Kearns went on to manage Mickey Walker and Joey Maxim, too. But after wandering verbally, perhaps filibustering to consume time and avoid grilling, he conceded that he visited Carbo's Miami Beach home, while countering by adding, "I was a bitter enemy" of the mobster. He waffled on whether he was part of Carbo's so-called Managers' Guild, while admitting further, "There is no doubt about it. Norris and Carbo run everything in boxing."[40] Kearns was outspoken about his ties to top racketeers.[41]

It is unlikely that this is the kind of company Gibson planned to consort with, as he was born into a strait-laced middle class family in Atlanta in 1912. His father was a rare figure, having graduated from Harvard in 1909 owing to aid from the formidable W.E.B. Du Bois, who also had done time in Cambridge, Massachusetts. The younger Gibson was admitted to Northwestern University by 1929 but, discouraged by the virulence of the racism he encountered, he

---

38. Clipping, 3 January 1951, Sub Group X, Series I, Box 4, HKBA.
39. *Life*, 9 July 1951, Sub Group X, Series I, Box 6, HKBA.
40. Testimony of Jack "Doc" Kearns, Hearings Before the Subcommittee on Antitrust and Monopoly Committee on Judiciary, U.S. Senate, 5-9 and 12-14 December 1960, 86th Congress, 2nd Session, Part II, Box 490, Kefauver-UTn-K.
41. *Miami Herald*, 22 May 1959, Sub Group VIII, Series I, Box 24, HKBA.

transferred to the University of Chicago, which at least was in a more friendly neighborhood in Hyde Park. A talented attorney and administrator, he toiled for the Negro Congressman William Dawson for a while and worked on the trailblazing high court case involving the elevated Hansberry family, which included the talented writer Lorraine and William Leo, the leading Africanist at Howard University. That case contributed mightily to the overall assault on Jim Crow in housing, and formed the basis for her prize-winning play, *A Raisin in the Sun*. "I had a good friend in Chicago," he recalled later, speaking of the pre-eminent Negro Communist, Ishmael Flory; as for Phileo Nash, the key New Deal aide, they were "socially friendly. He lived just a few doors from me in Washington," and both had ties to "Georgetown Day School...the first integrated school in the history of [the District]." He worked for the Roosevelt administration during the war but was unimpressed with the occupant of the Oval Office, finding him "really remote, a racist." Nash was also "friendly with Communists, as was I," Gibson reiterated, which brought grief to both men subsequently, including attacks by Senator Joseph McCarthy himself. "I was very indignant," sniffed Gibson.[42]

Besides being a Negro, Gibson was not the ideal match for the forces he was seeking to corral. Many were not happy when the capital of boxing shifted to Chicago, where he resided, away from Manhattan. It was more than just a geographic move: It also meant that those seeking to dip into the trough of riches generated by the sport were advantaged by being in the Midwest and disadvantaged if remaining in the Northeast.[43] Furthermore, Gibson said he was bent on "avoiding the mistakes of much criticized Madison Square Garden matchmaker Al Weill who has been accused of playing up racial and nationalistic antagonisms in setting up bouts."[44] Those who are left behind rarely enjoy being criticized by those who take their place, and this was particularly the case when what was at issue was playing upon "racial and nationalistic antagonisms" that had proven to be profitable, and admittedly dangerous, stretching back to Jack Johnson in Reno in 1910.

Besides tax matters, Gibson's partner, Joe Louis, was battling other problems. He "inadvertently" broke the leg of Lena Horne, the progressive chanteuse, which raised troubling problems about his ongoing problems with women. But despite this nettlesome issue, Louis had the advantage of global celebrity, while, said Gibson,

---

42. Oral history, Truman Gibson, HSTPL.
43. *Pittsburgh Courier*, 26 May 1951.
44. Undated report, Box 2, Gibson-LC.

"Norris and Wirtz boasted the riches of princes." So the foursome quickly ascertained that boxing and television was a compelling match, sating the appetite for bruising in a nation built on mass dispossession of Indigenes and mass enslavement of Africans (perhaps providing the latter with a soupçon of revenge for what they had endured historically). "Wednesday and Friday night fights," said Gibson, "consistently scored third and fourth in the [television] ratings." One problem was dealing with "Sugar" Ray Robinson, the logical heir to Gans, Johnson, Armstrong and Louis, though with a twist. He was reluctant to fly, making it difficult to move from the Atlantic to the Pacific (at a time when California was booming), not to mention London, where his prime opponent, Turpin, had a base of support, awaiting tapping. Perhaps aware of the bitterly sordid history of his profession, the exemplar of the "Sweet Science," said Gibson, "reads every line in his contracts and insists on changes that even his lawyers don't catch"; the "Sugar Man," he said, exuded a "sophisticated and stubborn knowledge of financial arrangements." But Gibson well knew that for good reason "allegations of mob influence stuck to boxing like Velcro," so Robinson had little choice but to flyspeck documents in response. After all, it was his boss, Norris, who tried to induce Gibson to use influence to help Anastasia foil deportation (his supervisor was "close" to this cutthroat), in a case heard by yet another Negro leader whom Gibson knew quite well—William Hastie, then a federal judge. Carbo offered to provide Hastie with a fancy home in the Virgin Islands as a further inducement, an archipelago where he had once served as a federal administrator in this ramshackle U.S. colony, suggestive of the snares brought by desegregation, which brought influential Negroes all too close to the corruption that inhered in U.S. imperialism. Gibson did not count this potentially tawdry episode as the reason for his imminent decline as a powerbroker. A man who lived by television began to die by dint of the same instrument when the televised congressional hearings led by presidential timber, Senator Estes Kefauver of Tennessee, placed this mild-mannered Negro lawyer under the national microscope when Jim Crow was still being enforced legally. This, to anticipate a phrase, did not make for compelling optics insofar as the Euro-American majority was known to despise "uppity" Negroes, i.e., those unwilling to accept blandly third-class status. Soon he was in a dispute with Wirtz, and then the crooner and actor Frank Sinatra, along with mobster Sam Giancana, were seeking to horn in on the filthy lucre delivered by televised boxing. By 1959, quite extraordinarily, the high court began to abandon the idea that sports were not subject to antitrust rules and declared the Louis-Norris-Wirtz-Gibson setup an improper monopoly. Soon Gibson was indicted and convicted. "My glory days as the nation's top boxing promoter were over," he lamented.[45] On the other hand, it was unavoidable that the glass ceiling had been dented, opening the gates for the post-Jim Crow entrance of Don King and a flock of other Gibson imitators, who at least were better compensated than the Chicagoan.

For Gibson had power but not wealth, much of which he was generating with his adept negotiating skill and adroit administrative ability. Moreover, as his federal trial suggested, there was danger in his associations, especially having to deal with plug-uglies like Carbo. "Carbo was no man to be trifled with," said Angelo Dundee, best known as a corner man for Muhammad Ali. He was "implicated in no fewer than five murders," likely a conservative estimate; he "ruled the sport, making its fights…. you couldn't make a move in big-time boxing without his blessing"; he was "boxing's hidden secret," said Dundee—a secret only to those not paying attention is my estimation. Though it remains true that "while everyone could see Carbo & Co. at ringside, few made mention of it," least of all sportswriters with their telescoped vision that admitted no notice of what occurred beyond the ring. Not only was Carbo seeking to control all boxers, he had formed a "managers' guild" too, which probably was the reason why a presumed dissenter, Ray Arcel, almost lost his life in an attack in broad daylight. Dundee certainly knew what was going on. His brother Chris Dundee, the top promoter in continuously growing South Florida, had a "casual friendship" with "Blinky" Palermo, Carbo's right-hand man; and Angelo Dundee knew that this torpedo with the fluttering eyes was the "behind-the-scenes manager" of Sonny Liston, the heavyweight whose defeat at the hands of the man who became Muhammad Ali led the sport into a new era.[46]

Dundee should have known about the gangsters behind the so-called Managers' Guild strikes of 1949, which blockaded boxing for a while.[47] Angelo Dundee, in turn, was frequently to be found in South Florida and pre-1959 Cuba, too, which sheds light on his being able to translate from Spanish to English—and vice versa—on behalf of Albany regulators.[48]

Ferdie Pacheco, the so-called "Fight Doctor" who also was an Ali corner man and a painter and Miamian, too, acknowledged that

---

45. Gibson, *Knocking*, 238-239, 242-243, 247, 251, 257-258, 261-262, 267-268.
46. Dundee, *My View*, 32-35, 45, 103.
47. Brady, *Boxing Confidential*, 76.
48. Minutes, 16 December 1960, NYSAC.

Chris Dundee "had come up the hard way from Philly club fights to Madison Square Garden under the watchful eye of mob boss Frankie Carbo, who controlled boxing." (The faux naïve Angelo Dundee could not understand why Ali's co-religionists in the Nation of Islam "thought that I was connected with the Mafia.") Pacheco knew that "boxing in the 1950s was pretty well controlled by the Mafia and Chris had to join the Boxing Union of Frankie Carbo," thus this Dundee brother had "a deep connection with Frankie Carbo and 'the boys.'" This cabal included the manager of boxer Doug Vaillant, who was "none other than Bernard Barker, who later went on to fame as being one of the Watergate burglars,"[49] a political crime in early 1970s Washington that led to the resignation of President Richard M. Nixon.

Coincidentally, Carbo was well-wired in Dundee's Philadelphia, just as "Mr. Gray" owned an expensive home in Dundee's Miami,[50] and congressional investigators already were scrutinizing the fact that "during the winter season, there is a great influx of Philadelphia gangsters in the Miami and Miami Beach areas."[51]

Stan Levey, the self-described "Jazz Heavyweight" who was present at the creation of the musical form known as "be-bop," was a topflight drummer, besides being a boxer of no small talent. He hailed from Philadelphia—in some ways the headquarters of organized crime insofar as boxing was concerned (as shall be seen, that Ali and his fiercest opponent, Joe Frazier, both resided there for a while was hardly accidental). "Fighting and drumming are both all about hitting and timing," said Levey, plus quick hands, good reflexes, the ability to pound—propelled by instinctive combativeness—and a masculinized environment. Levey's father was a "boxing manager" in the City of Brotherly Love beginning in the 1930s and held a "low level position in the national crime syndicate," too. Levey quoted approvingly a source who said the fighter/drummer "passed for black" and thus was in a position to substantiate his assertion that his hometown was "the number one boxing town in the country, if not the world"—and a seedbed for musical innovation too.[52] This merited "reputation [stretched] back to the nineteenth century

---

49. Pacheco, *Tales*, 2, 42, 88.

50. Wager, op. cit., Ellison-LC.

51. D.P. Sullivan to J.L. Nellis, 12 January 1951, U.S. Senate, 81st-82nd Congress, Special Committee to Investigate Organized Crime in Interstate Commerce, CR9 [rackets], CR10 [Juvenile Delinquency], Box 42, NAR-DC.

52. Gerald Horne, *Jazz and Justice: Racism and the Political Economy of the Music*, New York: Monthly Review Press, 2019.

but the city became the undisputed boxing capital in 1926 when it turned out a staggering one hundred thousand spectators for the Jack Dempsey/Gene Tunney championship bout." Both Carbo and Palermo had Philadelphia roots ("South Philly" remains a redoubt of racketeers); hence, Levey was in a position to know that Carbo was the "undisputed boss of boxing," and his "right hand man was a close associate of Dave Levey"—his father—i.e., Frank Palermo. The latter was a "South Philly wise guy known coast to coast as "Blinky." The two gunslingers "had the largest stable of fighters in the country and also controlled the Boxing Managers Guild," and from this pinnacle of the sport, the two mobsters "conspired together to throw fights." Levey recalled Palermo as a "medium sized guy, five seven" with a "slight build" and at least one "dark eye," while he referred to Carbo simply as "Mr. Gray. Everyone calls him Mr. Gray." Neither was a "small time crook"; this he knew since Levey's father and Palermo "conspired together to throw fights." He knew the tricks of the trade, such as, "for boxers who threw the occasional fight, pseudonyms helped avoid the scrutiny of regulators." Levey himself, before settling down behind a drum set, was a getaway driver for stickups. His father couldn't take the pressure and committed suicide—supposedly—in 1949, just as plummy profits were emerging, thanks to television.[53]

Levey may have known about a suspicious prizefight that took place in his hometown in 1950 and was typical of the odoriferous sport. A congressional investigator "witnessed" the event and "it 'smelled to high heavens'" to the point where George A. Fickeissen "contacted sports writers who covered that fight and they were of the same opinion." What happened was that "Tony Galento" was "booked to fight Henry Lewis but Galento was stricken with an attack of pneumonia" against this "top flight light heavyweight." So, "Otis Thomas...St. Louis Negro heavyweight...was substituted," and the fight proceeded. But suspicions arose since there was "very little betting on this fight as everyone felt that Galento was purposely being given a string of set-ups for a forthcoming fight"

---

53. Frank R. Hayde, *Stan Levey: Jazz Heavyweight, The Authorized Biography*, Solana Beach: Santa Monica Press, 2016, 9, 26, 31, 33-34, 49, 88, 97, 213. While Jack Johnson played a bass fiddle and "Sugar" Ray Robinson was a competent drummer, musicians like Miles Davis, Wallace Roney and Red Garland—who actually fought Robinson, completing the circle—were all boxers of varying ability. Also relevant is the point that Robinson also fancied himself as a dancer before finding fame as a boxer: Undated report, Odds and Ends on Boxing, Vol. XVI, UND.

with the heavyweight champion." Viewed without benignity was the point that "Bill Duffy," "Thomas' manager," was an "ex-convict" and the "purse was sizeable."[54]

Gibson was in way over his head. It remains unclear if he knew what he was getting into when he made the fateful decision to join a business with thugs, when, as a Negro, he was bound to be the fall guy if matters headed downward, which was unavoidable. Thus, congressional investigators for the longest time had cast a wary eye on Palermo. By 1950 they had a copy of his Pennsylvania driver's license, indicating that he was born in Philadelphia on 26 November 1905. That same year they had evidence that he had violated the rule that barred one from being a manager and promoter of a boxer—he slyly used a "front" to shroud his dual roles. Like so many in this unclean business, he too was close to Mickey Cohen, the former boxer now spearheading rackets in Los Angeles. Palermo also knew how to use his fists: In 1947 he was sentenced for aggravated assault and battery after administering a severe beating. By 1934 he was involved in illicit wagering. He had been arrested for larceny, threats to do bodily harm, along with assault and battery by automobile. Yet, after all these craven misdeeds, he was thought by at least one official—as of the early 1950s—to be leading an "exemplary and successful life" as manager of "lightweight champion…Ike Williams," a Negro pounder, along with "other high caliber fighters such as Billy Fox, Billy Arnold, Dosey Lay and Archie Wilmer." By then, he had five children: three daughters and two sons, ranging in age from 17 to 11, as he posed as a suburban dad. This pose, and perhaps undue influence, meant that by 1947 officialdom recommended that he be pardoned after he organized boxing matches for soldiers. In this, quite curiously, he received a letter of support from Judge Harry McDevitt of the Court of Common Pleas, who said, bizarrely, "those who do not like him try to connect him with racketeers like other fight promoters but I have been unable to find any connection between them." He was pardoned by the governor in January 1948, wiping the slate clean, allowing him to perpetrate more mischief. By 1950, as new vistas were opening for him in step with Gibson, the press indicated that he was also a partner in a "large numbers bank." A related story said that he had been sought "after a running gun battle" in South Philadelphia, as if he were starring in a newly minted show on the "boob tube"; it was all about "an unpaid numbers bet," i.e., he

---

54. George Fickeissen to John N. McCormick, 14 November 1950, Box 40, U.S. Senate, 81st-82nd Congress, Special Committee to Investigate Organized Crime in Interstate Commerce, NAR-DC.

"failed to pay off $350 on a 75 cent bet." By 1953 he was ensconced in an office in the Shubert Building in Philadelphia, 250 South Broad Street, like any other normal businessman.[55]

Because Palermo wielded such influence and had such leverage, he was able to extend his tentacles farther. Thus Frankie Palumbo managed Billy Fox, described as "colored," and this manager was "associated with Palermo, the 'Numbers King.'"[56] Ironically, perhaps consciously, Palermo became "King" in this presumably illegitimate commerce, as his Negro peers began to retreat, as desegregation mounted. For example, in nearby Chester, Pennsylvania, there had been a separate operation that involved, according to an investigation, "all Negro pick-up men and writers [who] meet about every two weeks," and "pick-ups...estimated at approximately $1500 a day." But "'Nig' Rosen's brother live[d] in Chester," too, which did not bode well for the future of this Negro operation in an age of "integration,"[57] which too often meant liquidation of Negro self-assertion.

Herman Goldberg, also known as "Muggsy" Taylor, was a close comrade of Rosen, too, and happened to "frequently entertain... members of the 'Big Mob' from Chicago in Atlantic City," within hailing distance of Philadelphia—and Chester.[58] Testimony before Senator Kefauver established that Taylor was a close comrade of Capone himself.[59] As for Rosen—his comrade Mickey Cohen explained that he was also known as Harry, "a Jew who hung out with black people, so was sometimes called 'Nigger' Rosen"[60]—"by coercion," said an investigator, he "seized control of the Maryland Athletic Club of Bladensburg Road and [the] District line," speaking of Washington. He was "fronted" by Taylor, a "local fight promoter, who has run gambling houses all his life," a marriage of corruption. Rosen was "closely associated with Meyer Lansky," and a "persistent rumor" contended that "the late 'Bugsy' Siegel was executed by a local henchman of Rosen's acting on behalf of the Rosen-Lansky interests." This claim was not interpreted as a step away from ethno-centrism insofar as Jewish mobsters were conspiring against each

---

55. Materials on Palermo, 1934-1953, RG 46, Box 109, ibid.
56. P.C. Murray to A. Klein, 22 November 1950, Box 39, ibid.
57. J.M. McCormick to H.G. Robinson, 27 October 1950, Box 40, ibid.
58. Alfred Klein to Mr. Halley, 6 September 1950, Box 40, ibid.
59. Testimony of Robert Taylor, Staff Investigator, Box 490, Kefauver-UTn-K.
60. Cohen, *Mickey Cohen*, 69.

other, but rather a step toward a long-promised synthetic and overarching "whiteness" and "integration."[61]

Still, this ethno-centrism remained prevalent. Hence, in 1950, Pennsylvania authorities were mulling if a certain man should be appointed to the boxing regulatory agency since it could encourage those of the "Jewish faith" to vote for the Republican Party.[62] But this inquiry reflected another trend: Post-1945, with the revulsion against the racist atrocity embodied in the Holocaust, the energy generated by the anti-Jim Crow movement, and the educational benefits directed to military veterans, there was a related boosting of the Jewish-American community, meaning fewer young Jewish boys and men battling out of their neighborhoods against Irish and Italian Americans, fomenting boxers like Benny Leonard, and an increase in the ranks of those like Bob Arum, who by the 1970s was competing with Don King to be "top dog" in the embattled sport, supplanting the Gibson-Norris-Carbo axis.

There were other diversions, too, for Jewish Americans. Matthew Feldman became a state senator in New Jersey, a post once generally barred to those like himself. "I earned respect because of my ability to handle myself," he related, sharpening his boxing prowess in Monmouth and later serving as a gunrunner during the 1948 war that led to the creation of Israel. He hid rifles, ammunition, handguns and other military materiel in what he called the "old Hackensack YMHA [Young Men's Hebrew Association] and facilitated their secret transfer to Freehold for shipping overseas under the Panamanian flag."[63] The support for this putatively illegal conduct arose from immense sympathy for the prime victims of the Holocaust, which then redounded to their general benefit. Also gaining sympathy was the heartrending story of Harry Haft, who learned to box in a concentration camp in Central Europe; like the "battle royal" he fought for the "amusement" of the "German guards," often "bare fisted," this after being "imprisoned at the age of 16." He spent "four and

---

61. D.P. Sullivan to J.L. Nellis, 12 January 1951, Box 42, U.S. Senate, 81st-82nd Congress, Special Committee to Investigate Organized Crime in Interstate Commerce, NAR-DC.

62. Dr. R.S. Davis to John Fine, 18 November 1950, Box 6, MS Group 206, John Fine Papers, Pennsylvania State Archives-Harrisburg.

63. Matthew Feldman in "The Jewish Veteran," July-August 1986, Sub Group IX, Series I, Box 8, HKBA. In the same collection, see also "American Weekly," 10 February 1957, Sub Group IX, Series I, Box 16: David "Mickey" Marcus was an "intercollegiate boxing champion" and also played a role in the formation of Israel not unlike Feldman's.

one half years in eleven different concentration camps," recounted a message to boxing researcher Hank Kaplan, and during this time was "shot, bayoneted and lashed by the Nazi guards," enduring "three and one half years...as a slave in the coal mines."[64] He was compared to a gladiator of yore.[65] Ineluctably, such riveting stories in the context of aforementioned trends, contributed to a noticeable decline in anti-Semitism in the U.S., pushing more Jewish Americans out of the ring in the process. As of 1957, an analyst could continue to claim that "Jewish fighters have been champions in every division—but heavyweight.... ever since the diminutive David upset the gigantic Goliath...Jewish fighters have been most successful in the lighter classes."[66] Soon, however, this conventional wisdom would fade into history.

Fortunately, fading with it were past odious practices from the intense days of ethno-centrism. Back then, according to writer Robert Cassidy, promoters were not above "hyping matches between a Jew and an Italian or Irishman," and it was done in a confrontational manner, not inimical to whipping up anti-Semitism. In those days, he said, "Jewish boxers took on different [names]. They changed their names, they even changed their ethnic connotation. Some became [sic] Irish or Italians."[67] Postwar, this was not so necessary, but at the same time, it may have consolidated a new iteration of "whiteness" as numerous Jewish Americans were accepted into this hallowed category, extending its shelf life.[68] However, as Jewish boxers receded from view, Jewish entrepreneurs did not. This lengthening list included Abe Saperstein—better known as a progenitor of the slapstick hoopsters, the "Harlem Globetrotters," who trafficked shamelessly in crude racist stereotypes—who also was a boxing manager.[69]

Congressional investigators also paid close attention to the man they called "Paul J. (Frankie) Carbo...an 'undercover' fight manager" who "purchased the contract of Bernie Docusen of New Orleans, partly with funds furnished by Frank Costello," widely

---

64. Harry Brooks Mandell to Dear Dave, 10 November 1948, Sub Group IX, Series I, Box 12, HKBA.

65. Report, March 1949, Sub Group IX, Series I, Box 12, HKBA.

66. Len Kanthal in "The Ring," December 1957, Sub Group IX, Series I, Box 14, HKBA.

67. Robert Cassidy in *Newsday*, ca. 1990s, Sub Group IX, Series I, Box 15, HKBA.

68. Horne, *Dawning*.

69. Minutes, 29 January 1960, NYSAC.

considered the boss of all crime bosses, an equivalent of Anastasia. Docusen's manager "of record" was Stanley Geigerman, "Costello's brother-in-law," while the "stable of fighters which Carbo is alleged to control," as of about 1951, included "Johnny Greco, 'Chalky' Wright"—recall how this boxer and former intimate of Mae West, wound up dead—"Cecil Hudson, Oelo Shans, 'Popeye' Woods, Jimmy McDaniels, Tami Mauriello, and Bill Poland" (recall his being implicated in illegitimate contests). Costello was a "star" of sorts at the televised Kefauver hearings that ensnared Gibson and was a target for the authorities. They knew that he had been indicted in 1939, along with James Brocato (alias Jimmy Moran), described as a former fighter and bodyguard of the assassinated Governor Huey Long: Illegal gambling—slot machines—were at issue.[70]

The Chicago Crime Commission also kept tabs on Carbo, "alias Frank Tucker, alias Frank Paul Castro," who was not averse to "do a gun job for pay...reported to spend most of his time in New York and Detroit," where the "Purple Gang" was hatched. He was described as having an "oval shaped face" with "close set eyes, [a] Roman nose, big ears," that were "set close to [his] head, bushy eyebrows and hair combed straight back." At the time of this writing, 1951, he was 45 years old. His "list" of "friends included" the mobster known as "Nig" Rosen, "Willie & Solly Moretti," Costello, of course, "Joe Adonis...Jimmy Doyle alias Palermo...Max Weisman and Quinn (fight promoters)" and, yes, "Jim Norris." He was also tied to middleweight Jake La Motta, later celebrated in cinema as the "Raging Bull." Carbo, a boulevardier of note, was often found in Jack Dempsey's fashionable bistro in midtown Manhattan, the nearby watering hole known as "Toots Shor," and other hotspots. Carbo was "active in fight promotions [in] Montreal, Providence, Boston, Cleveland, Detroit and Chicago." He was a "bookmaker's bookmaker," it was reported with seeming admiration, though he

---

70. Material "Taken from Records of U.S. Treasury Intelligence Unit," ca. 1950-1951, RG46, Box 78, U.S. Senate, 81st-82nd Congress, Special Committee to Investigate Organized Crime in Interstate Commerce, NAR-DC. This file includes *New Orleans Times-Picayune*, 10 October 1939, which includes the references to Costello and Governor Long. It also includes a handwritten letter to Senator Kefauver dated 19 March 1951, that pointed to the "common knowledge that Councilman Earl Brown"—who replaced the aforementioned Communist leader Ben Davis as Harlem's representative, after the latter was imprisoned—was "entirely supported by Frank Costello." See also Brady, *Boxing Confidential*, 61: Carbo "owned Bernard Docusen...[who] later went the distance with a peak Sugar Ray Robinson" and was also tied to Frank Costello.

was connected with the infamous Louis Lepke; the two "supplied goons for strike breakers in the garment district" in Manhattan and was "mixed up in murder," too. Like Palermo, he posed as a family man, with a wife "Jean" and a "daughter aged 7."[71]

But such poses could not obscure his connections to such ignobility as Ettore "Eddie" Coco, a thug who had the misfortune of becoming, as a reporter put it, "the first white man ever convicted in Florida for a killing [of] a [Negro]," an early casualty of the new dispensation delivered by desegregation, the flip side of Gibson in sum.[72] Actually, this former manager of the boxer and media personality Rocky Graziano was twice found guilty of murdering a Negro car washer and twice sentenced to life imprisonment.[73]

When Carbo visited Dempsey's bistro, he may have bumped into another insultingly named mobster who was a "personal friend" of the former champion. "Niggy" Rutkin and his various disreputable associates financed several of the pug-nosed boxer's business ventures, including his restaurant. In fact, Rutkin—who was also close to New Jersey crime boss Abner "Longey" Zwillman—and Dempsey were such close companions that their tie was subject to knowing stage whispers.[74] Rutkin was also viewed by the authorities as being in the suspicious category of the "heavy stock gambler," which brought him into close contact with Wall Street in his ramblings through Manhattan.[75]

The authorities knew quite a bit about the inner workings of these mobsters—though clearly not enough—because, as was admitted in 1950, there was the effort to "build a microphone into the house" of Mickey Cohen, the former boxer and then gangster in Los Angeles.[76] And for sensitive intelligence, there was Nat Fleischer, arguably the premier boxing journalist, who was described by one investigator as "my informant." Referred to was a "heavyweight prizefighter by the name of Rex Layne" who was "unable to a fight in [Madison Square Garden] because his manager" was "unwilling to give the New York mob a percentage"; hence, the unwitting Layne was "purposely

---

71. Ibid., Taken from Records of U.S. Treasury Intelligence Unit, Box 71.
72. Brady, *Boxing Confidential*, 61.
73. *Miami Herald*, 12 May 1955, Sub Group X, Series I, Box 13, HKBA.
74. J.F. Elich to H.G. Robinson, 10 July 1950, Box 39, U.S. Senate, 81st-82nd Congress, Special Committee to Investigate Organized Crime in Interstate Commerce, NAR-DC.
75. J.F. Elich to H.G. Robinson, 10 July 1950, Box 40, ibid.
76. H.G. Robinson to Boris Kostelanetz, 12 October 1950, Box 39, ibid.

matched against [Jersey Joe] Walcott in order to eliminate him.... Walcott is the fellow that the mob uses to beat down any fighter in the heavyweight class who is not controlled in whole or in part by the New York mob."[77] Walcott, who later served as a boxing regulator in New Jersey, had his own ties to Palermo through his aide Felix Bocchicchio, who, said a biographer, was "known or suspected to have fixed dozens of prizefights" over the years. (As was noted, the fact that reporters, too, were "on the take" hampered the ability to disseminate this news.[78]) In any event, Walcott's aide was supposedly so crooked he "had to screw his socks on."[79] Walcott was a cash cow for the morally purblind. In 1948, his bout with Louis increased revenue sharply in Albany, due in large part to a motion picture tax.[80]

But it was not just Walcott, who had roots in Camden, conveniently in reach of mob-infested Philadelphia. Walter Winchell, the tabloid gossip-monger, was told that "Frankie Carbo was very much in the [Rocky] Marciano background," referring to the undefeated heavyweight champion, whose ascendancy was viewed, by some, as restoring the "norm" before the arrival of Jack Johnson and Joe Louis, i.e., restoring the paramount role of men defined as "white" as the emperor of masculinity. Marciano was so heralded that the fabulously wealthy comedian Bob Hope—formerly a boxer known as Packy East—was seeking to produce a movie glamorizing his life. "Frankie Carbo was very much in the Marciano background" was the message transmitted, though this could be hard to glorify on the silver screen. Mr. Gray "had his henchmen trying to fix at least two fights against Rocky," that is, "Carbo was betting against Rocky" in that he "set up the first Joe Walcott-Marciano fight and bet heavily on Walcott," and tried to get the Italian-American puncher "blinded with…cayenne pepper."[81]

Marciano had his own potent allies. He was photographed more than once alongside Dwight D. Eisenhower, once with the president holding his massive fist.[82] Marciano's agent requested that the newly

---

77. Al Klein to Pat Murray, 21 November 1950, Box 39, ibid.

78. William Dettloff, *Ezzard Charles: A Boxing Life*, Jefferson, North Carolina: McFarland, 2015 (abbrev. Dettloff, *Ezzard Charles*), 19, 49.

79. James Curl, *Jersey Joe Walcott: A Boxing Biography*, Jefferson, North Carolina: McFarland, 2012, 44.

80. Report to Thomas J. Curran, 31 December 1948, NYSAC.

81. Vincent X. Flaherty to Walter Winchell, 23 May 1964, 4ZG40, Walter Winchell Papers, University of Texas-Austin.

82. Photo, 72-323.2.TIFF, Dwight D. Eisenhower Presidential Library, Abilene, Kansas (abbrev. DDEPL). At the same site, see also 72-232.1.TIFF.

inaugurated president be his guest during his 1953 bout with Ezzard Charles in Chicago.[83] Why would he not? By the time of their 1954 contest, there was spirited bidding for radio rights, claimed by Gillette, whose razor blades were flying off supermarket shelves and seemed to be part of the pugilistic landscape.[84]

Marciano also proved to be salve to the bruised egos of those who were disoriented by Negro domination of the heavyweight ranks: Louis, Walcott, Charles, et al. "Generally speaking," said one analyst in the hometown of Archie Moore, another contender, "Blacks had more opportunity in the lower weight classes, where if one of them beat a little white boy, it didn't seem so threatening to the pride of greater Caucasia [sic]"; thus, "in other places minority fighters could work only if they agreed to lie down for the white hopes."[85] It is hard to downplay the point that possibly the two best boxers of all time—featherweights Willie Pep, an Italian American, and Sandy Saddler of African ancestry with roots in the Caribbean—squared off more than once during this era, with the latter often triumphant, but this created hardly a stir, compared, for example, to the heavyweight bouts involving Marciano and his African-American competitors.[86] (The veteran journalist Bob Broeg was not alone in his assessment

---

83. Ben Bentley to James Hagerty, 28 March 1953, Box 190, DDEPL. At the same site see also Judith Tom to Dwight Eisenhower, 24 August 1948, Box 114, Principal File, Pre-Presidential Papers. This was an alleged fictional episode related to General Eisenhower: "Sometime during your mid-teens you—as Abilene's champion boxer—fought an exhibition match with a professional fighting under the name of Frankie Brown...admiring your skill, tried to persuade you to enter the ring professionally....you ended up convincing him that he should go back to school. Which he did." Eisenhower's predecessor George Washington was said to be a skilled boxer too: Undated Report, Odds and Ends on Boxing, Vol. XVII, UND.

84. Minutes, 8 October 1954, NYSAC.

85. Undated article on "The Ageless Warrior," likely a reference to Moore, in Moore material from the now defunct Hall of Champion Sports Museum, SDHC.

86. See undated report on Pep and Saddler, Odds and Ends on Boxing, Vol. XIX, UND: Saddler's roots were in Nevis and his father was a seafarer. There were "rumors" about a fixed fight when he knocked out Pep, an "accomplished drummer...born in Boston" but with roots in Hartford. Saddler fought quite a bit in Latin America; "he speaks Spanish," his "grandfather was Cuban," and he was on record as favoring boxing in Caracas more "than anywhere else."

that "Sugar Ray Robinson was great but pound for pound I thought Willie Pep was even better."[87])

As Gibson suggested, however, Robinson may have been "pound for pound" the most scrupulous of boxers in battling those across the negotiating table. In 1949, Robinson's team was complaining about a contract for a bout with Kid Gavilan that provided their man 40% of television rights and 16% to the Cuban. Robinson's team wanted to sell radio and television rights at a larger price than what was offered, and to that end brought in leading lawyer Arthur Garfield Hays to argue the point.[88] By 1957 Robinson was in a familiar posture, threatening to withdraw from a bout because of a dispute over closed-circuit television rights; he actually threatened to depart the ring if he detected radio or television transmission.[89] He had more options than most batterers: As of late 1952, regulators were wondering if he "planned to continue in the ring or adopt a theatrical career since he is now a successful song and dance performer."[90]

Yet Gibson, too, had cards to play: Regulators felt that no entity could match what he and his International Boxing Club could deliver in the form of "enormous television, theatre-television or movie profits."[91] It was hard to quarrel with Robinson's disputatiousness since his competitor as a pre-eminent boxer, Sandy Saddler, in 1951 was reduced to begging for a boxing license after a suspension. "Boxing is my bread and butter," he cried, "I have no other means of earning a livelihood."[92] His illustrious opponent Willie Pep was facing being barred from the ring as of 1954: "Willie's reflexes are gone" was the considered opinion, and also "gone" were ever lusher paydays.[93] "There comes a time in every athlete's life," said an examining clinician, "when it is time to retire," and besides, "Pep is over the hill."[94] Those who failed to emulate "Sugar Ray" often ended up like Saddler.

---

87. Undated report by Broeg, Sub Group X, Series I, Box 15, HKBA.
88. Minutes, 26 May 1949, NYSAC.
89. Minutes, 26 August 1957, NYSAC.
90. Minutes, 5 December 1952, NYSAC.
91. Minutes, 28 November 1952, NYSAC.
92. Sandy Saddler to Commissioner Robert Christenberry, 24 October 1951, NYSAC.
93. Minutes, 5 March 1954, NYSAC.
94. Minutes, 9 April 1954, NYSAC.

Hence, the leverage Robinson wielded was unusual—and justifiable—in an apartheid society. As the prime contests increasingly involved, for example, Ezzard Charles battling Walcott, or Turpin fighting Robinson, the declining Mike Jacobs asked querulously, "Have Negroes killed boxing?" He made the "claim that domination of [the] ring has caused [a] big slump at [the] gate.... this charge has been made increasingly during the past couple of years.... one Connecticut promoter even went so far to say, 'there is no chance in the ring for a white boy.'" There was an insistent rumble that maintained that "All Negro cards are bad bets": The "Ezzard Charles-Jersey Joe Walcott heavyweight title bout...which drew less than 25,000 is often cited as an example of the danger of matching two Negroes."[95] (The two punchers fought more than once and the audience may have declined owing to this factor as much as any other.) But what Jacobs did not contemplate, in any case, is a reconfiguring of two Negro contestants, featuring, e.g., Floyd Patterson (Negro good guy) vs. Sonny Liston (Negro bad guy), or Joe Frazier (Negro good guy) vs. Muhammad Ali (Black bad guy). This was how desegregation adapted to an older plot—from Johnson to Liston to Ali. And Jacobs may not have been an astute student of history: Did not the "battle royal" involve Negro combatants?

By late 1952, a reporter noticed that Chris Dundee was making plans for a "second all-Negro main event" at the "Miami Beach Auditorium," this "after being elated over the dividends last night's fight brought to his wallet.... the first had been a success, drawing the largest crowd in the history of the auditorium."[96] This was a feat in that Ferdie Pacheco, who was to become wealthier because of his association with Ali, recalled later in South Florida, "a rule prohibiting a bout between a white and a black man."[97] A problem, rarely glimpsed then, was that so many Negro men were bedazzled by the apparent riches accruing to Louis, Walcott, Robinson, Turpin, Saddler, and others, that in the absence of other opportunities in an apartheid society, they were pouring into boxing, creating unavoidable all-Negro matchups. Ezzard Charles's biographer noticed that during his subject's heyday there was a "Black Murderers' Row"

---

95. Report by Mike Jacobs, ca. 1953, Odds and Ends on Boxing, Vol. XXIV, UND.

96. *Miami Daily News*, 19 November 1952, Sub Group X, Series I, Box 37, HKBA.

97. Pacheco, *Tales*, 144.

among middleweights and lightweights, most of whom never got a title shot.[98]

Worse, from the viewpoint of apartheid, was that presiding over this Negro traffic jam at the top of the sport was yet another Negro, Truman Gibson. It would not be difficult to dislodge him, not least since his job involved consorting with racketeers, who were eminently fungible: Imprison one and replace him with another.

---

98. Dettloff, *Ezzard Charles*, 68.

Chapter 6

No "White Hope"?

As the 1950s unwound, Truman Gibson seemed to be cruising along nicely. He was graciously receiving encomia from legislators sending "heartiest congratulations" in his role as the face of the successful enterprise that was televised boxing.[1] Reporters from eminent periodicals like the *New York Times* were interviewing him as he pontificated about his sport being an essential part of the booming industry that was television and made to order for peddling beer, razors, and deodorant. "I keep in close touch with the Nielsen TV ratings and they do influence our thinking," he confided. Yes, his enterprise "always tried to provide sponsors with lively, free swinging showy fighters" since the "fight fan wanted to see knockdowns on his home screen," a cultural indicator that the man knowingly identified as "formerly Joe Louis' attorney" did not ponder.[2] But already there were troubling signs that he must have noticed, since he retained the newspaper articles that reflected the increasing jeopardy in which he found himself. For it was also in 1958 that, inaccurately and huffily, he told the *New York Herald Tribune*, "I have never associated with Frankie Carbo and won't start now." Almost daring his detractors to pounce, he mentioned offhandedly, "I have been accused of having 'capacious pockets and rapacious hands,'" a charge that he did not deny, as he may have raised dangerous echoes of the Jack Johnson era, except the Negro now was not a performer but ostensibly in charge. The reporter noted that he had a reputation for "proficiency as a poker player" but, ironically, he did not display the deftness expected of a card shark in this interview.[3]

For if he had paid attention to the reports emanating from his hometown he might have played his cards closer to his vest. A

---

1. James Thomas, New York State Assembly, to Gibson, 24 April 1958, Box 2, Gibson-LC.
2. *New York Times*, 23 April 1958, Box 2, Gibson-LC.
3. *New York Herald Tribune*, 23 April 1958, Box 2, Gibson-LC.

Chicago columnist referred to him contemptuously as "this phony, baloney guy" who wasn't simply "satisfied with controlling boxing. He also controls 2 colored insurance companies…[and a] hotel on the Southside of Chicago," that, he said with a mixture of wonder and unease, was "one of those plush affairs, wall to wall carpeting"[4]: The implication left hanging forebodingly in the air was that this was much too nice for the Negroes. Another column, oozing nastiness, spat out a troubling definition: "a leech is a double breasted bloodsucker like Truman K. Gibson…this burglar who is a licensed attorney." Amazingly, he compared the mild-mannered executive to Adolf Hitler. Ominously, this column was reprinted,[5] giving these unfounded charges added ventilation. Yet another commentator in 1956 referred to Gibson as "the man behind the scenes making the IBC [International Boxing Club] tick is a cunning 43 year old lawyer whose word is absolute law," an unusual position for a Negro to be in during the Jim Crow era. He was depicted as spending quality time with retired champion Joe Louis, and lolling around the Virgin Islands, where his comrade William Hastie had previously served as a colonial administrator.

Perhaps because of saturation of the airwaves, perhaps because of what Mike Jacobs had noted earlier (a surfeit of Negro boxers), perhaps because of a late blooming revulsion toward men pounding each other's skulls—or all of the foregoing—there were signs that the popularity of boxing may have reached a plateau in the 1950s. At least that was the conclusion of an aficionado and screenwriter who incorporated pugilistic themes in his cinematic creations. "Professional boxing has virtually died in New Jersey and many other states," groaned Budd Schulberg. Indicative that television plus Negro boxers might have been the underlying explanation of what he detected, was his assessment that "on the campus," e.g., Notre Dame, "it is a lively, major sport, outdrawing basketball, swimming, baseball and every other activity except King Football," which, too, featured a modicum of head-knocking. Boxing had "been a popular sport at Notre Dame since 1923 when it was first introduced by Knute Rockne,"[6] the football coach, whose fame also included the

---

4. *Nite Life* column by Jack Begun, August 1958, Sub Group X, Series I, Box 14, HKBA.

5. Column, August 1958, and *Plain Talk* [Miami], 16 August 1958, Sub Group X, Series I, Box 14, HKBA.

6. Schulberg column, *Sports Illustrated*, 4 April 1955, Sub Group X, Series I, Box 17, HKBA. For 1956 comment, see Clipping, February 1956, Sub Series VIII, Series I, Box 9, HKBA.

silver screen. It is worthy of mention that overwhelmingly, most of the boxers competing then in South Bend were of European extraction. It was not just so for Notre Dame, where boxing, as it was said, "ruled supreme": The Jim Crow University of Virginia could be seen similarly.[7] But soon, this intercollegiate sport began to shrink, and one possible reason was the proliferation of boxing on television, not only providing competition for spectators but reinforcing the sport's image as a Negro enterprise, spearheaded by a Negro—Gibson—and therefore inappropriate for "Fighting Irish" and "Cavaliers" both.

But it was not just university boxing squads that were impacted. According to writer Arthur Mann, "One by one television has emptied the little neighborhood and suburban fight club. Now it's killin' the small-city club. Who will pay two to five dollars to attend a local fight between third-raters, no matter how good, when they can stay home or hang out at a bar and get close-ups of big names?" It was also Mann who opined that "people attend fights, see idols destroyed and then mourn at their passing."[8] The problem for the sport was that too often the "idols destroyed" often resembled the majority population of the settler regime.

Another source in 1955 found "there were 17,487 native born licensed boxers in the U.S. during 1931" and "slightly more than 2000 today," a presumed staggering drop, made more complicated by the fact that those remaining at the top were mostly Negroes in a society still driven by Jim Crow. (Indeed, the seeming precipitous fall of boxers overall may have been connected precisely to the rise of Negro boxers and a reluctance of some to tangle with them.) Plus there was an attractive lure that may help shed light on why Carnera and Schmeling began to replace the likes of Braddock, for U.S. boxers were taxed 25 percent of their earnings in most European countries, but foreign fighters paid only five percent state and a small federal tax then.[9] For it was well established that the search for a "White Hope" did not rule out the crowning of a European, not just a Euro-American.

This desperate search for a "White Hope" may have led to the 1957 rebranding when boxer Ralph Dupas of Louisiana was adjudged to be "white"—and certainly not a despised person of color or a

---

7. Undated report by Bobby Goldstein, Sub Group X, Series I, Box 10, HKBA.
8. Undated narrative, Box 16, Mann-LC.
9. Report, ca. 1955, Sub Group X, Series I, Box 32, HKBA.

Negro—so he could contest fighters already so defined.[10] This to and fro was part of the racial reshuffling that accompanied the agonized retreat from the more egregious aspects of Jim Crow. Thus, Negro lightweight Joe Brown of New Orleans sued and a civil court judge upheld the decision of the Louisiana State Athletic Commission ban on "mixed" bouts; he cited a Texas decision allowing such.[11]

However, in 1959, in a monumental decision in retrospect, the high court in the U.S. invalidated the Pelican State's ban on athletic competition across the color line,[12] a belated reaction to Jack Johnson in Reno in 1910 and the beginning of desegregation of the sports juggernaut more generally: This created a cornucopia of wealth, some of which trickled down to Negroes, elevating their class status and increasing their ability to contribute to anti-Jim Crow causes more generally. The next year—1960—the boxer then known as Cassius Clay departed the Rome Olympics triumphant, and then instigated yet another new departure for the tortured and torturing sport.

* * *

It was also in the mid-1950s that Aldo Spoldi, an Italian visitor, underscored the difference between Europeans and those boxers he witnessed in the U.S. "In Europe we go in for science," he maintained. "The boxers try to pile up points; make the other fellows miss," utilizing "the technical angles of one man by his speed and skill trying to outpoint another...while in the United States fighters are sluggers, who try for the big kayo,"[13] a point validated by Gibson. "The fans want someone demolished." His interviewer, Ralph Warner, remarked that "of all European fighters, Frenchmen are the nearest to Americans,"[14] maybe a veiled reference to the late Marcel Cerdan who was associated with France, though he was of North African descent actually.

This preconception led to enhanced popularity for Ingemar Johansson, the Swedish heavyweight. Even the manager of "Sugar" Ray Robinson announced in 1958 that "I just want a white champion because the fight game desperately needs a white champion" and it would profit him, too, if one could be found, setting up what

---

10. *Miami Herald*, 28 August 1957, Sub Group X, Series I, Box 13, HKBA.
11. *Miami Herald*, 18 August 1955, Sub Group X, Series I, Box 13, HKBA.
12. *Newark Star*, 25 May 1959, Sub Group X, Series I, Box 13, HKBA.
13. *Miami Daily News*, ca. 1955, Sub Group X, Series 1, Box 39, HKBA.
14. *Miami Daily News*, ca. 1955, Sub Group X, Series I, Box 39, HKBA.

amounted to racial battles, that had proven their profitability, and danger, in Reno in 1910.[15] Things had gotten so desperate that the *Miami Daily News* said hopefully but incoherently, given international tensions, that Moscow had the "best 'White Hope'" for the "heavyweight championship."[16]

But then Floyd Patterson, who represented what amounted to the "Negro Restoration" after the brief reign of Marciano as heavyweight champion, felt compelled to deny that he was "raising" a "'White Hope' dispute before" his eagerly awaited bout with Euro-American contestant, Pete Rademacher. With a tad of tactlessness, the heavyweight with the peek-a-boo style, keeping the gloves high, blocking (it was hoped) blows to the skull, argued that "even if I did feel that way, I surely wouldn't say anything like that publicly." Others thought that Rademacher, a raw recruit in a sense, did not earn this lucrative match, but instead represented something often seen but rarely discussed in sport, "affirmative action" for Euro-Americans, boosting them into prominence over more qualified Negroes. (Though the rationale for this kind of positive discrimination was generally that the targeted group had suffered bias that this measure was designed to overcome, in this case, it was precisely the opposite: It was just a new form of a veritably eternal favoritism sculpted to benefit Euro-Americans.) Incautiously, Patterson declared that the "'White Hope' angle was the motivating factor behind the whole concept of the fight" in that "the Georgians who put up the money were thinking strictly in terms of a white man unseating a colored champion"[17]—and were to be disappointed when their man went down to defeat in the midst of stirring battles against Jim Crow, which they thought a Rademacher triumph could halt, at least temporarily.

President Eisenhower often temporized as these anti-Jim Crow struggles unfolded, though he did send troops to Little Rock, Arkansas, in 1957 to enforce desegregation at Central High School. Even then there were tremendous external pressures, including the U.S. losing "face" in Africa as Ghana surged to independence and as Moscow sent a satellite into outer space, garnering immeasurable prestige.[18] His experience as a boxer did not seem to help him in Arkansas, as he did not display nimbleness, nor the ability to land a

---

15. *Miami Herald*, 10 August 1958, Sub Group X, Series I, Box 7, HKBA.
16. *Miami Daily News*, 13 April 1950, Sub Group X, Series I, Box 9, HKBA.
17. *Miami Herald*, 2 August 1957, Sub Group X, Series I, Box 11, HKBA.
18. Horne, *White Supremacy*.

devastating blow. "When I was quite young," he said, "a number of us used to box."[19] Upon reaching the White House—and on the verge of a second term—he recalled that "boys in those days were raised for one-two things: work, and then they made their play, and if you couldn't play baseball and box and play football, why, your life was ended. That was in our boyish minds."[20] As president, Eisenhower sought to capitalize upon the popularity of boxing, especially among men, a trend propelled by the myth that he had boxed Knute Rockne, the renowned football coach at Notre Dame.[21] Lester Granger of the National Urban League, a grouping that served Negroes, sensed the president's pro-boxing sympathies and suggested he send Ezzard Charles on a tour of Ghana and Africa, which would lessen the sting in African minds delivered by Jim Crow and blunt any leanings toward Moscow.[22] Joe Louis, retired once more, sought to board this gravy train when he advised the Amateur Athletic Union, previously comfortable with Jim Crow but now pivoting toward the new order, that he would help them "to further international goodwill," which anti-racist measures would enhance.[23] Archie Moore, who was to controversially lambaste those engaged in civil unrest in Detroit in the following decade, sought the favor of the president when in 1955 he asked him to be his guest at his much-awaited bout with Marciano in Yankee Stadium.[24] (Maybe if the president had accepted, the "Mongoose" would have had better luck: "white fighters wouldn't fight me, the important guys," said Moore—a category that apparently excluded Marciano whom, to be fair, he came close to defeating. He blamed the referee—Harry Kessler—for his defeat, an irony since both had roots in St. Louis.[25] Another observer said that Moore "took" a "dive" in this bout.)[26]

---

19. Dwight Eisenhower to Charles Harger, 4 December 1946, Box 52, DDEPL.

20. Eisenhower Speech, 24 October 1956, Box 18, Speech Series, Ann Whitman File, DDEPL.

21. Congressman John Beamer to President Eisenhower, 28 May 1958, Box 190, Central Files/General Files, DDEPL.

22. Lester Granger to Max Raab, 29 March 1957, Box 190, Central Files/General Files, DDEPL.

23. Joe Louis to A.L. Neff, chair of International Great Northwestern Diamond Belt AAU Boxing Championship, 30 December 1955, Box 617, White House Central File/Official File, DDEPL.

24. Archie Moore to President Eisenhower, 21 August 1955, Box 190, Central Files/General Files, DDEPL.

25. Heller, *In This Corner*, 313.

26. Tosches, *The Devil*, 81.

Floyd Patterson was crowned the new heavyweight champion at a time when the political climate was not conducive to the re-emergence of an updated version of Jack Johnson; nor during a time when various iterations of progressivism were demonized as "Communism" was the time ripe for a version of Joe Louis circa 1947. Patterson was also lucky in facing overmatched opponents, like Tommy "Hurricane" Jackson, who incautiously "blamed" his mother for his losses, since "she was nagging him."[27] Yet there was momentum to eradicate the ugly stain of Jim Crow, at least officially, from the nation's escutcheon. Patterson, born in Shelby, North Carolina, returned to his hometown in 1959 for a bracing visit. Louis Lefkowitz, attorney general in the state of New York which he now called home, was told that "Floyd" during a recent visit to Shelby, "had…trouble finding a place to eat and sleep," which did not encourage him to pursue a plan of "building some motels with restaurants for his people."[28] Despite Patterson's public presentation as soft-spoken and the polar opposite of Johnson, the fact was that like many Negro celebrities, he consorted with Dr. Martin Luther King, Jr. at a time when he was still reviled as a "Communist sympathizer" and before his posthumous rehabilitation or distortion as a "safe," "vanilla" "moderate." They rubbed shoulders, said the boxer, "in Birmingham, at Jackson, then at Selma."[29]

But sending Ezzard Charles to Africa to trumpet the supposed new dispensation "for his people," while Patterson was enduring an enervating Jim Crow, was not a sustainable combination and eventually had to yield. The fact that Patterson as a result of his ring earnings now had the capital to build "motels" and "restaurants" gave impetus to this new order of things that was rapidly coming into being. Thus after the president's victorious re-election campaign in 1956, a writer for the *Pittsburgh Courier* was delighted to report that "the colored voters finally saw the light and voted in large numbers for President Eisenhower" and he wanted "this trend to continue in even greater numbers." How to do this given the heavy lift of overcoming more pleasant memories of the New Deal? "Floyd Patterson is the greatest hero of America since Joe Louis,"[30] so invite him and his manager, Cus D'Amato, to the White House.

---

27. Minutes, 28 April 1954, NYSAC.
28. Oliver Anthony to Louis Lefkowitz, 29 March 1960, Box 1055, Central Files/General Files, DDEPL.
29. *New York Post*, 8 April 1968, Sub Group XV, Series XIII, Box 46, HKBA.
30. James Edmund Boyack to James Hagerty, 8 July 1957, Box 1055, Central Files/General Files, DDEPL.

As other groups saw the benefits that flowed to Negroes from protest and a changed global climate, they, too, began to clamor. Just before the high court invalidated Jim Crow in 1954, James Ziccardi of Brooklyn complained to President Eisenhower that the Athletic Commission of the State of New York had "shown a tendency of discrimination" disadvantaging "Italian boxers;"[31] it was unclear what he meant. Still, this had the potential to lead in contrasting directions: either seeking to destabilize the anti-Jim Crow movement on the premise that it was in turn destabilizing white supremacy, or creating another rivulet to flow into a larger anti-bigotry agenda. As matters unfolded in coming decades, it appeared that the former proposition prevailed.

Italian-American mobsters already had to cede partial control of boxing to Negroes, suggesting that the anti-Jim Crow movement might not have been an unalloyed asset for this ethnic group. It was in 1958 that the FBI was investigating Patterson's bout with Roy Harris, the pride and joy of Cut and Shoot, Texas, and was on the trail of Carbo. This brought Special Agent Raymond J. McCarthy to Baja California, Mexico, for interviews, where he ascertained that Carbo had been spotted conferring with Al Weill, known to have ties to Madison Square Garden[32]—but that's as far as his investigation proceeded.

This FBI testimony was just another signal of how exposed Gibson was—whether he knew it or not. The nightmare was punctuated when Carbo had gone into hiding before the July 1958 indictment. He left his Florida home alongside what was described as a "well-formed" blonde companion, fleeing along a winding trail that led to Palm Springs then Reno, then Camden, New Jersey, across the bridge from his usual haunts in Philadelphia. He was captured on 31 May 1959 as he was observed watching a late night movie on television. He sprinted to a rear bedroom and climbed out of a window before being nabbed. Because of an ulcer, he was placed in a prison hospital.[33]

---

31. James Ziccardi to President Eisenhower, 11 April 1954, Box 1055, Central Files/General Files, DDEPL.

32. Affidavit, Raymond J. McCarthy, 2 December 1961, RG 21, U.S. District Court for the Central Court of California, Central Division (Los Angeles), Criminal Case Files, 27973, Box 1712, National Archives and Records Administration-Riverside, California. Hereafter abbrev. as Gibson Trial File-NAR-Riv.

33. Wager, op. cit., 46-49, 61, Ellison-LC.

Thus, when Gibson was put on trial beside Carbo and Palermo in Los Angeles in 1961, in a case involving attempting to muscle in improperly on the control of the compromised boxer Don Jordan, it was too late to recognize the jeopardy that had ensnared him. Just as the words in the trial often spoke to events in the 1950s when he was still riding high, the same held true for the damning testimony of Jack Leonard, also known as Leonard Blakely, a star witness for the prosecution. "I was a matchmaker and promoter of the Hollywood Legion Stadium," referring to the former citadel of Jim Crow. Before the tumult of this trial, he was meeting with Gibson, who received a call and said simply, "It's Blinky," speaking of the ill-regarded Palermo. He handed the phone to Leonard, who was told by the mobster that he and his crew would receive "Half" of the revenues of an upcoming fight—or it would not occur. Gibson then seemed to play the "good cop" to Palermo's "bad cop," counseling compromise, lest untoward consequences ensued—with the Philadelphian looming menacingly as to what those dire results might entail. Leonard repaired to Gibson's fashionable and comfortable bungalow at the Ambassador Hotel, where he resided when in the City of Angels, and to evade surveillance, called Palermo again, from a pay telephone, about the upcoming bout featuring the rising welterweight Jordan in contestation with Virgil Akins, whom the Philadelphian controlled. Matters seemed to be spinning out of control, for Palermo requested that Leonard fly to Miami to meet with the money man, Jim Norris. He did so, then watched agape as Chris Dundee and Carbo conferred with Mr. Gray becoming upset about perceived lack of flexibility on Leonard's part—so, naturally, the gangster threatened to "gouge my eyes out...I was really scared." Carbo was upset, and when that happened, mutilation could easily ensue.[34] The predictable occurred: By early June 1959, Leonard was found unconscious in his garage, after repetitive "threats of violence" were leveled at him by Gibson's co-defendants, but not the Chicagoan himself,[35] who apparently was too refined for such ruffian tactics. In addition to intimidating Leonard, this roughhouse method was a signal to others in the field, too, since the Californian was no novice, having arranged the boisterous bout between Bobo Olson and "Sugar" Ray Robinson in 1956.[36]

---

34. Testimony of Jack Leonard, 2 March 1961, Box 2483, Gibson Trial File-NAR-Riv.

35. Colloquy by Prosecutor Alvin Goldstein, 3 March 1961, Box 2483, Gibson Trial File-NAR-Riv.

36. Testimony of Jack Leonard, 7 March 1961, Box 2483, Gibson Trial File-NAR-Riv.

Leonard also happened to be in Chicago for Robinson's bloody battle with Carmen Basilio in 1958. "I went there to be bawled out by Mr. Carbo, not to make fights," he explained.[37] Basilio testified that he had visited Carbo's Miami home then, where Palermo was also present—curious associations for a leading boxer.[38] (Subsequently, this fighter's co-managers, Joe Netro and John De John, said they were "front men" for Carbo.)[39] Also managing Basilio was Gabe Genovese, who eventually was indicted for "being an 'undercover' manager."[40]

Thus, Mr. Gray's sallow complexion seemed to be purpling as he "bawled out" Leonard. He "got real mad at me," said Leonard, and "he said I should use [Al] Weill's fighters," speaking of the main man at Madison Square Garden, "because he had a made a lot of money with Weill...he was just shouting."[41] Earlier, Leonard had received an award for "doing the most for boxing" from Los Angeles sportswriters, who either were unaware of his more dastardly ties or chose not to burden their readers with the seamy details.[42]

Earlier, before departing the Ambassador, Gibson was "very indignant," according to Leonard, "that they shouldn't try to do something like that, especially in view of all of the heat that was on them at the time," a reference to the walls closing in on them all.[43] Gibson was being fingered by a number of witnesses, including the man once known as Jackie McCoy of Torrance, California (also known as Warren Wayland Spaw), who operated a liquor store and once sold used cars: He saw Gibson at an April 1959 match in St. Louis featuring Don Jordan, known to be mob controlled.[44] Coincidentally enough, according to St. Louis police officer Edmund Moran, Palermo, too, was at ringside during the Jordan fight, where 7500 were present, guaranteeing significant revenue to Jordan's

---

37. Testimony of Jack Leonard, 9 March 1961, Box 2483, Gibson Trial File-NAR-Riv.

38. Testimony of Carmen Basilio, 4-5 April 1961, Box 2485, Gibson Trial File-NAR-Riv.

39. *Miami Daily News*, 25 June 1959, Sub Group XV, Series VII, Box 34, HKBA.

40. Minutes, 14 February 1964, NYSAC.

41. Testimony of Jack Leonard, 10 March 1961, Box 2484, Gibson Trial File-NAR-Riv.

42. Ibid.

43. Testimony of Jack Leonard, 14 March 1961, Box 2484, Gibson Trial File-NAR-Riv.

44. Testimony of Warren Wayland Spaw, 16 March 1961, Box 2484, Gibson Trial File-NAR-Riv.

opponent, Akins, whose manager Eddie Yawitz was close to Morris Shenker, an attorney known to be close to Palermo.[45] (Just before this, promoter Jimmy White was indicted for seeking to fix Akins's bout with Cuban-born welterweight Isaac Logart).[46]

Also part of the Akins team was Bernard Glickman, a man of questionable ethics, who nonetheless informed congressional investigators "that Truman Gibson is a liar."[47] Glickman—and, to be fair, many managers and handlers—comported with the assertion of Allan Klein of the Pennsylvania Athletic Commission, who informed the U.S. Senate in 1959 that "probably anywhere from 65 to 75 percent of the boys now in boxing are Negroes," while the "largest number of managers, the majority of managers are white"[48]: This was the arc of the evolution of the sport since the days of Gans and Johnson.

Jordan was no choirboy, and it was an ominous sign when he turned up as a witness against Gibson. Born in the Dominican Republic, he once proclaimed astonishingly, "I killed thirty people in one month" as he was living the "life of a hired assassin [i.e.] to kill people.... we used poison dart, straight in the neck. Put fluid in the brain, it kills the body very quick," he said with confidence. This self-described "half breed Indian" spent a spell in a prison cell in the U.S., which coarsened him tremendously: "they used to beat the shit out of me," he said. It was possibly worse when he became a prizefighter. "The Cosa Nostra is a worldwide organization," he said. "You want to know why they control boxing? It's poor, hungry people," like himself: "I was like a slave to them.... fights I fought were prearranged, before I even entered the ring. I knew who was going to win," a boon to certain gamblers and a bane to others. But even the coarsening that he endured could hardly explain his coda: "I don't give a damn about a woman," he yelped, illustrating the worst aspects of the androcentric aspects of the sport and prison life, too. "A woman is a cow."[49]

Jordan may have been infected by the poisonous environment that surrounded him. The scandalous Mickey Cohen boasted that

---

45. Testimony of Edmund Moran, 24 March 1961, Box 2485, Gibson Trial File-NAR-Riv.

46. *Miami Daily News*, 11 July 1958, Sub Group X, Series I, Box 13, HKBA.

47. Testimony of Bernard Glickman, 5-9 and 12-14 December 1959, Hearings Before the Subcommittee on Antitrust and Monopoly Committee on Judiciary, U.S. Senate, 86th Congress, 2nd Session, Part II, Kefauver-UTn-K.

48. Testimony of Allan Klein, Senate Hearings, Box 490, Kefauver-UTn-K.

49. Heller, *In this Corner*, 359.

"I managed Don Jordan, the welterweight champion of the world" and "had him in the company of Judy [Garland] a few times." What choices did Jordan have in this respect? For Cohen was close to Harry Martin, "Boxing Commissioner" in the Golden State, who was married to the powerful gossip columnist Louella Parsons—"he was even a better friend to me [than she] was," he bragged, indicative of the influence he could wield on Jordan's behalf. "Very important to me," blabbed Cohen, was "who was the Chief of Police" in Los Angeles, since "I had gambling joints all over the city and I needed the police just to make sure they ran efficiently." The top cop "was chosen by the Board of Commissioners, so we had connections on the Board who were going to make sure another connection of ours got named." Furthermore, Cohen had his own "relationship with the legitimate Los Angeles banker, Harold Brown," suggesting he would not be deprived of access to capital. When crooner Frank Sinatra, who had his own interest in boxing, was "going pretty bad," it was Cohen who stepped up and "had this testimonial dinner for him at the Beverly Hills Hotel." It was no surprise, therefore, that Jordan would find it attractive to be yoked to Cohen—and just absorb the poison that oozed from every pore of this association.[50]

Moreover, as one drilled down deeper into the essence of boxing, it was possible to ascertain that boxers' choices could be terribly limited: If one were in a bout with a pre-arranged result, should one be the one who remains standing, arms aloft in victory—or bloodily prone on the canvas? The answer depended in part on who was slated to win—or lose—and not who was most talented. Thus, within days in 1956 the Negro puncher Tommy Campbell admitted that he agreed to lose a lightweight bout to Art Aragon (and another to Del Flanagan),[51] then Carlos Chavez admitted that he too agreed to lose to Aragon.[52] More often than not, working with Cohen meant that one was more likely to remain standing (and not permanently horizontal), enhancing one's future earnings in the process. Jordan was viewed as a premier fighter, yet he, too, once confessed that he threw a fight before denying same.[53] The corruption of the sport did

---

50. Cohen, *Mickey Cohen*, 88, 109, 146-148. Pianist and singer Nat "King" Cole also had a financial interest in boxing: Report to Robert E. Tiffany, Deputy Commissioner, 14 April 1961, NYSAC.

51. *Miami Daily News*, 21 March 1956, Sub Group X, Series I, Box 13, HKBA.

52. *Miami Herald*, 29 March 1956, Sub Group X, Series I, Box 13, HKBA.

53. See Los Angeles Police Department File on Jordan, 26 August 1959; *Los Angeles Mirror*, 6 November 1959; and undated picture of Jordan and

not just turn on "throwing" fights. The analyst Arthur Mann found that a "fighter's won or loss record depended largely on the speed of his manager in racing to the single telephone booth with a biased report or even an untruthful one," transmitting an often fabricated outcome to a credulous journalist.[54]

And the corruption did not end there either. What was described as "boxing's best kept secret" was "the 'opponent'" who "will rarely take an outright dive," said boxing commentator Steve Losch. "If he wins too often, promoters will shy away from him," so he had to lose credibly, making the victor look good. "Professional boxing is the only big time sport based on deception," and the "opponent" was an essential part of this framework. "Promoters often give out doctored records" in any event: *The Ring*, the official "record book," was notoriously studded with inaccuracies and incompletions—not to mention "only a fraction of the fighters in the world." The "latest gimmick," he said, "is for notorious black losers to adopt a Muslim moniker." They were a favorite "opponent" of Euro-American punchers, as if this were a re-creation of a religion *cum* race war (and perhaps underscoring Ali's ability to sell tickets to his fights). "Unemployed black teenagers" also were favored, as these youth were fodder for the boosting of tattered racial egos, and would fight for as little as $75. In Philadelphia, John Barr supplied these "tomato cans" and in New England the man to see was Vito Tallarita.[55]

Jordan's reversal in sum—admitting to corrupt matches, then denying it—was not just an indication that it was unwise to reveal dirty secrets that could expose cutthroats. It was also a muffled expression of the wider point that among all the various enterprises of racketeers—drugs, prostitution, restaurants, murder-for-hire, etc.—gambling, in the words of a keen observer, was becoming the "backbone" of their varied interests.[56] This was happening as Las Vegas was taking off, bringing Nevada back to the pole position it had abandoned, post-Reno 1910, a process that would accelerate further when the thugs were compelled to liquidate their interests in Havana after 1959. This had placed Gibson under further pressure,

---

Cohen in Box 129, RG 118, Records of U.S. Attorneys, Central Judicial District of California, Los Angeles, Selected Criminal Case Files, NA Identifier 38995426, NAR-Riv.

54. Mann, "Boxer Rebellion," ca. 1950s, Box 13, Mann-LC.

55. Steve Losch, "Boxing's Best Kept Secret," no date, Sub Group VIII, Series III, Box 48, HKBA.

56. *Chicago Daily News*, ca. 1955, Box 48, Kefauver-UTn-K. On Nevada's rise, post-1945, see Horne, *Jazz*.

as the riches generated by boxing rose sharply since the relatively tame time that he had entered the sport in 1949.

* * *

John Bonomi was flown to Los Angeles in order to impeach Gibson's credibility further during his federal trial in 1961. A lawyer, he had served on the staff of the U.S. Senate Subcommittee on Antitrust and Monopoly when Gibson was grilled there. Wisely, Gibson's attorney, William Ming, sought to forestall damaging testimony by stipulating that the earlier congressional transcript be admitted as evidence, but the prosecution balked and, instead, Bonomi unloaded on Gibson. He recounted in excruciating detail how Gibson had hired Viola Masters, Carbo's spouse, for a lucrative job in order to mask payments to Mr. Gray himself.[57]

Aileen Eaton, the rare woman who operated as a promoter—in her case for about two decades—confirmed that Leonard's reputation was not stellar. She and Leonard were the only promoters in Los Angeles then, she said, and thus she, too, was familiar with Carbo. She and Leonard competed, perhaps undermining her negative assessments; they competed for access to the Olympic Stadium, with 10,400 seats, since the Hollywood Legion Stadium, with 6,200, where Leonard had reigned, was now a "bowling alley."[58]

As for Gibson, he was president of the Norris-Carbo business known as the "International Boxing Club" which, he told the court, was "wholly owned" by Madison Square Garden, whereas the IBC in Chicago was owned by Norris and Arthur Wirtz. Gibson shuttled between the two cities and managed to arrange 104 fights in 1958 alone in the process; this involved hundreds of meetings and calls, though he denied owning interests in any fighters or even a tiny percentage of same. Under oath, he admitted that he had met Carbo as early as 1950 and knew Palermo and his fighters, too—Johnny Saxton, Ike Williams, Coolie Wallace, Young Jack Johnson, et al. He spoke with Palermo "frequently," he said.[59]

However, he insisted stoutly, "I have only one boss and that is James D. Norris," and less resolutely added, "neither Mr. Norris nor

---

57. Testimony of William Bonomi, 24 March 1961, Box 2485, Gibson Trial File-NAR-Riv.

58. Testimony of Aileen Eaton, 24 March 1961, Box 2485, Gibson Trial File-NAR-Riv.

59. Testimony of Truman Gibson, 20 April 1961, Box 2486, Gibson Trial File-NAR-Riv.

I have anything to do with Blinky," contradicting himself in response to Leonard calling Palermo "your boss."[60]

It was boxing, a sport increasingly dominated by Negro men, that provided the opportunity for him to ascend the ladder of success. Yet this was occurring in a Jim Crow society and thus he was bound to attract negative attention. What other Negro in 1958 had more than three offices? "A law office," he testified, and "an office in the insurance company with which I was connected," and "an office in the Chicago Stadium," and "an office in New York." But this bounty came with a stiff price. He walked a fine line, denying intimacy with Carbo but noting the obvious: "I am acquainted with him." Under intense questioning, he denied making payments to Mr. Gray. Yes, he said, "I was Vice-President of Telradio" and, yes, funds from this entity were funneled indirectly to Carbo via Norris and Viola Masters, the intimate partner of Mr. Gray—though he did not know this; however, he knew Masters well enough to recognize her as "the charming blonde lady in the first row."[61]

Gibson was portrayed admirably by the judge: "he does protect himself and answers the questions with an analytical approach" since he was obviously "well-versed in the use of the English language."[62] But the prosecutor was not so kind, calling him "evasive and non-responsive," and a "quibbler" besides.[63] The prosecutor, as matters evolved, had a keener sense of where this trial was going, in part because he took a lengthy transcript from a congressional hearing in which Gibson testified where the rules of evidence were inapplicable, and then wielded it like a cudgel against him in federal court, where such rules were very much applicable. Thus at the expansive U.S. Senate hearing, Gibson was asked if it were company policy to "cooperate with these underworld elements," and he replied "to live with them…to maintain a free flow of fighters…without strikes, without sudden illnesses, without sudden postponements…we decided to live with Carbo"—so, yes, they did "cooperate," and that in essence marked the beginning of the end of Gibson's spectacular rise.[64] He

---

60. Testimony of Truman Gibson, 25 April 1961, Box 2486, Gibson Trial File-NAR-Riv.

61. Testimony of Truman Gibson, 26 April 1961, Box 2487, Gibson Trial File-NAR-Riv.

62. Comment by Judge, 27 April 1961, Box 2487, Gibson Trial File-NAR-Riv.

63. Comment by Prosecutor, 28 April 1961, Box 2487, Gibson Trial File-NAR-Riv.

64. Testimony of Truman Gibson, 28 April 1961, Box 2487, Gibson Trial File-NAR-Riv.

was at the center of a spider web that linked organized capital (Norris and Wirtz, who generally escaped punishment) with organized crime (Carbo and Palermo, who, like Gibson, were made to walk the plank).

Wirtz led many companies, including the firm that controlled the professional hockey franchise in Chicago, the Blackhawks: "we are happy to say," he said, they had just won the "Stanley Cup," the sport's top prize. Yes, "I know him very well," he said unremarkably about Gibson (Wirtz was also vice-chairman of Madison Square Garden). "His compensation was straight salary," he said of Gibson, who delivered bountiful profits to him, making the suave attorney a man who continued to be constrained by the rigidity of Jim Crow. No stock options were proffered to Gibson, in short, even after Norris had a heart attack and "resigned as president. Mr. Gibson became president of the New York company" and was brought into closer interaction with Dan Topping (who maintained a major interest in the perennial champions, baseball's New York Yankees) and Ned Irish, both of whom in a later generation would be considered part of the "1%," the winners of capitalism. The Wirtz-Gibson relationship began in 1949 as rising television revenues began to have "effect on our attendance at Chicago Stadium," seating 20,000, and Madison Square Garden, holding 20,000.[65] At that point, Gibson and Louis appeared like manna from heaven, and these entrepreneurs were able to more than meet the challenge from this new household appliance by staging fights, then broadcasting them. But this brought them closer to an accommodation with the moral sewer that was boxing—a ticket to federal court, in other words.

Palermo did not aid Gibson's attempt to elude the authorities. "I know [Gibson] very well," he said brightly. And Norris? "I sure do" know him, too. How could he not? "I had the best stable in the country" of boxers, and Gibson and Norris were seeking same for television. Yet, he declared, "I have turned down opportunities of being co-managers of fighters…I have turned down a million offers like that," he bragged, i.e., "having a piece of a fighter"—since "good fighters are peddled by everybody." He may have vitiated the potency of his damaging testimony with his self-presentation, however. "I am just a character. I use any name I want," referring to his many aliases, including "Lou Gross"; "some people say I am Joey [Joe E.], look like Joey Lewis," a reference to a popular untalented comedian. "A lot of people took me for him"—but why should a federal court take seriously the testimony of such a "character?" "I didn't believe in no

---

65. Testimony of Arthur Wirtz, 3-4 May 1961, Box 2487, Gibson Trial File-NAR-Riv.

checking accounts," he added, and as for banks: "I should say not," suggesting his familiarity with cold, hard cash in brick-like amounts. The slight, diminutive blinker had a "missus"—Claire Cori—and a mistress, Margaret Dougherty, and a growing legion of problems, too. But with all the bluster and bloviating, the most startling aspect of his testimony was that it was Jack Dempsey who introduced him to his partner—Carbo—retrospectively raising numerous queries about this still reigning symbol of the sport, continually being introduced and taking a bow and receiving applause before big bouts.[66] (Gibson's boss, Jim Norris, met Carbo at the office of Mike Jacobs.[67])

But attention could hardly be diverted to the "Manassa Mauler" when Gibson was busily indicting still active pounders, including "Sugar" Ray Robinson, who, along with Patterson, was the contemporary face of the sport. "Ray Robinson is the only boxer who has ever been sued," he told the court. "[Mike] Jacobs had a lawsuit against Robinson for having taken $45,000 from him [then] signing a contract...for a Robinson-[Kid] Gavilan fight" contrary to the previous accord,[68] bolstering Gibson's continuing claim that "Sugar" Ray was too much of a clubhouse lawyer. He even had an astringent analysis of "Sugar" Ray's manager, George Gainford, also known to drive a crafty bargain. He had a "violent temper," scoffed Gibson; this he knew since "we have had numerous arguments over the years." Gainford undoubtedly was displeased when, before prosecutors, not shy about bringing indictments, Gibson announced that "Palermo...knew Gainford very well" because of their "long friendship."[69] "Sugar" Ray muddied the waters further when one day he said he had received countless bribe offers from "gamblers and hoodlums"[70]—then quickly retracted his statement.[71]

Just before this controversy, Norris suffered food poisoning, postponing a scheduled meeting with "Sugar" Ray.[72] This coinci-

---

66. Testimony of Frankie Palermo, 11 May 1961, Box 2488, Gibson Trial File-NAR-Riv.

67. Statement of James Norris, 5-9 and 12-14 December 1960, Hearings Before the Subcommittee on Antitrust and Monopoly Committee on the Judiciary, U.S. Senate, 86th Congress, 2nd Session, Part II, Box 490, Kefauver-UTn-K.

68. Testimony of Truman Gibson, 26 April 1961, Box 2487, Gibson Trial File-NAR-Riv.

69. Testimony of Truman Gibson, 26 April 1961, Box 2487, Gibson Trial File-NAR-Riv.

70. *Miami Herald*, 21 September 1957, Sub Group X, Series I, Box 7, HKBA.

71. *Miami Herald*, 2 October 1957, Sub Group X, Series I, Box 7, HKBA.

72. *Miami Herald*, 27 August 1957, Sub Group X, Series I, Box 7, HKBA.

dence raised suspicions, especially since Robinson was known to be friendly with the Negro mobster "Bumpy" Johnson, who was said to shield the sweet scientist away from traditional racketeering, dominated by Jewish and Italian Americans.[73]

Carbo, the unofficial czar of the sport, was said to be behind the attempt to sideline Negro punchers—or so said writer and boxing aficionado Budd Schulberg. Just as there were a number of Negro heavyweights, during the reign of Jack Johnson, who lurked in the shadows, Schulberg said there were "great black middleweights" who were "too tough, nobody wanted to fight them," and the same could be said for Ezzard Charles in the higher range. "The dapper... Carbo and the rest were not interested in promoting the careers of Black fighters" and drew a "pretty strong color line."[74] With the barring of "great black heavyweights" aiding Robinson's career immeasurably, and with the corruption that inhered in the sport, who could say credibly that this was merely coincidental?

Gibson also did not aid the case for Sonny Liston, who was to destroy Floyd Patterson, before inaugurating the Ali era by falling victim to the former "Louisville Lip." Liston was a kind of Jack Johnson without the left-leaning politics—his ties to mobsters virtually forbade such an eventuality. Gibson knew the St. Louis Slugger well enough to notice that "Liston's hands are about twice the size of the ordinary pugilist's hands so he physically could not use a normal size glove."[75] The prosecution sought to introduce Liston into the case, even presenting a handwriting sample from him—his cursive was decent—rebutting the idea that he was wholly illiterate.[76]

The intelligence unit of the police department in St. Louis, where the bruiser was residing for a good deal of the 1950s—before residing in mob-infested Philadelphia and Denver and mob-infested Las Vegas—detailed his ties to Carbo and Palermo and John Vitale, a

---

73. Interview with Jimmy Breslin, 26 June 1998, Box 91, Newfield-UT.

74. Transcript of interview with Budd Schulberg, 26 June 1998, Box 91, Newfield-UT.

75. Testimony of Truman Gibson, 21 and 24 April 1961, Box 2486, Gibson Trial File-NAR-Riv.

76. James E. Hamilton, Los Angeles Police Department to Lloyd Dunn, U.S. Attorney, 9 September 1959, RG 118, Records of U.S. Attorneys, Central Judicial District of California, Los Angeles, Selected Criminal Case Files, NA Identifier 38995426, Box 120, NAR-Riv., hereinafter abbrev. as Prosecutor's File. See also Assael, *Murder*, 41: Liston is listed here as being neither literate nor numerate.

mover and shaker in the Mound City with problematic connections.[77] Vitale once used a telephone at the local Negro weekly, the *St. Louis Argus*, to make a telephone call to Palermo, raising searching questions about both the caller and the site from where the call was made.[78] Subsequently, Frank Mitchell of this periodical was summoned to testify in Congress about these associations, but he invoked the Fifth Amendment, refusing to testify on grounds of possible self-incrimination. Adroit allusions in a volley of unanswered queries were made nonetheless about Vitale and his accused role in shooting of labor leaders; but Mitchell was also close to Harold Gibbons, a rare socialist-oriented labor leader with the mob-riddled Teamsters, and Raymond Sarkis, who was hostile to progressive labor.[79]

To an extent, this was to be expected of Liston, who was viewed widely as a "Bad Negro" devoid of humanity, as when he repeatedly destroyed his opponents in the ring with a viciousness rarely seen previously. Back in 1920, Negro heavyweight Sam Langford acted in movie simply entitled "The Brute"—Liston was thought widely to embody and live this role.[80] "I always say kill him when I'm in the ring with a white boy," was his reputed comment, which further punctuated the turnabout from the Negro as a "coward" and "soft" to the Negro as an "anti-white" brute, which dovetailed with anxieties about the coursing anti-Jim Crow movement and what it portended: revenge, perhaps, for centuries of horrors? Eventually, a mass-circulation magazine tagged him bluntly as "King of the Beasts."[81]

Liston's evident mob ties gave him even more an aura of menace. His "business advisor," Jack Nilon, told a nosy congressional panel that he did not ask questions—a smart policy in these circles—when

---

77. St. Louis Police Intelligence Unit to Lt. Colonel James Chapman, 11 August 1959, Box 120, Prosecutor's File: Prior to a bout between Liston and Bert Whitehurst in St. Louis on 24 October 1958, agents of the intelligence unit happened to be at the Lucky Athletic Club at 4524a Easton and there encountered John Wilson Green, identified as a Negro and a former state legislator, speaking with Millie Allen, "white female girl friend of John Vitale. Green is an ex-convict" and was "good friends" with Vitale and they "frequently played golf together" in Forest Park.

78. Virgil Peterson, Chicago Crime Commission to John Bonomi, 18 December 1959, Box 131, Prosecutor's File.

79. Testimony of Frank Mitchell, 5-9 and 12-14 December 1960, Box 490, Hearings Before the Subcommittee on Antitrust and Monopoly, Committee on Judiciary, U.S. Senate, 86th Congress, 2nd Session, Kefauver-UTn-K.

80. Moyle, *Sam Langford*, 319.

81. Tosches, *The Devil*, 136, 202.

Liston told him he wanted to "sign over valuable stock to Sam Margolis," a comrade of Carbo. It was well known that Liston had similar ties to Palermo, Vitale and Joe "Pep" Barone, a New Jersey tavern owner.[82] Liston also acted as a labor goon for St. Louis mob boss Raymond Sarkis, whose Syrian ancestry was indicative of how the entrance to "whiteness" was widening.[83] It came as no surprise when a reporter opined—drawing from intelligence provided by the St. Louis Police Department—that Carbo owned 52% of Liston's earnings, followed by Palermo's 12% and local racketeer John Vitale's 12%—leaving the boxer with a pittance after paying training and other expenses.[84]

Because razor-sharp racketeers had dug their sharpened claws so deeply into the sport, actual matches became an opportunity for them to congregate, bluster about "their" contestants, and make side bets on the outcome. Doubtlessly, senatorial ears leapt to alertness when at an "executive session" evidence was introduced to show that one of the pivotal encounters in mob history—when Capone met John Roselli, who went on to carry out various tasks for both Hollywood racketeers and U.S. intelligence alike—took place at a fight featuring Gene Tunney.[85]

In sum, Gibson was up to his neck in alligators, as he cast aspersions on "Sugar" Ray and did little to dispel swirling rumors that were tripping up Liston, mostly involving the business associates of the boxer and the Chicagoan: Carbo and Palermo. As if this agenda were not sufficiently full, Gibson then turned on Floyd Patterson, or at least his team led by his manager, Cus D'Amato (perhaps better known today as the handler of future champion Mike Tyson). Gibson was scalding in his evaluation of this manager. He was a competitor, a principal in the "Teleprompter Corporation that owned and controlled the closed circuit and television and motion

---

82. Undated report, Boxing Scrapbooks, Vol. XVII, UND. See also *New York Times,* 26 March 1964.

83. Column by Drew Pearson, 25 September 1962, Boxing Notes on Patterson-Liston, UND.

84. Wager, op. cit., Ellison-LC.

85. Testimony of John Roselli, Stenographic Transcript of Hearings Before the Special Committee to Investigate Organized Crime in Interstate Commerce, U.S. Senate, Executive Session, Chicago, 7 October 1950, Box 76, Kefauver-UTn-K. On Roselli and his ignominious death—his torso was found in an oilcan floating on the high seas after he was summoned to Washington to be interrogated about his various misdeeds—see Gerald Horne, *Class Struggle in Hollywood, 1930-1950: Moguls, Mobsters, Stars, Reds, and Trade Unionists,* Austin: University of Texas Press, 2001.

picture and radio rights for Floyd Patterson Enterprises…controlled by Cus D'Amato and Irving Kahn." Patterson was emulating his predecessor Joe Louis, who embarked on his own independent route in 1949: Thus Patterson never signed on with Gibson-Norris-Carbo and instead conflicted with them. Gibson, a bit contradictorily, said that his enterprise was not a competitor of Patterson's but that they "wanted to put us out of business not compete."[86]

Another source confirmed Gibson's sour assessment of D'Amato—but it is the former who wound up convicted in federal court. He "tried to set himself up as a Boxing Napoleon" was the conclusion, as he was the manager of Patterson—"and promote[d] his fights. And [took] TV rake-offs." Besides, his "boss" was Anastasia, who was Carbo's boss, too.[87] In brief, Carbo was sitting pretty, irrespective if Gibson or D'Amato prevailed. Gibson had designed a business model heavily dependent on the currency of Joe Louis, but as time passed, he was withered by repetitive battles with the taxman, opening the door for a new boxer (Patterson) with a similar idea (controlling the vast downstream profits of the sport), backed by the same force (mobsters).

For Albany regulators well knew that D'Amato was no saint. Charles "Charlie Black" Antonucci was his "trusted advisor and go-between…. whenever there is a Patterson fight, Black appears on the scene either with a part in the promotion or in the boxer management"; this character, in turn, was friendly with "Fat Tony" Salerno and "Trigger" Mike Coppola, as the regulator sniffed that Antonucci's "presence would [not] inure to the best interest of boxing," though via D'Amato he was a virtual "co-manager" of Patterson. D'Amato then sought to "dictate…the naming of [Harry] Davidow as [Ingemar] Johansson's manager," a blatant conflict of interest.[88] Eventually, D'Amato's license was revoked—for a while.[89]

But Patterson and D'Amato were to encounter some of the same piranhas with which Gibson had become all too familiar. An important East Harlem numbers racketeer—Salerno—was an essential part of the promotional operations for the first Patterson-Johansson

---

86. Testimony of Truman Gibson, 26 April 1961, Box 2487, Gibson Trial File-NAR-Riv.

87. Undated report, Sub Group XV, Series VII, Box 34, HKBA.

88. In the Matter of an Inquiry into Alleged Irregularities in the Conduct of the Promotion of the Patterson-Johansson World's Heavyweight Championship Contest Held at the Yankee Stadium on June 26, 1959, NYSAC.

89. Report to Caroline K. Simon, Secretary of State, 31 December 1960, NYSAC.

slugfest, and like many of this ilk, he was not interested in sharing profits with a boxer who had quite a bit to lose if his squeaky clean reputation were besmirched by revelations of involvement with racketeers.[90] At least Louis had retired before entering this dangerous business. The results were predictable. "I have not yet received one cent for the first Patterson fight," moaned the Swedish challenger. "I can't even get an accurate accounting of what I *might* receive," he complained [emphasis-original]. "My countrymen shout 'don't go back to America, Ingemar. You might not come back,'" a thinly veiled reference to the rampant organized criminality that prevailed on the west bank of the Atlantic. Yet his harshest barbs were reserved not for "Fat Tony"—but D'Amato.[91]

D'Amato's business colleague Bill Rosensohn sensed in advance of the fight that a pot of gold awaited. "We have had requests from newspapermen representing papers in all parts of the world," he exulted. Thus, regulators allowed "eight rows of working press seats" to accommodate varied requests, extraordinary for the time.[92] The interest of the press proved to be a telling indicator of the river of revenues that soon were to flow, generating in turn a waterfall of animosity and bruised feelings.

It was well for the Swedish boxer to be wary of returning to the scene of past triumph. For as he was gearing up to battle Patterson, the news was reported that "Sailor Joe" Stanley, the manager of Billy "Sweetpea" Peacock, was decapitated under the wheels of a locomotive; evidently he was despondent since he figured in two investigations in recent months which involved former matchmaker, Babe McCoy. Suicide was suspected, but the grisliness of the death left lingering questions as to the validity of that conclusion.[93] Perhaps more relevant was that Harold Johnson was said to be drugged prior to a nationally televised bout[94]—but then the excuse arose that mere "nose drops" were to blame for his damaged condition. It was safer to hibernate in Stockholm.

Still, Johansson need not worry that much. He had upset the "Negro Restoration," if only temporarily, by besting Patterson and, at least for some, assisting mightily a primary though frequently unacknowledged characteristic of the former slaveholders' republic: the correlation of forces racially, which was thought to have been

---

90. Wager, op.cit., Ellison-LC.
91. Undated report, Boxing Notes on Heavyweights, Vol. XV, UND.
92. Bill Rosensohn to Melvin L. Krulewitch, 5 June 1959, NYSAC.
93. *Miami Herald*, 18 May 1957, Sub Group VIII, Series I, Box 20, HKBA.
94. *Miami Daily News*, 7 May 1955, Sub Group X, Series I, Box 13, HKBA.

unduly upset when Marciano stepped away from the ring and Patterson took his place. Soon Congressman William Broomfield was contacting the White House, exploring the "possibility of arranging a meeting with [Eisenhower] and Ingemar Johansson."[95] Although he had defeated a U.S. national, the White House was magnanimously willing to embrace this Northern European battler—a throwback to "Battling" Nelson of Danish ancestry who fought Joe Gans—for whatever reason.

---

95. Congressman William Broomfield to Bryce Harlow, 20 June 1960, Central Files/General Files, Box 1055, DDEPL.

Chapter 7

Truman Gibson & Joe Louis: Down for the Count?

Truman Gibson was hit by double blows as the 1950s expired and the tumultuous 1960s began. Under unrelieved pressure from Patterson/D'Amato, various racketeers, and the federal authorities, it was the latter—in the form of the U.S. Supreme Court—which delivered a devastating blow, ruling that the International Boxing Club violated antitrust law. Justice Tom Clark, delivering the opinion of the court, told one and all that the "conspiracy began in January 1949 when appellants Norris and Wirtz...made an agreement with Joe Louis," who "agreed to give up his title after obtaining from each of the four leading contenders, exclusive promotion rights including rights to radio, television and movie revenues," which were then assigned to IBC, which forked over $150,000 in "cash plus an employment contract and a 20% stock interest and a 20% stock interest in IBC"; involved was a buyout of Mike Jacobs's interest at Madison Square Garden, too. This, it was thought, led to an effective and improper monopoly[1]—an ironic conclusion to reach as D'Amato/Patterson began pursuing Gibson and Co. avidly. (During his criminal trial, Gibson was quoted as lamenting that Patterson's manager had sought "to form some kind of organization to combat...the IBC.")[2]

Justice Felix Frankfurter, dissenting in the precursor case to this one, thought it would "baffle the subtlest ingenuity to find a single differentiating factor between other sporting exhibitions, whether football or tennis and baseball insofar as" antitrust is concerned.[3]

---

1. Tom Clark opinion, 12 January 1959, in International Boxing Club v. U.S.A., Box 452, Earl Warren Papers, Library of Congress-Washington, D.C. (abbrev. Warren-LC).
2. Comment, 7 March 1961, Box 2483, Gibson Trial File-NAR-Riv.
3. Felix Frankfurter dissent, January 1955, U.S.A. v. International Boxing Club, Box 575, Warren-LC.

Actually, a "differentiating factor" was having a Negro, Truman Gibson, in an executive post in boxing, but at this juncture it was difficult for polite (Euro-American) company to acknowledge the obvious. "Sports had not been considered as being within the purview of the Sherman Antitrust Act in a civil action," responded a dumbfounded attorney Gibson, in response: "we immediately stopped the practice of exclusive contracts with champions,"[4] and by the time of the trial he was out of boxing altogether[5]—but this was too little, much too late. The antitrust decision was rendered in 1959, which also was the year that an indictment was returned,[6] making truly for an *annus horribilis*.

Reinforcing this high court opinion was yet another when, following the indictment, in 1961 Gibson stood in the dock shoulder-to-shoulder with a quartet of unsavory characters—Carbo, Palermo, Joe Sica and Louis Dragna—whose presence alone sullied him. They were all found guilty after a 13-week trial and three days of deliberation. The prosecutor, Alvin Goldstein, was unsparing in assailing the "collusion between Gibson…and the underworld," all of whom were accused, *inter alia*, of trying to muscle in on the morally challenged boxer Don Jordan.[7] Jordan was presumed to be a valuable "commodity" in that the future billionaire Kirk Kerkorian also had once managed him.[8]

Indubitably, before the criminal trial, Gibson and his comrades were flying high. The prominent Manhattan-based journalist Arthur Daley termed the IBC—"Octopus, Inc.," with "control of Madison Square Garden, Chicago Stadium, Detroit Olympia and other arenas." Tossing caution to the winds, Norris had named one of his racehorses "Mr. Gray,"[9] flaunting their open connection to Carbo.

Defense counsel William Strong—who was part of the firm headed by the fabled San Francisco barrister Melvin Belli—disputed the prosecution, seeing instead a "very confusing case…a very hard case." Unlike the prosecutor, he was dismissive of Jack Leonard, key witness against Gibson and his co-defendants: "without Leonard there just isn't any case," he said, and he lacked credibility and was deceitful besides: "if you take Leonard out of this case, there is no

---

4. Testimony, Truman Gibson, 26 April 1961, Gibson Trial File-NAR-Riv.
5. Comment, 2 May 1961, Box 2487, Gibson Trial File-NAR-Riv.
6. Comment by Judge, 9 May 1961, Box 2487, Gibson Trial File-NAR-Riv.
7. *New York Times* clipping, ca. 1961, Box 209, Ellison-LC.
8. Minutes, 11 March 1961, NYSAC.
9. Arthur Daley, *Miami Herald*, 30 September 1960, Sub Group VIII, Series I, Box 16, HKBA.

case." Furthermore, the rotten roots of the sport itself could not be easily swept aside. "So long as we have a boxing world in this world, in this country, we will just have to put up with the way they talk and the way they deal."[10] He was largely correct, as Don King and Bob Arum loomed on the horizon—but the prosecutors begged to differ.

In a sense, the defendants were accused of seeking to "steal" Jordan from the grubby paws of Mickey Cohen and deliver him instead to Carbo. There was "considerable publicity in the local newspapers," said John Bradley, Dragna's attorney, "that the fighter Don Jordan was an associate and in constant company with Mickey Cohen."[11] According to press accounts, Cohen paid a visit to Jordan 18 hours before his pivotal bout with Denny Moyer; there were, it was said, press "reports in Los Angeles that the underworld was trying to take over Jordan."[12] Another journalist found that Jack Leonard had visited Carbo in the late 1950s to "Stand Trial," as if Mr. Gray were presiding over a state-within-a-state, which he was doing in a sense; this was during the time when Carbo was maneuvering "to muscle in on [Jordan]."[13]

"I managed Mickey Cohen when he was a fighter around Cleveland and I knew him," said Salvatore Casarona, a comrade of primary prosecution witness Jack Leonard, who also testified against the defendants.[14] Jordan was also tied to Donald Paul Nesseth of Covina, California, a used car salesman—"it was my major income until Jordan became successful," he said. But they were in dispute, which helped to drive him into the ethically mottled arms of Cohen; when the fighter journeyed to South America for bouts in 1959, Nesseth was upset that "Jordan wouldn't fight if I went along."[15]

"I am a professional fighter," countered Jordan, with "three or four bouts on national television." Yet Nesseth "told me I had to pay for getting the fight," speaking of his "first fight I fought on national

---

10. Comment by William Strong, 24 May 1961, Box 2489, Gibson Trial File-NAR-Riv.

11. Comment by John Bradley, 16 March 1961, Box 2484, Gibson Trial File-NAR-Riv.

12. *Miami Herald*, 11 July 1959, Sub Group IX, Series 2, Box 30, HKBA.

13. *San Francisco Examiner*, 10 March 1961, Sub Group VIII, Series I, Box 13, HKBA.

14. Testimony of Salvatore Casarona, 4-5 April 1961, Box 2485, Gibson Trial File-NAR-Riv.

15. Testimony of Donald Paul Nesseth, 14 March 1961, Box 2484, Gibson Trial File-NAR-Riv.

television"—a payment presumably brokered illicitly by Gibson.[16] Another telling witness against the defendants was Warren Wayland Spaw, also known as Jackie McCoy, a former boxer and manager before working with Nesseth, then D'Amato on the first fight between Patterson and Johansson,[17] in some ways the first notes of the swan song for Gibson.

Still, it was Jordan's testimony that remained near the heart of the case. He recounted his travails in the sport, especially when his manager was Harry Kabakoff, also surnamed as Himmelfarb, who once left him stranded after a bout in Mexico. Then future Las Vegas billionaire—and Don King partner—Kirk Kerkorian became his manager, this before Jordan became a car salesman. It was then that Nesseth tried to "forge" his names on various contracts; this manager, he contended, "would steal from anybody," it "got crazy." But it was unclear if Jordan's credibility remained intact when he spoke wistfully of Carbo as "The Man."[18]

It wasn't just D'Amato/Patterson and Cohen who were seeking to barge into a lush field that had been dominated by Gibson/Norris/Carbo. Witness William Daly, of Englewood, New Jersey, had been involved in the sport for decades by the time he reached the courtroom, as trainer, manager and promoter. He had been licensed in every U.S. state and 12 European countries, involving the managing of 175 boxers, including Lee Savold, who once fought Joe Louis. He had known Carbo for a quarter of a century—"I had a lot of dealings with him," he said—and over the years had scores of television deals with Gibson.[19] And yet he also was struck when he found that Frank Sinatra, a rising force in entertainment and politics, was seeking to buy a stake in boxing.[20] The attorney for defendant, Sica, may have overstated the case when he suggested that the authorities "wouldn't approve it, wouldn't approve anything that Sinatra had anything to do with."[21]

---

16. Testimony of Donald Jordan, 11 April 1961, Box 2485, Gibson Trial File-NAR-Riv.

17. Testimony of Warren Wayland Spaw, 16 March 1961, Box 2484, Gibson Trial File-NAR-Riv.

18. Testimony by Donald Jordan, 14 April 1961, Box 2486, Gibson Trial File-NAR-Riv.

19. Testimony of William Daly, 6 April 1961, Box 2485, Gibson Trial File-NAR-Riv.

20. Testimony by William Daly, 11 April 1961, Box 2485, Gibson Trial File-NAR-Riv.

21. Comment by Russell Parson, 25 May 1961, Box 2489, Gibson Trial File-NAR-Riv.

Wisely, William Ming, Gibson's counsel, sought to take advantage of the winds shifting against the odiousness of Jim Crow. "Quash the entire venire," he thundered, referring to the laborious process by which a jury is chosen. Of the "38 persons drawn by the clerk," he said beseechingly, "not one of those persons is a person of Negro citizenship." "We don't have to have Negroes in the venire," the judge insisted, hewing to the old-time faith. Ming's motion charging "systematic exclusion" was denied peremptorily, as was his attempt to separate his client from the unsavoriness of his co-defendants in a separate trial.[22] After the trial, the prosecution took note of the comment by an observant Negro journalist from Chicago who was upset that an "all-white jury" relying upon the testimony of a "liar"—Jack Leonard—had "convicted" Gibson.[23] This writer may have been even more upset if he had known that potential jurors considered for this weighty proceeding included a fan of "comic strips."[24]

The judge observed that the lead prosecutor, Alvin Goldstein, "has come upon the case at almost the last minute," a big gun deployed from a lucrative private practice in San Francisco; William Bierne, one of the opposing counsel, found this remarkable since the federal authorities "have a whole slew of United States attorneys…deputies, who have been working on this [case] for nearly two years," indicative of the importance to those in charge. It was not a good sign for the defendants when the judge declared skeptically, "I don't give a hoot for boxing…I just don't care for it," eradicating the possibility of the defendants being favored by a sports fan. "I have terrible problems with my bifocals," the judge muttered at one point, and thus he apparently did not waste his vision watching men bash each other. "Deafness is one of my frailties,"[25] said Bierne, and he was not interested in hearing stories about the moral frailties of his clients.

The prosecution was similarly obtuse toward the defendants and no less devastating. It was in late June 1961 when Alvin Goldstein stood in court and announced that this "married… Negro"—Gibson—was said to have perpetrated a "conspiracy to violate [the] anti-racketeering act [and] extortion via interstate communications and conspiracy." Noted conspicuously was Gibson's father, who founded Supreme Life, a prominent Negro business, and

---

22. Comment by Defense Attorney and Judge, 20-21 February 1961, Gibson Trial File-NAR-Riv.

23. *Chicago New Crusader*, 9 June 1961, Box 128, Prosecutor's File.

24. Note to Judge, 21 February 1961, Box 1711, Gibson Trial File-NAR-Riv.

25. Comments by Judge and Defense Counsel, 10 March 1961, Box 2484, Gibson Trial File-NAR-Riv.

was a graduate of Harvard Business School: "the family has always been a very wealthy and influential one," it was said. His 20-year-old daughter Karen was a student at the "exclusive" Sarah Lawrence College, while Gibson was deemed to be "one of the foremost leaders of his race…active in the religious practices and observances of his faith," too. He was a "well-known national and international figure," and "independently wealthy" too, it was said, as if they were inflating Gibson in order to deflate him more dramatically. (Their own report found that he had a mere $31,000 in cash on hand and a net worth of $10,000 more—Negro wealthy, yes, but hardly U.S. wealthy.)

The high court had consummated the unwinding of the IBC by 1959, but Gibson, it was thought, still merited severe punishment. Why? The prosecution's "evaluation" was that this was "another in the sad, disgusting, shocking and ever growing spectacle of American business bowing, kowtowing, using and being used by the hoodlum element." Gibson was no more than an exemplar of "moral decay," willing to wield "power for money—<u>MONEY</u> at any cost," he veritably shouted, as if this were a new concept. Hailed was the "deterrent value of the long sentence."[26] Considering that Carbo received five guilty verdicts, Palermo got seven—and Gibson only two—the Chicagoan was lucky by comparison.[27]

During the trial, the prosecutor referred to Gibson as "a very successful executive," and "he made a lot of money for them," referring to Norris, Wirtz, and his co-defendants.[28] This he knew for the trial was an exhaustive—and exhausting inspection of the defendants. There were over 70 witnesses, more than 300 exhibits, and Gibson's attorney, William Ming, predicted that his closing argument alone would last four hours.[29] There were 7,500 pages of trial transcript, embellished by what one attorney called "voluble and vigorous objections" that "were made to nearly every procedure" as "defendants' counsel were allowed a wide latitude in cross examination."[30] This case, said the judge, "is in its nature a long case," which turned

---

26. Report on Proposed Probation for Gibson, 29 June 1961, Box 120, Prosecutor's File.

27. Comment by Judge, 27, 29 and 30 May and 2 June 1961, Box 2489, Gibson Trial File-NAR-Riv.

28. Comment by Prosecutor, 25 May 1961, Box 2489, Gibson Trial File-NAR-Riv.

29. Summary, 19 May 1961, Box 2486, Gibson Trial File-NAR-Riv.

30. Memorandum, 29 November 1961, Box 1711, Gibson Trial File-NAR-Riv.

out to be an accurate evaluation.[31] "Whatever this case is," he said wearily, "it will never be noted as a case expeditiously tried by anybody."[32] As of 1951, the judge was handling 77 cases, but by the time of this marathon-of-a-trial he was handling over 150, though the present elongated trial seemed longer than all of those combined.[33]

"It is a difficult case," sighed the experienced jurist, who even then was handling "162 civil cases, besides a number of criminal cases,"[34] while the prosecutor remarked, "I assure you...I will be happy to get back to my private practice."[35] This remark was prior to Gibson's attorney denouncing him as a "liar." "What did you say to me?" Goldstein responded rhetorically. Ming upped the ante: "Go ahead and hit me," he implored: "I would just love that," he said unconvincingly. The judge, to little avail, demanded that "everybody... cool down."[36] The "length of the trial," said the judge, a master of obviousness, "has made people more irritable."[37] Shortly before this utterance, he said with a hint of resignation, that "this trial originally estimated at three or four, perhaps five weeks...is now either in its twelfth or thirteenth week."[38]

Ming's fiery broadside was part of a searing cleansing process, as the dirty linen of the sport was torched publicly, setting the stage for a new dispensation not dominated by Norris and Gibson (though Carbo and Palermo only disappeared temporarily). Jack Leonard, the prime prosecution witness, was characterized by Ming as a thief and fraudster—an "unmitigated liar and attempted blackmailer"; this is a "unique case," he insisted, a brazen attempt to bring down Gibson, "part of the world's most successful boxing promotion enterprise," which was not destined to survive.[39] Sure, Ming told the jury soothingly, Gibson defended Palermo's 1953 attempt to get a boxing license. But he only did so in order to gain access to Ike Williams, the boxer controlled by the mobster; plus, waiting in the wings was Sonny Liston, whom he also wanted to book and was

---

31. Comment, 12 April 1961, Box 2485, Gibson Trial File-NAR-Riv.
32. Comment by Judge, 12 May 1961, Box 2488, Gibson Trial File-NAR-Riv.
33. Comment by Judge, 20 April 1961, Box 2486, Gibson Trial File-NAR-Riv.
34. Comment by Judge, 28 April 1961, Box 2487, Gibson Trial File-NAR-Riv.
35. Comment by Judge and Prosecutor, 28 April 1961, Box 2487, Gibson Trial File-NAR-Riv.
36. Comments by Ming, Goldstein and Judge, 26 May 1961, Box 2489, Gibson Trial File-NAR-Riv.
37. Comment by Judge, 3-4 May 1961, Box 2487, Gibson Trial File-NAR-Riv.
38. Comment by Judge, 17 May 1961, Box 2488, Gibson Trial File-NAR-Riv.
39. Comment, 23 May 1961, Box 2489, Gibson Trial File-NAR-Riv.

also mob controlled. What about dealing with the mob-infested Hollywood Legion stadium? Why, said Ming, it was the "only building in the world...designed and built" for boxing.[40] Promoter William Daly, who had multiple dealings with Ming's client, concurred. It was "built exclusively for boxing," he gushed at the trial, it was a "dream of an arena. The cheapest seat was equivalent to the ringside," quite a feat.[41]

In testifying before Congress, Carbo dismissed the longstanding claim, including by the boxer himself, that Williams was victimized by Palermo. He "could not obtain fights until he secured the services of 'Blinky,'" he charged, and made over $1 million—but as of late 1960 he was working for a mere $96 every two weeks: So, he said triumphantly, how was this victimizing?[42] Williams, in his congressional testimony, presented a contrasting picture, recalling that Palermo tried to bribe him to the tune of $30,000 before one bout, which rose to $100,000 before he was slated to box Kid Gavilan—with presumably gamblers cashing in by plundering wagering counter-parties unaware that the fix was in. Williams was swimming alongside sharks then, conferring with Mickey Cohen and Benjamin "Bugsy" Siegel, among others—"Cohen was my very good friend," he volunteered.[43]

But this testimony helped to suggest why Gibson sought deals with the corrupt Jack Leonard, the chief prosecution witness. Moreover, Daly hardly helped his own challenged credibility when he discussed fondly his friendliness with Carbo and, in a burst of misplaced masculinity, admitted that "punch in the nose" and "hit in the head" were both "favorite expression[s] of mine."[44] The ostensible manager of Don Jordan, the welterweight near the center of the case, recounted at the trial that Gibson was "very indignant," while holed up in his comfortable bungalow at the Ambassador Hotel, when he fielded a call from Palermo about the boxer, when all should have known they were under strict surveillance. But, it was said, Gibson

---

40. Comment by William Ming, 26 May 1961, Box 2489, Gibson Trial File-NAR-Riv.

41. Testimony by William Daly, 6 April 1961, Box 2485, Gibson Trial File-NAR-Riv.

42. Testimony by Frankie Carbo, 5-9 and 12-14 December 1960, Box 490, Kefauver-UTn-K.

43. Testimony by Ike Williams, 5-9 and 12-14 December 1960, Box 490, Kefauver-UTn-K.

44. Testimony by William Daly, 7 April 1961, Box 2485, Gibson Trial File-NAR-Riv.

was so worried about "Gillette" and their "Christmas sales" that it seemed that caution was tossed to the winds and indiscreet conversations were held nonetheless.[45]

At times, Gibson was portrayed as going beyond this call of business, as when an official of the New York Police Department testified that he saw Gibson present an award to mob-connected Bernard Glickman in March 1958.[46] Glickman was a Chicago-based manufacturer of aluminum awnings who dabbled as a co-manager of Virgil Akins. He met Palermo in the early 1950s and admitted on the witness stand that "Mr. Palermo helped me along."[47]

This was a difficult needle to thread: Gibson was an innocent forced to do business with the guilty. When Palermo's accountant, Irving Sklar, was called to testify,[48] it was evident that rats were busily scurrying from the sinking ship, and Gibson would not survive. In any event, Palermo did not aid his co-defendant's case when he asserted at the trial, "I rendered some service for them with Liston, bringing Liston out of St. Louis, getting him all set up. I spent my money and got compensated for it."[49]

In a tantalizing thread unpursued in a case replete with them, Palermo said at one point, "Yes, I know him, an attorney named Morris Shenker,"[50] a reference to a prominent member of the St. Louis Jewish community, who happened to be close both to organized crime, and to the self-proclaimed "Millionaire Referee" Harry Kessler, who officiated in numerous bouts in which fortunes were wagered. In his subsequently published memoir, Kessler was candid in describing "our friends Morris and Lillian Shenker" and their 1963 visit to Israel.[51] Later, a reporter revealed to a mass audience that then-Mayor Alphonse Cervantes of St. Louis, assisted strategically by Shenker, focused heavily on "ghetto crime," obfuscating the reality that the former had "business and personal ties with gangsters," while the

---

45. Testimony by Donald Paul Nesseth, 14 March 1961, Box 2484, Gibson Trial File-NAR-Riv.

46. Testimony by Anthony Bernhard, 18 May 1961, Box 2488, Gibson Trial File-NAR-Riv.

47. Testimony by Bernard Glickman, 18 April 1961, Box 2486, Gibson Trial File-NAR-Riv.

48. Testimony by Irving Sklar, 18 May 1961, Box 2488, Gibson Trial File-NAR-Riv.

49. Testimony by "Blinky" Palermo, 12 May 1961, Box 2489, Gibson Trial File-NAR-Riv.

50. Testimony by "Blinky" Palermo, 12 May 1961, Box 2489, Gibson Trial File-NAR-Riv.

51. Kessler, *Millionaire*, 208.

latter was one of the "foremost lawyers for the Mob in the U.S." and a major backer of Israel, too.[52] The result of Cervantes's crusade was devastation of Black St. Louis by dint of mass incarceration and the construction of yet another gangster's paradise.[53]

Despite evidence to the contrary, Gibson denied closeness to Palermo and Carbo, too. He did recall a time when "Chris Dundee called me...then he put Carbo on the phone"; at issue were "Florida and Georgia rights, theater television rights for the Robinson-Basilio fight." This was during 1958, when "we had entered into a contract with Irving Kahn of Theater Network Television," a concession to D'Amato. "We were having difficulty making matches for Sonny Liston during this period," and the "fighter was very dissatisfied," since "in every fight we had made for him the opponent had gotten two to three times the amount of money that Liston had gotten." He added, "we had to guarantee very large sums in order to get these men to go into the ring with Liston," given his fearsome reputation. Less convincingly, he argued that Palermo was "looking to... sever all his connections with Liston." In any case, the brawler Nino Valdes got $11,000 to face Liston, who got a measly $5,000. But the long colloquy among counsel as to the meaning of the term "underworld" indelibly marred Gibson's testimony.[54]

As for Liston, his ascendancy as Jim Crow was retreating and Gibson was at the controls of the sport, seemed to be unnerving to certain Euro-Americans, raising searching questions about "race" and masculinity. After the burly Liston battered the hapless Euro-American Roy Harris to the canvas multiple times in the first round, leading to a TKO (Technical Knockout), a disgruntled and disappointed spectator put a gun to the victor's head and threatened to shoot him unless he confirmed that—results notwithstanding—he was a "yeller [yellow] nigger."[55] That is, in the throes of unsettling change, Liston was being commanded to confirm that the older and rapidly disintegrating conception continued to persist.

Furthermore on Liston, when a top British promoter, Harry Levene, insulted him odiously ("Black Gorilla...What a Bear I thought!...

---

52. Denny Walsh, "A Two-Faced Crime Fight in St. Louis: Both the Mayor and New Crime Commissioner have Personal Ties to the Underworld," *LIFE*, 68 (No. 2, 29 May 1970), 24-31, MoHS-SL.

53. Walter Johnson, *The Broken Heart of America: St. Louis and the Violent History of the United States*, New York: Basic, 2020.

54. Testimony by Truman Gibson, 27 April 1961, Box 2487, Gibson Trial File-NAR-Riv.

55. Tosches, *The Devil*, 138.

Neanderthal Man"), he may have been deviously seeking to capitalize upon deep-seated racist tropes in order to generate a larger audience,[56] while neatly driving down Liston's bargaining power besides.

Of course, by 1950 there were 1,800 boxers licensed by the British Boxing Board of Control, with 800 promotions keeping these fighters busy. But thereafter there were only 420 boxers and a mere 165 promotions, pointing up why an unprincipled promoter might want to play upon bigotry.[57] What was happening in part was that Gibson and his comrades had barged into this market. They had "shipped more fighters to England than William the Conqueror,"[58] said one droll commentator, possibly leading to a backlash against others crossing the Atlantic, e.g., Liston, and assuredly generating a mounting outcry against a boxing octopus with a Negro at the head.

The antagonists that Gibson had attracted in London did not help his case in Los Angeles. This list included Sam Silverman, born in 1912, who during his career had promoted over 10,000 fights, including 25 championship bouts, though he had varying encounters with Scotland Yard and, as one analyst put it, "the gangster boss of a London betting syndicate." But he was no fan of Gibson's entity either, especially after the IBC accused him of offering a fighter a paltry $100 to throw a fight—though he had so many enemies it was not easy to pinpoint IBC's culpability when he barely escaped injury from a rifle shot through his window and a dynamite explosion in the basement of a residence at a time when he and his family had just departed.[59]

* * *

The prosecutor, Alvin Goldstein, did not seem to be eager to leave the courtroom when he delivered a lengthy stem-winder, instructing the jury that "you have visited another world in this case...a world of deceit, perfidy and treachery, of clandestine meetings, of false rewards, false entries, businesses without names or domicile or

---

56. Undated report, Sub Group VIII, Series I, Box 13, HKBA.

57. Undated report by Frankie Goodman, Sub Group IX, Series I, Box 11, HKBA.

58. *Miami Herald*, 9 June 1963, Sub Group VIII, Series I, Box 16, HKBA.

59. *Miami Daily News*, 25 July 1961, and undated report, Sub Group VIII, Series I, Box 19, HKBA. Silverman was no friend of the U.S. generally, denouncing the champion basketball team, the Boston Celtics, while the hockey Boston Bruins were "foreigners playing a foreign game." The baseball Boston Red Sox? They "put you to sleep."

without offices....where threats of force and violence...are commonplace, a world where men travel incognito and under false names... men who laugh when told that others are afraid of them," i.e., "a sort of underworld." Yet a particular animus was directed toward the only Negro defendant, who was portrayed as voracious in his lust to derail competitors. The IBC "dominated" the boxing world, then Sinatra backed by Sam Giancana threatened this arrangement, and Gibson tightened his ties to the mob in response, leading to deeper exploitation of fighters.[60]

The family of chief witness Jack Leonard continued to endure difficulty. Future U.S. high court judge Byron "Whizzer" White, then a deputy attorney general, was informed that Leonard's "home was set afire...dyes were thrown into the swimming pool" and, resultantly, his "wife has been close to a nervous breakdown.... wife's mouth had become infected and she had her tooth pulled with a pair of pliers.... U.S. marshals have been living in their home" as a form of witness protection: Smuggling the family into a new town with new identities was considered. An analogy was drawn with Matt Cvetic, a key witness in anti-communist cases under the Smith Act that led to imprisonment of the Communist Party leadership, whose precipitous decline was enacted in part in Los Angeles.[61]

Before becoming a promoter, Leonard, 44 years of age, had endured scores of fights himself—amateur and professional—as a boxer, judging himself to be "mediocre," but he would have to unearth whatever craftiness he learned as a puncher in order to survive this particular ordeal.[62] Weeks into the trial, he declared himself bankrupt, not boding well for his future.[63] The destructive fire at his plush Northridge, California, home was the "work of the underworld," he charged.[64] Carbo, quite threateningly, thought that he was insufficiently generous in sharing his cut of Don Jordan's purses. It was hardly consolation when the chief of police in Los Angeles countered with the risible notion that thugs had not beaten him, a possible adjunct to the demonstrated reach of racketeers into this law enforcement agency.[65]

---

60. Comment by Prosecutor, 23 May 1961, Box 2489, Gibson Trial File-NAR-Riv.

61. Alvin Goldstein to Byron White, 14 June 1961, Box 126, Prosecutor's File.

62. Comment, 2 March 1961, Box 2483, Gibson Trial File-NAR-Riv.

63. Comment, 8 March 1961, Box 2483, Gibson Trial File-NAR-Riv.

64. *Miami Herald*, 28 July 1959, Sub Group VIII, Series I, Box 13, HKBA.

65. Undated report, Odds and Ends on Boxing, Vol. 42, UND.

Leonard, whom the prosecutor called the "principal witness in this case," had "received well over a hundred threatening phone calls"—even before the trial began—extending for a "two year period," and in one noticeably bloodcurdling call, he "was asked if he had ever seen a broad [sic] with her guts splattered on the sidewalk"; this alone illustrated the "desperate nature of these proceedings and the stake involved for these defendants." Tellingly, as the prosecutor put it bluntly, "defendant Sica [was] a defendant in a narcotics prosecution in which the principal witness was murdered."[66] (Sica was a suspect in two murders, including that of an attorney, Sam Rommel, along with the witness in the drug case, Abe Davidian.[67])

Interestingly, the judge in this lengthy trial suddenly died shortly after verdicts were returned.[68] "I'm a little nervous this morning," he said during the trial, "I forgot to bring my nitroglycerin."[69] At one point the judge reminded counsel, "everybody is getting awfully touchy,"[70] which was an understandable reaction given the stakes at play. This tense atmosphere notwithstanding, Hollywood actor George Raft, from his attractive home in Beverly Hills, wrote in enthusiastic support of Carbo, reminding the judge of the latter's patriotic service during the recent world war, as he toured military bases organizing boxing shows. He was a man of "good character," he insisted, recalling the "nice things he has done."[71] When the morally sloppy Palermo was detained at the airport in Los Angeles after caught red-handed while engaged in petty theft in May 1959, his initial call for rescue was to try to reach Raft: "They wouldn't let me talk to him," he said morosely.[72] Even Mickey Cohen knew that Raft's "idol was Owney Madden," a titan of corruption in boxing and throughout society, making comprehensible the desire to bar him from conferring with Palermo.[73]

---

66. Comment by Prosecutor, 20-21 February 1961, Box 1712, Gibson Trial File-NAR-Riv.

67. Comment, 9 May 1961, Box 2487, Gibson Trial File-NAR-Riv.

68. Memorandum, 29 November 1961, Box 1711, Gibson Trial File-NAR-Riv.

69. Testimony by Salvatore Casarona, 4-5 April 1961, Box 2485, Gibson Trial File-NAR-Riv.

70. Comment by Judge, 20-21 February 1961, Box 1712, Gibson Trial File-NAR-Riv.

71. George Raft to Judge Boldt, 14 July 1964, Box 1711, Gibson Trial File-NAR-Riv.

72. Testimony of "Blinky" Palermo, 15 May 1961, Box 2488, Gibson Trial File-NAR-Riv.

73. Cohen, *Mickey Cohen*, 115.

As for defendant Sica, he was a "TB [tuberculosis] suspect," a recent patient in rectal surgery that led to complications with most of his stomach removed: "He is wearing a mask," it was said at one point, which may have protected co-defendants and counsel from his suspected illness but may have underlined the point that masked men near courtrooms often were bent on felonies at that juncture. Defendant Dragna was the nephew of Jack Dragna, a long-time capo in the rackets in Los Angeles, which may have contributed to his conviction by association. As for Carbo, he had to be watched, said the prosecutor, since he was "the greatest lamster [a person liable to flee] in the world."[74] Carbo and his spouse were "hard of hearing," and the jury could well have drawn the inference that this was due to too many years of being too close when weapons were discharged into the unsuspecting.[75] But Carbo was sufficiently alert—according to a wiretapped conversation—to have developed his own ties to law enforcement, including Miami's, the coming citadel of organized crime: "the local ain't going to finger him [there]," providing him with wide latitude. He also had ties westward: "top mobsters, they get great fixes in Mexico…can't be extradited." This insider concurred with the notion that Mr. Gray was the "greatest lamster" of all.[76]

Despite the colorful cast of characters assembled at the courtroom in downtown Los Angeles—313 Spring Street, Courtroom #6—Gibson was in the unusual position of being portrayed as the Negro "brains" behind the entire operation, the linchpin, at the center of the web. Though it was noted early on in court that "this trial is being widely written up because we have such people involved in it," i.e., detailed "accounts from the newspapers" and "TV,"[77] it may have been the dearth of ordinariness—a Negro in charge?—that accounted for the general failure to focus on this relatively strange aspect. And yet, defendant Sica, then 49 years old and with a long rap sheet that included larceny and robbery, said he did not know Gibson—though he knew the blinker for 17 years—and also knew the man he called "the great colored pitcher," baseball hurler Satchel Paige.[78]

Sica was also linked to Chris Dundee, the Miami promoter and brother of the man who gained fame as Ali's trainer—Angelo Dundee. The Miamian and the defendant were both spotted as recently as the

---

74. Comment, 3 March 1961, Box 2483, Gibson Trial File-NAR-Riv.
75. Comment, 4 August 1961, Box 1711, Gibson Trial File-NAR-Riv.
76. Comment, 6 March 1961, Box 2483, Gibson Trial File-NAR-Riv.
77. Comment, 9 March 1961, Box 2483, Gibson Trial File-NAR-Riv.
78. Testimony by Joseph Sica, 3-4 May 1961, Gibson Trial File-NAR-Riv.

Patterson-Roy Harris bout in August 1958.[79] Dundee appeared at the trial as a witness for Palermo. Like so many involved in this trial, he, too, did not hear well (or maybe was seeking to evade answering questions adequately by pleading disability). He had known the blinker for three decades by then and, being the sole promoter in the growing urban node that was Miami, he also came to know Carbo well, too. "I spoke to Mr. Gibson quite often," unavoidably. But his hearing seemed to be unimpaired when he was asked why his name "was changed" from its Italian-sounding origin—"what difference does it make," he replied irritably.[80]

Though Gibson and his confederates were on trial, actually alongside them in the dock was the entire sport, as it had evolved in recent years. It wasn't just Jordan, trundled from one exploiter to another, forced to contend with the unappetizing choice of being corrupted by Kerkorian or Cohen or Carbo. It wasn't just the eloquent peroration—denunciation—by the prosecutor of the bestially sulfurous practices baked into the sport. In some ways, the ordinariness of the ugliness was most startling of all. Promoter William Daly was quite familiar with Doc Kearns, the former comrade of Jack Dempsey, who was still motoring along by the 1960s. They would commune at Kearns's abode—"everybody used to come there...I was his house guest," and that is where he met Carbo, the *éminence grise* of this entire story.[81] But then defense counsel William Bierne mentioned in passing that Kearns received 50% of Archie Moore's purse after he battled Joey Maxim "and he is still receiving that percentage,"[82] a jaw-dropping percentage in retrospect. (Just before the trial, in an explosion of cynicism and chutzpah, Kearns was working with the mob-riddled Teamsters union in an attempt to organize the entire boxing industry.[83]) By then Moore was reaching the end of a glorious career which he was desperately seeking to extend—jeopardizing life and limb in the process—not least since he was relinquishing so

---

79. File on Chris Dundee, circa 1961, Box 128, Prosecutor's File.

80. Testimony of Chris Dundee, 7 April 1961, Box 2485, Gibson Trial File-NAR-Riv.

81. Testimony by William Daly, 7 April 1961, Box 2485, Gibson Trial File-NAR-Riv.

82. Comment by William Bierne, 25 May 1961, Box 2489, Gibson Trial File-NAR-Riv.

83. *Miami Herald*, 8 December 1960, Sub Group VIII, Series I, Box 24, HKBA.

much of his earnings: "he washed the gray out of his hair," cracked Russell Parsons, attorney for Sica.[84]

The high court opinion and the criminal trial fundamentally ousted Gibson from the sport, paving the way for the subsequent rise of those like Don King and Bob Arum. Despite the unloading on him during the trial, he escaped with a probation and a fine. The crux of the case concerned extortion involving the purses of the besieged Don Jordan—in addition to Cohen and Carbo, the similarly oriented Ralph Gambina also claimed to have had him under contract at one time.[85] Gibson could well wonder why he and his outlaw comrades were on trial when the result could only benefit those like Cohen and Gambina. By August 1962 Gibson was petitioning the court in order to be allowed to travel abroad, Liberia in this case. "Gold Star Homes of which Mr. Gibson is an officer" was constructing "prefabricated home homes in Nigeria, Khartoum [Sudan]...Guinea...Liberia and Sierra Leone."[86] By April 1963 he was seeking to head southward, to the nation that became Belize.[87] His co-defendants were not so lucky as this light-skinned Negro with rapidly thinning hair and a face set off by horn-rimmed glasses. "In Alcatraz everybody had their own associations," said Mickey Cohen. Suggesting that the battle over control of Don Jordan could not obliterate deeper camaraderie, "in my group," said the diminutive racketeer, "was Frankie Carbo," and a kind of stand-in for Gibson: "Bumpy Johnson, a boss in Harlem"—not to mention "Alvin Karpis, [John] Dillinger's right hand,"[88] a reference to the slain bank robber.

* * *

The indictment and conviction of these defendants coincided with a change in administration in Washington, as President Eisenhower bowed out and was replaced by President John F. Kennedy, whose victory was significantly dependent upon a rush of Negro voters to the polls. This factor—along with a hastening of anti-Jim Crow

---

84. Comment by Russell Parsons, 25 May 1961, Box 2489, Gibson Trial File-NAR-Riv.

85. *International Herald Tribune,* 2 January 2006, Sub Group VIII, Series I, Box 9, HKBA.

86. Petition for Truman Gibson, 1 August 1962, Box 1711, Gibson Trial File-NAR-Riv.

87. Petition for Truman Gibson, 15 April 1963, Box 1711, Gibson Trial File-NAR-Riv.

88. Cohen, *Mickey Cohen,* 209.

activity—set the tone for his three-year tenure, climaxing weeks before his assassination with a massive March on Washington in August 1963. In a sense, this meant that Gibson's tenure as a boxing boss was premature; arguably, if he had been able to reach the peak of his influence later, he could have parlayed his clout as a former FDR advisor and influencer in Black Chicago to his benefit. Still, by early 1961 Senator Kefauver of Tennessee was in touch with the president's brother—future U.S. Senator and presidential aspirant, then U.S. Attorney General Robert F. Kennedy—about the attempt to "establish within the [Department of Justice] the Office of the National Boxing Commissioner." After a lengthy investigation, the legislator knew that "various states have been unable to solve this difficult problem," i.e., eliminating or even regulating the "racketeer element." Kefauver assured that "for the Commissioner to properly function, the services of the [FBI] are likely to be needed."[89]

But, alas, this concept did not take flight, becoming bogged down in bureaucratic snares and intense lobbying. Moreover, another instrumental event occurred, complicating life for mobsters and Washington alike. As early as 1950, Senator Kefauver was made aware of the strong bonds between Miami—a hotspot for racketeers, including Carbo—and "the West Indies, especially Cuba."[90] But by 1959, the *ancien régime* had been ousted, and by 1961, the attempt to dislodge its successor, led by Fidel Castro, had crashed figuratively, if not literally, into the Florida Straits. This heightened Cold War tensions, leading to what was called the October Crisis of 1962 in Havana and the Cuban Missile Crisis in Washington, as the world hurtled to the brink of nuclear catastrophe,[91] meaning it was difficult for the Kennedy Administration to focus on, by comparison, the relatively mundane matter of the malignant ills of boxing.

Nonetheless, the mandarins of the "New Frontier" in Washington were not particularly fond of Sonny Liston, quickly becoming a threat to dislodge Floyd Patterson. Patterson, by contrast, was viewed as the "Good Negro."[92] One who knew him contrasted Patter-

---

89. Senator Kefauver to Attorney General Kennedy, 8 March 1961, Box 229, Kefauver-UTn-K.

90. Letter from Lee Mortimer, 12 July 1950, Box 50, Kefauver-UTn-K.

91. Robert F. Kennedy, *Thirteen Days: A Memoir of the Cuban Missile Crisis*, New York: Norton, 1969.

92. See Patterson Narrative, ca. October 1960, Box 4, Mann-LC: In November 1953, Patterson was said to have impregnated a young girl. D'Amato counseled, "The only answer, Floyd, is a quiet marriage.... I was nearly 19. The girl was sixteen."

son with baseball legend Jackie Robinson, with the latter portrayed as a "sword rattler in the attaining of civil rights," while the boxer carried a comforting, hardly existent "silent message" more reassuring for those in power. Liston's image as a "Bad Negro" was a kind of replay of Jack Johnson without the anti-establishment politics but with the mob ties to which—at least publicly—the Kennedy team was hostile. Liston was also close to Ash Resnick, a wicked gambler and racketeer with roots in Las Vegas, Nevada, with the state making a comeback after hosting Johnson in 1910. Resnick placed the now fading Joe Louis on the payroll of the Thunderbird in Las Vegas as a kind of greeter, an ignominious end for a once great boxer who had hitched his fortunes to Gibson's and thus was destabilized when the suave attorney faced a criminal conviction.[93]

According to Harlem mobster Frank Lucas, he handed over a niftily huge sum to Louis in order for him to settle a claim with the taxman, further solidifying the former champion's debt to racketeers.[94] Louis repaid the favor when Lucas was on trial, and attended every day of this proceeding, often with the defendant's son in tow. After his conviction, Martha Louis—the champion's spouse—visited him frequently in prison. "I had a lot of respect for her,"[95] the inmate conceded.

Louis also repaid the favor when he was asked to testify on behalf of James Hoffa, Teamsters boss, then on trial, and, as Gibson recalled fondly, instead sat in the courtroom, his presence likely speaking more loudly to the jury than his inarticulate words might have.[96] Ironically, though Louis had styled himself as the anti-Johnson, not smiling after pulverizing Euro-American opponents, steering clear of public associations with Euro-American women, etc., in some ways his end was more inglorious than that of the Galvestonian. He married well when in 1959 he betrothed the woman who became Martha Louis, the first Negro woman to pass the difficult bar examination in California, qualifying as an attorney. Yet, she too fell upon hard times after he passed away, spending her declining years in a Farmington, Michigan, nursing home, poorly clad and with inadequate dentures, too,[97] a startling coda unfolding not far distant from where her spouse had shot to prominence in Detroit decades earlier.

---

93. Tosches, *The Devil*, 181, 185.
94. Lucas, *Original Gangster*, 218.
95. Ibid., 253, 283.
96. Gibson, *Knocking*, 262.
97. *Detroit News*, 21 March 1990, Sub Group VIII, Series I, Box 12, HKBA.

As the Kennedys were settling into newly found power in Washington, headlines blared about the former middleweight contender Jake La Motta, claiming that "Honest Fighters Finish Last." By then he was working as an actor, a route taken previously, albeit with more success, by former punchers like the then ridiculously wealthy Bob Hope. But now he had turned to the pages of a "Man's Magazine" blubbering about what had occurred years earlier when "to get a chance at the championship I had to make a deal with the fight mob, the crooked managers…[the] wise guys" and other barracudas. He unveiled at length in a kind of faux disgust "my notorious deal to throw the Billy Fox fight, the biggest fight scandal of my day."[98] Later, a journalist declared that "Blinky" Palermo—the man with the fluttering eyelids—was behind this notorious "fix."[99]

Despite the ongoing routing of Gibson, et al., racketeers continued to exert influence in the sport. "The Old Mongoose," Archie Moore, thought Patterson was overplaying his hand in refusing to fight Liston unless the challenger disassociated himself from the likes of Palermo and Carbo,[100] though this precondition may have been a useful cover for avoiding a potential beating in the ring, which is precisely what happened when they met in a one-sided match, then met again with the same result. Liston's smashing defeat of Patterson sealed his reputation as a boxer without peer—which then made his defeat at the hands of the man who became Muhammad Ali all the more startling, almost designed to catapult the former "Louisville Lip" into the top tier of boxing legends. (And almost designed to shrink the fortunes of bettors who wagered—unwisely but understandably—that Liston would prevail, while enriching obscenely counter-parties. "I made ends meet by betting," was the candid admission of Miami's Ferdie Pacheco, better known as a corner man for Ali—though he added quickly and unconvincingly that "all of my big wins came when I was outside of boxing."[101])

Chasing Gibson into Africa and Central America and placing his confederates behind bars did not necessarily deodorize the sport. Scenting the wealth to be made from the diverse revenue streams ranging from television to closed-circuit broadcasting, entering the fray was Roy Cohn, a former top lieutenant to the anti-communist bloodhound Senator Joseph McCarthy of Wisconsin (Robert F.

---

98. Jake La Motta, "Honest Fighters Finish Last," *TRUE, a Man's Magazine*, April 1961, Odds and Ends on Boxing, Vol. 43, UND.
99. *New York Daily News*, 25 October 1990.
100. Undated report, Vertical File-Archie Moore, SDHC.
101. Pacheco, *Tales*, 157.

Kennedy was also once at his side, too). "I owned a fight promotion company named Championship Sports, Inc.," said the future advisor to future boxing impresario and future U.S. President Donald J. Trump. "We put on the Floyd Patterson-Sonny Liston heavyweight title bout in Chicago on September 25, 1962." As often happened in prizefights, those a few minutes late in taking their seat at ringside could have missed the entire contest after Patterson was introduced rudely to Liston's massive gloved hands and then sniffed the canvas. "The IRS [Internal Revenue Service] seized all the proceeds of the fight, both the live gate and the closed-circuit theater gate." Still seemingly dazed years later, he said, as if his mind were boggled, "everybody's end was seized—the fighters', the theater owners', the managers,'"—"eight years later we were still owed $435,000," he concluded.[102] Cohn's entry into the sport did not bode well given his nasty roots. According to writer Arthur Mann, the Liston fight brought to promoters "more money than ever before drawn by a single fight," but the rookie, Cohn, the "mastermind" of the bout, went into debt in order to produce this result. Afterward, he wanted to control Patterson but was busy ducking creditors—he "donned false whiskers and fled secretly to Europe," this after the taxman had pursued him and his assets.[103]

D'Amato, and by implication, Patterson, was hostile to Cohn's partner, William Dennis Fugazy, president of Feature Sports. Just as Cohn had his own passel of government ties, so did his partner, since he had served in naval intelligence during World War II. Though Cohn was not an easy man to work with—Fugazy found him "quick to anger"—their relationship was close enough for him to name his youngest son after him.[104]

Before this contretemps erupted, Gibson told a congressional investigator that Fugazy was also in conflict with Carbo, adding ballast to the notion that intentional or not, the import of the 1961 trial in Los Angeles was to uplift one set of pirates over another. Revealingly, it was in this context, said Gibson, that Kearns was termed contemptuously as "nothing but a nigger lover," as the Cohn-Fugazy operation was noticeably devoid of Negroes in the top tier.[105]

---

102. Sidney Zion, *The Autobiography of Roy Cohn*, Secaucus, New Jersey: Lyle Stuart, 1988, 161-162.

103. "Behind the Boxing Bonanza," 1962, Box 5, Mann-LC.

104. *New York Times*, 13 March 1961, Sub Group VIII, Series I, Box 8, HKBA.

105. Testimony of Truman Gibson, 5-9 and 12-14 December 1960, Box 490, Kefauver-UTn-K.

The victory of Liston was just one more signpost on a road to the tumult that came to characterize the 1960s. Elaine Mokhtefi was at ringside both when the Black Panthers arrived in Algiers and—most important for the purposes of this book—seated at Madison Square Garden, when Benny Paret was pounded to death by Emile Griffith, an explosion of homophobia in that the vanquished had asserted derisively that the victor was "gay," a term just coming into common usage during this uproarious decade: "I watched, sickened, and helpless," she recollected, "as Griffith hammered Paret to death, the referee standing by" and—predictably, "the crowd demanding more" in a maddening outbreak of bloodlust—"until it was too late."[106] Paret was reputedly under the supervision of those tied to Carbo,[107] while his fellow inmate at Alcatraz, Mickey Cohen, expressed a likeminded homophobia.[108]

Paret's death was a defining moment for the sport, illustrating vividly the logical outcome of allowing two persons to pummel each other with ferocity. He appeared before regulators in the Empire State in early November 1958—just before Fidel Castro surged to power. He had arrived three months earlier from Santa Clara, Cuba.[109] His talent was recognized early, leading to a fierce struggle for control of his career, an unsteady path lubricated by his illiteracy and thumbprints deployed as a signature.[110] Ominously, when the authorities visited Paret's training camp, he was pronounced blandly "to be in good position physically and mentally," while Griffith was said to be "in the best condition of his sensational career"—with the difference in enthusiasm suggesting the outcome.[111] After the fatality, the tone shifted—perhaps to facilitate exculpation—and Paret was said to be in "excellent physical condition" beforehand.[112] Typically, the death was rationalized: There were "fewer serious injuries in professional boxing than in other sports, such as hockey, football, polo, skiing, auto racing," and the like. Yet despite giving Paret a clean bill of

---

106. Elaine Mokhtefi, *Algiers, Third World Capital: Freedom Fighters, Revolutionaries, Black Panthers*, London: Verso, 2018 (abbrev. Mokhtefi, *Algiers*), 33.

107. Heller, *In This Corner*, 364.

108. Cohen, *Mickey Cohen*, 223: "There are lots of queers in the joints [prisons].... I had owned these kind of joints where they were gay places.... the goddam joint [Springfield Prison] is crawling with queers all flying around."

109. Minutes, 7 November 1958, NYSAC.

110. In the Matter of: Inquiry into Contract between Manuel Alfaro and Bernardo Paret Crespo (Benny Paret), Boxer, dated November 7, 1958, NYSAC.

111. Minutes, 26 September 1961, NYSAC.

112. Report to Governor Nelson A. Rockefeller, 26 March 1962, NYSAC.

health, little was made of the technical knockout he suffered at the hands of Gene Fullmer in December 1961.[113] Increasingly, regulators were derelict, and not just in monitoring physical health. By 1966 they were mulling the possibility of providing a license to Clarence Ryan, though a Manhattan hospital concluded that he was "emotionally unstable...psychotic and a strange young man."[114]

Mokhtefi was also present in Algeria when representatives of liberation movements in South Africa and what became Zimbabwe arrived in search of succor and support.[115] It is unclear if they conferred about a leader of the rebel regime in what was then Rhodesia, and if so, if a leader of this outlaw state—Sir Roy Welensky—was discussed. He could have fit in well in the U.S., in that he was born Jewish in the hinterlands of Russia and Poland, but called himself a Swede. But like his counterparts on the west bank of the Atlantic he became a premier boxer in the raw and ruthless world of Rhodesian boxing, where one was lucky to be paid a pound for a round.[116] The man who became Sir Roy began as a lowly railway engineer, but not unlike George Wallace, when he became Rhodesian heavyweight champion in 1925, his ability to climb the class ladder was boosted and, like the Alabamian, his ability likewise to wreak havoc upon people of African descent was enhanced.[117]

Back in the U.S., climbing the rungs to prominence was a boxer with roots in Paterson, New Jersey, a former industrial powerhouse that had fallen on hard times, as evidenced by an increasingly distressed African-American community. Arising from these urban ashes was Rubin "Hurricane" Carter, described by one of his many biographers as "a rebel who refused to be intimidated by Paterson's white establishment" who feared his potential as a leader in the mold of Jack Johnson. He was, it was said, "threatening to shoot some New York City police if they continued to brutalize Blacks," and this militant stance led to a systematic and successful attempt to place the heavy-hitting middleweight behind bars, before a mass movement rescued him from oblivion.[118] The wise and articulate slugger was thought to be a "Malcolm X with fists," and even Muhammad

---

113. Dr. Marvin Stevens to Athletic Commission, 26 March 1962, NYSAC.

114. Minutes, 13 July 1966, NYSAC.

115. Mokhtefi, *Algiers*, 83, 104.

116. Don Taylor, *The Rhodesian: The Life of Sir Roy Welensky*, London: Museum Press Ltd., 1955, 13, 27.

117. Undated report, Sub Group IX, Series II, Box 26, HKBA.

118. Paul B. Wice, *Rubin 'Hurricane' Carter and the American Justice System*, New Brunswick: Rutgers University Press, 2000, 204.

Ali extended a hand of camaraderie to him, leading to retaliation targeting the heavyweight.[119]

Thus, even before Ali established an ineffable tie between Black Militancy and Black Boxers, this connection, for which Jack Johnson had established the template, was already in motion. There was something about using one's fists to earn a living that combined with the exceedingly dire plight of the communities from which they sprung, that contributed to—if not shaped—a renewed Black Militancy. And as Elaine Mokhtefi suggested, there was the role model presented by Southern Africa in popular, where racists were being challenged in armed revolts—a liberation process to which many Black Americans contributed.[120]

Hence, it was no surprise when a man considered to be a Founding Father of Black Studies in the 1960s—Nathan Hare, then of Howard University, later of the rebellious San Francisco State University—took to the ring, leading to a journalist's report that "once again Black Power won out over white power" as the scholar "flattened Dick Smith, an excellent white welter weight," and in the "first round," no less.[121] This career departure occurred after he had been sacked from the capstone of Negro education in Washington, D.C., after a typical display of militancy.[122]

Washington, D.C.—where the metropolitan area was to produce "Sugar" Ray Leonard, a face of the sport subsequently—was also to become a symbol of urban unrest, when civil explosions occurred nationwide in the 1960s. But unrest in the center of power—within walking distance of the White House and the Capitol—was qualitatively different from unrest elsewhere, and this city led the way when brawling among fans erupted at Golden Gloves bouts as early as 1961,[123] a foretaste of what was to erupt in the streets.

Richard M. Nixon of Southern California had served as Eisenhower's vice-president, then was defeated by Kennedy in 1960: He was said by one analyst to be the "Mafia's President" and certainly had ties as well to Southern Florida, where embittered Cuban exiles communed with a vibrant underworld. The man who embodied this trend of the underworld and Cuban exiles—and was also involved in management of boxers—was Bernard Barker, who in addition had

---

119. Report, 2 March 1988, Sub Group VIII, Series 1, Box 13, HKBA.
120. Horne, *White Supremacy*.
121. *The Hilltop* [Howard University], 8 December 1967.
122. *The Hilltop*, 1 December 1967.
123. Washington Post, 18 February 1961, Vertical File-Boxing, Special Collections, WDCPL.

links to real estate sales with seamy undertones. He appeared before Albany regulators during the pivotal year that was 1959 concerning a contract with boxer Doug Vaillant. "I work for [the] Cuban government," he said tersely, "the Treasury Department."[124] Yes, he was fired from the Central Intelligence Agency purportedly because of other connections, but he materialized a few years later as a burglar of Democratic Party headquarters in Washington, encapsulated later as the "Watergate" scandal, which caused Nixon to resign from the presidency in 1974.[125] And yes, this was the flip side of the tumult of the 1960s: a retrenchment and escalation by those that protesters were confronting and, ultimately, it was this retrenching trend that prevailed.

---

124. Minutes, 15 June 1959, NYSAC.

125. Don Fulsom, *The Mafia's President: Nixon and the Mob*, New York: Dunne, 2017, 39, 11, 145: Frighteningly, once Barker interrupted a speech by U.S. dissident Daniel Ellsberg, "shouting that he was a 'traitor' and a 'disgrace to the Jewish race.'"

Chapter 8

The Ali Regime

As the 1960s unwound, Cassius Clay—then renamed as Muhammad Ali—became the face of boxing, a successor to such eminences as Gans and Johnson and Armstrong and "Sugar" Ray and Joe Louis and the brief reign of Patterson. His knockout of Liston in 1964, his taunting destruction of Patterson in 1965, his unwillingness in 1967 to submit to acquiescence to conscription, meaning he would not fight in an increasingly unpopular war in Vietnam, his regaining his license in 1970 while using this three-year interregnum touring campuses in particular—and his regaining his title two more times before retiring in 1981—all this and more wrapped him in a unique mythos. Ali represented a Black Restoration, a lineal descendant of Johnson in the first instance in terms of his outspokenness about the war in Indo-China, which dovetailed neatly with a youthful rebellion catalyzed by the same tendency. The attempt to punish him by ousting him from the sport altogether because of his successful attempt to evade military conscription actually may have burnished his reputation, adding material sacrifice to his aura. His relationship with the Nation of Islam, cast prematurely into oblivion in the 1940s because of their reluctance to wage war against Japan in light of Tokyo's tantalizing slogan of being the "Champion of the Darker Races,"[1] also provided him with a beefy backup—embodied in the martial "Fruit of Islam"[2]—necessary and sufficient to confront the racketeers that still dominated the sport and, as Ike Williams and a legion of other punchers could well attest, had derailed more than one boxer's career.

In retrospect, his hiring of Angelo Dundee as a corner man—brother of Chris, whose ties to mobsters were well established—was

---

1. Horne, *Facing*.
2. A critical member of the Ali entourage was Gene Kilroy, who was formerly "Special Assistant" to Morris Shenker, noted mouthpiece of racketeers for years: Las Vegas Sports Book, 26 September 1980, Sub Group VIII, Series 1, Box 12, HKBA.

wise, his purported skills aside: Ishmael Reed contends that Angelo was a spy for the FBI.[3] His presence close to Ali's inner circle may have been comforting and calming to those who had dominated the sport up to that point. For with the surging anti-Jim Crow movement in the 1960s, there had to be adjustments to the status quo that had featured wise guys often plundering Negro gladiators, at times assisted by unfairly compensated Negroes like Truman Gibson. When total boxing revenue soared from about $5 million in the 1950s to $25 million, (likely an underestimate), by the 1970s—with African Americans claiming a larger percentage of a larger pie—a signal factor was the ubiquity of Ali.[4]

Ali made the historical moment but also was created by it: The means of transmission of his athleticism had increased as pay-per-view via television proliferated, which in turn dovetailed with rising Black Nationalism and antiwar activism—and his popularity enhanced the latter two ideological twists. "Muhammad is bigger than boxing," enthused promoter Don King in 1977, which remained true even though by then he was on the downswing of his enthralling career.[5] Even a decade before, when Ali was already controversial, the prime Albany regulator opined that "overall, Clay [Ali] has done a great deal for boxing. He has built up a worldwide interest in the game. Millions of people view him by reason of television (via Telestar)...he is arrogant but has done a lot for boxing." There were positive spinoffs too: "Everlast Sporting Goods is now selling 2600 pairs of gloves in a week...boxing is being stirred in colleges."[6]

Generally true—but Albany regulators who thrived on the revenue generated by boxing had other concerns. It was in 1969 that they were told that "boxing is declining as a prestige sport. Nationwide telecasting

---

3. Reed, *Complete Muhammad Ali*, 86.

4. Andrew R.M. Smith, *No Way But to Fight: George Foreman and the Business of Boxing*, Austin: University of Texas Press, 2020 (abbrev. Smith, *No Way*), 213. Foreman, in preparing for his epochal battles with Frazier and Ali, fought a number of questionable opponents which ill-served him as he confronted more worthy battlers: See *St. Paul Pioneer Press*, 9 February 1971: The "grotesque mismatch between...George Foreman and a nonentity named Phil Smith of Washington, D.C....a flabby opponent with three rolls of suet around his mid-section...30 pounds overweight...fiasco...helped stomp another breath of life out of pro boxing in this town." Foreman was "patriotically attired in red trunks with a blue stripe and a white waistband" and was "superbly conditioned."

5. Minutes, 4 October 1977, NYSAC.

6. Minutes, 2 February 1967, NYSAC.

is lessening the importance of New York State as a championship boxing center." Then there was the matter they were the reluctant to discuss publicly: "boxing is somewhat dominated by representatives of ethnic groups" (code for the Puerto Rican and African-American audiences); "the middle class" (code for Euro-Americans) "is hesitant to spend money to support matches between contestants from these groups." Then there were the "aggressive, excitable groups" that "release their tensions in a legal manner" at ringside: code again for Puerto Ricans, et al.[7] This suggested that once the Ali Regime was toppled, the sport was destined for decline.

Albany thought that "excitable" was a term that could be applied beyond Puerto Rico. Regulators believed that spectators in places like Quito, Ecuador, could also be so described. A referee from the U.S. was told "after he entered the ring" that "he would not be allowed to vote." The "medicine kit" of a corner man "was stolen"—then "his stool disappeared...the crowd became unruly" and threatened mayhem unless their compatriot was declared the victor. Since "more than 20,000 fans were present," their beseeching could not be ignored easily.[8] Then in 1967 at Madison Square Garden, the light heavyweight championship bout between Dick Tiger and Puerto Rican favorite José Torres ignited a disturbance. "Guards took away more than [25] whiskey bottles...hidden by fans under their coats."[9] Then in October 1969 Mike Quarry squared off against Ruben Figueroa and, it was said, "judges voted...to appease the Puerto Rican fans"; then Ali, who was present, "raised Figueroa's hand as the winner and the

---

7. Minutes, 10 January 1969, NYSAC. See also M.R. "Bob" Evans, President, World Boxing Association, to George Barton, ca. 1968, Boxing Board Records, 103.H.15.1B, MinnHS-SP: Evans, citing the writer Jack Drees, said, "The near death of professional boxing has created a void in the American sporting scene that deserves to be filled...the monetary rewards in boxing are very low...not enough fighters to supply the needs of small arenas... earning twenty to fifty dollars for a preliminary bout once, maybe twice a month...[yet] for all its low estate the American public still indicates boxing as its number one TV sports attraction. The Liston-Patterson fight a few years back, without home television, drew a radio audience of sixty-two million listeners. Liston against Clay drew close to seventy million radio listeners. These are the biggest audiences in the history of broadcasting." Still, awaiting elimination were the "'evils' of boxing...gangster influence, unscrupulous managers, larcenous promoters [emphasis-original]."

8. Cain Young, Manager of Ismael Laguna, to Commissioner Edwin Dooley, 28 May 1969, NYSAC.

9. Ned Irish to Governor N.A. Rockefeller, 17 May 1967, NYSAC.

booing increased."[10] Regulators fretted about wagering intersecting with ardent displays of fan enthusiasm to sway results: Albany was informed that "it is very likely you may have a riot before the fight is over with Puerto Rican boxers fighting."[11] How so? "Puerto Ricans are very excitable" was the insensitive conclusion reached.[12] After a further series of such reports trickled in to Albany, the decision was made to seek to "have only boxers of the same ethnic groups fight each other, for some time to come"—and "that a famous figure or Priest make a speech on good sportsmanship without getting didactic."[13]

Arguably, as a way to hem in and corral their meal ticket, Albany sought to restrain Ali—his alignment with Puerto Ricans was viewed with hysteria. The World Boxing Council affiliate in Manila was instructed to follow the "British Boxing Board...the Oriental Federation and the European group," "recognizing Frazier as the World Champion"—not Ali.[14] This restraint was mirrored at home when the so-called bible of the sport—*The Ring*—refused to name a "Fighter of the Year" in 1966 despite Ali's five successful defenses of his title; more telling is that this perverted decision was supported by mail from readers at a rate of six to one. The editors were adamant in asserting that "a boxer who defies the government of the USA to draft him" was unworthy of high honor. This decision was backed by the Boxing Writers Association, a model of quietude when it came to the real issue of racketeering influence.[15]

* * *

Clay's defenestration of the pugnacious Liston in early 1964 was a landmark in the sport, not only because it marked the advent of what could be called the Ali Regime. His second victory over the overmatched St. Louisan was of similar seismic impact, as it

---

10. Minutes, 6 November 1969, NYSAC.
11. Minutes, 1 December 1969, NYSAC.
12. Minutes, 12 December 1969, NYSAC.
13. Minutes, 8 December 1967, NYSAC.
14. Edwin B. Dooley, Chairman, NYSAC, to Hon. Justiniano N. Montano, Jr., WBA, 5 March 1969, NYSAC. At the same site and collection, see J. Onslow Fane, British Boxing Board of Control to Edwin Dooley, 16 May 1967: "your suspension of Muhammad Ali's license will be recognized and supported by this Board."
15. Undated clipping from *The Ring*, Sub Group IX, Series 2, Box 25, HKBA.

signaled that Ali would not be dislodged any time soon and that he and his Muslim co-religionists were now a force to be reckoned with, delivering consequences that have yet to be tallied altogether to this very day. Again, Reed argues that Liston took a "fall" in the second bout with Ali due to fear of "Muslim violence." (Then the vanquished St. Louisan fell victim to further violence—according to boxing insider Emmanuel Steward—who asserts that he was "murdered" and not a victim of a drug overdose, as widely believed.) He also asserts that Ali's religious comrades administered a beating to Bernard Glickman, an entrepreneur and boxing manager who had testified in Gibson's 1961 trial in Los Angeles. Irrespective of the veracity of these assertions—and I have no reason to doubt the accuracy of either—their very existence was a rebuff to the previous regime, suggesting that there was now an organized force that was more than ready to rumble, to coin a phrase. Reputedly, the Fruit of Islam also administered a severe shellacking to promoter Don King in Nassau, the Bahamas—conveniently beyond U.S. jurisdiction; it has also been reported that an actual showdown between traditional organized crime and the Fruit took place in 1965 in the context of the bout between George Chuvalo and Ernie Terrell.[16]

Ali needed all the help he could get at this point. The writer Norman Mailer says that the magnetic boxer told him that he was "living with threats against my life after the death of Malcolm X," in February 1965: "Real death threats."[17]

One columnist, commenting on the brutal Patterson fight, punctuated by Ali veritably torturing the loser in the ring because of his failure to address him by his chosen name—as opposed to his "slave" moniker—found a similar display beyond the ring: "there were four better fights in the audience," said Joe Falls, involving "four members of the Black Muslims. They terrorized the crowd, menaced the women and it took 20 cops—five for each—to beat them to the floor, handcuff them and drag them, screaming from the arena."[18]

---

16. Reed, *Complete Muhammad Ali*, 109, 135, 101, 173: Michael Buffer reportedly generated $400 million from invoking this "rumble" phrase that he was said not to have invented. On King and the Fruit, see Smith, *No Way*, 245. See also *New York Post*, 8 December 1981, Box 156, Newfield-UT: King was subjected to a "severe beating in his hotel room in Freeport [sic], the Bahamas" by "five unidentified men."

17. Norman Mailer, *The Fight*, Boston: Little Brown, 1975 (abbrev. Mailer, *Fight*), 166.

18. Column, 24 November 1965, Boxing Scrapbooks-Heavyweights, Vol. 18, UND.

Eventually, Ali was to befriend Major Benjamin Coxson, a major figure in the rise of organized crime in Black Philadelphia—which became the locus of this trend, an outgrowth of the anti-Jim Crow movement in that draconian racism had barred its full emergence previously. Before his gangland style slaying in 1973 in his comfortable home in Cherry Hill, New Jersey—the suburb where Ali too once resided—Coxson (or "The Maj" as he was known)—had absorbed 16 arrests and 12 convictions in the previous 20 years for various charges, including car theft, larceny, weapons offenses, interstate transportation of stolen vehicles, etc. "The country is run by racketeers" was one of the pithier conclusions of "The Maj," who happened to be one of the wealthiest African Americans in the vicinity of the City of Brotherly Love. He also became an agent for Ali and they spent time in each other's homes as the boxer called his comrade, "his 'gangster.'" When "The Maj" was gunned down in his home, then occupied by his spouse and two children, it was apparently by a group known as the "Black Mafia": The slaying was a result of an alleged drug deal that went sideways; this bloodily gruesome scene took place less than a kilometer from the home that Ali had purchased from Coxson and in the midst of the latter's attempt to become mayor of neighboring Camden, New Jersey, a town beset by multiple problems. Camden also had housed the mobster-connected boxer Jersey Joe Walcott. Interestingly, the Nation of Islam reportedly was displeased with Coxson because of his affable friendship with Ali.[19] And, of course, the ties of promoter Don King to organized crime in Cleveland are by now well-known.[20]

But was it fair to demand that Ali's circle include only angels and girl scouts when those he confronted were not so constricted? Thus, one of the "tomato cans" he battled, Chuck "The Bayonne Bleeder" Wepner, was managed by Anthony "Gary" Garafola,[21] who was said to be a "front for a powerful captain in the [Vito] Genovese crime family, James Napoli."[22] Napoli—or "Jimmy Nap," as he was termed—and his partner, Joseph "Joe Carlo" Calabro, also had their claws in Frankie de Paula, a ranking light heavyweight contender: The two racketeers were indicted for conspiring to pay huge sums

---

19. *New York Times*, 9 June 1973. For more on Coxson, see Kram, *Smokin' Joe*, 136, 139. See also Francis A.J. Ianni, *Black Mafia: Ethnic Succession in Organized Crime*, New York: Simon & Schuster, 1974.

20. Brady, *Boxing Confidential*, 331.

21. Minutes, 29 October 1954, NYSAC: The boxer Anthony Garafola assumes the "Ring Name" of Gary Garafola.

22. Assael, *Murder*, 96.

of money to certain fighters in order to entice them to agree to a preordained outcome of bouts. These two mobsters were also said to have links to Nino Benevuti, a middleweight contender.[23] Choirboy was not a term that could be affixed to de Paula: He and Garafola were arrested on federal charges of involvement in the March 1968 trucking theft of an $80,000 interstate shipment of copper destined for Newark, New Jersey.[24] Eventually, Anthony Joseph "Gary" Garafola was indicted for murdering de Paula,[25] suggesting that a topflight boxer who proceeded without some kind of backup was akin to a babe in the woods. Then another Ali opponent, George Chuvalo, had to survive a wave of negative publicity when one of his opponents was killed after he was reluctant to accept a deal whereby he would lose easily to the plodding Chuvalo.[26] Possibly because of the similarly beefy men who surrounded him, Ali managed to escape the ugly fate of one of his opponents, Cleveland Williams, who had been shot previously by law enforcement officers in Texas.[27]

Nevertheless, Ali became involved with questionable characters, his opponents aside. One of his promoters, James Anthony Cornelius, was linked to fraud.[28] Another fraudster, Harold Rossfields Smith—one of the names he deployed—was involved in yet another looting, this time with Wells Fargo bank, which he said was complicit.[29] (Ishmael Reed argues that Ali himself was witting in this crime, along with those of the shadowy Richard Hirschfield.[30]) This Negro received a ten-year term for bank fraud, this after he became one of the nation's most powerful boxing promoters as founder of Muhammad Ali Professional Sports, Inc.[31] He wound up serving five and a half years of this sentence meted out for embezzling a whopping amount from this bank. (When paroled in 1988, he was licensed to

---

23. *Detroit Free Press*, 17 December 1969, Boxing Notes on Muhammad Ali, Vol. 21, UND.
24. Minutes, 21 May 1969, NYSAC.
25. *United Press International*, 17 September 1970, Boxing Notes on Muhammad Ali, Vol. 21, UND.
26. *Detroit News*, 25 February 1972, Boxing Notes on Muhammad Ali, Vol. 21, UND.
27. *Miami News*, 11 June 1969, Sub Group X, Series II, Box 41, HKBA.
28. *Los Angeles Times*, 14 January 1982, Sub Group XV, Series VII, Box 35, HKBA.
29. *Los Angeles Herald Examiner*, 20 March 1981, Sub Group XV, Series VII, Box 35, HKBA. For more on this fraudster, see Brady, *Boxing Confidential*, 179.
30. Reed, *Complete Muhammad Ali*, 406.
31. *New York Times*, 2 June 1982, Box 156, Newfield-UT.

be a boxing manager, with this criminal background not derailing his application.[32]) Of course, the latter fraudster, as so often happens, had calling cards allowing him entrée into circles where Ali circulated; for example, "Smith" attended American University in Washington, D.C., a city that also housed Howard University, where the famed chanteuse and musician Roberta Flack spent her formative years: He was said to be her "chum."[33]

Black organized crime tended toward ethno-centrism, a counterpoint to what was coming to be called "La Cosa Nostra," not only disproportionately comprised of Italian Americans but Sicilian Americans, with the Nation of Islam's overtures to Arabs akin to LCN's relations to Jewish Americans, such as Mickey Cohen, "Bugsy" Siegel, Morris Shenker and others. Shortly after besting Liston, Ali praised G.A. Nasser, Egypt's leader, at a time when the Cairene was hardly popular among broad swaths of the U.S. population because of his steadfastness in confronting the U.S. ally in Israel.[34]

(A possible indicator of the fate of the Jewish-American backers of the latter arrived in late 1964 when Dick Wipperman was barred from wearing the Star of David on his trunks, as Jewish boxers had been doing for years; this occurred as Ali was gaining takeoff—and interpretively could be seen as further evidence of ushering this ethno-religious minority into the hallowed halls of "whiteness," paradoxically just as Zionism was assuming a firmer grip. The murder of Siegel in the late 1940s may have signaled that the integration of this minority into the formidable enterprise that was racketeering was bumpy—but, like the barring of the Star of David, it was proceeding nonetheless.)[35]

The hegemony of this ethno-centrism, especially among African Americans, was facilitated by the preceding eclipse of the kind of

---

32. *Los Angeles Times*, 4 May 1991, Sub Group VIII, Series I, Box 20, HKBA.

33. *Los Angeles Herald Examiner*, 7 April 1982, Sub Group XV, Series VII, Box 35, HKBA.

34. Report, 6 June 1964, Boxing Scrapbooks, Heavyweights, Vol. 17, UND.

35. Report, 20 November 1964, Sub Group IX, Series II, Box 26, HKBA. Mickey Cohen, leading Jewish-American racketeer, claimed inferentially in 1974 that his lengthy imprisonment may have had something to do with his ethno-religious ancestry. "I served a longer term on the income tax evasion charge," he groused, "than anybody in history. Even longer than Al Capone," was his sour assessment of his 11-year incarceration: *Los Angeles Times*, 13 November 1974.

militancy embodied by Paul Robeson—a militancy which placed emphasis on trade unionism—which was in similar decline.[36]

In sum, the transition from Clay to Ali—in every sense, from every angle—was unsmooth. By March 1963 the NAACP leadership was comprehensibly unaware of what was to come. While considering "Cassius Clay…in view of his mouthings," a reference to the doggerel, insults and perorations that then characterized the "Louisville Lip," the official concluded wrongly: "I am wondering if he has not presented us with a terrific opportunity to gain a Life Membership from him." This Association official exposed his misjudging of the situation when he recalled that "some time ago remarks quite similar to those of Cassius Clay were attributed to 'Fats' Domino" (the popular New Orleans singer and pianist) "and within a period of weeks an initial payment of $250…was received" by the NAACP.[37] As matters evolved, any donations from the boxer were likely reaching the coffers of the Nation of Islam, a factor that then altered the political calculus of Black America, setting the stage for the arrival of Black Power and a resurgence of Black Nationalism.[38]

Days later the bad news was delivered to the NAACP, which compromised its integrity in 1948 when it sacked the founder and patriarch of the organization—the legendary W.E.B. Du Bois—not least because of his closeness to the Progressive Party, then spearheaded by former FDR Vice President (and comrade of Joe Louis) Henry Wallace.[39] This unsightly purge contributed to an ideological vacuum, then filled by the Nation of Islam, which had been a minor force—until the organized left was put on a glide path to decline. In the short term, this purge kept the group afloat in the midst of anti-communist attacks led by those like Roy Cohn and his boss, Senator McCarthy; in the long term, it compromised the ability of the organization to appeal to restless African-American youth who then were eager to confront U.S. elites, rather than compromise with them. Thus, Maurice Rabb of Louisville told the Association, after meeting with Clay, along with his "brother Rudy, [and] his chauffeur, Mr. Frank L. Stanley," that the boxer himself "emphatically denied having made the anti-NAACP statements" attributed to him. Rabb was willing to accept this denial though "Cassius does

---

36. See Horne, *Paul Robeson*. See also Gerald Horne, *Red Seas: Ferdinand Smith and Radical Black Sailors in the U.S. and Jamaica*, New York: New York University Press, 2005.
37. NAACP to Maurice Rabb, 19 March 1963, Box III: A35, NAACP-LC.
38. Horne, *Fire*.
39. Horne, *Black and Red*.

not stop talking long enough for anyone else to complete a sentence. He interrupts constantly...he is 'way out,'" he said exasperatedly. But he was sufficiently grounded to proclaim that he "consented to join the NAACP if we would give him $250,000.00," indicating that he "seems to have been thoroughly exposed to the teachings of Elijah Muhammad," leader of the NOI: "he feels that five of our states should be turned over to the Negroes," he added with wonder. "He sneers at the fact that a Jew is the National President of the NAACP." On the other hand, "Cassius has the greatest respect for Jackie Robinson, 'Sugar' Ray Robinson...and...Archie Moore. Perhaps the best approach is through one of them." Above all, stressed this man who was part of the syndicate that backed Clay at the onset of his career, "<u>CASSIUS</u> makes all decisions concerning <u>CASSIUS</u> [emphasis-original]."[40]

A scant year later, after the upset victory over Liston, Clay had become effectively Ali, and Roy Wilkins, the staid and balding leader of the Association, rebuked the "persistence by the WBA [World Boxing Association] in harassing this young man," already threatening his career: Such a praxis, he insisted accurately, "will convince our membership and Negro citizens generally that Clay is being persecuted because of his race."[41] The WBA doubtlessly studying the political landscape with demonstrations by "Negro citizens" exploding regularly, "subsequently announced," said the Association, "that no action would be taken against the champion 'at this time'"—those final three words not to be ignored.[42]

The WBA had its own problems. Albany regulators were told that in the mid-1960s the association was weakened when the "World Boxing Council...pulled out" and embarked on their own path. Moreover, it was said that their leader Luis Spota "is an out and out Communist," a descriptor bound to be taken seriously.[43]

Also not to be ignored were the furious protestations by Liston's scruffier backers, who apparently thought that their alleged payment of $50,000 to the victor's team provided them with the right

---

40. Maurice Rabb to Morris de Lisser, 25 March 1963, Box III: A35, NAACP-LC. See also Minutes, 9 February 1962, NYSAC: Question to "Cassius Clay...this contract is for three years. You get two-thirds and the manager gets one-third. Is that clear?" Response from "Mr. Clay...Yes."
41. Roy Wilkins to Edward Lassman, 24 March 1964, Box III: A35, NAACP-LC.
42. Press Release, 26 March 1964, Box III: A35, NAACP-LC.
43. Minutes, 17 November 1966, NYSAC.

to choose his future opponents and promote his future fights[44]—a deal akin to what Joe Louis had to broker in negotiating with Braddock decades earlier. The Liston crew thought they would be able to garner a future share of Ali's bounteous revenue based on their man's supposed dive in the first fight.[45] A report subsequently maintained that Liston earned his stripes with racketeers by "breaking up strikes," a contention that adds credence to the various rumors surrounding his defeats at the hands of Ali.[46]

Liston's road to prominence was stony indeed. At the age of 14 he was incarcerated, and by the time he became 17, he was facing a prison term of four years: robbery and larceny were the charges; then came a charge of assault with intent to kill, then impersonating a police officer and disorderly conduct, among other accusations. Albany regulators looked askance at his relationships with mobsters, including "Blinky" Palermo, who owned a bistro where Liston's wife toiled as a waitress and cook.[47] Like flies to honey, racketeers flocked to Liston: His 1962 Chicago bout with Patterson brought the burly heavyweight $250,000 from television alone. His 1963 contest with Patterson brought him a cool $1.6 million, while his 1964 bout with "Clay"—where an easy victory for him was predicted—brought Liston from the gate, closed-circuit television and radio $720,000. After his 1965 defeat at the hands of Ali, the record revealed that he had taken home almost $4 million for his championship fights.[48]

Closed-circuit TV was driving the sport in general. When Patterson faced Chuvalo in early 1965, regulators were gleeful, since the mass ability to watch this bout—along with 19,000 spectators surrounding the ring—meant that a leading Manhattan daily "carried the outcome of the fight on its front page in banner headlines, similar to news stories of international importance." The problem for Albany was the seeming inability to tax revenues generated outside of the state. This was also an issue for Nevada. The Ali-Patterson bout in Las Vegas in 1965 had a gross in closed-circuit revenues over $3 million in the U.S. and Canada alone.[49]

---

44. Tosches, *The Devil*, 208.
45. Assael, *Murder*, 194. See also Brian DeVido, *Every Time I Talk to Liston*, New York: Bloomsbury, 2004.
46. *Guardian* [U.K.], 17 February 1991, Box 151, Newfield-UT.
47. Decision Denying Sonny Liston a License, 27 April 1962, NYSAC.
48. Minutes, 31 August 1967, NYSAC.
49. Report to John P. Lomenzo, Secretary of State, and Governor Rockefeller, 31 December 1965, NYSAC.

Liston had his own issues, separate and apart from closed-circuit revenues: He embarked on an uphill climb after his two shocking defeats at the hands of Ali. There are few individuals more pitifully pathetic than the fearsome villain unmasked as an ordinary mortal, not unlike the classic scene from the film *The Wizard of Oz*, when the ogre behind the curtain with the booming voice is revealed to be a mere pipsqueak. This "Bad Negro" was expected to put the loquaciously rebellious Ali in his place—and failed miserably (unless, of course, you wagered that he would fail). Even the discussion of the multi-talented performer Sammy Davis, Jr. becoming his manager was not enough to repair his tattered reputation.[50] Liston's organized crime connections and his own rap sheet meant that he would face difficulty in gaining a license to pursue his fistic career. Such was the case in Minnesota in August 1968 at the height of unrest in the U.S. for which Ali had become a reigning symbol. But his stinging defeat by the obstreperous Ali had reduced his usefulness to those determined to uphold the increasingly challenged status quo. "Lift the ban imposed upon Boxer Sonny Liston" was at issue. But then began a lengthy recitation of his various transgressions: "administering a serious physical beating to a policeman in St. Louis...in which the policeman suffered a broken leg; curbing a woman at 3:00 A.M. in a public park in Philadelphia; and threatening a policeman in Denver...who arrested him for driving 70 miles an hour in a 35 mile zone." Underscored were the curious results of his matches with Ali: "All this in addition to the conduct in the ring in two fights with Cassius Clay," featuring a phantom punch from Ali and the purported torpedo that was Liston wilting like a wet firecracker, sitting slumped on his tool and unable to return to combat, unable to answer to the bell. Yet Liston had leverage in the federal union that had propelled the sport in the first place, as Negroes fled west to Nevada, then eastward to New York, in the early 20th century. Liston still could box in California and maybe Nevada, too—not to mention abroad—so despite his lusterless record, it was agreed "unanimously" that he would be licensed in Minnesota [emphasis-original].[51]

Ignored was the purported reason why fights with Liston did not occur in Nevada. Art Lurie of the boxing authority there found it suspicious that when Liston was knocked down in the second fight the

---

50. Picture and inscription of Liston and Davis, 14 November 1967, Odds and Ends on Boxing, Vol. 46, UND.

51. Minutes, State Athletic Commission, Boxing Board Records, 103.H.15.1B, MinnHS-SP.

referee purportedly had to be instructed to start counting.[52] Besides, the Sagebrush State was undercutting New York busily, as major bouts fled to Las Vegas. Albany was contemplating cutting taxes on these events to become more competitive in a downward spiral; non-resident boxers were taxed at 14% of the income derived from the contest, and slashing this figure was the proposed remedy, with little concern about the concomitant impact on education and health care. For as Albany saw matters, competitors in Texas, Nevada, Florida and New Jersey, did not then "have a state personal income tax, except Pennsylvania with a 2.3 per cent state personal income tax"—rates that jeopardized the possibility of staging future Ali bouts, which were registering significant revenues.[53] The ability of boxers to engage in arbitrage, manipulating one jurisdiction against another, may have influenced baseball star—and GOP stalwart—Jackie Robinson to demand that Albany license Liston immediately.[54]

Helping to protect Ali and his own leverage from the unfortunate fate that had chased Jack Johnson into exile and "Chalky" Wright to a premature death was his manager, Herbert Muhammad, an offspring of Elijah Muhammad. More contemporarily, Ernie Terrell, who once sang alongside his sister Jean Terrell (who replaced Diana Ross in the "Supremes"), in yet another mob-dominated business,[55] seemed to fight a losing battle when racketeers sought to install the disgraced Bernard Glickman as his manager.[56] "I do feel I can beat the present champ, Cassius Clay," said the tall boxer, sincerely but wrongly.[57] Muhammad's presence was an informal guarantee that what befell Terrell would not ensnare Ali. When the portly manager leapt on the apron of the ring to confer with his client in his bout with Zora Folley in 1967, it was emblematic of his hard-charging style.[58] For the formidable presence of Muhammad, backed by the

---

52. *Las Vegas Review Journal*, 1 June 1986, Sub Group VIII, Series I, Box 13, HKBA. See also Oral History, Art Lurie, 25 April 1986, UNV-LV.
53. Minutes, 2 May 1973, NYSAC.
54. Jackie Robinson to Edwin B. Dooley, 6 February 1968, NYSAC.
55. Benjaminson, *Story of Motown*, 105.
56. Report, 29 March circa 1966, "Chicago Tribune Service," Boxing Scrapbooks, Heavyweights, Vol. 18, UND. See also Minutes, 29 July 1966, NYSAC: Another "investor" in Terrell's career was George A. Hamid of Margate, New Jersey, advertised as a "part owner of the Miami Dolphins Football Team." His presence was just one more example of how boxing intersected with other sports. See also Minutes, 14 September 1956, NYSAC: Legendary football star Bronko Nagurski registers as wrestler.
57. Minutes, 26 March 1964, NYSAC.
58. Minutes, 22 March 1967, NYSAC.

Fruit, assumed management of Ali shortly after his contract with the syndicate in Kentucky expired. Like many of the "royal family"—the name affixed to the offspring and closest co-religionists of Nation of Islam leaders—he resided near the University of Chicago campus. His home, however, was designed by an Arab architect and carried like cultural influences, redolent of what amounted to an oppositional stance, as the U.S. itself backed Israel during repetitive wars in the region—then endured the transformative backlash of the oil embargo of 1973. Still, the two telephones encased in his Cadillac echoed an elite U.S. lifestyle far distant from the bulk of African Americans nationally. Unruffled, and in decided contrast to others in his tax bracket, the pudgy manager told an inquirer, "I've had more bugs put in my rooms and on phones," reflective of the hysteria-generated surveillance that greeted the gladiatorial attainments of his primary client. He was well compensated—reportedly receiving the normative one third of Ali's purses—and as matters evolved, was quite profitably adroit in playing off the two promoters who picked up the baton once carried aloft by Mike Jacobs, then Truman Gibson—Don King and Bob Arum. He was accused of allowing Ali to fight well past the time he should have retired, thereby jeopardizing his health, but such an analysis presupposes that the boxer himself was eager to desert the spotlight, a difficult argument to mount.[59]

Moreover, it is difficult to evaluate Muhammad in isolation or absent comparison to the sport in general. For example, as Ali was en route to garnering multi-million dollar purses, Bob Foster, though a lanky, bomb throwing light-heavyweight champion, was receiving mere hundreds of dollars for a non-title fight.[60] Even the predictably somnolent sportswriters of the *New York Times* demanded that Albany in 1968 do something, since "everyone connected with boxing knows that Foster is owned and controlled by Washington's Kingpin mobsters, namely Joe Nesline and Charles 'The Blade' Tourine…they have already quietly flooded the country with bets on Foster" in his bout with Dick Tiger, which Albany sanctioned.[61] (Tiger, a Nigerian—an Ibo—had another problem: His manager was in the region known as "Biafra" then in the throes of a brutal civil war with

---

59. Mark Kram, "On the Throne Behind the Power," *Sports Illustrated*, 27 September 1976, Sub Group VIII, Series I, Box 15, HKBA.

60. *Washington Star*, 7 December 1969, Vertical File-Boxing, Special Collections, WDCPL.

61. Sports Editor of *The New York Times*, 30 April 1968 to State Athletic Commission, NYSAC.

the Lagos administration.)⁶² Foster's other purported manager, Morris "Mushky" Salow was, said Albany, "known to the West Hartford Police as a gambler" and owner of a watering hole "frequented by hoodlums," not to mention a lengthy rap sheet.⁶³ The unctuous Salow spoke glowingly of the "deserving boy" he managed—i.e., the man who was not only a prime contender but an Air Force veteran who served five long years.⁶⁴ Yet, said a key Albany regulator, "Foster is in need of money and has obligations to his home and family," a situation worsened by the presence of Salow, who "is associated with undesirables. We have doubts about his integrity." This meant that "the gamblers took over Foster." Thus, Albany was "convinced" that the bout between him and the ethically challenged opponent de Paula was a "fixed match and that de Paula 'threw' the match."⁶⁵

Tommy "Hurricane" Jackson, who once fought Patterson, was said to have an "'undercover' manager" too, in the person of John "Sonny" Franzese, a "known hoodlum involved in shylocking, narcotics and prostitution" as "leader of the Mafia in Queens," New York.⁶⁶ On the other hand, the FBI maintained that a son of Muhammad threatened promoter Don King after a separate court case involving Murad Muhammad to the point where the matchmaker "feared for his life."⁶⁷ Given the heinous circumstances that accompanied the sport, it was not easy to disparage a boxer who desired extra layers of protection.

For Ali was an expert promoter of his prizefights, drawing upon strains stretching back decades when promoters noticed that money was to be made by dethroning the boxer so bold as to challenge the "Great White Hope," a vain search that resumed with a vengeance in the mid-1960s, leading to much publicity and healthy purses for the likes of journeymen like Jerry Quarry.⁶⁸ By 1968 the "Bible" of boxing—*The Ring*—was sifting through on the average about 100 letters monthly from boxing fans who were lusting to see Quarry become champion.⁶⁹ Another writer in the "Bible" reflected upon

---

62. Minutes, 10 January 1969, NYSAC.
63. Minutes, 15 May 1968, NYSAC.
64. Morris Salow to Edwin B. Dooley, 6 December 1967, NYSAC.
65. Minutes, 12 December 1969, NYSAC.
66. Report, ca. May 1968, NYSAC.
67. FBI Document, 4 March 1982, Box 156, Newfield-UT.
68. Column by Eddie Muller, 17 April 1966, Sub Group VIII, Series III, Box 33, HKBA.
69. Dan Daniel, "Quarry Revives White Hope Yammer," *The Ring*, 47 (No. 4, May 1968): 10-11, 62, 11, Box 156, Newfield-UT.

224   THE BITTERSWEET SCIENCE

earlier eras when "prospects" for this racially coded title "came from every conceivable line of industry—railroad yards, farms, cattle ranches, lumber camps, docks, street cars and office buildings.... White Hope tournaments sprung up all over the world."[70]

With a jujitsu-like maneuver—prefiguring the "rope-a-dope" tactic, allowing his opponent to exhaust himself by punching a (presumably) well-protected Ali, leaving the former vulnerable to a late-round flurry—Ali well knew that certain spectators would pay handsomely to see him receive a comeuppance or at least absorb well-placed blows. Hiding in plain view was Ali's adept fusing of "race," the factor that undergirded an enriching and rebellious slavery, and "religion," with his Muslim faith harking back to the existential threat perceived by Western Europeans in the wake of the Christian ouster from Constantinople in 1453, followed by the titanic battle for Iberia, culminating in 1492 with the impending advent of settler colonialism itself. It was particularly this matter of religion, adherence to Islam with hundreds of millions of adherents globally, that helped to bolster Ali's popularity, leading him to receive fan mail globally, some merely and inadequately addressed "care of Ali's trainer"[71] (most of the letters from Africa were from the southern cone, indicative of the resonances between Jim Crow and apartheid).[72]

Also hiding in plain view was the unavoidable fact that the audacity of Ali's promotional acumen paled in comparison to past efforts that would have made P.T. Barnum blush. Thus, in 1939, Joe Jacobs, in order to hype a bout between his client, "Two Ton" Tony Galento and the "Brown Bomber," claimed with intentional falsity that Joe Louis had "knocked out Max Schmeling," his other client, by placing in his gloves "a small metal cylinder with knobs on each end... slipped into the palm of Louis' right hand." After the pulverizing of the German, "Julian Black one of [Louis's] managers "leapt into the ring and "took the gadget from Louis' glove." But when hauled before the authorities, Jacobs backpedaled furiously, saying weakly, his falsehood was "strictly for publicity purposes...something had to be done to enliven that fight up" and "it did get a lot of publicity at the time." He demurred when instructed sternly that "you might have set back boxing back fifty years in making such a charge."[73]

---

70. Jersey Jones, "The White Hopes," *The Ring*, 45 (No. 6, July 1966): 16-20, 36-37, 36, Box 156, Newfield-UT.
71. See Folders of Fan Mail, Sub Group XIX, Series II, Box 1, HKBA.
72. Horne, *White Supremacy*.
73. Testimony of Joe Jacobs in Minutes, 11 July 1939, NYSAC.

Jacobs was manipulating the inner recesses of the weak-minded, who thought that a Negro could beat an Aryan only by dint of cheating. Ali's taunts and doggerel—predicting correctly that Archie Moore would fall by round four—never stooped this low. (Set aside the allegation that Moore agreed to a preordained outcome of this contest.[74] Since Moore was close to Jack "Doc" Kearns, who in turn was thought to be "paying out to the underworld in St. Louis," this allegation was taken seriously.[75])

Instead, Ali placed himself broadly within the ranks of the mass dissent that bubbled to the surface in the 1960s, driven by the anti-Jim Crow and antiwar movements. The other symbol that merged these two potent forces was Nobel Laureate Dr. Martin Luther King, Jr. Tellingly, when Ali was prosecuted because of his reluctance to be conscripted, FBI agent Courtney Evans revealed that "evidence" against this "prizefighter" was derived from a "telephone tap [that] had been in operation against [Dr. King],"[76] unveiling the details of their consultations. And though Ali was criticized sharply for the manner in which he derided his many opponents—especially South Carolina's and Philadelphia's "Smokin'" Joe Frazier—some of the hostility generated was beyond his immediate control. For his other principal opponent, Texas's George Foreman, emphasized his "Christian identity," converting his battles with Ali into something that may have been deeper than the continuing "race" conflicts of the "Great White Hope" era: religious war.[77]

When Foreman, the future pastor, not only wore his religious beliefs on his sleeve but also waved the U.S. flag after triumphing in the Mexico City Olympics—this after two victorious sprinters, Tommie Smith and John Carlos, shoeless and defiant, raised clenched fists on the podium in protest of maltreatment of Black Americans—the Houstonian was juxtaposed to Ali, to the latter's detriment, at least among the bulk of Euro-Americans across class lines. Then Frazier was characterized as the "blackest White Hope in history," signifying that what was at stake was wounding and dethroning the often bombastic Ali, which would then serve as a proxy for uplifting the opposing form of racial masculinity that he was thought to undermine. Of course, there were not as many differences between and among these pugilists as were imagined. In a remarkable united front, Ali, Frazier and Patterson all backed the victorious Republican,

---

74. Smith, *No Way*, 80.
75. Minutes, 14 February 1964, NYSAC.
76. Oral History, Courtney Evans, 5 January 1971, JFK.
77. Horne, *Dawning*.

Ronald Reagan, in his re-election race in 1984,[78] while Foreman flashed his true colors once more when over strident objection by activists, he chose to visit apartheid South Africa.[79] Ali seemed incongruously aligned in this rightward maneuver, yet it was Frazier who chose to be represented by militant African-American attorney Bruce Wright, who at one point faced Ali's lawyer, the unprincipled Bob Arum.[80]

Patterson, on the other hand, got a plum appointment as a regulator of the sport in Albany, providing an opportunity for various payoffs and "legal graft" in a state dominated by the GOP governor for years, the munificent Nelson A. Rockefeller.[81] It was then that Don King, citing his adversary Bob Arum, argued that "[Madison Square] Garden runs the Commission," which suggested that Patterson was now in bed with a previously close colleague.[82]

Since Patterson contended that "Mike Burke"—the Garden's majordomo—"does not want to do business with Don King," the promoter with the electrified hairdo might have had reason to question both the Commission and the Garden alike.[83] While shunning King, the Garden evidently had no such qualms about dealing with Carbo, the reigning racketeer.

Albany was told in 1967 that "the Garden would have lost money if they did not have the [Emile] Griffith fights in the past three or four years."[84] Yet, like the ascension of Truman Gibson, Patterson's rise was a further desegregation of the highest rungs of the sport. But it did not mean desegregation altogether since it was Patterson the regulator who announced: "I am still against women boxing" since they, allegedly, "are not structured or built to box as men are. Women's bones are more brittle than men['s]," he argued.[85]

---

78. Reed, *Complete Muhammad Ali*, 93.
79. Smith, *No Way*, 9, 66, 211. On the 1984 presidential race, see Reed, ibid., 93.
80. Minutes, 25 January 1974, NYSAC.
81. Minutes, 27 September 1977, NYSAC.
82. Minutes, 29 September 1977, NYSAC.
83. Minutes, 30 December 1977, NYSAC.
84. Minutes, 18 September 1967, NYSAC.
85. Minutes, 16 December 1977, NYSAC. At the same site and collection, see also Report, 31 December 1964, and Minutes, 1 January 1965: "The Commission discussed at great length the matter of licensing women wrestlers.... there are 45 states out of 50 which license women wrestlers. Our rule in not licensing women wrestlers is invalid." See also: Minutes, 22 March 1967: license denied to a "mute" [male] boxer. At NYSAC see also Report, 7 March 1967: There had been "very excellent deaf boxers in the past 30 years...it is very possible that his handicap, rather than constitute a detriment to his

The overall climate was complicated, as signaled by the fact that in 1964 Kid Gavilan had run afoul of the authorities in Cuba, then, as now, blockaded by Washington, because of his close association with the religious formation, the Jehovah's Witnesses, accused of refusing to respect civil authority.[86] Even Archie "The Old Mongoose" Moore, a true light heavyweight, was praised lavishly by the two icons of the Republican Right—Nixon and Reagan—after he denounced those in Detroit in 1967 who rebelled against police misconduct in a major explosion of civil unrest,[87] suggesting that he was unwilling to confront the real snakes, and possibly paving the way for his post-retirement metamorphosis as a well-compensated actor. This perception received confirmation when in the wake of the Detroit Rebellion he appeared before the House Un-American Activities Committee, and rather than emulate Robeson's performance about a decade earlier when he berated his interlocutors uncompromisingly, the "Mongoose" fled from the snakes and, instead, declared in summary that "Reds Await Race War."[88]

It was not just the heavyweights—and those who fought them—who found themselves on the same side as the primary antagonists of Black America. By the early 1960s, "Sugar" Ray Robinson, facing a career in terminal decline, evidently agreed to violate an internationally recognized boycott by fighting in Johannesburg.[89] By the early 1980s, even Ali—in league with promoter Bob Arum—was said to be contemplating fighting Henry Clark in Johannesburg (with typical flim-flam, the promoter promised "sticky seating arrangements for whites and 'colored,'" an indecipherable locution and probably intended).

Having said that, it does appear that Frazier—he of the devastating left hook—beat most of his competitors in leaning to the right. Even Foreman, who spectacularly bounced the Philadelphian on the canvas in their short-lived contest in Jamaica—raising the specter of a reprise of Liston, without the distasteful associations—could hardly match Frazier in this regard. Richard M. Nixon termed

---

ability in the ring, might prove the reverse." See also Jeff Leen, *The Queen of the Ring: Sex, Muscles, Diamonds and the Making of an American Legend*, New York: Atlantic Monthly Press, 2009 [emphasis-original].

86. Report, ca. June 1964, Boxing Scrapbooks, Vol. XVII, UND.

87. Moore and Pearl, *Any Boy Can*, 162.

88. *United Press International*, 26 October 1967, Odds and Ends on Boxing, Vol. 46, UND.

89. *New York Daily Mirror*, 4 February 1962, Sub Group VIII, Series I, Box 16, HKBA.

Frazier a "fine guy." This "fine guy" also had become quite fond of the Philadelphia police and their hardline chief and future mayor Frank Rizzo, who had a reputation for brutality that made his peers—e.g., in the Los Angeles Police Department, responsible for two major conflagrations in 1965 and 1992—seem pusillanimously pussy-footed by comparison.[90] Then again, Frazier's role as Ali foil generated hefty incomes for both, suggesting why he might want to adhere to the GOP mantra of lower taxes. On 8 March 1971, the two combatants drew 19,000 spectators to Madison Square Garden with a live gate revenue of $1.3 million. The Garden was paid $4.5 million for so-called "ancillary rights," and in that vein total world receipts amounted to $16 million—with the Albany taxman carting away almost $350,000 apiece from each fighter[91] (and that does not include federal taxes).

Ali, the pitchman, generated these impressive sums with his P.T. Barnum-like promotions, though he was assisted by others. Albany regulators recounted how before the second contest between the two, they became embroiled in a brawl at a Manhattan studio with commentator Howard Cosell being blamed for encouraging the fray, a maneuver that might have generated a bigger box office to the benefit of his broadcaster employer. Ali had thrown oil on the simmering fire by denigrating his opponent's intelligence, instructing his sparring partners to don a gorilla mask supposedly to prepare for the alleged simian-like Frazier. This odiousness capitulated to the basest instincts of the Euro-American majority. The television host Dick Cavett was also culpable, insofar as he played up this trope for his sizable audience.[92]

Then again, the preceding era was indelibly stained by the sidelining of principled combatants like Du Bois (an equivalent of Henry Armstrong in holding multiple titles as leading intellectual and organizer) and Robeson (whose rugged physique was reminiscent of Ali's); ideological space was thereby reduced for the kind of militancy that the historical moment demanded.

With Negroes—make that Blacks—erupting in important urban nodes, including Washington, D.C., and embarrassing the U.S. abroad by protesting at the Olympics, Ali became one of their heroes. By refusing to step forward and enter the war machine, he became a hero for many of these dissidents and, correspondingly, a villain for those on the other side of the political barricades. When

---

90. Kram, *Smokin' Joe*, 160.
91. Minutes, 2 May 1973, NYSAC.
92. Minutes, 24 January 1974, NYSAC.

the Boxing Board in Minnesota convened in 1966, Ali's detractors were breathing fire, unleashing their flamethrowers in his general direction. Jay Frawley was foremost amongst them: "I move that our Commission go on record," he thundered, "as refusing to grant a license or permit to any organization or individual to show the closed circuit of the heavyweight fight between Cassius Clay and George Chuvalo anywhere in the state of Minnesota." Why? This was "out of respect for all servicemen of the past and present; for our American boys now fighting in Vietnam; and for all loyal American citizens." As was the trend nationally, "the motion was seconded and carried unanimously."[93] Although Minnesota was supposedly one of the more "liberal" U.S. states, having sent Democratic Party warhorses Hubert H. Humphrey and Walter Mondale to within a heartbeat away from the presidency, this Upper Midwest outpost was akin to its counterparts further south when it came to assessing Ali. In February 1970, "Clay's reinstatement again was brought up," and it was adjudged that "nothing be done further on this matter."[94] (The reluctance to use his chosen name "Ali" became a symbol of disobedience to the strictures of the new political dispensation.)

Letters flowing into the White House from disgruntled voters attested to the sensitive nerve that Ali had touched. The citizen who called herself "Mrs. L.R. Mitchell" thought she had registered a rhetorical triumph when she equated the boxer to Dr. King and the "Black Power" advocate then known as Stokeley Carmichael.[95] Leveraging Dr. King's relationship with President Johnson, so essential to passing civil rights legislation, was turned against the Texan, especially the cleric's "remarks backing" the boxer, as the occupant of the White House was told.[96] Even Morton Susman, the U.S. attorney in Houston—and thus subject to the whims of the president and responsible for the jurisdiction where Ali refused to step forward to be conscripted—in reaching White House aide Barefoot Sanders chortled prematurely that "Clay is on his way to prison to receive the

---

93. Minutes of State Athletic Commission, 17 March 1966, Boxing Board Records, 103.H.15.18, MinnHS-SP.

94. Minutes of State Athletic Commission, 16 February 1970, Boxing Board Records, MinnHS-SP.

95. Mrs. L.R. Mitchell to President Johnson, 1 May 1967, Box 260, White House Central Files, LBJPL.

96. Fred Panzer to Robert Kintner, 2 May 1967, Box 260, White House Central Files, LBJPL.

reward he richly deserves for his action: this conviction will stick!"[97] That premature conclusion was echoed in Albany, where the boxer was investigated. By their own admission, regulators there prepared a "detailed report," noting when he registered for the draft on 18 April 1960, then ordered to report for induction on 28 April 1969, after being convicted by jury in June 1967, leading to a five-year sentence and $10,000 fine.[98] What these premature jailers did not envision, it seems, was that a movement would arise to rescue the boxer. The "Committee for Muhammad Ali" denounced the "punitive frenzy" enveloping their hero, along with the "bitter attacks on him,"[99] which served to channelize the gathering antiwar and Black Liberation movements that saved him from the military. The New York Civil Liberties Union's decision to "strenuously protest" the mistreatment of Ali was further evidence of the broadening of his political base.[100]

* * *

Despite the increased attention to the sport delivered by the Ali Regime, in some ways there was stark continuity from the immediate past. Ali did not create spectacle in the sport, but it did seem that the blinding wattage of his persona discombobulated an already addled band of promoters. Hence, when the idea was bruited of Ali taking on basketball superstar Wilt Chamberlain—all 7'1" and 275 pounds of him—a Minnesotan sought to top this notion by proposing a battle between the hoopster and Jim Beattie of St. Paul, weighing in at 240 pounds and 6'8½". The authorities in the state objected since the proposal "smacked so strongly of a burlesque atmosphere" and "would be ridiculed by the news media and boxing public"[101]— i.e., would not be a winner in the box office.

Actually, it was worse. At least Chamberlain was a world-class athlete, a dominant rebounder and scorer, as evidenced by

---

97. Morton Susman to Barefoot Sanders, 3 August 1967, Box 260, White House Central Files, LBJPL. In the same box, see also Philip Kelly to President Johnson, 5 May 1967: "I do not think that it is right to draft Cassius Clay and not George Hamilton," a reference to the deeply tanned actor and purported paramour of the president's daughter.
98. Minutes, 14 October 1969, NYSAC.
99. Minutes, 4 March 1968, NYSAC.
100. Aryeh Neier, NYCLU, to Edwin B. Dooley, 3 May 1967, NYSAC.
101. Minutes of State Athletic Commission meeting, 15 March 1967, Boxing Board Records, 103.H.15.1B, MinnHS-SP.

his once tallying 100 points in a game: Hundreds of games in the professional ranks have been played without an entire *team* scoring as many. But even a World Boxing Association official, a body often eager to sanction contests of any sort, felt that Beattie "should be retired from boxing for the sake of his future health" in that he suffered "respiratory difficulty" and exhibited "signs of asthma"; his "bronchial asthma" was "precipitated by arduous physical exertion," which even a burlesque bout would deliver: "continued fighting could result in a fatality from heart failure," which was too much even for the indelicate tastes of routinely supine boxing authorities.[102] A physician was found, Jan H. Tillisch, to dissent from this conclusion,[103] but a second opinion was delivered by Dr. Robert Winter, who found that Beattie, in addition, had a "bulging lumbar disk," likely a "fracture" that brought "extreme pain."[104]

Thus, as the man who became Ali was in the process of startling the sport by upsetting Liston, due north Marvin Westmoreland, a Chicago boxer, was hospitalized for four weeks after a match against Brian O'Shea. Governor Karl Rolvaag of Minnesota was told that the Chicagoan was the "victim of a so-called SYSTEM meaning a clique of Chicago handlers of boxers who did not have the physical welfare of their pugilistic protégés at heart; and were willing to sacrifice… boxers' physical welfare" in order to "make a 'fast buck.'" [emphasis-original][105] Part of what happened to this unfortunate pugilist was that he was said to be not in proper physical condition, since he "weakened himself by reducing twelve pounds in twenty-four hours before the fight…[then moved] from 152 pounds to 144," an all too common practice in the sport which seemed to spawn extreme dieting and its untoward consequences ineluctably.[106] Another investigator found that the loser "looked like he never had boxing gloves on his

---

102. Leon Feldman, World Boxing Association, to George Barton, 30 March 1966, Boxing Board Records, Box 112.f.5.3b, MinnHS-SP.

103. Jan Tillisch to George Barton, 18 March 1966, Boxing Board Records, Box 112.f.5.3b, MinnHS-SP.

104. Robert Winter to George Barton, 20 October 1967, Boxing Board Records, Box 112.f.5.3b, MinnHS-SP.

105. George Barton, Commissioner and Executive Secretary to Governor Rolvaag, 6 February 1964, Boxing Board Records, 103.H.15.1B, MinnHS-SP.

106. Minutes of State Athletic Commission meeting, 27 December 1963, Boxing Board Records, 103.H.15.1B, MinnHS-SP.

hands more than half a dozen times before fighting O'Shea."[107] He was "dizzy" after the bout, said one who saw him, not a good sign.[108]

A St. Paul promoter, George Weir, was irate at this turn of events. "A nationwide 'system,'" he spat out, "controls boxing for the purpose of taking boys off the street and throwing them into a ring just to get a 50 percent cut" and, in return, "fighters get their heads beaten in."[109] He was referring to the uncertain fate of Westmoreland, who remained in critical condition.[110] But the situation was both worse and more banal than originally suspected. An official investigation found that "Westmoreland" was actually "Bobby Shack," using the old trick of changing one's name to flout rules against multiple bouts in short bursts of time. He claimed that he had a "twin brother," a dubious proposition leading to a request for inspection of "finger print cards, photos, tattoos, distinguishing marks," etc.[111]

Meanwhile, the funhouse mirror reflection of boxing—i.e., wrestling—continued to pile outrage upon outrage. A few years after the Shack/Westmoreland travesty, Guy Taylor, a professional wrestler, expired following a televised match. Minnesota at that juncture was one of the few states in which professional wrestling was unsupervised by the relevant authorities, turning the "sport" into an anarchistic "Wild West."[112]

Hundreds of miles from the cool and pristine lakes of Minnesota were the steamy deserts of Arizona, but the scene involving these roughhouse sports was eerily alike. By 1964, Phoenix had passed a law that gave promoters or matchmakers, said a dumbfounded official in Salt Lake City, "the right to choose their own officials for a professional boxing match," which, said F.J. Kilholm of the Utah State Athletic Commission in a masterpiece of understatement, "opens the door to collusion."[113] Given the sordid history of the sport, it was

---

107. George Barton to Emmett Keller, Boxing Club of St. Paul, Box 112.f.5.3b, Boxing Board Records, MinnHS-SP.

108. Johnny Coulon to George Barton, Box 112.f.5.3b, Boxing Board Records, MinnHS-SP.

109. Report, 28 December 1963, Box 112.f.5.3b, Boxing Board Records, MinnHS-SP.

110. Report, 16 December 1963, Box 112.f.5.3b, Boxing Board Records, MinnHS-SP.

111. Report by Roy Tennison, Assistant Chief Inspector of Athletic Commission, 17 October 1966, Box 112.f.5.3b, Boxing Board Records, MinnHS-SP.

112. George Barton to State Representative John Johnson, 3 May 1968, Box 112.f.5.5b, Boxing Board Records, MinnHS-SP.

113. F.J. Kilholm to Arizona State Athletic Commission 18 December 1964, RG1, 36:380, SG 19, Series 2, Box 036, 3.4.6, ASA-P.

akin to allowing one team to hire the umpires and/or referees—then place knowing wagers—or allowing one set of litigants to select the judge. This was not just a hypothetical concern: A leading Albany regulator in 1967 observed that "millions of people watched the fight between Cassius Clay [sic] and Ernie Terrell in Houston...I would say about sixty million." Yet the referee received only $700 for the fight, making him susceptible to all manner of blandishments.[114]

It is indicative that as boxing continued its normative chaos, wrestling was beset by what amounted to pandemonium. The latter "sport" had a theatrical aspect, like a kind of performance art, that played upon the "blood and guts" theme that thrummed in U.S. culture. Thus, by 1965 at one noticeably wild Arizona wrestling match, a woman spectator was "thrown out bodily" and, typically for the nation, it was ascertained that management of the venue "discriminates against Indians, Mexicans and Negroes."[115] "I had no idea that we had such devoted wrestling fans in the state of Arizona,"[116] said an aide to the governor months after the foregoing words were recorded, apparently unaware of the squalid depths to which the state had sunk—and the chord it struck with some.

It is possible that as revolts erupted in Watts in 1965, and anti-war protests in Washington became more militant, this anti-authority stridency was then refracted through the culture, including wrestling. Certainly, some of the chaotic scenes happening in Arizona wrestling matches cry out for explanation. Thus, by the summer of 1967—as Detroit was exploding in flames—in Tucson at "one of the wrestling matches," Mike Quihuis of State Athletic Commission became "engaged in an altercation with one of the deputies and punched the officer.... the deputy is supposed to have called [this official] a name which related to his nationality unfavorably,"[117] a euphemism for an insult to a man of Mexican ancestry. Weeks later, a correspondent of the governor had had enough: Yes, "wrestling is mentioned" in the "Bible," said F.A. Belsey, which apparently provided the requisite authenticity and historicity: It was "the oldest sport known to man," but what was happening in the arenas of the Grand Canyon

---

114. Minutes, 9 March 1967, NYSAC.

115. Minutes, Arizona State Athletic Commission, 1 May 1965, Reel 76.1.1, ASA-P.

116. Tom Hall, Research Assistant—Office of the Governor, to Manuel Pena, Executive Secretary of State Athletic Commission, 26 July 1965, RG 1 31: 271 SG 19 Series 1 5S3, Box 031, 3.4.6, ASA-P.

117. Referred to Stan Worner, Executive Office, State House-Phoenix, 18 July 1967, RG 1, SG 20, Box 406, 3.5.9, ASA-P.

State was "disgusting"; there were "gutter fights" and "eye gouging, trunk pulling, choking, nose and ear biting, men flung around the ring by their hair," and successful efforts to "deliberately break a man's leg." Worse, at these spectacles, "swarms of youngsters" ranging from "eight years of age to eighteen" were present, lapping it all up. There they learned to "become brutes" and contribute to "juvenile delinquency" in a venue where "rules and regulations mean nothing"[118]—the latter being not the lesson deemed appropriate for youth.

As suggested by the fracas that engaged Commissioner Quihuis, wrestling—like its cousin, boxing—tended to play upon gender, racial and ethnic sensitivities. Albany, as late as the tumultuous 1960s, did "not permit women to wrestle or be licensed," using traditional patriarchal rationales.[119] Still, beyond New York, at times these contests involved women, e.g., the "African Lioness" who paraded in a black mask, and "The Most Ferocious Negro Masked Girl Wrestler" who, naturally, was scantily clad, leaving little to the imagination.[120] Women were more likely to be found in wrestling than in boxing, in part—I think—because the former created more voyeuristic opportunities for the salacious male gaze. By 1965, Mary Horton was plugged as the "First Negro Woman" in the "sport," while Olivia Mangho "from the Congo" was hailed. Then there were "Babs Wingo" and "Ethel Johnson," seen as "superbly equipped" since "they are on the average bigger and heavier than their white rivals."[121] Eventually, it was reported that for the "first time in the whole world Negro Girls World Tournament" would be staged, with scattered references to the "African ferocious Black Pussycat" in competition for the "Negro Girls World's Title and Championship Belt."[122]

Just as boxers moonlighted as musicians, and vice versa, Bobo Brazil, born in East St. Louis, had been a star player with the "Negro House of David semi-pro [baseball team]." He was a thickly muscled 6'7" and 280 pounds, and billed as the "sensational giant Negro champion" who faced the "Wild Samoan Bushman," meaning "Prince Maiva, Samoan Chief" who, insultingly, was said to

---

118. F.A. Belsey to Governor Williams, 4 September 1967, RG 1 SG 20 Box 406, 3.5.9, ASA-P.
119. In the Matter of Silvia T. Calzadilla vs. New York State Athletic Commission, 18 January 1968, NYSAC.
120. See Broadsides from 1960s particularly in Box 119, Pfefer-UND.
121. "Ring Wrestling," 1965, Box 150, Pfefer-UND.
122. Undated Broadside, Box 150, Pfefer-UND.

"resemble…a monkey."[123] There was also "Jungle Boy" who was a fixture in Detroit, rapidly undergoing rapid racial change, who sported a large bush of hair, and in his corner was an "Exotic Slave Girl!"[124] (exclamation point in original).

There were Native American grapplers portrayed insensitively also, especially Chief Don Eagle,[125] who was not able to subdue "Gorgeous George,"[126] though the victor intentionally subverted traditional notions of masculinity with his preening, his strut, his affect, his wardrobe, his flashy blond coiffure, his dramatic use of perfume—or should I say, cologne? The Gorgeous One was an early cowardly villain, a recurrent trope in the "sport" and, possibly, a stand-in for how settler colonialism was built. He also was "passing" in that he had a heterosexual marriage and two children whom he "shielded" from the public, so as not to disrupt his image.[127] Residing in the 1960s in a fashionable abode at 8272 Sunset Boulevard in Los Angeles, he ran afoul of regulators when his routine—a woman preceding him into the ring (she "disinfects it for me," he explained) was flummoxed since "no girls are allowed in the ring in Brooklyn."

Still, he appeared to subvert masculinity—a punishing grappler who seemed to be effeminate?—just as Ali and other punchers continued to contradict the continually discredited idea that Black men were somehow cowardly. Like Ali, who emulated him, he also wrestled with alimony: "between the Internal Revenue and my ex-wife whom I am supporting and my children," he felt his income was draining.[128] (The sport may have been more sexually fluid than it appeared at first glance. The writer Ishmael Reed has referred to the "bi-sexuality" of "Sugar" Ray Robinson, while revealing that the broadcaster Howard Cosell made likeminded sexualized overtures to Ali's tormentor Larry Holmes.)[129]

The Chief was depicted as "copper colored"[130] and sported a headdress,[131] which became a routine signifier for Native Americans generally, though it was actually unique only to certain ethnicities among this diverse group. Still, he was depicted as "one of the

---

123. See Broadsides from 1950s in Box 120, Pfefer-UND.
124. *Detroit Wrestling News*, 8 March 1951, Box 123, Pfefer-UND.
125. *Cleveland Plain Dealer*, 24 May 1950, Box 122, Pfefer-UND.
126. *Chicago Sun-Times*, 27 May 1950, Box 122, Pfefer-UND.
127. *Chicago Tribune*, 27 December 1963, Pfefer-UND.
128. Minutes, 26 February 1960, NYSAC.
129. Reed, *Complete Muhammad Ali*, 201, 150.
130. *New York Journal American*, Box 122, Pfefer-UND.
131. *Sports Pointer*, 1 April 1950, Box 122, Pfefer-UND.

greatest if not the greatest Indian wrestlers of all time"[132]; his stature was such that at one point he was slated to wrestle Carnera, with Dempsey serving as referee.[133]

The once feisty "Mauler," by then in his dotage, managed to get in on the theatricality by punching the Italian.[134] Dempsey was also pictured in Cleveland as a referee, poised to slug "The Great Moto" in his "honorable Japanese jaw."[135] Even after the end of the Pacific War, Japanese villains remained prominent, including "The Great Togo."[136] As if the incursions westward centuries past to the gates of Europe had yet to be forgotten, numerous grapplers were advertised as "Mongol," though since many of them were masked, it was hard to tell if they were truly of this ethnicity.[137] However, it was "Chief Little Wolf" who was the "creator of the famous Indian Death Lock,"[138] one of the more punishing moves deployed in the ring.

The Gorgeous One was not the only blond in the sport; there was also Buddy Rogers, often found in St. Louis, who was billed as the "Atomic Blond," an explosive mixture of two important signifiers.[139] In one riotous match Rogers took a swing at the referee, Jersey Joe Walcott, who plastered the aggressor with a wicked right cross—and awarded the victory to "Bearcat" Wright and "Sweet Daddy" Siki, Negroes both, representing a kind of racial united front that was then being expressed in the streets.[140] For mimicking their boxing counterparts, wrestling matchmakers reveled in pitting grapplers of European ancestry, Gene Kiniski and Waldo von Erich, for example, versus Africans like "Sweet Daddy" Siki and Bobo Brazil. This latter contest took place just before the Watts Revolt of 1965 in Los Angeles.[141]

Earlier, one Native American grappler was portrayed as a "Navajo on the warpath" made of "copper skinned dynamite." This "full blooded Navajo" was poised to wrestle with "Jagat Singh, the Hindu grappler," though it was unclear who was being referenced when a

---

132. *The Mat*, June 1950, Box 122, Pfefer-UND.
133. *Wrestling News Pictorial Pulse*, 14 December 1950, Box 122, Pfefer-UND.
134. Report, 1950, Box 122, Pfefer-UND.
135. Undated Broadside, Box 123, Pfefer-UND.
136. *Amsterdam Evening Record*, 25 October 1950, Box 130, Pfefer-UND.
137. See the thick files on "Mongols" in Box 136, Pfefer-UND.
138. Undated report, Box 123, Pfefer-UND.
139. *In the Ring* [St. Louis], 11 November 1950, Box 123, Pfefer-UND.
140. Report, 19 September 1960, Box 149, Pfefer-UND.
141. *Washington Post*, 15 February 1965, Box 149, Pfefer-UND.

particular maneuver was said to have been "used from ancient time by the Indians to torture their victims to death."[142]

Wrestling found certain nationalities fungible; thus, there was "Emir Badui" who entered the ring turbaned with an earring, initially listed as an "Egyptian poet" then as the "Clean Wrestling Persian" (Iran was no antagonist of the U.S. then).[143] Then there was "Chief Lone Eagle" of "Cherokee" ancestry; he was "ably assisted," it was reported, "by Princess Bonita…she beats the tom toms when she senses danger of defeat."[144]

Boxing also utilized these drearily hoary stereotypes. There was "Big Chief Knockout," for example, who sported a headdress, too, but to the casual observer resembled a Negro.[145]

Still, it is possible that the rise of Ali Regime also provided a jolt of popularity to wrestling, as the former Louisville Lip continued to generate fortunes for many.

---

142. *Sport World*, 4 March 1935, Box 122, Pfefer-UND.

143. *Ocean Park Arena News*, 2 June 1939, and *Medford Mail Tribune*, undated, Box 126, Pfefer-UND.

144. *Wrestling as You Like It*, 8 July 1950, Box 122, Pfefer-UND.

145. Undated column by Lester Bromberg, Sub Group X, Series I, Box 21, HKBA.

Chapter 9

Tales of Don & Bob

In the early 1960s, Bob Arum, by his own admission, "handled a big case that involved boxing, the seizure of funds in the Patterson-Liston fight," while he was employed by the "Tax Division" of the Justice Department, and from there, because of contacts made, he was catapulted into the front ranks of boxing promotion. He was sufficiently wise to stand beside Ali in 1967 during the conscription controversy, which involved a short-term loss and long-term gain. "I became a pariah and it affected my parents and everything," he said ruefully later: "it wasn't a pleasant time." But that gained him credibility in the circles that mattered, those of Ali in the first place, allowing him to decamp to commodious offices in Nevada. "My experience with Muslims was very good,"[1] referring to the heavyweight champion and his retinue, and his vast fortune was proof positive of this assertion. It should not be gainsaid that Arum's standing alongside Ali when he was under fire was hardly trivial. Fellow Las Vegas resident Marc Ratner recalled later that back then the heavyweight champion was "hated" because of his anti-war posture, and the backwash splattered those who were sympathetic to him, which would have included Arum.[2]

It was not just "Black Muslims" who captured Arum's fancy. He emerged from what was described as a "Conservative Jewish family," although it was yet another African-American star athlete—footballer Jim Brown—who introduced him to Ali in 1965, when the lawyer was toiling for the firm of celebrated attorney and author Louis Nizer.[3]

Also gaining traction with Ali was Arum's rival, Don "The Kid" King, who got his start as a teenager involved in gambling near the campus of Kent State University in Ohio. Later, according to a

---

1. Oral History, Bob Arum, 20 October 2016, UNV-LV.
2. Oral History, Marc Ratner, 23 August 2016, UNV-LV.
3. Report, ca. 1995, Sub Group VIII, Series I, Box 1, HKBA.

journalist, "his house was blown up," then he was convicted of second degree murder by what was described as an "all white jury"; he served four years, where he apparently used his time wisely, reading voraciously. By 1971 he was paroled—later he was pardoned after gaining prominence—and it was his association with Ali (convincing him to participate in a benefit performance) that put him on the path to untold wealth.[4]

Eventually, the exiled Nevadan's influence in the sport was so pervasive that the ostensible governing body, the WBA [World Boxing Association], was renamed familiarly as the "WBArum." The competing body, the World Boxing Council, was viewed more benignly by King, Arum's rival, containing delegates from 156 member nations—"the strongest boxing authority in the world," said one analyst. Their ranking of contenders was important, taken seriously by credulous sportswriters who then took to their columns to create momentum for yet another "super fight." Purportedly, Arum sought to bribe one publisher of a boxing newsletter by buying 4,000 subscriptions, with slanted coverage as the quid pro quo. Arum's wealth allowed him to consider purchasing a professional basketball franchise.[5] (Reportedly, Arthur Conan Doyle was a budding boxing writer and considered covering the pivotal Johnson-Jeffries bout in Reno in 1910[6]: This should remind us that it would require a Sherlock Holmes to ferret out all the malfeasances perpetrated by boxing scribes.)

King's route to the top was circuitous, but provided him with variegated experiences that allowed him to flourish as a promoter. From 1951 through 1966, as a numbers boss in Cleveland and arrested five times in the process, he honed a head for mathematical calculations with a wiliness that allowed him to escape Houdini-like from tight spots. During this era, whose distinguishing feature was the erosion of rigid Jim Crow, he survived gang wars, shootings and trials. After his career in boxing accelerated, rising like yeast as well were the purses of fighters and the employment of more African Americans in ancillary roles as reporters and broadcasters.[7] As with so many similarly situated, like Ali's erstwhile comrade Malcolm X, King used his time behind bars wisely: "I read Karl Marx," he informed writer Norman Mailer, "a cold motherfucker, Marx. I learned a lot

---

4. *TRUE* magazine, September 1974, Box 54, Newfield-UT.
5. Brady, *Boxing Confidential*, 209, 223, 230.
6. *Sports Illustrated*, 13 March 1961, Sub Group VIII, Series I, Box 6, HKBA.
7. *Details*, November 1990, Box 151, Newfield-UT.

from him."[8] It was doubtful if King's journey to Moscow in 1988 was an ideological quest, however.[9]

Though not flyspecked so relentlessly as King, it is evident that in climbing the greasy pole of fame and fortune, Arum had incurred a modicum of wrath. José Torres, a Puerto Rican boxer and, arguably, the leading athlete-intellectual of the 20th century, recalled a "time when Cus D'Amato was being interviewed...and...was saying that Bob Arum was the worst human being in the Western Hemisphere and he was asked what about Don King. And Cus says I have not dealt with Don King...but...God cannot make the same mistake twice."[10] D'Amato notwithstanding, Elbert "Duke" Durden, well-known Nevada matchmaker and member of the state's Athletic Commission, too—who also happened to be African-American—was not singular in suggesting that the repetitive "FBI probe[s]" of King were "racially motivated" in that others with spotty records were not subjected to as much scrutiny, as if his existence on the top rungs of the economic ladder were an affront to the status quo. Durden himself was also seen as not above investigation, and the criminal inquiries of both, he said, were hardly coincidental: "We both happen to be Black."[11] Arum could afford to be generous, in sum, and at one point echoed positive assessments of his eventual rival, describing King as "a business man in Ohio who has impressed me as being a very intelligent and decent man"[12]—a view that was not to be widely shared subsequently.

By 1972, Ali had absorbed a rift with Arum, which did little to harm his relationship with King. Brusquely, he informed the Harvard-trained attorney turned promoter, that he was "retaining Ramsey Clark as my own attorney," a former U.S. attorney general on a steady march to the left; the charismatic prizefighter said he "would appreciate your turning over to his office all of my personal, business, tax records and other matters."[13]

The jousting between King and Arum defined the sport, beginning in the 1970s and continuing into the 21st century. This was nothing new. The conviction of the Gibson-Carbo-Palermo cabal

---

8. Mailer, *Fight*, 119.

9. *United Press International*, 6 March 1988, Sub Group VIII, Series II, Box 25, HKBA.

10. Transcript of José Torres, 12 June 1991, Box 151, Newfield-UT.

11. Report, 24 January 1981, Sub Group VIII, Series I, Box 7, HKBA.

12. Minutes, 23 August 1973, NYSAC.

13. Muhammad Ali to Bob Arum, 9 October 1972, Box 173, Ramsey Clark Papers, LBJPL.

was thought to have cleaned up the sport, but only served to create openings for such disgustingly immoral figures as Mickey Cohen and Roy Cohn. King, like Gibson, was singled out in the press for his transgressions—though admittedly there was a modicum of good reason for this. Heavyweight champion Larry "The Easton Assassin" Holmes was particularly harsh toward the promoter with the unique hairdo. He convinced Ali, said this bruiser, that together they "could put boxing under the control of Black fighters [and] Black promoters," e.g., King, reprising what Gibson and Joe Louis had attempted in 1949. Yet King's comrade Al Braverman said Holmes, "had plans for his own heavyweight, a white hope named Dino Dennis," since a "manager could always make money with a white heavyweight who wasn't a total waste...and Don went right along him,"[14] an emblem of his utter hypocrisy, according to the Pennsylvanian.

Again, this view of the sport through a "racial" lens was part of U.S. culture generally. It was in 1980 that the popular writer Pete Hamill—writing on the stationery of the *New York Times*—made a request to "Dear Angelo [Dundee]": "There's a promising young white heavyweight [that] you should manage," a racial designation he was careful to specify. "He's the son of the actor Danny Aiello... who starred in 'Knockout' on Broadway," and "Danny," he said familiarly, "is talking about putting together a syndicate with Robert de Niro, Ben Gazzara...to finance the kid's career,"[15] giving him an immeasurable boost over others similarly situated.

Clearly, it is no excuse for Arum that others were operating along parallel racial lines. Still, Arum was no saint but for some reason did not receive as much negative attention in the mainstream press—the inadequacies of sportswriters was a particular whipping boy of Holmes—despite the promoter's repetitive collaborations with an abhorrent apartheid South Africa.

Arum visited Johannesburg in 1982[16]—not necessarily his first trip—during the high tide of apartheid and in violation of the boycott propounded by the African majority. According to investigative journalist Robert Friedman, Arum worked closely with Sol Kerzner in the land of apartheid. "Both are Jewish," he wrote and "being Jewish has helped Bob Arum to do business in and with Pretoria." Certainly, Arum made a fortune there as Africans were being slaughtered in the

---

14. Larry Holmes, "Boxing Politics," Box 156, Newfield-UT.

15. Pete Hamill to "Dear Angelo," 10 December 1980, Sub Series VIII, Series I, Box 10, HKBA.

16. David Bloch to Hank Kaplan, 27 July 1982, Sub Group IX, Series I, Box 35, HKBA.

streets. "[I made] more money from the concessions" on one fight in 1979 there "than I do from a whole promotion in the U.S.," he gushed. He matched, and may have exceeded King in deviousness, which is why Friedman found that that "few men in the sport of boxing are more intensely disliked," though a caveat is required: The Arum-King "cartel" meant the former was tied to the CBS television network and the latter to ABC and, as suggested, King was with the World Boxing Council and Arum with the World Boxing Association. By 1980 Arum was "at war" with Madison Square Garden—possibly engendering his move westward to Las Vegas—and King was not, and thus maintained a posh office within walking distance of this sports mecca.[17]

Hence, the entities tied to King "intensely disliked" Arum, and vice versa. Intriguingly, one of Arum's predecessors as a potential titan of the sport, who was also "intensely disliked," once bumped into Arum, shook his hand and then, said a beaming Roy Cohn, "I've finally made it."[18]

The presence of Cohn underlines why Arum may not have been the most "intensely disliked person" who ever disgraced the sport; likewise, sadly, the Nevadan was not the only boxing personality to truck with apartheid. Tellingly, boxing as we know it, took shape simultaneously in both ends of settler colonialism—South Africa and the U.S. Some of these punchers from Johannesburg wound up in the U.S. Rudy "Boer" Unholz was knocked out by Gans in 1908, anticipating Johnson's earthshaking defeat of Jeffries in 1910. "Boer" Rodel fought some of the republic's best before expiring in Los Angeles in 1956. And, yes, the traffic was in both directions, from which U.S. promoters sought to profit.[19] Actually, it was not just S.A. and the U.S.A.: Completing the circuit was a group of Australian fighters who helped to establish the sport in the southern cone of Africa.[20]

By 1979, Dundee was in touch with Reg Layton of Brisbane, Australia, a promoter there who had met the Ali trainer in Sydney and now wanted aid in penetrating the U.S. market.[21] This circuit

---

17. Robert Friedman, undated article in "Inside Sports," Sub Group VIII, Series I, Box 1, HKBA.

18. Mark Kram, undated article on Arum, Sub Group VIII, Series I, Box 1, HKBA.

19. Chris Greyvenstein to Hank Kaplan, 2 January 1978, Sub Group VIII, Series I, Box 9, HKBA.

20. Chris Greyvenstein to "Dear Bill," 28 November 1978, Sub Group VIII, Series I, Box 9, HKBA.

21. Reg J. Layton to "Dear Angelo," 24 December 1979, Sub Group VIII, Series I, Box 12 HKBA.

was facilitated by the ascension of apartheid's H.W. Klopper as the president of the World Boxing Association—or WBArum—as the Nevadan was deepening his potency within the sport.[22]

Thus, as Arum was jetting across the Atlantic to southern Africa, Angelo Dundee, then installed in Ali's entourage, was consorting with the South African National Boxing Control Board in Johannesburg, and making a "promise of future contributions to [the] museum there.... sponsors are desirous of urgently learning the dates when you will be able to travel and remain there." Graciously, Stanley Christodoulou, secretary of this morally stained group, offered generously "booking of first class airfares for yourself and your wife," along with the "best hotels here."[23] The two men had conferred in Washington earlier in 1978, leaving the apartheid man to gush about the "honor of meeting you" and thanking Ali's trainer for the "hospitality and friendship extended to me.... I will certainly take up your kind invitation to correspond with you in regard to any of your fighters coming to South Africa," which would presumably include his prime client, the heavyweight colossus himself.[24] Dundee was in touch with the right man to whitewash apartheid in that Christodoulou was one of the few men who had refereed 100 world title fights—"in each of boxing's seventeen weight divisions," one commentator enthused and, it was added "unquestionably South Africa's best known boxing ambassador."[25]

Dundee also consulted with a premier promoter in the land of apartheid, Reg Haswell.[26] "I wish we could get Ali here," he said wistfully in May 1976, weeks before the Soweto Uprising that placed the apartheid regime on a glide path to extinction. "He would draw a 100,000 crowd," he insisted, "like [Jack] Dempsey used to do." Assuming the role of pitchman, he implored, "we wouldn't have a stadium big enough to get everybody in," before descending into reality, adding "it really is a shame we can't get him here. I would still give a million dollars to handle the gate only, the television and other ancillaries I would leave to the promoters of Ali, I would just

---

22. Report in Spanish, 18 August 1982, Sub Group VIII, Series I, Box 12, HKBA.

23. Stanley Christodoulou to Angelo Dundee, 1 February 1980, Sub Group VIII, Series I, Box 4, HKBA.

24. Stanley Christodoulou to Angelo Dundee, 4 July 1978, Sub Group VIII, Series I, Box 4, HKBA.

25. Undated report, Sub Group VIII, Series I, Box 4, HKBA.

26. Reg Haswell to "Dear Angelo [Dundee]," ca. 1986, Sub Group VIII, Series I, Box 10, HKBA.

like to prepare the venue for the fight and give a guarantee of a million dollars."[27] If Ali would not come to South Africa, at least not then, Haswell thought he could entice Dundee with the prospect of an association with "the next champ in young Gerrie Coetzee (pronounce it Cootsee)."[28]

Dundee was part of a transatlantic network, a kind of "White Atlantic" that was determined to uncover and exploit Black Boxers. Thus, by 1978 Wolfgang Kuhlmann of Hamburg informed "Dear Angelo" that he "just came back from South Africa where I have been many times in the last 3 years with fighters from everywhere."[29] Then there was Cedric Kushner, in a class by himself, who had migrated to the U.S. in 1971 from South Africa "with $400.00 in his pocket," he said. He crossed the Atlantic as a "deckhand on a German freighter" and somehow wound up in business with major rock stars, e.g., Fleetwood Mac, Rod Stewart, the Rolling Stones, Joni Mitchell, as the republic continued to be a magnet of untold riches for the Pan-European world. As a fellow South African came to play a major role within the WBA, he switched smoothly to boxing, promoting "Sugar" Shane Mosley, along with a number of Africans from the land of apartheid, including Cassius Baloyi, Zolani Petelo, Jacob Mofokeng—and the German Sven Ottke. Still, he promoted himself as managing a "roster of eleven world champions…at the forefront of the international boxing business" and the "most active promoter of championship bouts worldwide."[30]

Hank Kaplan, known globally as an expert on the sport from his perch in Miami, and a close comrade of the Dundees as a result, was consulted by Chris Greyvenstein of Cape Town: "I could be offered a contract to be boxing consultant for a new tv network (pay tv) started by four major newspaper groups in this country. If I take the assignment I could well find that there is some need for some connecting link in the States and who would be better than you." He realized that "South African connections are hardly an easy thing in the States these days," because of the burgeoning anti-apartheid movement, but this was not a heavy lift, he thought, since there were

---

27. Reg Haswell to "Dear Angelo [Dundee]," 25 May 1976, Sub Group VIII, Series I, Box 10, HKBA.

28. Reg Haswell to Angelo Dundee, 27 April 1977, Sub Group VIII, Series I, Box 10, HKBA.

29. Wolfgang Kuhlmann to "Dear Angelo," 18 March 1977, Sub Group VIII, Series I, Box 10, HKBA.

30. Undated promotional material, Sub Group VIII, Series I, Box 11, HKBA.

"plenty of American fights on local tv already."[31] Besides, Greyvenstein admitted that he had "quite a lot of friends in the States,"[32] a product of an enriching—for some—bilateral relationship.

Hence, when Anthony Morori, described as South Africa's junior lightweight champion, arrived in New York City to train at Gleason's Gymnasium—along with his manager, Theo Thembu, a leading African sportswriter in Johannesburg—it was unclear if Christodoulou (or Dundee) facilitated the journey.[33]

It was unclear because it was not just Dundee, or Arum, who were blazing a trail to Pretoria. Simultaneously, G.G. (or "Gee Gee") Maldonado made his way to a so-called "bantustan" or a crude equivalent of an Indian reservation, though not recognized internationally, to serve as punching bag for South Africa's Kallie Knoetze. Not much interest was stirred—unless fight fans came disguised as empty seats—in that only 6,000 were present in a facility that held 90,000. Antonio Cervantes of Colombia made mincemeat out of South African challenger Norman "Pangaman" Sekgapane in another mismatch.[34]

* * *

When King encountered various difficulties in the 1970s, Holmes said that "Arum knew about all of Don's legal problems and was taking advantage of the opportunity to try to steal some of his fighters," and the Easton resident "spoke to some people who believed Arum was the guy who put the government on to Don in the first place. That wouldn't surprise me a bit." Then Holmes threatened to sign with Arum himself, and King threatened to break his legs—and Holmes bought a pistol in response.[35] Given the longstanding ties between organized crime and law enforcement, it was not outlandish to suspect that the latter could be manipulated easily.[36]

---

31. Chris Grevenstein to Hank Kaplan, 21 October [ca. 1978], Sub Group VIII, Series I, Box 9, HKBA.

32. Chris Greyvenstein to "Dear Bill," 28 November 1978, Sub Group VIII, Series I, Box 9, HKBA.

33. Dewey Fragetta to "Dear Friend Sailor," 10 December 1970, Sub Group VIII, Series I, Box 8, HKBA.

34. Report, no date, Professional Licensing Agency/Boxing Commission/Boxing Show Results and Ratings/1979-1982/Series 83-786. A2563, Box 1, Indiana State Archives-Indianapolis (abbrev. ISA-A).

35. Larry Holmes Manuscript, "Boxing Politics," Box 156, Newfield-UT.

36. Michael F. Rizzo, *Gangsters and Organized Crime in Buffalo: History, Hits, and Headquarters*, Charleston: History Press, 2012 (abbrev. Rizzo, *Gangsters*);

Both promoters were exceedingly well compensated, and as Holmes saw things, this was at the expense of boxers like himself. By 1986 the grizzled Holmes was testifying before the authorities in New Jersey: By then the Garden State was one of the "Big Four" that mattered in the sport, which also included the Empire State, Nevada and California.[37] "In the last three years," said the lisping fighter who remained sufficiently sagacious to put forward numbers that disguised his overall income, while revealing that of others, "I paid over $8 million to Uncle Sam," while "Bob Arum made $30 million one year and Don King made $40 million." With barely contained disgust, Holmes recounted how promoters promised, say, $1.2 million and then by dint of salami slices that would do a butcher proud, this would be cut downward with precision. Unsurprisingly, he suggested that bribes to judges were part of the corrupt process. An announcement of who won each round could curb this corruption, he thought.[38] (Even Arum, in a position to know, said judging of bouts in "boondock areas like Tennessee or Rhode Island" was quite dicey: "anything can happen."[39])

Yet, despite Holmes's frequent pillorying of King, somehow they managed to share close quarters on a plane to El Paso for a fundraiser for John Hill in the midst of a losing race for governor of the Lone Star State in 1978.[40]

It remained unclear from his testimony how much Holmes took home after paying his gargantuan tax bill, but the wider point was that as U.S. imperialism continued its post-World War II boom, as the more egregious aspects of Jim Crow eroded, some African Americans (and some Jewish Americans, too) were able to profit handily.

But what Holmes revealed was the expansion of revenue that arrived in the latter decades of the 20th century. Arum asserted that

---

Anthony M. DeStefano, *Top Hoodlum: Frank Costello, Prime Minister of the Mafia*, New York: Kensington, 2018 (abbrev. DeStefano, *Top Hoodlum*).

37. "Public Hearing Before Assembly Independent Authority and Commissions Committee on the Promotion and Conduct of Boxing Matches in New Jersey," 19 January 1983, Belleville, New Jersey, New Jersey State Library-Trenton (abbrev. NJSL-T).

38. "Public Meeting Before Assembly Independent and Regional Authorities Committee on Testimony on Status and Possible Reform to Boxing in the State of New Jersey," 19 May 1986, Trenton, NJSL-T.

39. *Las Vegas Sports Book*, 5-11 August 1983, Sub Series VIII, Series I, Box 1, HKBA.

40. Report, 19 September 1978, Professional Licensing Agency/Boxing Commission/Boxing Show Results and Ratings, 1979-1982, a2563, Box 1, ISA-I.

the new departure arrived ca. 1991 with the advent of satellite "pay-per-view," with boxing extravaganzas delivered to millions of living rooms. "That's when everything exploded," he said in 2016, still seemingly spellbound by the thought, "and these fighters started making enormous amounts of money" (at least some and including promoters like himself).[41] Thus, in 1992, when Larry Holmes faced off against Evander "The Real Deal" Holyfield, the pay-per-view was expected to be delivered to 20 million households in addition to more than 1,000 domestic closed-circuit locations in over 100 countries—all engineered by Arum and his associates.[42]

For whatever reason, the mainstream press concentrated heavily on King's transgressions—Arum, not so much—as if they were *sui generis* and only appeared with the arrival on a scene of this Black multi-millionaire. Thus, when the boxer, then writer, José Torres, was deposed in a contentious trial, he reflected on these tensions. This former Olympic silver medalist and light heavyweight champion was no novice, but was a veteran of the grittiness of New York City politics, having worked for former mayoral hopefuls Paul O'Dwyer and Andrew Stein (he also appeared in movies alongside star actors such as Barbra Streisand). Hence, he recalled when the federal authorities contacted him about King, looking toward prosecution, and his penchant for having his son be a manager of a fighter whose bouts he was promoting. He reminded them of the Dundees (trainer and promoter) and the case of Dan Duva, a promoter, whose father was a manager.[43] George Gainford, involved in the management of "Sugar" Ray Robinson, was said to have "owned an interest in the welterweight champion, Kid Gavilan" while the two were in the process of battling each other.[44] Earlier, he had offered to have Danny "Bang Bang" Womber—whom he called "my fighter"—challenge the Cuban Kid.[45] Joe Glaser, the rude and crude mob associate who managed the career of Louis Armstrong and other notables expired in 1969, and Gainford's main client, "Sugar" Ray, joined Yankee baseball luminaries Mickey Mantle and Phil Rizzuto—along with television personality and columnist, Ed Sullivan—as an honorary pallbearer.[46] Harold Lederman, often found at ringside as a

---

41. Oral History, Bob Arum, 20 October 2016, UNV-LV.
42. Report, June 1992, Box 202, Stardust Resort and Casino Records, UNV-LV.
43. Transcript of 12 June 1991 Deposition, Box 151, Newfield-UT.
44. Minutes, 26 March 1954, NYSAC.
45. Minutes, 1 May 1953, NYSAC.
46. Report, September 1969, Sub Group VIII, Series 1, Box 9, HKBA.

judge, often importuned Angelo Dundee for opportunities to judge matches—a clear conflict of interest since the trainer or his brother often had an interest in who prevailed in the ring. "I could use someone to put a word in with Jose Sulaiman, for me," president of the World Boxing Council, "so maybe I can get a good fight...maybe some day you'll let me work with you on CBS [television network]," he said hopefully.[47] Al Weill, best known for his involvement with Marciano, was interrogated "relative to his acting as a matchmaker and as a manager of boxers at the same time," an offense thought to be unique to King.[48]

No litany of transgressions would be complete without reference to Sonny Liston: By 1972, his erstwhile manager, John Nilon, was accused of assisting in the making of a $100,000 payment that was linked to alleged bribes of politicians in New York state,[49] whose Athletic Commission had tremendous sway over the sport. To act as if the former Cleveland numbers runner was wholly unique, a departure in a sport where it was joked that bouts should have taken place in sewers—if only there was sufficient headroom[50]—was riotously laughable and reflective of the poor understanding of history that seems to be endemic nationally.

For example, Lou Duva of the famed family also served as president of a Teamsters local in New Jersey; he insisted that "the next best thing" to controlling a "heavyweight champion" would be "to have a white contender." Why? "Look at all the money Jerry Quarry makes because he's a pretty good fighter who's white"; as was widespread in the republic, he pooh-poohed the notion that a matter as quotidian as racism was a factor: "it's a matter of economics," argued this trucker and bounty hunter, not "discriminatory motives."[51] Like musicians, union bosses who also found it necessary to use their fists from time to time also often came from boxing backgrounds. This included Paul Hall, a leader of both the seafarers union and the AFL-CIO [American Federation of Labor-Congress of Industrial Organizations]—and like most labor bosses, a fierce anticommunist—and former middleweight battler.[52]

---

47. Harold Lederman to Angelo Dundee, 26 January 1975, Sub Group VIII, Series I, Box 12, HKBA.
48. Minutes, 23 December 1935, NYSAC.
49. Report, 4 May 1972, Boxing Notes on Muhammad Ali, Vol. 21, UND.
50. Kram, *Smokin' Joe*, 65.
51. *Bergen Record*, 18 August 1974, Sub Group VIII, Series I, Box 7, HKBA: In the same box, see also *USA Today*, 3 April 1991.
52. Obituary, 24 June 1980, Sub Group VIII, Series I, Box 10, HKBA.

Nevertheless, even positing bias, conceivably King's missteps may have exceeded those of the competition; for example, Mike Tyson, who became the face of boxing in the late 20th century, succeeding Gans, Johnson, Louis, and Ali, employed King's daughter as the head of his fan club, though it is not clear if this protégé of Cus D'Amato was aware of this.[53] The problem, in brief, was that the misdeeds of the hirsute King were all too real. Heavyweight Tim Witherspoon asserted that "he made me sign blank contracts. He made me use his son as my manager. He warned me never to talk to a lawyer or an accountant…I had no rights." Boxers may have been expert at the right cross, while promoters were masters of the double cross[54]—which was more effective and deadly.

King was not above flaunting his underworld mettle in order to extract concessions from boxers, invariably younger and less experienced than himself. As he told one puncher, "You can leave here, make a call and have me killed in half an hour. I can pick up the phone as you leave and have you offed [murdered] in five minutes."[55] It would have been unwise for the naïve to ignore such bravado, for King had ties not only to Carl Lombardo, a wealthy businessman in northern Ohio, a card-carrying member of the U.S. elite, but also to John Gotti, a so-called "Mafia Godfather," at least, according to the FBI.[56]

King's Cleveland, like many metropolitan regions, had more than its share of racketeers. Among them was Morris Kleinman, once designated as a "senior member of the Cleveland syndicate" in "alliance" with "[Moe] Dalitz"—who then moved to Las Vegas where Arum wound up—and Sam Tucker. Kleinman had investments in boxing, and like many—for example, Mickey Cohen—was a former puncher himself, starring as a champion amateur boxer. Depicted as the "Al Capone of Cleveland," he also had investments in poultry, and before that bootleg liquor and rum running—then he, too, moved to Southern Florida, the citadel of Carbo and Chris Dundee.[57] As for Cohen, also with roots in Cleveland, he was once a top

---

53. Affidavit of Joseph A. Mafia, in U.S. District Court for Southern District of New York, ca. 1990, Box 54, Newfield-UT.

54. *Details*, November 1990, Box 151, Newfield-UT.

55. Mailer, *Fight*, 117.

56. See Memo from Special Agent of FBI-Cleveland, 14 August 1980, Box 54, Newfield-UT. On King and Gotti see in same box, *New York Post*, 7 October 1992. For more on this topic, see *New York Daily News*, 15 August 1992.

57. *Miami Herald*, 12 November 1965, Sub Group IX, Series I, Box 15, HKBA.

gambler in Los Angeles, the city that helped to give birth to modern Las Vegas: Raking in a hefty $80,000 a month, the 5'3" dynamo lived lavishly in a Brentwood mansion in a neighborhood festooned with Hollywood royalty.[58]

Las Vegas, where Arum eventually shut up shop, made this Ohio town seem like small potatoes in comparison. Bedecked with casinos and brothels within hailing distance, the state where Jack Johnson was propelled to fame in 1910 had returned to boxing prominence post-World War II. Strikingly, Morris "Moe" Dalitz, with roots in Cleveland but who then sunk roots in Las Vegas, was the connective tissue between the two cities. He endeared himself to the local Jewish-American community, of which Arum was a leading member by, in the words of a local observer, delivering "large sums of cash… to the synagogue."[59] Dalitz was a close colleague of the infamous Meyer Lansky—often denoted as the "brains" behind organized crime nationally (he completed the triangle, given his residence in Southern Florida). But it was Dalitz who was awarded the "Torch of Liberty Award" by the Anti-Defamation League of B'nai B'rith by 1982.[60]

Walter Weiss was a former fighter himself, having endured almost 40 amateur fights and about 10 professional, along with serving as sparring mate of Tommy Collins, the featherweight battler of the early 1950s, earning up to $20 a round. "Meyer Lansky's partner got me a dealing job at the Sands," he recalled, speaking of a local casino/hotel, and he "spent six years on Wall Street," too. As Ali was soaring—bringing King and Arum along with him—Weiss noticed that "at that time the Jews were heavily involved in the mob…at one time the Jews owned every hotel here except the Tropicana…it was the mob" actually "but the front were all Jews." The ecumenical Dalitz shrewdly covered his flanks when he "contributed heavily to the building of the Catholic Church" and he "contributed significantly to the building of Ner Tamid Temple," a Reform Synagogue. It was his "Cleveland outfit" that "had the Desert Inn," while the respectable developer Irving Molasky was Dalitz's "legitimate partner."[61] These "legitimate partners" provided camouflage in that despite his many sordid activities, Dalitz generally was able to escape severe penalty.

---

58. *Miami Herald*, 29 July 1976.
59. Oral History, Marc Ratner, 23 August 2016, UNV-LV. At the same site, see also Oral History, Lovee Arum, 1 November 2016.
60. *Las Vegas Review Journal*, 3 September 1989, Biographical File on Moe Dalitz, UNV-LV.
61. Oral History, Walter Weiss, 2 November 2010, UNV-LV.

Much has been made, including in these pages, about the revelations provided by the senator from Tennessee after inspecting the multiple crevices of organized crime, but Dalitz breezily dismissed the "Kefauver investigation" since it "had no impact on anyone in Las Vegas to my knowledge."[62] Just as the authorities seemed to be more interested in King than Arum, Kefauver's inquiries tended to focus more on the region sprawling eastward from St. Louis to the Atlantic—though it is not clear if this were accidental.

Dalitz's arrogant dismissal of the possibility of his prosecution, and his very position in the Nevada hierarchy, also represented a major turnabout from decades earlier insofar as representatives of the Jewish-American community had disappeared for the most part from the ring but had intensified their representation at the top ranks of the sport nonetheless. This was an outgrowth of the post-World War II dispensation which entailed not only a retreat from the more horrid aspects of Jim Crow but an opening for more opportunity to benefit this ethno-religious minority, too. "Right now," said Arum in 2016, "I don't think there are more than two or three Jewish fighters," likely an underestimate but still reflective of the dimensions of the issue.[63]

Thus, Arum, who was Jewish-American, and King, an African-American, presided over an ethnic succession in the sport no less momentous than what was attempted by Gibson and Carbo and Norris. For by 1974, as Ali was hitting his stride, the main matchmaker at Madison Square Garden asserted that "today 75 percent of the fighters in the States are Hispanic," heavily Mexican and Puerto Rican and Dominican, as the Cuban pounders from years back had been removed from the market as a result of the blockade of the 1959 Revolution. Yet, one factor remained constant: "[the] amount of Hispanic officials, judges and referees is less than 10 percent." This regulator was then reflecting on "the third we-wuz-robbed riot of 1974," when "White Hope" "Mike Quarry won a unanimous decision over Pedro Soto, a Puerto Rican" with a spark for this conflagration being "none of the officials…were Latin."[64] An Albany regulator was thinking along similar lines when in 1973 he claimed, "I believe we have too many foreign champions."[65]

However, given the harassment of Ali, it was apparent that some were not too happy with certain native-born champions either. The

---

62. Oral History, Moe Dalitz, 4 November 1977, UNV-LV.
63. Oral History, Bob Arum, 20 October 2016, UNV-LV.
64. Report, 12 December 1974, Sub Group VIII, Series I, Box 3, HKBA.
65. Minutes, 27 March 1973, NYSAC.

problem was that as Jim Crow barriers eased, African Americans, too, were finding other outlets for their talents. By 1969 Minnesota regulators were observing with concern the drop in "Negro participation in...Golden Gloves (this year)...and it has been agreed that it was because they weren't as hungry and the old deal of wanting to get into it, has diminished."[66] Not only were these African Americans not as "hungry," Minnesota regulators thought they were not as talented. "Many Negroes had entered" the Golden Gloves, it was reported, "but had been eliminated before reaching the Midwest finals."[67] Minnesotans should have been more self-critical however, for, like many, they too had sought to bar Ali during his draft troubles, thereby sending a forbidding signal to youthful African Americans who saw him as a hero and may have wanted to walk in his footsteps. "How could we, as veterans," state regulators were told unnecessarily, "face our youngsters without feeling we are betraying them...if we allow a draft dodger like Cassius Clay to have his way."[68] This was the sport's self-inflicted wound, for a few years later St. Paul regulators were pondering the point that "boxing—both professional and amateur—is at a low ebb" in the republic.[69]

This low ebb was not necessarily prevalent in Las Vegas; there the arrogant Dalitz was reflective of the callousness that often was the handmaiden of those incapable of understanding the larger forces that propelled them. "We didn't have any black people" as workers in Las Vegas, he said gruffly. Why? "Because none were adept. They weren't qualified," said this partner of yet another respectable member of the U.S. ruling elite, Merv Adelson, real estate baron and television producer.[70] Though speaking venomously in ardent tones that dripped with anti-Black racism, many of these same forces spoke in *sotto voce* about the rampant stories about Howard Hughes—aviator, film producer, mogul, sexist—and his anti-Semitism. One principal at Caesar's Palace recounted a story about his interviewing a woman who was seeking employment as a cocktail waitress and was enticed to undress in the process. Hughes's hotel employees,

---

66. Minutes, 14 March 1969, Boxing Board Records, 103.H.15.1B, MinnHS-SP.

67. Minutes, 17 February 1969, Boxing Board Records, 103.H.15.1B, MinnHS-SP.

68. United Military Veterans Council to Harold Levander, 20 February 1970, Boxing Board Records, 103.H.15.1B, MinnHS-SP.

69. Richard Plunkett to R.C. Schwartz, 25 January 1975, *Boxing Board Records*, 103. H.15.1B, MinnHS-SP.

70. Oral History, Morris "Moe" Dalitz, 4 November 1977, UNV-LV.

said Mike Unger, were "predominately Mormon...I hid the fact that I was Jewish" when toiling on his plantation. And when Clifford Perlman "took over" Caesar's in the "early seventies, it was very definitely mob-controlled," for arriving, too, were Meyer Lansky and a "lot of [South] Florida money,"[71] meaning a marriage with boxing.

Still, Arum was not immune to such dishonorable associations. There was Frank Gelb, for example, touted as an Atlantic City impresario by an official body in the Garden State. He was also a manager of successful punchers, but by 1980 had become the boxing consultant for Resorts International, an opulent, garish hotel/casino in Jersey. He managed to be close to both King and Arum—but noticeably so to the latter. Hauled before an investigative body, he exhibited what was described charitably as "unwarranted evasions and memory lapses" garnished with a "lack of candor." He denied ever meeting Nicodemo "Nicky" Scarfo, the Philadelphia mob boss, and as for Palermo, he suggested that he had not met the blinker until the late 1970s. Still, he was busily booking fights overseas as well as nationally, which inevitably brought him, and his questionable associations, closer to King and, more so, to Arum. By 1980 there was a spate of gangland rub-outs: Angelo Bruno in March, Philip Testa a year later in 1981; then there was the horrific beating of Frank "Flowers" d'Alfonso in October 1981. Investigators sensed a Gelb connection. Viewed skeptically were Gelb's ties to Palermo's mouthpiece Robert Gabriel, not to mention d'Alfonso and the alleged "processing [of] mob money through a legitimate enterprise such as a closed circuit tv boxing show," e.g., the Ali-Holmes bout of 1980, staged conveniently in Las Vegas. Gabriel admitted that d'Alfonso provided a "'loan'" to Gelb for this latter fight and said further that the "transaction was discussed with and partly financed by the mob...I sought out Mr. Palermo's advice," he confessed.[72] Eventually, "Frankie Flowers" was plucked, gunned down in an assumed gangland execution.[73]

In the aftermath of this Nevada spectacle, more blood was shed. Richard Green, the first Negro referee in the Sagebrush State, who was the third man in the ring during the 1980 contest and many other title clashes, was found dead of a gunshot wound.[74] Richard Steele,

---

71. Oral History, Mike Unger, 21 January 2016, UNV-LV.

72. Testimony of Frank Gelb, "Organized Crime in Boxing. Final Boxing Report of the State of New Jersey Commission of Investigation. 1985. 974.90 162, NJSL-T.

73. Report, 1895, Sub Group VIII, Series 2, Box 25, HKBA.

74. *Valley Times*, 5 July 1983, Sub Group VIII, Series I, Box 9, HKBA.

a former boxer, actor and police officer who worked with fellow thespian Ryan O'Neal when he portrayed a pugilist, recalled with sorrow the "bullet in his chest," referring to Green. He seemed skeptical of the official judgment that this was a suicide. "This happened several times in my lifetime when people said that they committed suicide and I knew better."[75]

As so often happened, this now gloried 1980 contest in the Nevada desert took place against the backdrop of feuding mob factions: St. Louis and Detroit, this time. Showy mobsters often saw the occasion of a bout in Vegas as a chance to display their ill-gotten wealth at casino tables and ringside alike, as if this exhibition of affluence could intimidate a plug-ugly with an itchy trigger finger and dreams of eliminating the competition. Thus, looking back at this event, Mike Unger, who was there, assayed that "we made thirty one million dollars that weekend of the fight" at Caesar's Palace, a monument to garishness and greed: this, he said, on an investment of $8 million. "I have no idea what the other hotels made," he said, leaving the impression that an even greater bonanza was recouped by them. Yes, he said with a sense of immense satisfaction, the Ali-Holmes contest was "the first big, big fight not only in Las Vegas but ever."[76]

One of King's closest business comrades, Al Braverman, was said by the *New York Post* to be a "disciple" of "Blinky" Palermo, suggesting that the 1961 trial in Los Angeles did not resolve the underlying issues.[77] At one point, one "informant" of the Bureau "had a meeting" with King, who told him that "he was going to Philadelphia… to meet with Frankie D [Delaphonzo] to plan the killing of Richie Giachetti," an associate of Larry Holmes. "King was livid at Giachetti because Giachetti had tape recorded conversations with King and Larry Holmes for the past three years and Giachetti had turned these tapes over to the FBI." In passing, it was observed that the former numbers boss "would like to have Arum's legs broken."[78]

Giachetti was worried, fearing there was a contract to kill him. "They would make it look like a mugging," said this former trainer of Holmes, who seemed to have insight into this kind of brigandage. He also thought that King, who once aspired to become an undertaker, was well acquainted with sophisticated means of murder. He recalled King's sharp clashes with a fistic master, Jewish-Hungarian

---

75. Oral History, Richard Steele and Zakeisha Steele-Jones, 2 February 2015, UNV-LV.
76. Oral History, Mike Unger, 21 January 2016, UNV-LV.
77. *New York Post*, 26 May 1996, Box 54, Newfield-UT.
78. Memorandum, 29 May 1981, Box 54, Newfield-UT.

mobster Alex "Shondor" Birns, over the numbers racket and related underworld rackets—a turning point in the rise of Black Gangsters regionally, if not nationally—which ended with the latter and his 1975 Lincoln town car falling victim to a car bomb. King did not escape unscathed either: A bomb exploded on the porch of his home, he was shot in the head, back and neck—this while he was supposedly under police protection in a case involving Birns (possibly another case of why it was folly for Black Gangsters to concentrate on economics to the detriment of political influence).[79]

Because of King's mystique, Holmes declared that "bookmakers have taken a Don King fight off the board when they think something didn't smell right." Holmes, a former sparring partner of Ali, then his successor, realized he needed backup, a potent factor provided to the former "Louisville Lip" by the Nation of Islam. Holmes knew all too well of "good fighters who never got anywhere...it didn't matter how much talent you had...Don knew that an unknown fighter like me needed him more than he needed me." Thus, when he signed with King, the Clevelander received 25% of his purses, the trainer—Giachetti—got 12%, and the manager, Earnie Butler, got 10%.[80]

Holmes may have put an end to Ali's glorious career, but it was "Smokin'" Joe Frazier and George Foreman whose own bruising excellence pushed the former "Louisville Lip" to ever greater heights. Yet, while Foreman, as of this writing, is a millionaire many times over, the stocky Frazier died in 2011 with few if any assets, despite involvement in fights delivering millions in revenue. He did have a liking for gambling, but even Atlantic City, within reasonable distance of his Philadelphia home, is insufficient to explicate what happened to him. Like others who had fought their way to the top, he had rich experience in battling racists—especially in his birthplace, South Carolina—and this transferable skill was then deployed in the steamy gyms of the City of Brotherly Love: These equivalents of slaughterhouses were often in decrepit edifices amidst rubble-strewn lots. Striding from these ruins were not only Frazier but a bevy of battlers including Bennie Briscoe and "Gypsy" Joe Harris, and later the ultimate contenders: Bernard Hopkins, Dwight Muhammad Qawi, Matthew Saad Muhammad, et al. It was not just the dangers of the concrete canyons of this increasingly distressed metropolis that shaped and hardened these fighters; it was also the reality experienced by those like Bobby Carmody, who won the bronze medal in the Tokyo Olympics of 1964, then three years later died as a soldier in

---

79. *New York Post*, 8 August 1981, Sub Group VIII, Series I, Box 9, HKBA.
80. Larry Holmes, "Boxing Politics," no date, Box 156, Newfield-UT.

an ambush in Indo-China. It was evident that a bloody gym was to be preferred to a battlefield in Vietnam, and thus, after the city predictably went up in flames in 1967 in a burst of unrest, one of the central gyms was among the few buildings with windows not shattered. Though Frazier became well known for his curious associations with right-wing pols, like Mayor Frank Rizzo, even he was sufficiently sensitive to become inflamed by the horrid treatment of Dick Allen, the proud and brooding Black slugger of the baseball Phillies.

Frazier was also upset with Ali's baiting of him in increasingly insensitive terms, comparing him to various animals, which upset many besides the man with the powerful left hook, a tendency likely exacerbated because of the baiter's lighter skin color. This raw conflict generated an electric intensity that characterized their three ferocious bouts, especially the "Thrilla in Manila," promoted by King.[81]

But this ferocity was also present at Madison Square Garden in 1971 during their first match. As was so often the case with heavyweight championship contests, there was quite a bit of peacocking. The self-described "Original Gangster," Frank Lucas, effused that presence at ringside "separated the boys from the men. Anybody who was half of somebody was there." Unavoidably, boasted Lucas, "I was there, front and center…Ali came down and also gave me a hug before going into the ring" while Frazier, "he winks at me on his way into the corner." The authorities knew that gladiatorial combat tended to draw those who often were involved in gambling and other activities deemed questionable, which also meant that the predators of the peacocks also showed up. "Ever since" that bout, rued Lucas, when he "made that bet at the Ali-Frazier fight, the feds had their eyes on me." It was not just prosecutors who saw prizefights in the same light as lions viewed gazelles on the savannah. Ali's return from purgatory, after his escape from the possibility of prosecution for draft evasion, took place in Atlanta in 1970. "That's when my trouble started," said Lucas, a fixture at such spectacles, referring to Ali versus the perennial "White Hope" Jerry Quarry. Again, as the ballers and shot-callers amassed in enough fur to ignite an animal rights protest, criminal investigators were espying their own quarry.[82] And so were would-be ballers and shot callers: In an episode from one of the so-called "Blax-ploitation" movies then trending, scores of fight fans were not only robbed of their wads of cash and flashy jewelry at festivities following the fight, but just as Quarry

---

81. Kram, *Smokin' Joe*, 8-9, 33, 40-41, 53-54, 129.
82. Lucas, *Original Gangster*, 238-239, 233.

was figuratively undressed in the ring by Ali, exposed as a poseur, the partygoers too were undressed, compelled to hand over their often elegant duds to the fleeing bandits. Seven months later two of these robbers were found murdered in the Bronx: perversely appropriate, the two victims—McKinley Rogers, Jr. of Brunswick, Georgia, and James Henry Hall, 25, of Atlanta—were found slumped in a stolen Cadillac.[83]

* * *

It was not just African-American bruisers who were exploited so relentlessly. As Jim Crow came under assault and those like Ali were able to claim a larger share of the wealth they were creating, the idea arose to go straight to the source—Africa—and find new candidates for exploitation. Like a latter-day explorer in a pith helmet, it was left to Thomas "Sarge" Johnson of Indianapolis, one of the planet's top amateur boxing coaches, to visit the continent,[84] once routinely described as "dark." His mission was to provide instructions in the art of what used to be called manly self-defense. There would also be the ancillary benefit of winning hearts and minds in the ongoing Cold War, as Moscow was shaping mentalities by subsidizing the ongoing struggle against apartheid and colonialism.[85]

Johnson was not the first prospector of what was routinely referred to as "Black Gold" in Africa. In 1968, authorities in Phoenix were seeking to attract a Nigerian boxing coach to Arizona to learn the tricks of the trade.[86] But for some reason, by 1973 Phoenix was backtracking, arguing that invitations to boxers from Port Harcourt, Nigeria, to come train in the desert were not authorized officially, suggesting that the baggage Johnson was carrying to the continent was fuller than imagined.[87]

By the summer of 1977, "Sarge" Johnson was exuberantly informing the State Department that "there is Black Gold in African boxing," this after the Ivory Coast had hosted the "first ever African Regional

---

83. *United Press International*, 26 May 1971, Boxing Notes on Muhammad Ali, Vol. 21, UND.

84. *Indianapolis Star*, 12 August 1979, Sub Group VIII, Series I, Box 11, HKBA.

85. Horne, *White Supremacy*.

86. Minutes, 13 May 1968, Reel 76.1.1., Arizona State Athletic Commission, ASA-P.

87. Leo Crowley to Port Harcourt, 30 May 1973, RG1 SG20, Box 680, ASA-P.

Boxing Clinic." Though not necessarily because of Johnson's ministrations, a steady flow of battlers from that nation did emerge in coming years (Azumah Nelson of neighboring Ghana, John Mugabi of Uganda, and Nigeria's Dick Tiger much earlier setting the pace). It became clearer that winning hearts and minds during the Cold War by seeming to extend U.S. largesse was a critical matter for these "clinics." West Africa, said Johnson, "has already provided us with more local and international coverage than we've had for quite some time." "Mission accomplished!" he clucked.[88]

By May 1979 Johnson was in Zambia, then a headquarters for liberation movements on the verge of seizing power in Zimbabwe (then Rhodesia), Namibia (South West Africa), and South Africa itself. His two-week course was advertised as the first of its kind in Southern Africa. Nairobi, and even the Seychelles, were on his agenda.[89]

Naturally, Johnson contacted Angelo Dundee, the informal broker of boxing flesh. First he chose to "thank" the Ali trainer "for your support in trying to help [obtain] boxing equipment for the Upper Volta [Burkina Faso] boxing team" since "this country of West Africa...is definitely without a doubt...**BLACK GOLD**!" he veritably shouted. "I have never seen so much raw talent in my life," he exclaimed. It appeared that he was hyping West Africa in order to create opportunities for himself: "Why don't you bring [this] to the attention of your good friend Mr. Howard Cosell about the possibility of me being a scout for you and ABC [American Broadcasting Corporation]. Official or unofficial." Scheming in a manner congruent with the lineaments of the sport, he added, "I would see to it that all top amateur boxers because of your choice be directed to you and ABC."[90] It is unclear if Dundee or Cosell—the boorish broadcaster whose career as a ringside analyst was solidified as a result of less than insightful interviews with Ali—ever replied. Months later, Johnson was seeking to ingratiate himself with the trainer, referring to himself familiarly as "your pal Tom" and revealing that he had "heard that Muhammad Ali will be going to Swaziland for an exhibition."[91]

---

88. Air-gram to State Department from Ivory Coast, 18 July 1977, Sub Group VIII, Series I, Box 11, HKBA.

89. *Zambia Daily Mail*, 9 May 1979; *Nairobi Times*, 30 April 1979; *The Nation* [Seychelles], 1 June 1979, Sub Group VIII, Series I, Box 11, HKBA.

90. Thomas Johnson to Angelo Dundee, 18 April 1977, Sub Group VIII, Series I, Box 11, HKBA.

91. Thomas Johnson to Angelo Dundee, 11 February 1978, Sub Group VIII, Series I, Box 11, HKBA.

Ali did venture to the continent in 1974 to the nation now known as the Democratic Republic of the Congo (then Zaire), which was ruled dictatorially by the kleptomaniac once known as Joseph Mobutu: He had blood on his hands because of his key role in the murder of the heroic Founding Father, Patrice Lumumba. Tagging along was the celebrated writer and informal pugilist Norman Mailer; and as so often happens, his journey to the heart of darkness apparently stirred darker impulses within him. This was during a time when the very term "Black Power" seemed to spur a severe bout of angst among certain Euro-Americans, as if they were jolted back to the early days of settler colonialism, when they were perpetually besieged. Pretentiously referring to himself in the third person, the logorrheic Mailer—whose father had decamped to South Africa before arriving in the U.S.—revealed what he should have kept hidden: "he no longer knew whether he loved Blacks or secretly disliked them." His purpose in the Congo was "not only...to report on a fight but to look a little more into his own outsized feelings of love and—could it be?—sheer hate for the existence of Black[s] on earth."[92]

There Ali pulled off one of his exalted maneuvers, turning the African audience against his opponent: "those Africans are anti-America," said Ali who often was grouped among this cohort, "they remember how you waved the flag at the Olympics," and many had yet to forgive or forget the U.S.'s own dastardly role in Lumumba's assassination and the subsequent thieving misrule. Foreman's vigorously affirmed faith in capitalism did him few favors in a nation where socialism was hardly discredited. Per usual, typical shenanigans followed the fighters and their vast entourages across the Atlantic. Both camps were accused of seeking to bribe the referee, evoking images of a then popular film starring mega-stars Sidney Poitier and Bill Cosby. The fight was capped off by Ali's signature move that has launched a thousand metaphors: the "rope-a-dope," whereby he lay back against the evidently loosened ropes of the ring and allowed his opponent to exhaust himself (and perhaps do lasting damage to Ali's innards) by punching himself into seeming exhaustion. But again, the thinly veiled story of the fight was the explosion of revenue delivered by closed-circuit broadcasts, which poured more money into King's pockets, and further incentivized Arum to best him.[93]

---

92. Mailer, *Fight*, 35, 37.
93. Smith, *No Way*, 131, 162, 172, 193, 204.

Chapter 10

The Return of the "Great White Hope"?

By the late 1970s, Don King seemed to be flying high, raking in millions in revenue, perambulating around the globe, consorting with celebrities—few of whom exceeded his own level of wealth and notoriety (or infamy). But then he absorbed incoming fire that would have shot down a less nimble businessman. Meanwhile, the counter-revolution against racial equality continued apace, culminating in the 1980 election that thrust Ronald Reagan into the White House; unavoidably, these retrograde forces helped to give rise to malignant forces in boxing—including the Return of the Great White Hope.

As for King, he managed to arrange a boxing tournament, in league with television network ABC, that managed to expose a scandal. The qualifications to reach a vaunted appearance on the small screen were based on rankings in the supposed boxing bible, *The Ring*, which revealed that the sport was desperately in need of a Martin Luther. For their "rankings" were replete with errors and rooted in quicksand—maybe ignorance at best. One matchmaker argued that if this were the bible, a "New Testament" was now in order. It was even more scandalous, said Bert Sugar, a boxing expert himself, in that all sides proceeded even though there were "about 200 people out there who do nothing but compile fighters' records for a hobby." In short, there were about 200 people looking over the shoulders of King and ABC to make sure their rankings were well-grounded, meaning scandal was virtually baked into the process. The "bible" was no cipher, having a companion Spanish version with a combined monthly circulation of about 140,000. But it was co-founded by the late promoter Tex Rickard, the colorful figure from the "Roaring Twenties," and aficionado Nat Fleischer, which suggested that it was almost designed to promote the former's contests; by the time of the scandal it was administered by Fleischer's son-in-law, Nat Loubet.[1]

---

1. *San Francisco Chronicle,* 14 August 1979, Sub Group VIII, Series I, Box 13, HKBA.

Again, though King was rightfully pilloried for this travesty he could righteously reply that those without sin should cast the first stone. A few years after this scandal, Frank Valenzano (who managed Roger Mayweather, then handled Floyd "Money" Mayweather—one of the best of all time) declared that "boxing is handled by some dishonest people. They'll get a guy from Timbuktu, rate him No. 6 and then get him a title shot."[2] In other words, what King was doing was not uncommon. In any case, King had insulated himself to a degree with his bleating about his success being representative of a trend "Only in America," while consorting with those like Sonny Werblin, a former agent for Ronald Reagan, who went on to raise gobs of funds for the president's campaigns, at the same time being a major shareholder in the Gulf & Western conglomerate (known colloquially as "Engulf & Devour").[3] Moreover, King did not organize this tournament alone—what about the complicity of ABC?

Yet even given the moth-eaten standards of boxing, the brazenness of King and his partners was breathtaking. One investigator found not only "phony rankings" but "rigged results," "bribes" and "kickbacks."[4] Kenny Weldon said he paid to get a fight—then had to kick back 10% of the fee.[5] Another boxer, Ike Fluellen, said that *The Ring* credited him with victories in bouts that did not include him.[6] He was ranked as the Number 3 Junior Middleweight without fighting for a year, and after he blew the whistle he began receiving a steady stream of harassing phone calls. Fluellen knew a thing or three about intimidation, having served on the police force of an unfashionable Houston suburb, and thus well concluded, "If this isn't organized crime, I'm not a policeman," as he was "afraid to start my car without looking under the hood."[7]

Though dimly recognized at the time, what was happening was that the declension of the Ali Regime coincided with a retreat of the anti-Jim Crow movement, which had seemed to reach a zenith in 1968. As progressive forces were forced to back down, this had knock-on effects downstream, including the recrudescence of malignant forces that had not disappeared in boxing in any case. Thus, the latest King scandal was accompanied by—in retrospect—an astonishing array

---

2. Report, 1 May 1984, Sub Group VIII, Series 1, Box 22, HKBA.

3. *New York Daily News*, 11 May 1980, and undated column by Phil Berger, Sub Group VIII, Series 1, Box 22, HKBA.

4. *Miami News*, 6 April 1977, Sub Group VIII, Series 2, Box 25, HKBA.

5. *Houston Chronicle*, ca. 1977, Sub Group VIII, Series 2, Box 25, HKBA.

6. *Washington Post*, 17 April 1977.

7. Report, 20 April 1977, Sub Group VIII, Series 2, Box 25, HKBA.

of murders, beatings and the like impacting a diverse array of boxers, managers, referees, even promoters. This did not bode well for the sport, at a time when a 1972 poll cited by boxing maven Bert Sugar indicated that 1% of the U.S. audience actually followed the sport.[8] Perhaps unavoidably in this challenging environment, the search for the Holy Grail, or Great White Hope, re-emerged.

* * *

By 1980, Ali was in visible decline as a boxer, a reality that was punctuated when Larry Holmes disassembled him in the ring the following year. By 1980 Ali was not the same kind of lightning rod that he had become in 1967 when he refused to be conscripted. By 1980 the flames of unrest that had swept through Detroit and Newark and Los Angeles generally had been suppressed, meaning a differing political equation.

And, thus, by 1980, Ali took off for Africa on a Washington-sponsored diplomatic mission—a reversal from 1967: This was the beginning of his startling transformation from firebrand to cuddly teddy bear, consummated when he lit the Olympic torch in Atlanta in 1996, albeit trembling visibly from the onset of a degenerative disease doubtlessly sparked by too many blows to head and body. An evidently defanged Ali was easier for many to swallow and, in the process, pay penance and seek absolution for militantly opposing him and seeking to derail his career years earlier.

The transformative process was in its infancy. It was then that on behalf of President Jimmy Carter and his Georgia comrades who were swept into influence by his rise—especially Andrew Young, recently defrocked as U.S. ambassador to the United Nations, after serving as a mayor and congressman in Atlanta—Ali jetted to Africa to persuade dubious leaders that they should join Washington in boycotting the Moscow Olympics because of the 1979 Soviet intervention in Afghanistan. This led to a U.S. alliance with religious zealots that in turn led to these former allies, after coming to power in Kabul, becoming complicit in an attack on New York and Washington on 11 September 2001, followed by a U.S. intervention in that country that continues as of this writing.

Another former Negro Olympian, Mel Whitfield, conscripted for this questionable project, admitted that the boxer was not exactly greeted with sweets and roses by those who encountered him, his immense popularity notwithstanding. Instead, said Whitfield,

---

8. Smith, *No Way*, 102.

there was "some negative coverage," an understatement at best. In his comprehensive report, the pugilist was more forthcoming. "Many countries lean more towards Russia [sic] than the U.S.," he acknowledged, since "Soviets are viewed as advancing the cause of liberation and freedom in Southern Africa, rather than us." Wallowing in the liberal angst that was becoming au courant among African Americans, he cried, "this pains me as a Black American." But as a globetrotter, he should not have been surprised by this turn of events, since he should have known beforehand what he wrote: "Africans know we did not join their boycott of the 1976 Montreal [Olympics]...this disappointment was universally expressed. I, too, feel that this was a mistake." That is, Africans were expected to accept rubbing shoulders with Rhodesians and apartheid masters in Canada and shun those who opposed them, a naked endorsement of neo-colonialism that should have compelled Ali to reject this dicey diplomatic portfolio. "In Lagos," rapidly becoming the heavyweight of the continent, "my discussions with officials were polite but certainly strained. I know no Nigerian leader worth his salt wishes to fall in line." There was "heavy resistance" in Nigeria, making it "hard to have good discussions." On a more positive note for the U.S., he also detected some skepticism of Moscow and was "impressed with the great political importance the Africans attach to sports,"[9] which played to Washington's strength in turning out a steady stream of talented athletes.

Ali's very presence was an exemplar of the magnetic appeal of African-American athletes. He did receive fan mail from Asia (notably India, Pakistan and Sri Lanka),[10] Europe and Australia, but most came from Africa. Typical was the missive from Obed Montene of apartheid South Africa addressed to "Dear Brother (The Champ)," wherein he adopted the talking points of Ali enunciated before his next fight: "we have confidence," he said, "that you will beat the daylight out of self appointed Uncle Tom's champion, Larry Holmes."[11]

Ali continued to stir controversy in the ring, too. When he fought Chuck "The Bayonne Bleeder" Wepner, the purported inspiration for a series of movies featuring Sylvester Stallone, Ali accused his opponent of throwing "rabbit punches" or blows to the back of the head or the base of the skull, and he retaliated in kind. But, said

---

9. Mel Whitfield to "Dear Colleagues," 1 May 1980 with attached: Muhammad Ali, "Summary of my Findings," Sub Group XIX, Series 8, Box 9, HKBA.

10. See bulging folder in Sub Group XIX, Series 2, Box 3, HKBA.

11. Obed Montene to Ali, no date, Sub Group 2, Box 1, HKBA.

Ali, the referee, Anthony Perez, reprimanded him without rebuking the originator of this foul praxis. Ali then slurred the referee, calling him a "white motherfucker," and Wepner was addressed similarly. Perez brought suit in response to Ali's display and argued that after Ali had administered a crushing "knockdown" of the hapless challenger, it appeared that it was [Ali's] intention to kill Wepner"; and, he continued, Ali "stated...he did have the intention of killing Wepner,"[12] leading to this unavailing lawsuit to collect $20 million from Ali's coffers.[13]

Three years after being pummeled by Holmes, and four years after his ill-fated expedition to Africa, Ali was examined by the eminent Dr. Stanley Fahn of the medical school at Columbia University for signs of "Parkinson disease." The diagnosis was not altogether reassuring, though he did find his patient's "mind" to be "impressively alert and well-oriented," though this would not have been the pleasant conclusion of Perez.[14]

Assuredly, Ali was sufficiently alert to seek to capitalize upon his vast popularity. Just before his Africa journey, Sammie Marshall, on behalf of "Muhammad Ali Professional Sports," the entity that led to the jailing of the aforementioned Harold "Rossfields" Smith because of embezzlement involving a major California bank, reached out to him. This was the boxer's attempt to turn the tables on the promoters and, like Joe Louis and Truman Gibson, grab a slice of a continuingly expanding pie. It was then that Marshall sought a "promoter's license" for a bout in Minnesota.[15] But like Louis before him, Ali's venture would also encounter formidable obstacles, for instance when there was fervent denial that a building in Dover, Minnesota, "was not available," because "black boxers" were allowed previously to "compete in the boxing matches."[16] However, the Land of 10,000 Lakes seemed to have a similar number of ways to express racism, which was bound to make life more complex for

---

12. Anthony Perez vs. Muhammad Ali, U.S. District Court, Southern District of New York, 1975, Sub Group XIX, Series 2, Box 29, HKBA.

13. *New York Daily News*, 17 April 1975, Sub Group XIX, Series 2, Box 29, HKBA.

14. Report by Dr. Stanley Fahn, 20 September 1984, Sub Group XIX, Series 2, Box 1, HKBA.

15. Sammie Marshall to Mr. O'Hara, 4 October 1979, Boxing Board Records, 103.H.15.1B, MinnHS-SP.

16. Layton Ernst, Board of Education, Dover-Eyota Public Schools to Governor Wendell Anderson, 14 December 1972, Boxing Board Records, 103.H. 15.1B, MinnHS-SP.

Marshall and MAPS. "Derogatory remarks made by fans during... bouts in regard to race or color" were at issue, along with a "question of long hair and beards," a product of the counterculture then on the march. The response? A "clean shaven stipulation" was mandated, but the authorities were not so decisive in confronting racism.[17]

But Marshall and MAPS were not necessarily flummoxed by this not-so-novel twist. As Ali was contemplating a voyage to Africa, Marshall in Minnesota was planning an "all women's card" and, besides, "working with a gay fighter."[18] At the time, state authorities were fielding "a few complaints" about the "holding of Bikini Contest[s] at Boxing shows."[19]

Marshall insisted stoutly, "I do believe in free enterprise," hardly at issue, as he contrasted MAPS feebly with "lots of people [who] were coming in to Minnesota to make a bundle of money and to run and leave."[20] This may have been a subtle jab at the competition, the man with the electrified hairdo, Don King, who was then seeking a "license" for the wildly lucrative "closed-circuit television boxing bouts." Harry Davis, Chairman of the state's Boxing Board, desired a share-the-wealth proviso, however, and King could well wonder if Arum would have been confronted similarly: That is, he wanted King to partner with a "live boxing franchise" in the state.[21] (Few things convert certain Euro-Americans to the virtues of socialist wealth sharing, more than the sight of a Negro with a fortune.)

A better course would have been for the Minnesota authorities to focus more intently on the health and welfare of boxers. Boxers continued to fall into life-defying comas after exiting the ring.[22] Sadly, this kind of tragedy was hardly peculiar to Minnesota; due southwest in Arizona, a fighter who had a demonstrated history of what

---

17. Minutes, 16 February 1970, Boxing Board Records, 103.H.15.1B, MinnHS-SP.

18. Minutes, 3 August 1979, Boxing Board Records, 103.H.15.1B, MinnHS-SP.

19. Minutes, 11 September 1984, Boxing Board Records, 103.H.15.1B, MinnHS-SP.

20. Transcript, 15 February 1980, Boxing Board Records, 103.H.15.1B, MinnHS-SP.

21. Harry Davis, Chair of Boxing Board to Don King, 10 October 1980, MinnHS-SP.

22. Report from law office of Fred Allen, Minneapolis, 22 October 1971, Boxing Board Records, 103. H. 15.1B, MinnHS-SP.

was described as "nausea and right kidney pain" was allowed to box 10 rounds—then "passed several kidney stones."[23]

Still, in 1981, the Minnesota authorities officially posed a query rarely raised, i.e., "what happens to a boxer when he adds weight and then takes off weight...at a rapid rate...to make the weight for a bout"; there was no evidence of action taken, though fighters spiraling from light-heavyweight to middleweight, or middleweight to welterweight, was not an uncommon phenomenon.[24]

Again, St. Paul was not singular in its nonfeasance, for Phoenix was in hot pursuit of this dubious distinction. Torpor was the response when boxer Jesse Garcia made a complaint about small-time promoter Kenneth Palmer, who provided him with a "cash bond of $500" after a bout—along with $2,500 in "outstanding bad checks."[25] Garcia's attorney was livid at the "unjust treatment" accorded his client, which he said was due at least partially to his being a "Mexican citizen," an increasing tendency of maltreatment as the ascent of boxers from south of the border began.[26] Robert W. Lee, a would-be boxing czar in New Jersey, railed against the rankings of boxers as designated by the WBA, denouncing the "wrongs done to boxers and particularly the American boxers," but Garcia and his team would have dissented.[27]

In some ways, the descent of the sport, as the sorrowful case of Garcia symbolized, accelerated in concert with the decline of Ali's health and the concomitant rise of an enervating conservatism, which spelled ill for the fortunes of the U.S. working class, making this sprawling entity more susceptible to ever more outlandish proposals. Among the latter was the ascension of what was termed by Midwest authorities as "tough man contest[s]" and "bar-room brawling." In other words, a kind of free-for-all was at play, with the ultimate beneficiary being orthopedic surgeons in for-profit hospitals. "I am definitely not in favor," said Dr. Lacey Walker of

---

23. Dr. George Fickas, "To Whom it May Concern," 1 May 1972, Reel 76.1.1, ASA-P.
24. Minutes, 16 January 1981, Boxing Board Records, 103. H. 15.1B, MinnHS-SP.
25. Jay Edson to Harold Rucker, 17 September 1973, RG1, Box 680, 1.5.9, ASA-P.
26. Harold Rucker to Governor Jack Williams, 5 September 1973, RG1, Box 680, 1.5.9, ASA-P.
27. Robert W. Lee, Deputy Athletic Commissioner-New Jersey, to Rodrigo Sanchez, WBA President, 20 November 1979, Professional Licensing Agency/Commission Meeting Files/83-789, 221-a-4, Box 2, ISA-I.

Michigan, though, typically, he realized that "such contests have regularly taken place in Arizona and some western states," where the culture continued to be marred by a relatively recent routing of the Indigenous, many of whom had managed to retain a portion of their once vast landholdings. Dr. Walker fretted that "spontaneous death" was the unavoidable result, not least since the "general state of health of the participants is at best poorly known," meaning "unnecessary medical and legal problems for both the physician and boxer involved."[28] Undeterred, by 1980, arriving from Illinois and decamping in Schererville, Indiana, was a spectacle billed as an "All Women Mud Wrestling Team"—the "Chicago Knockers"—at $4.00 per ticket.[29] By mid-1981, regulators in the Hoosier State were warning one of these organizers of performances designed for the leering male gaze, that "unlicensed 'whipped cream' wrestling matches between female contestants" should cease. For these grotesque exhibitions were illegitimate, since the State Athletic Commission was the "sole and exclusive authority" mandated to "sanction and license wrestling matches."[30]

Boxing was taking a toll, as Ali's increasingly shaky movements and slurred speech indicated—and "tough man contests" (and even women grapplers in unregulated environments) would drive injury further down the ranks. Unhappily, the virus had crept across the border in that by 1980 even Canada was complicit, although the "Great White North" did not possess the martial, perpetual warfighting culture that, it was thought, was a *sine qua non* for "tough man contests" and the like. By 1980 this huge nation had been sponsoring for two years "heavyweight 'tournaments' open to any person who could claim to have a heartbeat," according to an astringent critic. "You could kick, you could chop, you could slap," a bloody exhibition facilitated since mere boxing was "frowned" on. "Posters advertised for 'truck drivers, loggers, motorcycle raiders,'" all of which struck a responsive chord since "fans broke down the door to attend these rip-offs." For those times, "seats" were "not cheap," averaging "$10 to $15," and yet there were "crowds drawing 5000

---

28. Dr. Lacey Walker to Charles Davey, Boxing Commissioner, Troy, Michigan, 15 October 1979, Box 2, PLA/Commission Meeting Files/83-789, 221-a-4, ISA-I.

29. Advertisement, 24 April 1980, Box 2, PLA/Commission Meeting Files/83-789, 221-a-4, ISA-I.

30. Richard E. Bossung, Chairman of Indiana State Athletic Commission to Jack Brinson, 22 June 1981, Box 2, PLA/Commission Meeting Files/83-789, ISA-I.

or more suckers." In a throwback to slavery, indicative of the atavism involved, there were "'free for all' battle royals," though "top pay" was "$2500," a good deal of which would have to be directed to medical expenses since "teeth are knocked out, jaws broken, testicles squashed, faces gashed, kidneys and livers damaged"—and "brains seriously injured."[31] Ignored was the axiom, now hanging by a thread—attributed to trainer Victor Machado, who worked alongside the great Wilfredo Benitez: "Anyone can fight but not everyone can box."[32]

A few rungs below Ali on the totem pole of boxers was "Bad" Bennie Briscoe, the quintessential Philadelphia fighter, a wide category that conceivably could include Liston, Frazier—and Ali himself. Like a "Black Robot," which was one of his nicknames, he moved forward launching hammer blows, refusing to retreat, with opponents' punches seemingly bouncing off ineffectually from his iron jaw. For two decades, from 1962 to 1982, he constantly challenged for the middleweight crown, but as early as 1980, Pennsylvania sought to suspend "permanently" his license "for his own physical wellbeing." This maneuver was executed by J. Russell Peltz, director of boxing at Philadelphia's Spectrum arena, whose supposed concern for Briscoe's well-being had to be viewed cautiously, since expressing sympathy was not normatively part of his occupation's makeup. But, he continued, "since 1969 I have seen all but one of Briscoe's fights" and "I have promoted or co-promoted more than 75 percent of them." The brawler was once the "most feared boxer in the middleweight division"—"his record of 63-20-6 with 51 knockouts is testimony to that fact"; but now he was a shadow of his former self. Father Time was undefeated thus far and Briscoe was no exception to this dictum. He was now 37, elderly for a puncher—at least before the resurrection of George Foreman in his 40s. As for Briscoe, said Peltz, "in recent years, his physical deterioration has become quite apparent."[33]

Those quick with a quip had long suggested that those who chose to make a living as a boxer needed their head examined—before, after, and even during their bouts. As with many acid-tongued

---

31. "Canvas Quotes," 17 April 1980, Box 2, PLA/Commission Meeting Files/83-789, 221-a-4, ISA-I.

32. *Las Vegas Sports Book*, 8-14 July 1983, Sub Group VIII, Series 1, Box 13, HKBA.

33. J. Russell Peltz to Howard McCall, Commissioner, Pennsylvania State Athletic Commission, 9 April 1980, Box 2, PLA/Commission Meeting Files/83-789, 221-a-4, ISA-I.

ripostes, this one, too, carried a kernel of truth. Such a lens might be a useful way to view Curley Lee, a heavyweight once knocked out by Cleveland Williams, who in turn pushed Ali to mount one of his finest performances—before succumbing in a technical knockout in the third round. As for Lee, he escaped conviction for murder of his four children, drowned in a bathtub, because of diminished mental capacity. He also had been charged with the murder of his brother-in-law, John Hunter, 17, beaten to death with a crowbar. The judge concluded that Lee's insanity was "due to a vicious beating in the ring."[34] His contemporary, Billy Collins, once fought 10 brutal rounds at Madison Square Garden and departed with a damaged right eye, a fractured cheekbone, a broken nose, which may have been induced since his opponent fought with the padding removed from his gloves and converted this contest into a one-sided bare-knuckled brawl. It would have been understandable if the battered and bruised Collins had left the ring so depressed that he would have committed mayhem on any nearby.[35]

Eddie Machen, who provided Joe Frazier with a spirited tussle, was also found to be "mentally ill," suffering from "acute schizophrenia," a "danger to himself and others" who had "gone beserk [sic] on at least two occasions."[36] He was found dead in San Francisco after a fall from a second-story apartment window—though it was unclear if it was an accident, murder or suicide.[37] Apparently, clinical depression was the diagnosis. Oscar Bonavena, an Argentine pounder in the tradition of Luis Firpo, battled Patterson, Ali and Frazier; however, it is unclear if his last battle—skirmishing with a brothel owner in Nevada who shot and killed him after being accused of sleeping with his spouse—was due to a mental lapse or physical urge (or both). Buster Mathis fought Ali and Frazier, too, but left the ring beset by a medical textbook compendium of health maladies, leading to his weight ballooning to a staggering 550 pounds—leading to predictable result: a fatal heart attack at the age of 51. Jerry Quarry—once thought to be a "White Hope" when he battled Ali, was ultimately unable to feed or dress himself, claimed by what one writer termed "dementia pugilistica"—formerly known as being "punch drunk" and induced by repeated and traumatic

---

34. *United Press International*, 18 February 1973, Odds and Ends of Boxing, Vol. 47, UND.

35. *Philadelphia Inquirer*, 10 July 1991, Sub Group VIII, Series 1, Box 13, HKBA.

36. Report, 9 December 1962, Odds and Ends on Boxing, Vol. 44, UND.

37. *New York Times*, 8 August 1972.

blows to the head—with mental and physical debilities. He expired at the age of 53. His younger brother Mike, once a contender himself, would expire for similar reasons shortly thereafter. When before a heavyweight battle, one of the contestants said he would bring along two attorneys in case he had to appear at an arraignment to respond to a criminal complaint, perhaps for battery or murder, it was hard to say if this were a joke or for real.[38]

Earlier, Johnny Saxton, once a welterweight champion who battled Carmen Basilio, Kid Gavilan, Virgil Akins and other contenders, eventually was confined to a mental institution after having been arrested in a burglary attempt. Truman Gibson's IBC took pity on him and gave him a pittance, since he had "been a very active fighter" during the Chicago Negro's heyday.[39] The writer Arthur Mann spoke movingly of Saxton and Johnny Braxton, "both recent welterweight champions, both in their early thirties and both…'half-dead' in mental institutions."[40] Later, referee Mills Lane recalled a bout between Oliver McCall and Lennox Lewis where the former, a mentally troubled puncher, apparently had a breakdown in the ring, as he stumbled around crying and dazed and refused to defend himself.[41]

It is possible that a co-factor in the breakdown of so many fighters were some of the archaic, unwritten rules foisted upon the sport. Chris Dundee, South Florida promoter and brother of the Ali trainer Angelo Dundee, long had insisted that fighters over whom he held sway should steer clear of romance and marriage, thereby depriving these men of human relationships that could have steadied them in choppy seas of emotion.[42]

Evidently, one boxer capsized in these troubled waters. Tim "Doc" Anderson felt he had been drugged after promoter Rick Parker had arranged a bout with former New York Jets defensive end, Mark Gastineau. He left the ring with severe liver and kidney damage (possibly the result of poisoning by a compromised corner man) this after—he claimed—Parker had offered him a compensatory $500,000 if he allowed the footballer to prevail. Apparently, Parker

---

38. Kram, *Smokin' Joe*, 341, 291.
39. Testimony of Truman Gibson, 27 April 1967, *Records of the District Court for the United States, Central District of California, Central Division (Los Angeles), Criminal Case Files, (Transcripts) 27951- 27973*, RG 21, Box 1712, NAR-Riv.
40. Arthur Mann, "Tears for the Half-Dead," no date, Box 16, Mann-LC.
41. Undated article on Mills Lane, Sub Group VIII, Series 1, Box 12, HKBA.
42. Report, 3 April 1938, Sub Group VIII, Series 1, Box 13, HKBA.

thought Gastineau, who frolicked with minor celebrities, was yet another "Great White Hope" in the making. This former opponent of Holmes and Foreman, instead, systematically pumped bullet after bullet into Parker's writhing body, reloading at one point, as he dispatched a man who was another kind of "White Hope": He termed himself the "White Don King," a nickname bound to receive negative attention.[43] Anderson was accompanied into the ranks of accused criminals by Bobby Halper, a boxer and ex-convict who was shot in a clothing store by gunmen. By 1980 he was acquitted of arson after being accused of destroying 13 stores in the Bronx. Known as "Crazy Bobby," he served 17 years of hard time for kidnapping.[44]

It was not just promoters who fell victim. Larry Rozallia, a U.S.-based referee who was in the ring for the Super Bantamweight title match in South Korea claimed he was coerced into giving the decision to Yom Dong Kyun over Rigoberto Riasco of Panama, after this official reportedly had been beaten by gangsters who threatened his life.[45] Mills Lane, the referee of choice for many high-stakes battles, was treated similarly in Venezuela. In 1972 he was there for a flyweight bout, and the Filipino challenger defeated the local favorite. "They chased me out of the country," he recalled later. "They had a riot...they spit on me, threw beer on me."[46]

Managers were not exempt either. Thomas Eboli, also known as Tommy Ryan, was already bathed in infamy in 1952 when he assaulted a promoter and referee after "his" fighter did not prevail in a match in New York. It was Al Weill who was attacked by "Ryan," and it was Ray Arcel, later clubbed senseless on an urban sidewalk, who sought to interrupt the fracas.[47] That contretemps did not halt Ryan's steady climb up the racketeering ladder, virtually to the top as a crime boss. But this ascent was brutally halted in the 1970s when he was discovered immersed in his own blood on Lefferts Avenue in Brooklyn: Five slugs were lodged in his body.[48]

---

43. *Orlando Sentinel,* 11 February 1996; Undated report, ca. 1985, Sub Group VIII, Series 1, Box 16, HKBA.
44. *New York Times,* 26 January 1980, and report, 27 May 1978, Sub Group IX,. Series 2, Box 12, HKBA.
45. Report, November 1976, Sub Group VIII, Series 1, Box 18, HKBA.
46. *Las Vegas Review Journal,* 8 March 1984, Sub Group VIII, Series 1, Box 12, HKBA.
47. Undated Report, Circa 1952, Sub Group VIII, Series 1, Box 24, HKBA.
48. *Newark Star Ledger,* 18 July 1972, Sub Group VIII, Series 1, Box 18, HKBA.

Battles for control of boxers' fortunes continued to roil the waters, though fortunately not eventuating in gangland killings in Gotham. Aaron Pryor, a welterweight champion whose windmill style of launching a left then ducking right, and vice versa, signed a deal with celluloid boxer Sylvester Stallone, though Dan Duva, increasingly challenging the Arum-King duopoly, claimed that he had a valid contract with the Ohioan.[49] Speaking of Stallone's *Rocky*, a blockbuster at the box office, the model for the flinty old fight manager played by Burgess Meredith was supposedly Howie Steindler. One of his clients was Danny "Little Red" Lopez, one of the premier Native American punchers. It was also in the 1970s that Steindler was found suffocated in the back seat of his gaudy car. He had been beaten severely about the head and body. He was slain the day after he contacted the Golden State's Athletic Commission about issues that apparently played a role in his demise. The rising star "Sugar" Ray Leonard, as charismatic as his namesake, provided the eulogy and was a pallbearer.[50]

Meeting a similar fate was yet another manager, Vic Weiss. He was found with two bullets in his head in the trunk of a Rolls Royce. He had been beaten badly and shot in the face with a shotgun besides, hogtied—bound at the ankles, waist and neck—and then daintily placed in a yellow blanket. It had all the earmarks of a gangland murder since a robber would have removed the valuable jewelry. He had just met with sports moguls Jerry Buss and Jack Kent Cooke—the latter had helped to finance the first Ali-Frazier contest.[51]

In yet another aspect of the bittersweet nature of a besieged sport, Bert Sugar, leading analyst and journalist, was roughed up in the office of his *Boxing Illustrated*, while the premises were vandalized and his telephone lines were slashed.[52] He had been fired from *The Ring* in 1983.[53]

As had been the case for some time, boxing was like a "Typhoid Mary," a super-spreader of microbes of corruption. Leading sports broadcaster Jack Buck, the voice of the St. Louis Cardinals baseball squad, sued Edward Yawitz, claiming that his name, reputation and earning power had declined because of his association with

---

49. Report, ca. 1982, Sub Group VIII, Series 1, Box 20, HKBA.

50. On Steindler, see *Tampa Tribune*, 11 March 1977; Report, ca, 1977; Report, July 1977, Sub Group VIII, Series 1, Box 20, HKBA.

51. *Los Angeles Herald Examiner*, 20 June 1979, Sub Group VIII, Series 1, Box 22, HKBA.

52. Undated report, Sub Group VIII, Series 1, Box 20, HKBA.

53. Report, 21 November 1984, Sub Group VIII, Series 1, Box 20, HKBA.

this finagler. The slippery Yawitz was also accused of bilking Dal Maxvill, the slick fielding, light-hitting shortstop and his teammates. Yawitz had been investigated for associations with organized crime, but what had allowed him entrance to these rarefied circles was the time he had managed Mound City pounder Virgil Akins.[54]

* * *

What was happening in part was also a product of the so-called "Reagan Revolution," formally inaugurated in early 1981 with the former mediocre actor moving into the White House. At the same moment, Christine Jarrett, executive secretary of Louisville Wrestling Enterprises (actually based in Nashville), warned the authorities in neighboring Indianapolis to refrain from the impulse to follow the deregulation impulse which was now part of the official mantra. She "heard it was being considered to dissolve the Indiana State Athletic Commission," and beseeched them not to do so, since "if there is no active state athletic commission," matters would devolve as in Tennessee where the "outlaw 'so-called' promoters" did "not only smoke pot and take pills, they sell it" to any so inclined, including most likely pugilists. These rebels with a cause also were known for "leaving unpaid newspaper and radio advertising" in their wake.[55] Mike De Fabis, president of Preston-Safeway Foods in Indianapolis, concurred. There were "key dangers in having no commission and no control over boxing," he stressed, since "our borders would be open to unscrupulous, dishonest promoters who would not be forced to agree upon participants' purses"; there would also be "potential for serious injury" with no doctor at ringside, another fruit of deregulation. "There is no national governing body for professional boxing," he emphasized, accurately dismissing the WBArum and the World Boxing Council; thus, it was "better to have no professional boxing in Indiana than to have it not controlled." Instead, he saluted "amateur boxing" which had a "strong internationally recognized governing body (the United States Amateur Boxing Federation)."[56]

Yet despite the best wishes and efforts of Midwesterners, their exertions were unlikely to have national impact. Charles Davey, a

---

54. *St. Louis Post-Dispatch*, 29 January 1975, Sub Group VIII, Series 1, Box 23, HKBA.

55. Christine Jarrett to Indiana House of Representatives, 19 February 1981, Box 2, PLA/Commission Meeting Files/83-789, 221-a-4, ISA-I.

56. Mike De Fabis to State Athletic Commission, ca. early 1981, Box 2, PLA/Commission Meeting Files/83-789, ISA-I.

boxing regulator in Michigan, acknowledged that "California has more professional boxing than any other state" and a "proportionate amount of the good fighters," to the point where "in our latest ratings California fighters are rated in the top 7 weight divisions."[57] Of course, to get a fairer analysis of the sport, one would have to survey next-door Nevada, along with New York and its next-door neighbor in New Jersey (and its next-door neighbor in Philadelphia, too), but the point remained that the Midwest may have been in the vanguard in football, even basketball—but not boxing.

Indiana authorities took note of the flailing situation unfolding due west in Colorado, where the authorities' push toward deregulation preceded Reagan's seizing the White House. "Official meetings are rare," it was said of the sport's regulators, and "record keeping is unorthodox," forestalling learning from the past. Some of the commission's records were kept at the home of Ralph Blossom, the part-time executive secretary, which defied best archival practice. "Arbitrary" was the descriptor attached to their meetings, all of which was "counter to the sunshine law," meant to expose the decisions of shrouded meetings to public scrutiny. This administrative anarchy was complemented by "archaic procedures." The Denver commission also had a leader who had served for more than four decades, creating fertile soil for corruption and self-dealing. Eddie Bohn, an imposing and gruff former heavyweight boxer, had also been a state senator. "We're scared to death of Eddie Bohn," said one who knew him and wisely kept his identity hidden, as if it was feared that the ethos of the sport—"knock people senseless"[58]—would be applied to leakers. As had been the case since earlier in the century when Negro boxers flocked west to Nevada, then nimbly executed a U-turn eastward to New York, promoters, too, had manipulated federalism to their benefit, engaged in a kind of pugilistic arbitrage, taking advantage of weaker jurisdictions like predator piranhas gobbling guppies.

* * *

After Holmes beat Ali mercilessly, the "Easton Assassin" strode in the large footprints of the man he vanquished in a pedigree that stretched back to Jack Johnson and continuing through Joe Louis.

---

57. Charles Davey, Troy, Michigan, to James E. Baiz, 2 August 1978, Box 1, PLC/Boxing Commission/SAC/83-786, a 2554, ISA-I.

58. *Denver Post*, 22 February 1976, Box 1, PLC/Boxing Commission/SAC/83-786, a2554, ISA-I.

Holmes felt he did not receive the respect of his predecessors, a fair point, but what was at play, in part, was the diminishing of a sport based on "knocking people senseless"; even in the Age of Reagan, this was a difficult sport to maintain, akin to justifying dueling at 20 paces. And then there was the revival of the "Great White Hope" trope, embodied in the person of "Gentleman" Gerry Cooney, a challenger to Holmes, who himself embodied the aphorism that uneasy rests the head that wears the crown. For while Ali could have manipulated racial, and religious, sentiments to create a bonanza at the box office, Holmes was uneasy with being cast as a kind of "race warrior." Yet even before Cooney had burst onto the scene, Angelo Dundee was being briefed by a Louisiana entrepreneur, Norman Lockwood, who inferentially revealed the lengths (or depths) to which those searching for a "Great White Hope" would descend: "I have a white heavy just turning pro…looks pretty good," he announced breathlessly in 1977: "he is Lebanese…may have found one."[59] Dundee had an unusual job: broker to find the next "Great White Hope." Vito Tallarita was pushing into the spotlight a number of punchers. From his abode in fashionable Enfield, Connecticut, he mentioned some to "Dear Ang": "all three are white and are all available," he said enthusiastically.[60] Felix "Tuto" Zabala told "Dear Angelo" he was willing to "offer" to him a boxer who was "white."[61]

Apparently Dundee was not involved when "Tropic" Kenny Klingman appeared as a newly minted "Great White Hope," with the distinctive feature of a "Star of David" on his trunks.[62] As political upheavals engulfed São Paulo and Bueno Aires, Abe Katznelson arrived in the U.S. with five boxers from South America in tow and, instead, turned them over to Gil Clancy, a competitor of Dundee: this was also an indicator that boxing was seen by many as a quick way to exit political and economic instability, enhancing the value of the increasingly mythical "Great White Hope."[63]

However, Holmes had reason to adopt this pose of combating racism forcefully. His former trainer, Richie Giachetti, taped his

---

59. Norman Lockwood to Angelo Dundee, 15 June 1977, Sub Group VIII, Series 1, Box 13, HKBA.

60. Vito Tallarita to "Dear Ang," no date, and *Miami Daily News*, 9 February 1984, Sub Group VIII, Series 1, Box 21, HKBA.

61. "Tuto" to "Dear Angelo," 20 February 1978, Sub Group VIII, Series 1, Box 23, HKBA.

62. Report, 7 May 1978, Sub Group IX, Series 1, Box 15, HKBA.

63. Report, February 1970, Sub Group VIII, Series 1, Box 12, HKBA.

conversations with the boxer, then fed same to the FBI.[64] When these tapes were played for the fighter at a grand jury session in 1981, he was dismissive: "'I paid the man $1.5 million,' he said as he scoffed, "which is very good for someone just pouring water, putting in my mouthpiece and saying 'Time.'"[65] Giachetti could have responded that this was only the objective functioning of the political economy of racism: nothing personal. But instead, what he did say was that boxers like Holmes were participants in bouts with preordained outcomes, including his battle with Ken Norton—who once broke Ali's jaw. The same held true for Norton and Jimmy Young (a former Ali sparring partner) and the battle of the Frenchmen: Scott Ledoux vs. Johnny Boudreaux. Don King, his fellow Ohioan, said the trainer, bribed higher-ups in the World Boxing Council in exchange for profitable high rankings for boxers he promoted. Even Ali was implicated, he said, since he personally met with "Mafia people" about the Ali-Holmes bout for reasons that remained unclear but certainly were devilish.[66] But Holmes was fixated on King, not "race" and his being bilked. Though Holmes claimed the former numbers runner made $25 million in one year, another source in 1983 said the figure was more like $25 million over 9 years;[67] yet Holmes would have claimed that either figure was accumulated at his expense.

Still, Holmes, contrary to his self-presentation, was not so unlikely a combatant in the drama co-starring Cooney. The champ recalled a bout with Ibar Arrington, in which the latter fighter, though strong as a bull elephant, absorbed what Holmes termed a "fearful beating." And he "took the beating because of his trainer. Angelo Dundee was working his corner and shouting to his fighter: 'That nigger ain't shit—kick that nigger's ass. He did the same thing to me," said a disgusted Holmes, "when he worked Rodney Bobick's corner in Manila." Though this only inspired Holmes further[68] and, arguably, the racial hype surrounding the Cooney bout inspired him likewise.

But like too many, writer Jack Fiske seemed almost giddy about the prospect of a "race war" in the ring: "and now the White Hope hunt begins anew," he crowed, seemingly salivating over the "greater financial significance of a white vs. black matchup" and

---

64. *New York Post*, 22 May 1981, Box 156, Newfield-UT.
65. *New York Times*, 22 May 1981, Box 156, Newfield-UT.
66. FBI document, 5 June 1981, Box 156, Newfield-UT.
67. Document, 6 January 1983, Box 156, Newfield-UT.
68. Larry Holmes, "Boxing Politics," Box 156, Newfield-UT.

"that's where Cooney comes in."[69] Indeed. Overly stimulated flacks in Las Vegas billed Cooney falsely as the "sensational challenger from South Africa," which was only accurate in the sense that the White Hope trope did implicate apartheid.[70]

Holmes tried to deflect the role of lightning rod—which found him anyway. Later it was revealed by an inquiring journalist that throughout the prelude to this ordeal, Holmes was subjected to venomous racist slurs; bullets were fired at his home, too, and his mailbox was blown up. In an overly optimistic maneuver a special telephone hookup had been established in Cooney's dressing room by the U.S. Secret Service, so that President Reagan could talk to the newly crowned king of masculinity—a conversation that was thwarted by the fierce beating taken by "Gentleman" Gerry.[71] Understandably grating on Holmes's already frayed nerves was the fact that he had to split the lucrative purse 50-50 with what one observant journalist called "an unproven fighter with skimpy credentials." "Does it really matter that [a] white man is not champ," it was asked querulously. The answer seemed to be "yes." What else could explain why Cooney—and not the hard-hitting Ernie Shavers or the wily Jimmy Young –"rated $10 million?" Seemingly slumping onto his keyboard, the journalist answered, "when he is white evidently," noting that "for Holmes this became the source of great bitterness."[72]

Holmes was also in business with some questionable characters who were a source of bitterness for countless others. There was Joseph Hand, for example, a successful promoter in league with organized crime in Philadelphia. Before that he was a police detective—"in the intelligence unit," he said—where he came to know Joe Frazier. In these overlapping circles he came to know "Blinky" Palermo and Frankie "Flowers" d'Alfonso, who met an unfortunate end in a gangland slaying. Hand partnered with Frank Gelb, an Atlantic City impresario for the Ali-Holmes contest in 1980, and Robert Gabriel, who once worked in the office of the district attorney in Philadelphia. (Note: Ties to intelligence and law enforcement gave Hand

---

69. Column by Jack Fiske, undated, Sub Group VIII, Series 3, Box 39, HKBA.

70. "Suggested Copy for Invitation" from Phil Arce, President; Dennis Gomes, Vice President; and Bill Robinson, Vice President, 1982, Box 29, Frontier Hotel and Casino Collection, UNV-LV.

71. *New York Times*, 11 March 1985, Box 156, Newfield-UT.

72. *Las Vegas Review Tribune*, 12 June 1982, Sub Group VIII, Series 1, Box 24, HKBA.

and Gabriel access to all manner of leverage and information.) Hand alone promoted the Holmes-Cooney closed-circuit enterprise in Pennsylvania and West Virginia.[73]

Also involved in the lush deal that placed Holmes and Cooney into the ring was Anthony "Butch" Cristelli, who was a close comrade of the blinker, the now elderly Palmero, who he denied was a mobster in the face of massive evidence to the contrary. He did consult with Palermo on closed-circuit telecasts for this mega-fight and was aided by his uncle, who happened to be close to "Frankie Flowers." He got involved in boxing as a manager and therein became friendly with Thomas del Giorno, an influential soldier in the gang controlled by "Nicky" Scarfo, yet another Philadelphian. He was also close to Rocco Auletto, who fought professionally as "Roxy Allen" and was knocked out by Jersey Joe Walcott in 1935. Bookmaking and loansharking were part of their portfolio. Cristelli, too, was a former Philadelphia police officer who managed to escape to the monthly payments provided by the social welfare program targeting those with a disability.[74]

The outcome of many a fight, including the Holmes-Cooney contest, could have been thwarted by the third man in the ring, referee Mills Lane. He grew up on a former rice plantation, a whopping 13,000 square miles alongside the Combahee River in South Carolina, where enslaved Africans had toiled desperately. His grandfather owned the largest bank in Georgia, and his father employed a large staff of Negro families. In the daytime, the children of the latter attended a substandard school on the plantation, while Lane and his siblings took a bus ride for 20 minutes to a rural and also segregated school. A gun-carrying Republican, he eventually migrated to Nevada, where he became a referee. Although Lane agreed with the consensus that Ernie Shavers—who fought Ali to a standstill—was probably the hardest puncher he ever saw, after watching Holmes whip Cooney into submission, he may have wanted to amend his opinion.[75]

The misrepresentation of Cooney as being a citizen of the land of apartheid was reflective of the growing salience of South Africa in the political discourse of the U.S., as the struggle for democracy

---

73. "Organized Crime in Boxing: Final Boxing Report of the State of New Jersey Commission of Investigation," 1985, 974.90 162, NJSL-T.

74. Ibid.

75. *New York Times*, 20 July 1987, undated article on Mills Lane, Sub Group VIII, Series 1, Box 12, HKBA.

increased in intensity. Though Arum, as noted, was not above dealings with apartheid, a new promoter on the scene—Butch Lewis—distinguished himself in opposition to this inhumanity. The husky, chocolate-colored entrepreneur attached himself to the Spinks brothers—Leon and Michael—and ascended as they rose, as Don King had done with Ali. Michael Spinks, like his brother with roots in St. Louis, backed Lewis's anti-apartheid activism, proclaiming that he was prepared to jeopardize his flourishing career to do so.[76] Lewis was sufficiently audacious to challenge the Arum-dominated WBA: Beginning in 1982, he had pressured the group to break ties with apartheid, though he backed the ethically challenged Robert Lee as president in order to do so.[77] Congressman John Conyers of Detroit, a founder of the Congressional Black Caucus, a powerbroker in Washington, hailed him.[78] Presidential aspirant Senator Joseph Biden of Delaware saluted Spinks by way of bringing attention to the promoter.[79] Yet another perennial presidential aspirant, Senator Edward Kennedy of Massachusetts, praised Lewis directly.[80] Even the staid *New York Times* implied there was something awry about the WBA and the new kid on the block, the International Boxing Federation, collaborating with Pretoria.[81]

Lewis's anti-apartheid stance was all the more remarkable since his cohorts continued to be mired in Pretoria's muck. Angelo Dundee, Ali's trainer, was foremost among them, collaborating on bouts featuring apartheid's top heavyweights, organizing clinics in South Africa to uncover future battlers[82] and—said one observer from Natal—"endeavoring to use our top referee Stan Christodoulou to work [an] Ali bout."[83] This observer, Doug "Duggie" Miller, was no ingénu: "my lad is doing compulsory Army training and

---

76. Statement of Butch Lewis, 1 October 1986, Sub Group VIII, Series 1, Box 13, HKBA.

77. Butch Lewis to Gilberto Mendoza, 18 August 1986, Sub Group VIII, Series I, Box 13, HKBA.

78. Congressman Conyers to Butch Lewis, 30 September 1986, Sub Group VIII, Series I, Box 13, HKBA.

79. Senator Biden to Michael Spinks c/o Lewis, 30 September 1986, Sub Group VIII, Series I, Box 13, HKBA.

80. Senator Edward Kennedy to Butch Lewis, 10 October 1986, Sub Group VIII, Series I, Box 13, HKBA.

81. *New York Times*, 2 October 1986.

82. Report, 25 October 1981, Sub Group VIII, Series 1, Box 20, HKBA.

83. Doug "Duggie" Miller to Angelo Dundee, 8 July 1977, Sub Group VIII, Series 1, Box 15, HKBA.

was out on a special training course in the bush for 10 days," he told his U.S confidant at a time when Pretoria was embroiled in "bush wars" in Mozambique, Angola, Namibia and elsewhere.[84] Miller also encountered former Ali opponent Chuck Wepner in South Africa, and even though his contest was a stinker, the presence of "The Bayonne Bleeder" was a de facto vote in favor of apartheid's legitimacy.[85] At a time when Butch Lewis was gathering kudos from powerful politicos, Hank Kaplan, a comrade of the Dundees, was fielding compliments from Eric Moolman of the South Africa Veterans Boxing Association and fishing for a Beau Jack autograph.[86]

The "Great White Hope" moniker eventually settled on apartheid's finest, Gerhardus "Gerrie" Coetzee, who was crowned as a WBArum champion in the early 1980s. During his undistinguished career, he fought such boxers as Greg Page, James "Quick" Tillis, Michael Dokes, Renaldo Snipes, Mike Weaver, Leon Spinks, et al. Typical was his bout with John Tate, a Negro who fought him in the heart of darkness that was Pretoria in 1979. Looking back from the vantage point of 1984, one observer told Kaplan: "I gave Tate some articles I had from South Africa," said Philip Paul, "on his bout with Coetzee. He was rather pleased with them. I doubt if he could read them. Five years ago he couldn't read or write but could sign his name."[87] As for Coetzee and those around him, they embodied a kind of moral illiteracy. Soon Coetzee was domiciled in New Jersey and represented by Arum. "I want to fight Larry Holmes," he brayed. But given his national origin, the WBC did not rank him, meaning a title bout with the "Easton Assassin" was unlikely at best, unless he could win the WBArum title and then seek a contest to unify the two titles.[88]

It seems that Dundee and those of that ilk were essential cogs in a trans-oceanic Pan-European community that had retreated somewhat in the U.S. but remained potent in South Africa—and also Australia, which reflected the dueling opinions about those not

---

84. Doug Miller to Angelo Dundee, 1 June 1978, Sub Group VIII, Series I, Box 15, HKBA.

85. Doug Miller to Angelo Dundee, 12 February 1977, Sub Group VIII, Series 1, Box 15, HKBA.

86. Eric Moolman to "Dear Hank," 13 March 1985, Sub Group VIII, Series 1, Box 15, HKBA.

87. Philip Paul to Hank Kaplan, 15 February 1984, Sub Group VIII, Series 1, Box 16, HKBA.

88. Report, ca. 1980s, Sub Group VIII, Series 1, Box 22, HKBA.

viewed as "white" when a journalist referred to the Indigenous population of this continental island as "two legged animals"—and the best boxers.[89] This dualism at once reflected the rancid racism that governed the lives of too many—yet propelled them simultaneously into fistic glory.

---

89. Undated report on Australia, Sub Group VIII, Series 1, Box 15, HKBA.

Chapter 11

Corruption, Reform—and Beyond

The tidal wave of revenue generated by new technologies to deliver boxing contests to ever larger audiences combined with a preexisting trend of organized crime influence to create more instability overall.

With the advent of casinos in Atlantic City, New Jersey, these two trends intersected and, like a cold front meeting a warm front over the plains of Nebraska, a tornado of tumult ensued. By 1985, the authorities in the Garden State had zeroed in on Andrew Licari of Livingston, a "Luchese Crime Family associate" in their opinion. He had a "financial interest" in Bobby Czyz, the light heavyweight contender with potential to generate a payoff as yet another "Great White Hope." Czyz was also tied to Lou Duva, a member of a family that was profiting as much as any from the increased revenue streams flooding into boxing. Then there was Carlo de Iuliis, also known as Carlo Dee, who was a comrade of Alfred Certisimo, who answered to the name Al Certo; the latter was ostensibly a tailor in Secaucus, but was better known as a "Genovese crime family associate" and agent for Mustafa Hamsho, a hard hitting contender of Arab origins, who once battled "Marvelous" Marvin Hagler. Visitors to Certo's shop were not only well-groomed mobsters but Robert Lee, a boxing commissioner with the charge of regulating the sport. Certo was also a promoter who was accused of specializing in arranging fights for known losers with long criminal records and therefore susceptible to acquiescing to preordained results.

Atlantic City was known as a "Mob Mecca," and the rogues' gallery of cutthroats that flocked there did little to erode this tarnished reputation. There was Barry Shapiro, who also had a scrap metal business and was close to Nicodemo "Nicky" Scarfo with ramified ties in the mob haven that was South Philadelphia. By 1985 he had about a dozen fighters under contract and about 20 more in his orbit. "I spent about four to six months with Larry [Holmes] traveling,"

Shapiro confided (they were in business together) and had "dealings with Don King," too: "he was like teaching me," he said beamingly. He owned about 5% of the purses of the puncher once known as Dwight Braxton: "he trains in my gym," he said. Shapiro had a number of business partners, including the racketeer Martin Taccetta: "Marty was interested in purchasing a property in Haiti...a casino type of property."

In an unsurprising conclusion so mundane that it seemed like self-parody, the New Jersey investigators found that "one product of organized crime's presence in boxing could be an increase in 'fixed' fights," i.e., the "outcome of a fight can also be all but guaranteed by merely recruiting inexperienced or otherwise inferior fighters to compete." Implicated here was Steve Traitz, a business agent of Roofers' Local 30, who also operated the Montgomery County Boys Club, which was often visited by the now elderly "Blinky" Palermo (convicted in 1961 during the trial that involved Truman Gibson). He once testified as a character witness on the blinker's behalf. In turn Traitz also had two sons who boxed.

Boxing in South Jersey and the fertile vineyard of punchers that was Philadelphia were infested thoroughly by racketeering parasites. Used car dealer Joseph Elentrio was part of this cabal and was exceedingly close to Thomas del Giorno, a close comrade of "Nicky" Scarfo: The latter was at the top of the pyramid of regional gangsters. Then there was Joseph Verne, a promoter and said to be a wholesale furniture distributor. He had business ties to one of Joe Frazier's sons, along with Joey Giardello, Jr., namesake of the former top boxer. Verne had loaned money to the prizefighter known as Dwight Braxton and all the while he, too, had comfortable connections with Scarfo and Edward "Ricky" Casale, a roofer ostensibly, and also a Scarfo confidant, along with Palmero and Certo. Also part of this network was John Barr, known as the "Fix Man," who was in the lucrative sideline of supplying an endless array of losers to rings regionally, whose job was to improve the record of others by agreeing to wind up on the canvas, down for the count. Close by was Robert Botto of Swedesboro, who carried the titles of supermarket owner, manager, sausage maker and promoter (though in the latter instance you definitely would not want to know how the product was made).

Press reports indicated that Robert Lee, a statewide regulator of the sport, was all too close to these unpalatable elements. With a *savoir faire* that would have dazzled the most talented flack, racketeers then moved that retired baseball star Larry Doby—a Negro, besides—replace Lee. By then the slugger had a liaison post with the then New Jersey Nets professional basketball franchise, yet another indicator of how corruption in boxing was a "super-spreader" to other sports. Doby was also friendly with fellow North Jerseyan, Chuck "The Bayonne Bleeder" Wepner, who in turn was implicated in this region's sink of venality. Doby, who starred with the unfortunately named Cleveland Indians baseball team, moved to Montclair, New Jersey, in the 1950s, and then became friendly with local sports bettor Frank Scaraggio, from whom he purchased a Cadillac, the vehicle of choice for the up-and-coming then. His other purchases were targeted similarly, buying clothes from Certo and buddying with others of that ilk. Their political link—state legislator, Buddy Fortunato—refused to testify when an investigation was made of these curious linkages.[1]

There was an interlocking directorate that enveloped these characters subject to investigation in New Jersey and related to an earlier generation. For example, the aforementioned Robert Gabriel acted as an attorney for "Blinky" Palermo, while speaking on his behalf was the union boss Traitz. Palermo was said to have an interest in Jimmy Young, a competent heavyweight, who was also related to these dubious figures. These relations came in handy when Palermo was seeking to set up a bout between Ali and Young.[2]

Statewide authorities well knew that the explosive growth of casinos in Atlantic City not only lubricated the path for more boxing but its accoutrement: racketeering. Bringing in "Jersey" Joe Walcott as a regulator was akin to placing a wolf in charge of the henhouse, given his distasteful managerial connections during his starry boxing career. Part of the problem was the curious relation between Philadelphia law enforcement and rackets and boxing. Joseph Guinan, who died in 1986 at the age of 87, was emblematic of this trend. He had been a police officer and a boxer, wailing away in 60 fights as a lightweight. Then he joined the police department in 1927 and developed a specialty in prostitution and racketeering. His squad was not shy about wielding their fists, nightsticks and guns. Brute force was their calling card, and apprising suspects of rights was seen as effete. This culture became endemic and then bled effortlessly into maltreatment of Negroes: The moral corruption proved conducive to the

---

1. "Organized Crime in Boxing: Final Boxing Report of the State of New Jersey Commission of Investigation" 1985 974.90 162, NJSL-T.

2. Report of Investigative Activity," 9 February 1978, RG 7, #7.88, Records of the General Assembly, Pennsylvania Crime Commission, Investigation Case Files and Exhibits, 2-1050, Carton 49, 120-1-23, Assembly-Pa.

flourishing of other kinds, ironically serving to enhance the mobsters who were supposedly the initial target.[3]

Like others who migrated from law enforcement to boxing, Robert Lee moved from a post as a cop in Scotch Plains, New Jersey, to regulator of boxing, where he was said to influence Walcott profoundly. During their reign, record keeping was abysmal, which thwarted accountability. Lee was said to realize also that "some boxing organization rankings might be rigged," a reality that should have been gleaned from the Don King-ABC debacle of 1977.[4] This was not the only complication encountered by those seeking an accurate evaluation of the sport. Called to testify, the veteran corner man Ray Arcel—infamously clubbed to the brink of death decades earlier in a reputed mob hit—managed to observe that he had started in the sport in 1917 and since then had helped to develop 19 champions. But after that, he was less communicative, perhaps wary of retribution: Again, "I don't hear very well," he said at one point, though he did state the obvious—"boxing is controlled by the networks." That Assemblyman Fortunato chaired the hearing, when he refused to testify as a witness before other legislators, also raised eyebrows.[5] It was also not reassuring when Randy Neumann, a former boxer who became a popular referee, was compelled to deny mob ties.[6]

However, traditional racketeering faced multiple challenges beyond statewide investigations in New Jersey and elsewhere. In fact, these investigations can be viewed retrospectively as a reflection of the impending erosion of the hegemony of the "traditionalists," which accelerated with stiffer competition emerging from Eastern Europe with the fall of the Berlin Wall in 1989.[7] As suggested, the very ascension of Don King was an indication that, unleashed by the anti-Jim Crow movement, Negro racketeers were able to muscle in on traditional bastions. It was in 1988 when the authorities in

---

3. *Philadelphia Inquirer*, 31 January 1986, Sub Group VIII, Series 1, Box 10, HKBA.

4. "Interim Report and Recommendations of the State of New Jersey Commission of Investigation on the Inadequate Regulation of Boxing," 1984, 974.90 I 52, NJSL-T.

5. "Public Hearing Before Assembly Independent Authority and Commissions Committee on the Promotion and Conduct of Boxing Matches in New Jersey," 19 January 1983, NJSL-T.

6. "Public Meeting Before Assembly Independent and Regional Authorities Commission on Testimony on Status of and Possible Reforms to Boxing," 16 June 1986, NJSL-T.

7. Robert Friedman, *Red Mafiya: How the Russian Mob Has Invaded America*, Boston: Little, Brown, 2000.

Pennsylvania noticed that "blacks, Hispanics and Asians who were involved in illegal activities were never approached by the LCN [La Cosa Nostra traditionalists] for 'Street Tax.' In fact, [it was said] the mob feared...they would shoot back if approached. The blacks were bad debtors [sic] and the 'shake' would not be worth the aggravation." By way of contrast, "news media added to the Scarfo mob's alleged strength by printing stories about how strong it was. As a result, many independent white criminal groups paid the street tax when pressured," while those who were not "white" often were less susceptible to the reach and content of the mainstream "news media."[8]

But history showed, for example, when the sport fled to Nevada then eastward afterward, that unscrupulous entrepreneurs took full advantage of federalism and, per usual, engaged in manipulative arbitrage, deserting one state for another. Thus, almost as a rebuke to the extensive investigations of the sport in New Jersey, shortly thereafter Roy Jones knocked out "Derwin Richards" in the first round in Pensacola—but, it turned out, he actually floored Tony Waddles, a 19-year-old staffer for an auto dealer.[9]

At any rate, investigations of wrongdoing in boxing had become like a theatrical performance with mobsters in expensive suits hauled before legislative investigators eager to preen before the cameras and gain an advantage in the unending quest for higher office. Hence, just after Jones's exercise in padding his already impressive record, Senator Fred Thompson, a Tennessee Republican, who had a profitable sideline as an actor and had garnered national attention during the "Watergate" scandal that ousted Richard M. Nixon from the presidency, convened the latest performance in congressional theatre. Stepping into the spotlight was Salvatore "Sammy the Bull" Gravano, who had turned against his erstwhile fellow mobsters. The "Gambino Family," of which he had been an essential part, had left boxing in the early 1960s—just as Carbo, Palermo and Gibson were walking the plank. But Gravano still dabbled: "I often attended fights," he said, "including the Mike Holmes-Larry Holmes fight in 1988," where he was accompanied by the so-called "Dapper Don," John Gotti. "I tried to set up a fight between [Renaldo] Snipes and

---

8. Report of Investigative Activity, 13 January 1988, Records of the General Assembly, Pennsylvania Crime Commission, Investigation Case Files and Exhibits, RG7, #7.88, 2-1050, Carton 49, 120-1-23, Assembly-Pa.

9. Kelley C. Howard, "Regulating the Sport of Boxing—Congress Throws the First Punch with the Professional Boxing Safety Act," *Seton Hall Journal of Sports Law*, 7 (No. 1, 1997): 103-127, 103, Box 72, FT-UTnK.

Francesco Damiani," who had roots in the old country: "our family had close ties with the Italian family." Then there was the mob tailor, Al Certo and Gambino family associate, who managed Buddy McGirt, a rising contender. Boxing was just a part of the conglomerate which also involved control of unions and related industries such as construction, shipping, garment, garbage disposal; however, for the longest period, these latter revenue streams came to surpass that of boxing, while the latter had a further impediment: more scrutiny. But at a certain juncture they returned to the sport with a vengeance, especially after pay-per-view and closed-circuit broadcasts delivered profits too bountiful to ignore. And this brought them closer to casino magnates like future president Donald J. Trump and Las Vegas's main man, Steve Wynn. "Snipes was close to me," too, he confided. "I'm sure we would have no problem in convincing Snipes to lose" to Damiani. Paul Castellano, another racketeering comrade, had the gumption to turn down a meeting with Don King.[10]

Given that "Big Paulie" was gunned down in midtown Manhattan in 1985,[11] he should have been seeking any meeting (and colleague) he could secure. Certainly by then, King was a force to be reckoned with, able to dodge criminal investigations as he powdered the air with a fusillade of sonorously orotund verbiage: "Only in America" was his ill-conceived motto. The FBI thought it had reason to believe that the ebony-hued man with the striking bouffant had a corrupt deal with Jim Spence of ABC-TV sports: King, it was said, "kicks back money to Spence for the right to show King's fights." As was typical, some extraordinarily close-mouthed reporters were part of the bargain since "both he and King have paid off journalists for favorable articles in the New York newspapers."[12] Castellano might have benefited from King's favored relationship with certain scribes. Mark Kram lost his job at *Sports Illustrated* after being accused of too fawning coverage of the promoter, while *The Ring*, as noted, cooked the books to facilitate King's varied promotions, hailing boxers who should have been critiqued.[13]

---

10. Testimony of Salvatore "Sammy the Bull" Gravano, "Corruption in Professional Boxing-Part II. Hearings Before the Permanent Subcommittee on Investigations of the Committee on Governmental Affairs. U.S. Senate 103rd Congress, 1st Session. 10 March and 1 April 1993," Box 72, FT-UTnK. On Certo and McGirt, see New York *Newsday*, 2 April 1993, Box 156, Newfield-UT.

11. *New York Times*, 17 December 1985.

12. FBI Report, 5 June 1981, Box 156, Newfield-UT.

13. Smith, *No Way*, 227, 226.

Perhaps "Big Paulie" Castellano did not keep up with the news—not a good move for an entrepreneur with vast interests, like himself. For in a continuation of a historic pattern, Don King had spread his capacious wings beyond numbers, then boxing, to music. As "Big Paulie" was about to journey to the great beyond, the man with the puffy hairdo was involved in promoting superstar singer and dancer Michael Jackson in Philadelphia in conjunction with another boxing crony, Joseph Hand, one of his closest collaborators, and "Frankie Flowers" d'Alfonso, soon to be murdered.[14] (Since Hand had a penchant for all cash transactions, it was neither simple nor easy to trace his various business dealings.)[15]

A boxer who should have been critiqued for different reasons was the former amateur John Franzese, a mobster who boasted bonds to Rocky Graziano, boxer turned media personality, and the once diminutive, then corpulent crooner Frank Sinatra. Franzese went on to become an elder statesman in the feared Colombo crime family, and from that hallowed perch obtained an exceedingly lucrative stake in the enormously profitable 1972 pornographic film *Deep Throat*—an investment in this nastiness was normative for racketeers. Likewise, he invested astutely in another business where his ilk was often found: music or, in his case, Buddha Record Company. The wider point was that there was a kind of cross-infection that polluted boxing and other entertainments. Despite his thick catalogue of villainy, Franzese passed away quietly at the overly ripe age of 103 in 2020.[16]

The testimony of "Sammy the Bull," a confessed mass murderer, reminded those who had not been paying attention that despite the 1961 Los Angeles trial that ensnared Truman Gibson, what had occurred was that one faction of corrupters simply had replaced another. This was confirmed by a counsel to Senator Thompson's subcommittee. W. Leighton Lord III charged that "organized crime currently exerts the type of influence over the sport of boxing that it did in the 1940s and 1950s." He pointed to the relationship between world champion Iran Barkley and Lenny Minuto of the "Luchese Crime Family" and the relations between Bobby Czyz and not just the Duvas but also Andrew Licari, a "Luchese soldier." The

---

14. Report of Investigative Activity, RG7, #7.88, Records of the General Assembly, Pennsylvania Crime Commission, Investigation Case Files and Exhibits, 2-1050, Carton 49, 120-1-23, Assembly-Pa.

15. "Organized Crime in Boxing: Final Boxing Report of the State of New Jersey Commission of Investigation" 1985 974.90 162, NJSL-T.

16. *New York Times*, 25 February 2020.

attempted refutations provided by Al Certo, who cut his testimony to fit the mob fashion in denying all and denouncing "The Bull,"[17] convinced only the naïve and deluded.

Despite Certo's admonitions to the contrary, "The Bull" had a point: The flooding of more revenue into prizefighting did attract the morally questionable. When the apparent successor to Ali—Mike Tyson—fought Frank Bruno in early 1989 in Las Vegas, executives at the Stardust Resort and Casino seemed to be engaged in a collective heart palpitation as they swooned over "average bets of $150 and above for 4 hours of play per day" goosed by "credit lines of $10,000 and above," virtually designed to attract those with a dearth of impulse control and a high tolerance for massive losses.[18] The nexus of gambling, Las Vegas, corruption—and boxing—was combustible and seemingly engineered to produce untoward results. Thus, when Tyson was on the verge of an upset defeat, both Don King and Jose Sulaiman of the WBC sought to reverse the decision based on a technicality: The Brooklyn flame-thrower had become too valuable a commodity with large sums wagered in his favor.[19] The rampant dishonesty of the sport could also serve to feed rumors about the legitimacy of contests. Thus, when Ken Norton—he of the devastating overhand right punch—battled the slick Jimmy Young, rumors flew that the fight was "fixed," which, if so, would have led to a bounty for those in the know.[20] A similar miasma of rumor attached to the fabled Holmes-Cooney contest, where, it was said, even the loser told his pals to bet on the winner. Similar preordained outcomes were said to inhere in the bouts of former champion Vito Antuofermo, who once battled "Marvelous" Marvin Hagler.[21] Even the heralded Joe Louis, on a steep slope of decline, was said to use his strategic post as Las Vegas "greeter" in hotel-casinos to influence wagering by hyping underdogs,[22] as he whispered what was thought to be wise intelligence into the ears of the unsuspecting.

---

17. "Organized Crime in Boxing: Final Boxing Report of the State of New Jersey Commission of Investigation" 1985 974.90 162, Hearings on Corruption in Boxing, Testimony of W. Leighton Lord III and Al Certo, NJSL-T.

18. Memorandum, 8 January 1989, Box 201, Stardust Resort and Casino Records, UNV-LV.

19. Statement of Randy Gordon, New York State Athletic Commissioner, 11 August 1992, Box 54, Newfield-UT.

20. Memorandum, 29 May 1981, Box 54, Newfield-UT.

21. *New York Newsday*, 13 August 1992, Box 54, Newfield-UT.

22. Smith, *No Way*, 121.

But it was not just the Sin Capital that was Nevada which descended into the bog of corruption. Due northeast in Minnesota, a self-described "veteran fight manager" denounced the "conflicts of interest" he noticed. Biff Holstein, a "cut man, sold boxing equipment to fighters, managers and promoters," irrespective of his relationships to fighters with whom he was contracted.[23] It was also in Minnesota that "Simmie Black fought under Kenny Louis' name," a corrupt practice that was becoming commonplace.[24] In that state, thought to be a lodestar of good governance, a key regulator had a son who boxed, while a leading referee also controlled a boxing gym, suggesting he could favor a puncher who emerged from his enterprise.[25]

In a microcosmic episode of a troubled sport, Meldrick Taylor defeated "Roberto Medina" on national television in a punishingly bruising bout—except Medina was actually the escaped convict John Garcia, who was arrested and handcuffed after being pummeled: His colorful tattoos were a dead giveaway.[26] Near the same time, exiting prison restrictions, after serving over five years, was Harold Rossfields Smith, whose crime was embezzlement of $21.3 million from Wells Fargo, which, he said, was his more than complicit partner. This former promoter associated with Ali, then sought to become a boxing manager, where his slipperiness would have fit nicely.[27]

For one of the bastions of pugilistic excellence was Detroit, from which emerged Joe Louis earlier and Thomas "Hit Man" Hearns later. During this latter era, the Kronk gym, hotspot for the sport, patrolled by Emmanuel Steward, also contained Ricky Womack, an armed robber with an undefeated record by the early 21st century (he had pistol whipped a clerk and stolen some tapes). William "Caveman" Lee was a bank robber. Du Juan Johnson murdered a drug dealer. Bernard "Super Bad" Mays died at the age of 33, not at the hands of a fellow boxer or a jealous husband but as a direct result of the malt liquor he imbibed daily since his teen years. Duane Thomas defeated one of Africa's best—John Mugabi—in 1986, then was shot to death in a drug dispute. Manager and promoter Johnny

---

23. Memorandum, 8 April 1998, Boxing Board Records, 103. H. 15. 1 B, MinnHS-SP.

24. Jim O'Hara, Boxing Board, to Jimmy Lyons, Mississippi Athletic Commission, 24 November 1993, Boxing Board Records, 112.f.5.3b, MinnHS-SP.

25. Undated memorandum from Jerry Collin, Boxing Board Records, 103. H. 15. 1B, MinnHS-SP.

26. *Los Angeles Times*, 21 July 1985, Sub Group XV, Series 7, Box 35, HKBA.

27. *Los Angeles Times*, 4 May 1991, Sub Group X, Series 1, Box 20, HKBA.

"Ace" Smith was arrested in a drug deal gone bad—220 pounds of phony cocaine were involved—then was gunned down.[28]

Given the environment into which they were thrust, it would be a flagrant error to assume that those who were caught up in iniquity were doomed to remain on that path. Boxing historically had been a way out for these young men and a return to a kind of righteousness. For example, the now famed television star, director and producer Charles Dutton had been a boxer nicknamed "Roc" who killed a man, then served a lengthy term in prison for manslaughter, before recovering as a credentialed actor.[29]

Also becoming commonplace was the ever tighter link between an apartheid regime increasingly under fire and various U.S. states that should have known better. By 1991 Stanley Christodoulou, an old friend of Angelo Dundee, was in touch with Jim O'Hara, a leading boxing regulator in Minnesota. The good news, however, was that the cultural boycott was apparently working, since boxers of inferior quality were more prone than others to risk crossing activists. After Ricky Rice was flattened in the third round by apartheid battler Francois Botha, Christodoulou was irate, berating the vanquished since he "had no idea what boxing is all about and had his boxing ability been equal to his ability to clown there might have been a contest." He attached an article from the hometown *Natal Mercury*, wherein an observer "watched in amazement" at the antics of this "unbelievably inept boxer" who "would [have] been better suited to boxing tomatoes than the burly Botha"; Rice was "one of the worst boxers ever seen in a professional ring" and "didn't know the difference between a right cross and the Red Cross," which should have been at ringside to attend to the prostrate visitor.[30] Still, if Rice's performance in Finland was an indicator, he was not so feckless a fighter as he appeared. The Professional Boxing Federation there noted that before his journey to the southern tip of Africa, he floored Jouni Kopola in Helsinki.[31]

Tyson, a meteor who flashed across the sky before crashing rudely to earth, was admired greatly by Las Vegas mogul Kirk Kerkorian,

---

28. *Detroit News*, 11 February 2001 and Undated Report, Sub Group X, Series 1, Box 20, HKBA.

29. Tommy Davidson, *Living in Color: What's Funny About Me*, New York: Kensington, 2020, 169.

30. Stanley Christodoulou to Jim O'Hara, 19 February 1991, Boxing Board Records, 112.f.5.3b, MinnHS-SP. See also *Natal Mercury*, 20 February 1991.

31. Professional Boxing Federation of Finland to Boxing Board, 24 August 1990, Boxing Board Records, 112.f.5.3b, MinnHS-SP.

a business partner of Don King, the latter a man the heavyweight came to despise. Kerkorian had experience with the sport, successful as a welterweight (winning 33 of 37 bouts while never being knocked out), but his older brother left the ring with cognitive issues and slurred speech. The purported billionaire retained the instinct to go for the jugular that Tyson possessed, as suggested by his musing that "the most beautiful feeling in the world is when you know it's the other guy that's going down." Kerkorian also formerly managed Don Jordan,[32] another welterweight, who not only had had ties to Mickey Cohen, crime boss of Los Angeles, but the struggle to control his career had led to the prosecution of Carbo, Palermo, and Truman Gibson.

And just as Gibson was followed by King, then supplemented by Butch Lewis, by the 1990s they were joined by Rock Newman, who was close to then Mayor Marion Barry of Washington, D.C., heading his transition team and also active in the "Million Man March" of 1995, spearheaded by Minister Louis Farrakhan of the reconstituted Nation of Islam, which Ali had departed by then.[33] The feisty, rapidly balding and chunky Newman displayed his own fighting acumen when he rushed angrily toward Andrew Golota, who had executed a deft low blow against Riddick Bowe, the heavyweight he promoted.[34]

Nevada may have been the seedbed of this trend of this corrupt influence on the sport, but as the foregoing has suggested, it was hardly alone. Corruption was so vast in the sport that it even managed to incorporate the long dead. By 1991, forged autographs of Sonny Liston were still being peddled.[35] The market, already frothy, had become even more bubbly once those like Frank Stallone became active; brother of Sylvester of the same surname, who had made a fortune playing a character that resembled Chuck "The Bayonne Bleeder" Wepner, Frank Stallone—boxer, singer and actor—also made a splash as a collector of fight memorabilia.[36]

Politically questionable, as well, was the flacking for the heralded showdown between Thomas "Hitman" Hearns and "Sugar" Ray Leonard in 1989. As U.S. imperialism was unleashed by the

---

32. Rempel, *Gambler*, 17, 27, 302.
33. *Las Vegas Review Journal*, 5 November 1995, Sub Group X, Series 1, Box 16, HKBA.
34. *New York Times*, 13 July 1996, Sub Group X, Series 1, Box 16, HKBA.
35. Memorandum from Tom Solecki of Universal Autograph Collectors Club, 8 April 1991, Sub Group X, Series 1, Box 19, HKBA.
36. Report, 6 May 1979, Sub Group X, Series 1, Box 20, HKBA.

imminent erosion of the socialist camp, the typical Las Vegas chorus lines were repurposed as "dance troops in battle fatigues," as even the frivolous were now seriously contemplating war. Promoter Bob Arum alluded ominously "to the Japanese attack on Pearl Harbor and the German invasion of Poland" in order to provide the bellicose atmosphere seen as *de rigueur* for high-stakes bouts. Arum declared that "this contract signing is a declaration of war" and the tagline for the bout itself minced no words: "The War." The press announcement began with film clips of German troops marching through Paris, then bombs burst in the air and fighter planes began shooting deadly projectiles. Then to bring it all back home, there followed images of dancing Indigenes and Wild West saloon brawlers: As one observer put it, "violence in all forms, was fair game."[37]

The luminosity of the newest "Sugar" Ray suggested that yet another sub-heavyweight could generate the requisite interest and revenues for the sport, allowing dollars to trickle down to the many others so dependent upon the sport for their livelihoods. Angelo Dundee, who was part of Leonard's retinue, implied that like so many champions before him, he cooperated with suspicious characters, like Goldie Hearns, "who controlled boxing in Washington, D.C.," adjacent to the middleweight's suburban Maryland home.[38]

Large or small, boxers were promoted with themes that dovetailed neatly with the dangerous times. It may not have been coincidental when Leonard battled his nemesis, the Panamanian Robert Duran, on the anniversary of the bombing of Pearl Harbor in the hinge year 1989, which seemed to augur a renaissance for U.S. imperialism in light of the collapse of the Berlin Wall weeks earlier. "War December 7" was the tagline.[39] Boxing increasingly was becoming bound up in geo-politics. New York was insisting earlier that Duran's title defense be held there, while General Omar Torrijos, the president of Panama, was insisting just as firmly that it be held in his bailiwick,[40] an insistent demand that did not disappear when this charismatic leader perished in a suspicious air crash.

The elevation of the grizzled Panamanian was symbolic of another transition in the sport. As Jewish-American battlers receded from view, to be replaced by African Americans, they in turn were being crowded by boxers from south of the U.S. border. This presented

---

37. Report, 1989, Box 201, Stardust Resort and Casino Records, UNV-LV.

38. Dundee, *My View*, 34.

39. Brochure on Leonard vs. Duran, 1989, Box 201, Stardust Resort and Casino Records, UNV-LV.

40. Minutes, 2 May 1973, NYSAC.

cultural matters that U.S. elites thought they were poised to address. This came clear in Las Vegas in 1992 when the boxer of Mexican origin, Julio César Chávez, fought Héctor "Macho" Camacho of Puerto Rico. The Stardust Hotel in Las Vegas decided that "in room movies will be turned off during Mexican fights and we'll keep track of which rooms the Mexicans are in"; naturally, there would be "Spanish speaking cocktail servers" and, yes, "keep our restaurants open later for the Mexicans since they eat later and often do not show up on time."[41] Stereotyping was hardly peculiar to Nevada. Teddy Brenner, the premier matchmaker at Madison Square Garden, referred to the people stretching from Argentina to Mexico with a broad brush: "they are emotional people," replete with "explosiveness." Perhaps it was nervousness about their alleged explosiveness that impelled Brenner to assert that "with the preponderance of Puerto Rican fighters, I suggest the Commission appoint more Latin officials."[42] Regulators knew as early as 1951 that there were special issues pertaining to the influx of Latinx pugilists though they studiously ignored this gathering reality. When Louis Ramos appeared before them, he conceded that he had "very little" knowledge of the English language (articulated via translation) and added revealingly that "when the referee tells me something, I do not understand. I only understand a little,"[43] which could be crucial in tense moments in the ring, granting an advantage to the English-speaking.

By the time of Chávez's arrival on the scene, promoters should have been well-prepared to handle Spanish-speaking boxers, given the long-term presence of Cuban boxers, including Kid Chocolate and Kid Gavilan. After the 1959 Revolution more islanders arrived on the mainland, including Luis Sarria, "Sugar" Ramos, José "Mantequilla" Nápoles, José Legrá—and many more. Yet, this presence evidently did not well equip promoters for what was to come.[44]

The arrival of more boxers, monolingual in Spanish, did more than recreate cultural stereotypes. Earlier in Minnesota, a "rumor prevailed" about a "rough fight," and the manager of one of the combatants "not speaking English" presented a problem: "it was necessary to call in a linguist from the Mayo Clinic, who talked

---

41. Memorandum, 21 October 1992, Box 202, Stardust Resort and Casino Records, UNV-LV.
42. Minutes, 21 November 1974, NYSAC.
43. Minutes, 19 January 1951, NYSAC.
44. *Miami Herald*, 25 November 1991, Sub Group X, Series 1, Box 17, HKBA.

Spanish and who could translate our instructions."[45] Nationally, state regulators seemed quite ill-prepared to confront a predictable issue: providing translators for non-English speakers.

Perhaps knowledge in languages other than English would have been beneficial to those boxers who were jetting abroad in increasing number. Thus, when Hearns—the self-proclaimed "Detroit Hit Man"—battled Virgil Hill in 1991, he exceeded previous militarist expectations by actually preparing for the battle by spending 10 days in October visiting U.S. troops then based in Saudi Arabia; he was billed as the only U.S. athlete to make such a trip. "One of the reasons I went to the Middle East," said the compliant boxer, "was to boost the soldiers' morale." He had nothing to say about the gender apartheid that characterized the regime. But he was made an honorary general by General Norman Schwarzkopf—or "Stormin' Norman" as he was called. Touched, he donated a hefty $50,000 to the USO [United Service Organizations], designed to supplement the welfare of U.S. troops, while his Michigan hometown continued to deteriorate.[46] This inattention to gender was even more stunning, since Hearns was one of the few punchers who had a woman—Jackie Kallen—who managed his career from the time he was a stripling of 20. "From the first time we met," he said sincerely, "she took charge, organizing my life and helping me shape my career."[47]

It was not just would-be militarists who flocked to the sport. The presence of racketeers in the sport—a tendency that never really disappeared but was curbed somewhat by the ascension of Ali and his Fruit of Islam colleagues—surged as competing forces went into eclipse, not least the once vibrant challengers to white supremacy. Quite dangerously, a leading boxing judge and referee, John Moriarty, was also known as Lieutenant John Reich, redolent of his neo-Nazi background. His portraiture featured a picture of Adolf Hitler and a swastika—though, fashionably, he portrayed himself as no more than an anti-communist.[48] Henry Lamar, Harvard's boxing coach and Bay State regulator of the sport, did not overtly avow similarly odious ideas, though he came from a similar background.

---

45. Minutes, 6 October 1971, Boxing Board Records, 103. H. 15. 1B, MinnHS-SP.

46. Brochure, 1991, Box 202, Stardust Resort and Casino Records, UNV-LV.

47. Jackie Kallen, *Hit Me with Your Best: A Fight Plan for Dealing with All of Life's Hard Knocks*, New York: St. Martin's, 1997, Foreword by Thomas Hearns, xi.

48. *Detroit News*, 23 February 1992, Sub Group VIII, Series 1, Box 12, HKBA.

His great-grandfather of the same surname was a proud Mississippian, leading the state into secession, and after ignominious defeat becoming a strident opponent of rights for the formerly enslaved.[49] Lamar's fondness for the sport represented a now bygone era following World War I when the U.S. elite thought the sport would enhance manliness, an ideology that declined overtly as a search for a Great White Hope became fruitless, as Jack Johnson was followed by Joe Louis, then Ali. (Noted referee Mills Lane argued that college boxing, once a staple at elite universities, went into decline following severe injuries—including death--in the ring in the 1960s.[50])

As Lane's comment suggests, the health of fighters remained a pressing matter. By 1984, former Olympic medalist and contender for championships, "Sugar" Ray Seales, was en route to blindness, as a result of repeated blows to the tissue around his eyes.[51] This was nothing new. For as early as 1943, Albany was considering the perilous condition of Henry Armstrong's eyes, pounded repeatedly during his illustrious career; this was in the context of examining his upcoming fight with Beau Jack, a defining bout in light of the latter's economic distress. Injury and poverty were too often the characteristic traits of boxers, even at the elite level. (Naturally, the bout was authorized duly.)[52]

By the late 1980s, the Minnesota regulators were seeking to constrain the use of steroids, thought to increase muscle mass and strength—albeit with tremendous side effects, including uncontrolled rage and fatalities.[53]

Health concerns were not as straightforward as they appeared at first glance. This was also manifested in the 1980s when the state debated the issue of a "homosexual" who "was scheduled to box in a kick boxing match. His opponent requested him to take an AIDS test, he refused, so the bout was not made." This received no evident censure from regulators; instead, praised was "outstanding work in working with the referees and corner men on dispensing rubber medical examination gloves to prevent them coming in

---

49. Obituary, 30 September 1985, Sub Group VIII, Series 1, Box 12, HKBA.
50. *Las Vegas Review Journal*, 8 March 1984, Sub Group VIII, Series 1, Box 12, HKBA.
51. *Washington Post,* 22 January 1984, Box 151, Newfield-UT.
52. Minutes, 12 March 1943, NYSAC.
53. Minutes, 21 June 1989, Boxing Board Records, 103.H. 15.1b, MinnHS-SP.

contact with hepatitis or AIDS. The vote was unanimous."[54] Jerry Coughlin, a key regulator, issued guidance on AIDS, instructing that "coaches, seconds, referees, doctors and other ring personnel face potential exposure" and, thus, "must wear rubber medical examination gloves."[55] Subsequently, the U.S. Olympic Committee warned of the "transmission of infectious agents during athletic competition," including HIV,[56] the virus leading to the disease that is AIDS.

Yet, while rubber gloves were being strapped on busily, fatalities otherwise continued to mount. It was in 1994 that amateur boxer Donell Lindsay suffered a head injury in the ring and died a day later from traumatic brain injury from blows to the head.[57] Minnesota was the site but the trend was reflective of national characteristics. It was in 2019 that a rising heavyweight, Deontay Wilder, bragged that "this is the only sport where you can kill a man and get paid for it at the same time. It's legal. So why not use my right to do so?" he asked rhetorically, while adding unnecessarily, "this is not a gentlemanly sport."[58] As ever, promoters were able to take advantage adroitly of federalism and migrate to jurisdictions where regulators were absent or pliable or bribable. An audit of the Athletic Commission in Arizona found that this body had "not fulfilled its responsibility" or subscribed to "statutory requirements. As a result, some unlicensed individuals have participated in professional boxing."[59]

Boxing generally managed to escape the kind of scrutiny that fatalities and corruption demanded. Like any other capitalist, those involved in this grinding sport consorted with politicos for the betterment of both. Typically, it was in 1986 that the governor-elect of Florida, Bob Martinez, saluted Chris Dundee: "thank you again," he enthused, "for everything you did to help elect me 40th Governor" of the Sunshine State; "heartfelt gratitude for your hard work on my

---

54. Minutes, 15 July 1987, Boxing Board Records, 103.H. 15. 1B, MinnHS-SP.

55. Memorandum from Jerry Coughlin, 4 June 1987, Boxing Board Records, 103. H.15.1B, MinnHS-SP.

56. Memorandum from USOC, May 1996, Boxing Board Records, 112.f.5.3b, MinnHS-SP.

57. Louis Robards, Assistant Attorney General, to James O'Hara, 12 April 1994, Boxing Board Records, 112.f.5.3b, MinnHS-SP.

58. *Los Angeles Times*, 16 May 2019.

59. Office of the Auditor General, "A Performance Audit of the Athletic Commission," December 1981, Report to the State Legislature, State of Arizona, University of Arizona-Tucson.

behalf."⁶⁰ Dundee benefited from the "light touch" regulation that characterized the state's treatment of the sport. Mike Scionti of the State Athletic Commission was peppered with inquires about a television event that rightfully should have been addressed to a national body: And that was precisely the point, in that multiple jurisdictions meant that probing queries fell between and amongst stools. Still, Scionti was interrogated about the "slugfest" on the USA Network, an upstart cable television channel scrounging for viewers. Robert "Mike" Cahill, the inquirer, wondered if there was a "payoff" to judges and suspected "gambling's influence.... this is why our country has become cynical," he scoffed.⁶¹ The fight complained about featured Terry Ray vs. Robert Daniels; the former was "my fighter," said Angelo Dundee as he issued a "protest" if a special scrutiny emerged, where influence with Martinez's Republican Party would have aided him and his charge immensely.⁶²

Inescapably, African Americans, even those with a debatable grip on ethics, by the nature of their existence, were forced to veer—somewhat. Don King, for example, was harshly critical of the "Negro-phobia" which he said correctly inhered in U.S. society. Sadly, those who were not of African ancestry rarely pointed to this obvious aspect of the republic, which then increased the importance of the hirsute one's insight, endearing him further to the community from which he sprung and making it more difficult for politicos or prosecutions to target him. His then protégé and soon-to-be adversary, Mike Tyson, burst into tears when—escorted by King—he visited Auschwitz and espied the crematoria, a journey rarely taken and an expression rarely rendered by boxers in the late 20th century.⁶³

The star-crossed relationship between King and Tyson, with the latter charging, not unfairly, that he had been traduced by the former (looted in fact) illustrates yet another theme of racism and the political economy of the sport. For even Tyson has looked back fondly at his initial mentor, Cus D'Amato, who has been portrayed angelically. Yet the record reveals another story, giving impetus to King's allegation of "Negro-phobia" in that the message rendered was that

---

60. Governor-Elect Bob Martinez to Chris Dundee, 26 December 1986, Sub Group XVIII, Series 3, Box 2, HKBA.

61. Robert "Mike" Cahill to Mike Scionti of State Athletic Commission, 25 October 1996, Boxing Commission Records, 000331, S2080, Box 1, Florida State Archives-Tallahassee (abbrev. FlSA-T).

62. Angelo Dundee to Mike Scionti, 2 October 1996, Boxing Commission Records, 000331, S2080, Box 1, FISA-T.

63. Gonzalez, *Inner Ring*, 155, 171.

it was acceptable for Euro-Americans to engage in hijinks and dirty tricks—but not others. For it was as early as 1959 that regulators in the Empire State charged that the then manager of Floyd Patterson was associating with "Charley Black...a convicted gambler," acted as "promoter and matchmaker without license," sought to gain an interest in Patterson's main challenger, Ingemar Johansson—a textbook definition of conflict of interest—and, crucially, "disobeying the rule that a manager must give an itemized report on distribution of a boxer's purse within five days after a bout."[64] New York regulators studied these points intently. The record reveals that "Ingemar Johansson testified that he did not think he would have received the bout [with Patterson] had he not accepted [D'Amato's choice] as his manager...he would have to have a manager who was acceptable to Mr. D'Amato...at first D'Amato had suggested giving 33 1/3 percent of his earnings on a five year contract to a new American manager but they finally agreed to ten per cent." Presumably, the shrewdly corrupt D'Amato stood to benefit, irrespective of who prevailed in the bout.[65] Perhaps if boxing writers had been better at their jobs, an alert Tyson would have known that by 1966, Patterson was suing D'Amato for $250,000, an amount he claimed he was owed.[66] And perhaps as well, he could have avoided the alleged plundering he suffered at the hands of a onetime manager, Bill Cayton,[67] who of course was not a Negro.

Negro corruptors did not have the advantage of their Euro-American counterparts in being able to twist politics to their advantage by dint of non-prosecutions—or otherwise. Frank Costello, the so-called "Top Hood" of racketeering, wielded influence in Tammany Hall—the Democratic Party in New York City—and reputedly had a role in selecting the 1932 nominee for U.S. President; this influence extended downward to local courts and cops. The close embrace of New York and South Florida also meant influence extended southward to the winter haven of mobsters. When an attempt was made in 1957 to liquidate Costello, the hit squad consisted of a two-man team of driver Tommy "Tommy Ryan" Eboli, a notorious manager of boxers and over-the-hill boxer Vincent "The Chin" Gigante. Eventually, "Tommy Ryan" himself was liquidated in 1972 after he had climbed the greasy pole to the virtual top of racketeering.[68] Due northwest

---

64. Minutes, 5 November 1959, NYSAC.
65. Minutes, 21 May 1959, NYSAC.
66. Minutes, 13 July 1966, NYSAC.
67. *Los Angeles Times*, 30 July 1988.
68. DeStefano, *Top Hoodlum*, 144, 209, 243, 259.

in Buffalo, racketeers were said to have prevailed in the selection of Dennis Vacco as U.S. attorney, with power over federal prosecutions.[69] It is gross understatement to suggest that King, or Negro mobsters, had comparatively lesser influence.

* * *

There were numerous attempts over the decades to reform the status quo but, alas, impenetrable obstacles impeded change. Inexorably, these reformative proposals reached an apogee as forces of the status quo were placed on the defensive by the anti-Jim Crow movement; yet, finaglers continually took advantage of federalism to play off one jurisdiction against another. Hence, it was in 1965 that Jack Urch, a regulator in California, lamented that "since 1959 we have consistently expressed our belief that a Federal law is in the national interest and is a necessity if boxing is to be re-established as a worthwhile sport…. numerous examples," he continued, "can be given where a state has conducted an extensive examination and found an applicant undesirable in some respect; this person is denied a license, however, he soon reappears in another state conducting business as usual with complete impunity. Thus," he said, "those jurisdictions which attempt to eliminate the undesirables in boxing soon find themselves eliminated from consideration for any of the big boxing attractions." Acute reference was made to the "recent Clay-Liston fiasco" in that "as soon as Massachusetts attempted through its legal representatives to investigate the promoters of the fight, the promoters promptly took the fight" to Lewiston, Maine. Regulators generally were "supported by taxes on the gate receipts of the boxing events held within their state or community, thus the very fights which might be controlled by hoodlums also are the very fights which the most local commission is most desirous of having," since racketeers' fights generated many rivulets of revenues. As matters evolved, said Urch, "those states which 'welcome everybody' reap the benefits," and those states that tended to scrutinize promotions often were evaded. "The states cannot and will not take necessary action," a situation that cried out for federal response.[70]

Yet, as I write in 2020, the promise of federal regulation of the sport has yet to become a reality. In some ways, the situation has

---

69. Rizzo, *Gangsters*, 176.

70. Memorandum from Jack Urch, Executive Officer of the Athletic Commission of California, 24 June 1965, Box 26, Folder 32, Jeffrey Cohelan Papers, University of Oklahoma-Norman.

worsened for fighters. Wrestling, a kind of burlesque of boxing, has been increasingly supplanted by mixed martial arts or UFC [Ultimate Fighting Championship] which the late Senator John McCain of Arizona castigated as no more than a "human cockfight," which might be a characterization that is too generously sympathetic.[71] UFC rose in popularity in the aftermath of the Muhammad Ali Boxing Reform Act passed by the U.S. Congress in 2000, which was thought to have cleaned up this sewer of entrepreneurship. Yet it was in 2020 that presidential aspirant Andrew Yang inferentially displayed the flexibility and elusiveness of combative sports when he endorsed the campaign to facilitate unionizing drives among mixed martial artists, whose sport was seemingly en route to surpassing boxing in popularity.[72]

Investigators in New Jersey in 1984 demanded that "cut men," those designated to stanch the bleeding after a fighter stumbled back to his corner, required more regulation: What potions precisely were they using, and could they harm those treated, along with those they were fighting? Also demanded was universal urine testing given growing suspicions about the misuse of steroids and other substances.[73] Testifying before New Jersey legislators in 1986, "Smokin'" Joe Frazier demanded pensions for fighters, presumably through taxing promoters, arenas and the like.[74] Larry Holmes also made it to Trenton in 1986 and though he had not fought since 1983, he continued to have regular brain scans and various stress tests. He felt that ringside authorities should pay attention to later rounds, since boxers were injured generally, he said, "from round six...seven on up"[75]—though maybe the option should be Olympic-style bouts of three rounds or even headgear for fighters, per the quadrennial exposition. UFC lawyer I. Lawrence Epstein pooh-poohed the idea that the size and nature of gloves should be altered, since "big

---

71. Quoted in Oral History, I. Lawrence Epstein, 24 August 2017, UNV-LV.

72. *Washington Post*, 9 May 2020.

73. "Interim Report and Recommendations of the State of New Jersey Commission of Investigation on the Inadequate Regulation of Boxing," 1984, NJSL-T.

74. "Public Meeting Before Assembly Independent and Regional Authorities Commission on Testimony on Status of and Possible Reforms to Boxing," 16 June 1986, NJSL-T. Frazier opposed gloves without thumbs, and added that a knockout of an opponent was executed via a blow along the "chin line" and not the head.

75. "Public Meeting Before Assembly Independent and Regional Authorities Commission on Testimony on Status of and Possible Reform to Boxing in the State of New Jersey," 19 May 1986, NJSL-T.

gloves don't protect your brain,"[76] though Holmes, who admittedly had more direct experience with gloves, thought changing gloves should be considered. Above all, Holmes had soured on the very idea of promoters and "wouldn't mind," he said with earnestness, "if I saw government come and take over the promoter's position."[77] This was putatively an advanced ideological position: Nationalizing the industry was rarely a view taken by the most advanced workers in any sector. Nevertheless, the man who had the most to lose from such a takeover—Bob Arum—instead was recorded as advocating "for federal control"; possibly such a reform could allow him more access to politicos to squeeze, then eliminate his hairy competitor, Don King, then revert to private control under the Nevadan's aegis.[78]

As the aforementioned "Sugar" Ray Seales, and countless others, could well attest, boxing was deadly for the eyes. But what if a boxer had ophthalmic issues in the first instance? Minnesota regulators were in "total agreement that hard contact lenses should not be used by boxers," yet there was a lingering "problem with soft contact lenses," too, i.e., the "possibility of dislocation of the lens from the cornea actually causing a foreign body sensation." Still, quickly quelling the idea that they were reformist regulators, they swiftly began to debate earnestly "whether or not we should allow children under age ten to box."[79] Nonetheless, at a meeting of the latest iteration of the WBArum—the U.S. Boxing Association and the International Boxing Federation—Minnesotans collaborated in forging a "joint resolution" that was "passed" seeking to "discourage boxers from fighting beyond the age of 35 for safety purposes," while "barring any fighters with detached retinas from being rated by either the IBF or USBA."[80]

---

76. Oral History, I. Lawrence Epstein, 24 August 2017, UNV-LV: "Headgear doesn't do anything to protect your brain...big gloves don't protect your brain." See also the remarks of George Gainford, manager of "Sugar" Ray Robinson, who was paraphrased as saying in 1951 that "boxers will not wear the headguards if they could possibly avoid doing so": Minutes, 5 January 1951, NYSAC.

77. "Public Meeting Before Assembly Independent and Regional Authorities Commission on Testimony on Status of and Possible Reform to Boxing in the State of New Jersey," 19 May 1986, NJSL-T.

78. Minutes, 15 July 1987, Boxing Board Records, 103.H. 15. 1B, MinnHS-SP.

79. Minutes, 20 February 1979, Boxing Board Records, 103.H.15.1B, MinnHS-SP.

80. Minutes of USBA Convention in Virginia, 15 July 1987, Boxing Board Records, 103.H.15.1B, MinnHS-SP. See also Kelley C. Howard, "Regulating

Boxing continued to wrestle spasmodically with the matter of gender equality. It was only in 1974 that the first woman judge was christened in the Empire State—though Carol Polis happened to be the spouse of Bob Polis, a referee of longstanding, suggesting that nepotism and cronyism continued to plague the sport.[81]

Albany regulators continued to be pressured to yield on the related issue of licensing women boxers. The chairman of the Athletic Commission was hesitant: "There is a danger to the stomach and the breast. It is all wrong.... there are some activities," he insisted, "that women don't belong in." A comrade opted for the trifecta: "I don't think women should be referees, judges or boxers," said one commissioner, while another chimed in by expressing reluctance about "getting into Women's Lib. They don't [know] enough about the game."[82] Finally, there was a capitulation in 1975, and quickly emerging was the reputed "Female Ali," speaking of Jackie Tonawanda, who won all of her 36 bouts and even decked a male opponent. Much of her training and sparring was with men since, she asserted, "The women don't show me anything and they can't take my power." She paved the way, ironically, for Laila Ali (daughter of the heavyweight champion) and Jacqui Frazier-Hyde (yes, daughter of Muhammad Ali's primary opponent). Tonawanda died in 2009 bereft of life insurance, pensions and savings, delivering an unfortunate aspect of gender equality.[83]

If Albany had studied its own record it would have been discovered that as early as 1931 there was evidence before regulators that "Kid Chocolate," the Cuban flash, "could not possibly have won his bout with Tony Canzoneri at Madison Square Garden as the officials were fixed and only a knockout would have been scored in Chocolate's favor."[84] Maybe if officials had spent less time seeking to block women's equality, they would have had more time to confront what they were debating at the same time: the "violent outburst" at Madison Square Garden in August 1974, noticed by the chief regulator, featuring "the throwing of bottles and by the igniting of torn seats," accompanied by "open gambling around the ring."[85]

---

the Sport of Boxing—Congress Throws the First Punch with the Professional Boxing Safety Act," *Seton Hall Journal of Sport Law*, 7 (No. 1, 1997: 103-127, Box 72, FT-UTnK.

81. Report, 17 July 1974, NYSAC.
82. Minutes, ca. September 1974, NYSAC.
83. *New York Amsterdam News*, 7-13 May 2020.
84. Minutes, 27 November 1931, NYSAC.
85. Edwin Dooley to Teddy Brenner, 6 August 1974, NYSAC.

Or more time could have been spent eliminating the underlying conditions that led to the impromptu sacking of Joe Bostic, a Garden announcer who happened to be African American. His hiring had been an upgrade; typically, his predecessor, Pat Mascia, had been the chauffeur of Mayor John V. Lindsay, while—typically—the relatively overqualified Bostic asserted, "I speak Spanish, French and Italian," all useful in appealing to a cosmopolitan clientele. Times had changed: Bostic had pledged to appeal to a bevy of African-American elected officials, including Congresswoman Shirley Chisholm, on the heels of her path-breaking attempt to reach the presidency, and Percy Sutton, then serving as Manhattan Borough President.[86]

Nevertheless, a few years later, as legalizing women boxers was well in motion, Albany found that "there are only a few women boxers licensed in the approximately 13 states which permit it; no state permits boxing under rules substantially similar to those applying for boxing by men. In all of these states, women may only box with other women; they are generally allowed to box fewer and shorter rounds than men, and they are usually required to wear both specific protective devices (chest protectors) and to use more heavily padded gloves." There were other measures designed to protect these combatants—though regulators did not consider seriously if such measures would be conducive to the health of male boxers, too.[87]

Yet as early as 1963, Albany regulators were mulling over mandating headguards, 10-ounce gloves and "4 ropes in the ring" and moving away from "6 oz. gloves." They recalled what happened in 1961, when Charlie Mohr competed in the boxing finals of the "Intercollegiate Championships in Wisconsin...he wore a headguard and 10 ounce gloves" and "was killed. The Intercollegiate Boxing was eliminated"—however, the authorities did not draw the inference that the sport might be inherently dangerous.[88]

By 1974 Albany was facing a problem that had dogged the sport ever since it had attained a veneer of legality decades earlier. The august *New York Times* had editorialized in favor of banning the sport. Regulators argued that "during the three years prior to the enactment of the Walker Law which restored boxing legally in 1920, 35 ring deaths occurred" at a time when "bouts were held clandestinely in barrooms and on barges and the bodies of boxers were

---

86. Minutes, ca. September 1974, NYSAC.
87. Minutes, 16 September 1977, NYSAC.
88. Minutes, 20 May 1963, NYSAC. Cf. Pacheco, *Tales*, 158: When boxer Davey Moore was killed in the ring, "there were only three ropes...a fourth rope would have caught Davey's head."

found in the river, on hospital steps and in alleys." The implication was that there was some pervasive human impulse—or U.S. cultural reflex—which demanded boxing, and it was better to legalize and regulate it. Besides, it was said with a hint of triumphalism, "more people watch a Heavyweight Championship on television than view any other single sport," generating tax revenue that would be difficult to replace.[89]

By 1977 regulators were informing Governor Hugh Carey that "two hundred...events...held under the Commission's auspices provided approximately $1,250,000 in revenue" to New York.[90] Yet giving momentum to the new abolitionists was the continuing corruption that had not eluded regulators in that also by 1977, regulator, and Democratic Party honcho, James Farley "suspended himself" from the Commission because of his overly cozy relationship with Don King, involving lush "expenses—airfare, hotels" and other perks.[91]

This was a step forward but certainly not enough. As early as 1962, while reaffirming the decision to deny a license to Sonny Liston, Albany regulators opined that "the necessity for federal licensing control," in order to wrong-foot the arbitrage that allowed playing off one state against another, was "crystal clear."[92] Leading regulator and former boxer Floyd Patterson also tellingly proposed in December 1978 a "Pension Plan for Fighters," which could have been funded via taxes on promoters and matchmakers and the like. Intriguingly, the much reviled Don King contributed $5,000 for a "study" of this proposal, though the record did not reveal a like contribution from his competitors, e.g., Arum.[93]

Something had to be done. For it was in 1979 that Albany, including Patterson, concurred "strongly" with a *New York Times* opinion that asserted that "boxing is on its deathbed." This was in the context of the regulators demanding before the U.S. Congress—once more—"federal...regulation and control of boxing within the United States." This would involve, inter alia, "standardization of rules and regulations...computerization of boxers' records...a nationwide comprehensive Insurance Plan for All Boxers.[94]

---

89. Edwin Dooley to *New York Times*, 26 June 1974, NYSAC.
90. James A. Farley to Governor Carey, 19 April 1977, NYSAC.
91. Minutes, 4 May 1977, NYSAC.
92. Minutes, 3 October 1962, NYSAC.
93. Minutes, 18 December 1978, NYSAC.
94. *New York Times*, 21 March 1979; Testimony of the New York State Athletic Commission Before the Committee on Education and Labor of the United States, House of Representatives, 29 March 1979, NYSAC.

By early 2020 the *New York Times*, a frequent jouster with boxers and regulators alike, found that "boxing in the city is not what it used to be…. all over Brooklyn and Manhattan expensive boutique boxing gyms with names like Shadowbox and Rumbles have popped up, supplanting the city's bare bones fight clubs," featuring yuppies and Wall Street henchmen toughening themselves for exploitative escapades. This was occurring while "professional boxing's slow retreat from New York City" continued to be "a phenomenon… driven by high insurance rates and the steep overhead costs of presenting fights in the city."[95] Although Las Vegas continued to be a lodestar for boxing, there was a slow but steady retreat from the halcyon days of the Ali Regime.

Still, despite the goodwill of regulators and the philanthropy of Don King, if the sport were to be saved and reformed it would have to occur—as with any of the oppressed—by organizing from below in league with allies. And this brings us to 1977, when the Teamsters proposed an organizing drive within the sport.[96] Their checkered record notwithstanding (my father was part of this union and fell victim to their consorting with racketeering and looting pensions, including one that would have benefited me personally), this was a proposal worth considering. This was not an isolated event since by 1996, regulators in Florida were debating if "boxers should have a labor union and that participants in the boxing industry should provide for medical care and retirement [pension] for boxers"—though, typically, this was deemed to be not "realistic," and the authorities "went on to other business."[97] The admirable proposal—and the swift deep-sixing of it—too were part of the bittersweet reality that continues to animate boxing.

---

95. *New York Times*, 1 March 2020.
96. Minutes, 29 September 1977, NYSAC.
97. Minutes, 29 July 1996, 000331, S2080, Box 1, Boxing Commission Records, FlSA-T. See Newsletter of the "American Association for the Improvement of Boxing," Summer 1999; the "Professional Boxing Safety Act of 1996"; HR 2716: Bill "to establish in the Department of Labor a Federal Boxing Board to Prescribe and Enforce Fair Labor Standards Applicable to the Conduct of Professional Boxing"; S305: "Muhammad Ali Boxing Reform Act," Box II: 863, Moynihan-LC.

Index

AAU. *See* Amateur Athletic Union
Abrams, Georgie, 87
Adelson, Merv, 253
Afghanistan, 263
AFL-CIO. *See* American Federation of Labor-Congress of Industrial Organizations
Africa, 3–5, 166–67, 258–60
African Americans: Ali, M., influencing, 264; ancestry denied by, 9; anti-Jim Crow and, 164, 200–201; anti-labor climate and, 43–44; Arum, B., as, 252; in boxing, 9–11, 210–11; Eisenhower, D., voting by, 167; Euro-Americans attacking, 42, 47–48; Golden Gloves participation of, 253; in Harlem, 50; in Nevada, 31–32; organized crime and, 216; outside fights for, 9–10; racism protests by, 104; soldiers, 114; systematic exclusion of, 189; urban eruption of, 228–29; white supremacy against, 41, 110. *See also* Black issues
aggravated assault, 149
Ahearn, Goldie, 84
Aiello, Danny, 242
Akins, Virgil, 169, 193
Ali, Laila, 304
Ali, Muhammad, 5–6, 16, 203; African-American athletes and, 264; African audience of, 260; Black Militancy of, 206–7; Chamberlain taking on, 230; Clay's transition to, 217–18; Cohen and example of, 98; decline of, 263; Dundee, A., hired by, 15, 72, 84, 198, 209–10, 244, 280; as face of boxing, 209;

Foreman's battle with, 210n4; Frazier and, 22–23, 225–26, 257; health jeopardized of, 222; for heavyweight championship, 229; Holmes bout with, 254–55, 275–76; IndoChina war opposed by, 22; King, D., and, 210, 239–40; Liston's battles with, 220; military conscription evaded by, 209; mistreatment of, 230; mixed fights of, 83–84; Muslim violence and, 213; Parkinson disease signs of, 265; Patterson, F., fight with, 219; popularity of, 224, 265; prizefight promotion by, 223–24; questionable characters and, 215; rabbit punches accusations by, 264–65; in Rome Olympics, 164; rope-a-dope tactic of, 224, 260; Swaziland exhibition for, 259; Wepner fight with, 264–65
Ali regime, 209–10, 212–13, 262, 307
Allen, Dick, 257
Allen, Millie, 179n77
"All Women Mud Wrestling Team," 268
Amateur Athletic Union (AAU), 128, 131
Ambers, Lou, 89
American Federation of Labor-Congress of Industrial Organizations (AFL-CIO), 249
American Legion, 103–4
American Youth Congress (AYC), 101–2, 123–24
Anderson, Tim ("Doc"), 271
Andrade, Cisco, 127
Andrews, Bobby, 109
Angola, 4, 281
Angott, Sammy, 110

anti-apartheid movement, 245, 280–81
Anti-Defamation League, 107, 251
anti-Jim Crow, 214, 225, 262, 286, 301; African Americans contributing to, 164, 200–201; Ali, M., and, 210; Eisenhower and, 165; Italian Americans and, 168; white supremacy and, 168
anti-labor climate, 43–44
anti-racketeering act, 189
anti-Semitism, 7, 94, 152
antitrust law, 145–46, 185
antiwar movement, 225
Antonucci, Charles ("Charlie Black"), 181
Antuofermo, Vito, 290
Aragon, Art, 172
Arcel, Ray, 119, 139, 146, 272, 286
Argentina, 24, 61n23, 295
Arizona, 72–73, 232–33, 298
Armenian Assassin, 18
Armstrong, Henry, 35, 87–90, 119; eye problems of, 297; Legion Stadium fight of, 104–5; Robinson, S. R., fighting, 127
Armstrong, Louis, 248
Arno, Nat, 107
Arouch, Salomo, 7
Arrington, Ibar, 277
arsenal of democracy, 107
Arum, Bob, 14, 17–18, 226; as African-American, 252; dishonorable associations of, 254; funds seizure case of, 239; Johannesburg visit of, 242–43; King, D., jousting with, 151, 241–42; in Las Vegas, 251; newsletter bribe from, 240; revenue of, 247; of WBA, 243–44
Arum, Lovee, 15n56
Atlantic City, 96, 150, 254, 256, 278, 283–84, 285
Attell, Abe ("The Little Hebrew"), 36, 42, 68–69, 120
Auletto, Rocco, 279
AYC. *See* American Youth Congress
Azikiwe, Nnamdi, 21

Babs Wingo, 234
Backus, Frank, 32
Baer, Max, 85–86, 93
bantustan, 246
Barbaro, Frank, 114
Barcelona, 24
bare knuckle boxing, 29–30
Barker, Bernard, 147, 207
Barkley, Iran, 289
Barone, Joe ("Pep"), 180
Baroudi, Sam, 122
Barr, John, 173, 284
Barry, Marion, 293
Bartfield, Jake ("Soldier"), 68
Basilio, Carmen, 170, 194
Battle of Waterloo, 12
battle royals, 3, 3n1, 110–11
battle royal wrestling, 83
Battling Siki, 78–80, 99
Beattie, Jim, 230–31
Belcher, Julius, 6
Belize, 200
Belli, Melvin, 186
Belsey, F. A., 233
Benevuti, Nino, 215
Benitez, Wilfredo, 269
Bennett, Ray, 66
Bernstein, Jack, 67
Bethel African Methodist Episcopal church, 32
betting coup, 61
Biden, Joseph, 280
Bierne, William, 189
Big Chief Knockout, 237
bigotry: fascism and, 94; toward Jews, 33–34; Johnson, Jack, fighting, 27–28; whiteness and retreat of, 77
Birns, Alex ("Shondor"), 255–56
Biscailuz, Eugene, 97
Black, Charley, 300
Black, Simmie, 291
Black issues: Black Gangsters, 256; Black Gold, 258–59; Black Liberation movements, 230; Black Mafia, 214; Black Militancy, 206–7; Black Murders Row,

Index   311

158; Black Muslims, 213, 239;
Black Nationalism, 217; Black
Panthers, 205; Black Power, 229;
Black Restoration, 209; Black
Supremacy, 13
Black Sox scandal, 36, 120, 139
Blake, Eubie, 41–42
Blakely, Leonard, 169
Blease, Cole, 49
blindness, from boxing, 63–64
Bloom, Phil, 36
Blossom, Ralph, 275
Blumenthal, Nessie, 91
Blunt, Eddie, 120
Bobick, Rodney, 277
Bobo, Harry, 120
Bocchicchio, Felix, 155
Bodner, Allen, 37, 69
Bohn, Eddie, 275
Bonavena, Oscar, 270
Bonomi, John, 174
bookmaking, 16n63, 279
Bostic, Joe, 305
Botha, Francois, 292
Botto, Robert, 284
Boudreaux, Johnny, 277
boxing: African Americans in, 9–11, 210–11; African candidates for, 258–59; Ali, M., as face of, 209; all-Negro matchups in, 158; Argentina's regulation of, 61n23; Attell in, 36; bare knuckle, 29–30; blindness from, 63–64; boys taken off street in, 232; in California, 275; Carbo, F., ruling, 146–47; concentration camps learning, 151–52; control of, 112; corruption in, 15–17, 66–67, 121–22, 172–73; deception in, 173; dictator, 112; diminishment of, 276; dirty linen of, 191; eastward spread of, 55; ethnic groups and, 211; Europe giving points in, 164; fatalities in, 25n102, 122, 298; fighters breakdown in, 269–71; film revenue from, 61; financial problems in, 118; Frazier and, 6–7, 210n4, 302–3, 302n74; Friday Night fights, 145; Gans and scientific, 38; Georgetown University team in, 62; in Great Britain, 57; Great White Hope in, 73, 164–65; heavy betting in, 117–18; Jewish Americans changing names, 152; Jewish Americans in, 7, 19, 25, 42; Jim Crow laws influencing, 12–13; Johnson, Jack, and control of, 86; King, D., and, 250, 261; legislative bill banning, 131; Madam Bey's attraction to, 100; masculinity in, 58–59; Masterson's interest in, 56; mining camps sponsoring, 42–43; mobsters in, 5–6, 14–15, 14n53, 99, 145; Negro boxers representation in, 124–25; in Nevada, 32–33; New York epicenter for, 80; Paret's death in, 205; participation decrease in, 135; phoney fights in, 109; physical toll from, 24–25, 27, 27n114; political interests in, 20–24; popularity of, 162, 166; post-Jim Crow era of, 14; prizefighting legalized in, 37, 73; punch drunk from, 25, 64–65, 270–71; racketeers and, 15, 97; radio revenue from, 84; referee scrutiny in, 89–90; reforms of, 302–3, 302n74; regulators in, 90, 108, 111; revenue from, 72, 210–11; ring name changes in, 94–96; Robinson, S. R., scrupulous in, 157; Roosevelt, T., promoting, 33; segregation in, 37–38; Sinatra buying in to, 188; Smith, B., fixed fight in, 117; sport and abolishment of, 49–50; tax collection from, 82–83; Teamsters union and, 307; on television, 145; tournament, 261; tuberculosis in, 26–27; Tunney refusing to, 65–66; as unsanitary sport, 25–26; weight changes for, 267; between white men, 48–49; women in,

boxing (continued)
226, 304. *See also* fighting; Negro boxers; prizefighting
boxing license: in Britain, 195; decreases in, 163; Dempsey's deferred, 76; Graziano's revoked, 119; Liston denied, 306; for Moore, 109; of Negro boxers, 103–4
Boxing Managers Guild, 148
Boxing Writers Association, 212
box office draw, 83–84
Braddock, James, 13, 84
Bradley, Frederick Van Ness, 131
Brady, Jack, 93
brain scans, 302
Brandeis, Louis, 35
Brantford, John Louis, 105, 105n127
Braverman, Al, 242, 255
Braxton, Dwight, 284
Brazil, 234, 236, 272, 294
Brazil, Bobo, 234
Brenner, Teddy, 295
Brent, Sidney, 105
bribery: by Arum, B., 240; episode, 88, 119; Nilon's political, 249; by Palermo, 192
Briscoe, Bennie, 256, 269
Britain, 57, 195
British Board of Boxing Control, 122
Brocato, James, 153
Broeg, Bob, 156
Broomfield, William, 183
Broughton, Jack, 29
Brown, Aaron. *See* "Dixie Kid"
Brown, Earl, 153n70
Brown, Frankie, 117, 156n83
Brown, Harold, 172
Brown, James Boyd, 118
Brown, Jim, 239
Brown, Ray, 118
Brown, Thomas, 70
Bruno, Angelo, 254
Bruno, Frank, 290
"The Brute" (film), 179
Bryan, Ned, 121

Buchalter, Lepke, 69, 139
Buck, Jack, 273
Buckley, Jim, 101
Buffer, Michael, 213n16
Bullard, Eugene, 40
Burkina Faso, 259
Burley, Charles, 109
Burley, Dan, 90
Bush, George H. W., 22
Buss, Jerry, 273
Buxbaum, Jacob, 96

Caesar's Palace, 253, 255
Cahill, Mike, 299
Calabro, Joseph ("Joe Carlo"), 214
California, 275
California Athletic Commission, 13
Camacho, Héctor ("Macho"), 295
Campbell, Frankie, 86
Campbell, Tommy, 172
Cannon, Speedy, 109
Canzoneri, Tony, 304
capitalism, 16
capoeira (choreographed combat), 4
Capone, Al, 34, 91, 150, 180
Caracas, 156
Carbo, Frank, 14–15, 34, 112, 138, 200; boxing ruled by, 146–47; capture of, 168; Chicago Crime Commission watching, 153; color line drawn by, 178; congressional testimony of, 192; Docusen contract purchased by, 152–53; Dundee, A., comments on, 146; Dundee, C., known by, 142; Fugazy in conflict with, 204; Gray payments denied by, 175; guilty verdict of, 186, 190; mobster ties with, 198; Raft supported by, 197; Siegel, B., selecting, 139; trial of, 169
Carbo, Paul John, 139–40
Carey, Hugh, 306
Carlen, Ray, 109
Carmichael, Stokely, 22, 229
Carmody, Bobby, 256

Index

Carnera, Primo ("The Ambling Alp"), 21–22, 90–92, 102, 111, 163
Carpentier, Georges, 26, 66, 79
Carry, George, 71
Carter, Jimmy, 141, 263
Carter, Rubin ("Hurricane"), 206
Casale, Edward ("Ricky"), 284
Casarona, Salvatore, 187
Cassidy, Robert, 152
Castellano, Paul, 288–89
Castro, Fidel, 201, 205
Caucasian race, 8–9
Cavett, Dick, 228
Cayton, Bill, 300
CBS. *See* Columbia Broadcast System
Cerdan, Marcel, 164
Certo, Al, 283–85, 288, 290
Cervantes, Alphonse, 193–94
Cervantes, Antonio, 246
Chamberlain Wilt, 230
Championship Sports, Inc., 204
Charles, Ezzard, 122, 156, 178; African tour of, 166–67; Walcott battling, 65n40, 134, 158
Chase, Robert, 121
Chavez, Carlos, 172
Chávez, Julio César, 295
Chicago Blackhawks, 176
Chicago Crime Commission, 153
"Chick Champ of the World," 4
Chile, 25
China, 22, 50, 102, 128, 208
Chinese Americans, 8
Chisholm, Shirley, 305
Choynski, Isidore Nathan, 36
Choynski, Joe, 36, 36n37
Christian, Henry, 118
Christian identity, 225
Christodoulou, Stanley, 244, 280, 292
Chuvalo, George, 213, 215, 219, 229
Civilian Board of Boxing Control, 12
civil rights, 82, 107, 202, 229
Clark, Henry, 227
Clark, Ramsey, 241
Clark, Tom, 185

Clay, Cassius Marcellus. *See* Ali, Muhammad
Claybourn, Jack ("Black Panther"), 102
clinical depression, 270
closed-circuit television, 219, 266
closing arguments, 190
Coco, Ettore ("Eddie"), 154
Coetzee, Gerrie, 245, 281
Coggins, Jack, 121
Cohen, Mickey, 15, 18, 141–42, 149, 192; Al Capone of Cleveland of, 250; Ali, M., as example from, 98; ethno-religious ancestry of, 216n35; Jordan managed by, 171–72, 187, 293; as mobster, 96–97, 154
Cohn, Roy, 203–4, 217, 243
Collins, Billy, 270
Collins, Tommy, 251
Colombia, 246
Colorado, 275
color line, 122–23, 129–30, 178
Columbia Broadcast System (CBS), 137–38
Comanches, 55, 56
"Committee for Muhammad Ali," 230
Compitello, Rocky, 135
Communists/Communist Party, 23, 44, 100, 102, 104, 105, 113, 123, 124, 130, 136, 140, 142, 143, 144, 153, 167, 196, 218
concentration camps, 151–52
concussion, of Tunney, 61
Congo (Zaire), 18, 234, 260
congressional testimony, 192
Conn, Billy, 114, 121
Conn, Mark, 135
conservatism, 23–24
Conyers, John, 280
Cooke, Jack Kent, 273
Coolidge, Calvin, 8
Cooney, Gerry, 276–79
Coppola, ("Trigger") Mike, 181
Corbett, James J., 38–39, 47

Cori, Claire, 177
Cornelius, James Anthony, 215
corruption, 16n63; in boxing, 15–17, 66–67, 121–22, 172–73; color line and, 129–30; with gambling, 120–21, 173–74; Jordan admitting bout, 173; in Las Vegas, 290; material incentives for, 141–42; in sports, 36, 139–40
Cortez, Joe, 108
La Cosa Nostra, 216, 287
Cosby, Bill, 260
Cosell, Howard, 228, 235, 259
Costello, Frank, 152–53, 153n70, 300
Coughlin, Jerry, 298
Coxson, Benjamin ("The Maj"), 214
Crawford, Matt, 104
Cribb, Tom, 30
criminal investigations, of King, D., 288
criminal trial, 200
Cristelli, Anthony ("Butch"), 279
Cuba, 33, 85, 109, 146, 156, 157, 171, 201, 207, 208, 227, 248, 252, 295, 304
Cuban Missile Crisis, 201
Curley, Eddie ("Newsboy"), 69–70
Curley, Richard, 39n51
Cvetic, Matt, 196
Czyz, Bobby, 283, 289

Daley, Arthur, 186
d'Alfonso, Frank ("Flowers"), 254, 278, 289
Dalitz, Moe, 15, 19–20, 97, 250–52
Daly, William, 188, 192, 199
D'Amato, Cus, 167, 180–81, 185, 204, 241
Damiani, Francesco, 288
Dana, Charles, 8
Daniels, Billy, 115n38
Daniels, Robert, 299
Davey, Charles, 274
Davidian, Abe, 197
Davidow, Harry, 181
Davis, Al ("Bummy"), 96

Davis, Ben, Jr., 130–31, 153n70
Davis, Harry, 266
Davis, Howard, Jr., 129
Davis, Karl, 102
Davis, Sammy, Jr., 98, 220
Dawson, William, 144
Death by Lynch Law, 41
de Coubertin, Pierre, 58
Deep Throat (film), 289
De Fabis, Mike, 274
defensive strategy, 44–45
de Iuliis, Carlo, 283
De John, John, 170
Delaney, Billy, 93
Delaphonzo, Frankie D., 255
del Giorno, Thomas, 279, 284
democracy, arsenal of, 107, 279–80
Democratic Republic of the Congo, 260
Dempsey, Jack ("Manassa Mauler"), 8, 57, 59, 177, 244; betting coup with, 61; boxing license deferred of, 76; Carpentier fighting, 26; controversy following, 60; negro boxers avoided by, 73; New York bout of, 60–61; Tunney fighting, 62, 64–65; Wills fighting, 12, 74
de Niro, Robert, 242
Denmark, 40, 83
Dennis, Dino, 242
de Paula, Frankie, 214–15, 223
desegregation, 24, 158, 164–66
desperados, 46–47
di Benedetti, Joseph, 71
Dickerson, D. S., 45
Dickerson, Earl, 136–37
Diddley, Bo, 21
Dillinger, John, 200
discrimination, 12–13
Divodi, Andy, 117n47
Dixiecrats, 126
"Dixie Kid," 39
Dixon, George ("Little Chocolate"), 38
Dixon, Tommy, 27n114
Dixon, Willie, 21

Dobbs, Bobby, 31
Doby, Larry, 284
Docusen, Bernard, 13, 152–53
Docusen, Viola Lytel, 13n50
Donavan, Arthur, 89
Don Eagle (Chief), 235
Dorazio, Gus, 115
Dougherty, Margaret, 177
Douglass, Frederick, 4, 37
Doyle, Arthur Conan, 240
Doyle, Jimmy, 122, 122n67
Dragna, Jack, 198
Dragna, Louis, 186
Driscoll, Alfred, 116
Du Bois, W. E. B., 143, 217, 228
du Mole, Jean Baptiste, 13n50
Duncan, Charles, 82
Dundee, Angelo, 147, 259, 271, 299; Ali, M., hiring, 15, 72, 84, 198, 209–10, 244, 280; Ali regime and, 209–10; Carbo, F., comments by, 146; Hamill's request to, 242; Hearns, G., and, 294; Layton in touch with, 243–44; Lockwood briefing, 276; matches judged by, 248–49; transatlantic network of, 245; working his corner, 277
Dundee, Chris, 169, 250, 298; as boxing promoter, 72, 146–47, 271; Carbo, F., knowing, 142; Gibson, T., called by, 194; Negro boxers comment of, 84; Sica linked to, 158, 198–99
Dupas, Ralph, 163
Duran, Roberto, 10, 23, 294
Durden, Elbert ("Duke"), 241
Dutton, Charles, 292
Duva, Dan, 17, 248, 273
Duva, Lou, 249

Earp, Wyatt, 40, 143
Eaton, Aileen, 174
Eboli, Thomas ("Tommy Ryan"), 135, 272, 300
Eckstine, Billy, 115n38
Edwards, Danny, 12

Edwards, Edward, 26
Egan, Pierce, 30
Eisenhower, Dwight D., 155, 165–67
Elentrio, Joseph, 284
Ellis, George, 32
Ellison, Ralph, 50
Empie, Adam, 11, 57
England, 11, 25, 29, 30, 86, 123, 173, 195
Entenza, A. P., 120
Epstein, I. Lawrence, 302
Equiano, Olaudah, 4
"Ethel Johnson," 234
ethnic groups, 211
ethno-centrism, 150–52, 216
ethno-religious ancestry, 55, 86, 216n35, 252
Euro-Americans, 88; African Americans attacked by, 42, 47–48; Johnson, Jack, with women as, 51; Negro boxers and, 49, 122; prostitutes, 46; race and masculinity of, 194
Europe, 39, 164
Evans, Bob, 211n7
Evans, Courtney, 225
Everlast Boxing Record and Blue Book, 72
eye damage, 119

fagnorolahy (violent dance), 3
Fahn, Stanley, 25, 265
Fall, Louis Mbarick. *See* Battling Siki
Falls, Joe, 213
Farley, James, 59, 74, 306
Farrakhan, Louis, 293
fascism, 92–94, 107
fatalities, 56, 150; in boxing, 25n102, 122, 298; spontaneous, 268
Fats' Domino, 217
Feldman, Matthew, 94, 151
Ferrell, Lew, 15
Fickeissen, George A., 148
Fields, Jackie, 7
Fifth Amendment, 179
Fighter of the Year, 212

316 Index

fighting, 5, 5n14, 19, 269–71, 302
Figueroa, Ruben, 211
Filipinos, 9, 13, 88, 103, 272
film revenue, 61
financial problems, 118
Finch, James, 45–46
Fine, David, 70
Firpo, Luis, 60, 67
Fishbaugh, F. M., 63
Fiske, Jack, 277
fist-fighting, 19
Fitzpatrick, Sam, 34
Fitzsimmons, Bob, 47
fixed fights, 66, 129; Attell and, 36; gambling and, 120; from mobsters, 148; Moore agreeing to, 225; Smith, B., in, 117
Flack, Roberta, 216
Fleischer, Nat, 11, 15, 52, 90, 154, 261
Fletcher, Eddie, 70
Florida, 146, 154, 168, 194, 201, 207, 221, 250, 251, 254, 271, 298, 300, 307
Flory, Ishmael, 144
Flowers, Tiger ("Georgia Deacon"), 76, 79–80
Fluellen, Ike, 262
Flynn, Ed, 77
Folley, Zora, 221
food poisoning, 177–78
football, 65n40
Ford, Sammy, 96
Foreman, George, 18, 88, 210n4, 225–26
Fortunato, Buddy, 285
Foster, Bob, 222–23
Fox, Billy, 150, 203
France, 39, 40, 59, 164
Frankfurter, Felix, 185
Franzese, John ("Sonny"), 223, 289
Frawley, Jay, 229
Frazier, Joe, 13, 147, 270, 278; Ali, M., and, 22–23, 225–26, 257; Allen, D., treatment and, 257; boxing and, 6–7, 210n4, 302–3, 302n74; desegregation and, 158; died with few assets, 256; fighter pensions demanded by, 302; Foreman's battle with, 210n4; leaning to right, 227–28; World Boxing Council and, 212
Frazier-Hyde, Jacqui, 304
Friday Night fights, 145
Fried, Leo, 70
Friedman, Robert, 242
Friedman, Walter ("Good Time Charlie"), 50
Friedman, William, 70
Fruit of Islam, 213, 221–22
Fugazy, William Dennis, 204
Fullmer, Gene, 206
Fulton, Fred, 60
fund seizure case, 239

Gabriel, Robert, 254, 278, 285
Gainford, George, 119, 177, 248
Galento, Tony, 148, 224
Gambina, Ralph, 127, 200
Gambino Family, 287
gambling: boxing with heavy, 117–18; corruption with, 120–21, 173–74; fixed fights and, 120
Gans, Joe, 26, 34, 37–38, 40–43, 83
Garabedian, Charles B., 94
Garafola, Anthony ("Gary"), 214–15
Garcia, Ceferino, 88
Garcia, Jesse, 267
Gardener, Kid, 31
Garner, John, 129
Gaskin, George, 119
Gastineau, Mark, 271–72
Gates, Leo, 79
Gavilan, Kid, 135, 157, 192, 227, 248, 295
Gazzara, Ben, 242
Geigerman, Stanley, 153
Geisler, Jerry, 104, 125
Gelb, Frank, 254, 278
gendered theories, 10
Genovese, Gabe, 170
Genovese, Vito, 18, 214
Georgetown University, 62

German, Fred, 118
German gym, 85
Gersh, Ed, 128–29
Getty, J. Paul, 35
Ghana, 165, 166, 259
Giachetti, Richie, 255, 276–77
Giancana, Sam, 145, 196
Giardello, Joey, Jr., 284
Gibbons, Harold, 179
Gibson, Karen, 190
Gibson, Truman, 5–6, 18, 26, 111, 133; antitrust law violation and, 185; bringing down, 191; criminal trial influencing, 200; Dundee, C., calling, 194; Glickman award presented by, 193; as IBC president, 174; indictment of, 146; Jordan witness against, 171; Leonard, J., deals sought by, 192–93; Leonard, J., witness against, 186–87; matchmaking and, 14; mob liaisons of, 91, 149, 159, 175–76; modest salary of, 136–37; negative article about, 162; Negro soldiers and, 114; Norris testifying at trial of, 139; operation linchpin, 198; opportunities for, 82; Palermo and, 174–77; Patterson, F., impressing, 180–81; punishment of, 190; sordid events and, 142; Topping interactions with, 176; traveling abroad, 200; trial of, 169, 174; troubling signs for, 161–62; witnesses reporting, 170
Gibson, William, 65
Gigante, Vincent ("The Chin"), 300
Glaser, Joe, 248
Glickman, Bernard, 171, 193, 213, 221
Godfrey, ("Old Chocolate") George, 78, 91
Godfrey, Hy, 67
Goldberg, Herman. *See* Taylor, ("Muggsy")
Golden Gloves, 20, 98, 131; African Americans participation in, 253; brawling fans at, 207; Negro boxers represented in, 128–29
"Goldfield in Turmoil" headline, 43
"Goldfield Rag" (Blake), 41
Goldstein, Alvin, 186, 189, 195–96
Golota, Andrew, 293
Gordon, Cupie, 69
Gordon, Harry, 68
Gordon, Waxey, 69
Gordy, Berry, 21
"Gorgeous George," 235–36
Gotti, John, 287
Graham, Billy, 135
Graham, Shirley, 130
Granger, Lester, 166
Grant, Bertram, 140
Gravano, Salvatore ("Sammy the Bull"), 17, 287–89
Gray (Mr.), 169–70, 175
Graziano, Rocky, 119, 154, 289
Great Britain, boxing in, 57
Great Depression, 83, 87
The Great Togo, 236
Great White Hope, 163, 166, 223–25, 263, 281; in boxing, 73, 164–65; Cooney as, 276; Gastineau as, 272; Quarry, M., as, 252, 257, 270; tournament to develop, 114; white supremacy and, 50–51
Greb, Harry, 68, 76, 79
Green, Johnny, 36–37
Green, John Wilson, 179n77
Green, Richard, 254
Greenbaum, Gus, 14–15
Greenberg, Benny, 97
Greenberg, Harry, 34
Greyvenstein, Chris, 245–46
Griffith, Emile, 10, 10n41, 205
Grupp, Billy, 68
guilty verdict, 186
Guinan, Joseph, 285
Guinea, 200

Haft, Harry, 151
Hagler, Marvin, 17, 283, 290
Haley, Patsy, 39n51

Hall, James Henry, 258
Halper, Bobby, 272
Halper, Lou, 107
Hamid, George A., 221n56
Hamill, Pete, 242
Hamsho, Mustafa, 283
Hand, Joseph, 278, 289
Hansberry v. Lee, 137
Hare, Nathan, 207
Harlem, 50
Harlem Globetrotters, 152
Harris, Bobby, 70
Harris, ("Gypsy") Joe, 256
Harris, Roy, 168, 194, 199
Hartley, Fred, 129
Harwick, Luis ("Cocoa Kid"), 116
Hastie, William, 137, 145, 162
Haswell, Reg, 244
Haughton, William, 120–21
Haupt, Lewis, 63
Havana, 9, 45, 57, 73, 116, 173, 201
Hawkins, Augustus, 104
Hay, Jack, 76
Hayden, Jimmy, 109
Hays, Arthur Garfield, 157
Haywood, ("Big Bill"), 43
headgear, 303n76
health issues, 268–69
Hearns, Goldie, 294
Hearns, Thomas ("Hitman"), 17, 293, 296
heavyweight champion, 59, 121, 165; Ali, M., and Chuvalo for, 229; interest in, 137; Louis, J., as, 81; mixed race not approved for, 76; Patterson, F., as, 167; revenue increase from, 83; tournaments for, 268; white, 242. *See also* weight class
Hecht, Gerhart, 143
Heege, P. C., 63
Hemingway, Ernest, 34
Hergot, John, 39
Herman, "Kid," 42
Herzog, Chaim, 108n3
Hill, John, 247

Hill, Virgil, 296
Hirschfield, Richard, 215
Hitchcock, Alfred, 100
Hitler, Adolf, 85, 93, 296
HIV/AIDS, 297–98
Hoff, Max ("Boo Boo"), 91
Hoffa, James, 202
Hofheinz, Fred, 21
Hollandersky, Abraham, 68
Hollywood Legion Club, 104–5, 124–25, 192
Holmes, Larry ("The Easton Assassin"), 235, 242; Ali, M.,'s bout with, 254–55, 275–76; brain and stress tests of, 302; Cooney fighting, 279; Holyfield fighting, 248; King, D., difficulties of, 246–47; questionable characters, 278; racism combated by, 276–78; revenue expansion of, 247–48
Holocaust, 151
Holstein, Biff, 291
Holyfield, Evander ("The Real Deal"), 18, 248
homophobia, 10, 205, 205n108, 297
Hope, Bob, 155, 203
Horne, Lena, 144
horse racing, 16n63
Horton, Mary, 234
Hubert, Tee, 129
Hughes, Howard, 253
human rights, 130, 134
Humphrey, Hubert H., 229
Hunt, Sam, 138
Hunter, John, 270

IBC. *See* International Boxing Club
imperialism, of U.S., 81, 130, 247, 293
incarceration, 216n35
Indian Death Lock, 236
IndoChina war, 22
Indrisano, Johhny, 98
International Boxing Club (IBC), 137–38, 157, 162, 174, 185
International Boxing Federation, 303

Index 319

International White Hope Association, 9
interracial ban, 38, 52, 55
Ireland, 108
Irwin, Fred, 97
Islam, Nation of, 6
Israel, 108, 151, 193, 194, 216, 222
Italian Americans, 70, 72, 79–80
Italy, 92, 102, 111, 116
Ivory Coast, 258

Jack, Beau, 3, 3n1, 110–11, 141, 297
Jackson, Michael, 289
Jackson, Peter, 38–39, 84
Jackson, Tommy ("Hurricane"), 167, 223
Jacobs, Joe, 92, 177, 185, 224
Jacobs, Mike, 110–13, 119, 137–38, 158, 162
Japanese Americans, 126
Japan/Japanese, 9, 25, 35, 85, 102, 209, 236, 294
Jarrett, Christine, 274
Jeannette, Joe, 74–75
Jeffries, Jim, 8, 44, 47, 74, 93
Jehovah's Witnesses, 227
Jennings, Harry, 72
Jerome, Frankie, 56
Jewish Americans, 87, 216, 252; anti-Semitism and, 7, 94, 152; Attell's combativeness as, 68–69; bigotry toward, 33–34; boosting of, 151; as boxers, 7, 19, 25, 42; boxers changing names, 152; Green, J., boxing as, 36–37; intimidation of, 67; opportunities for, 79–80; in professional prizefighting, 68–69, 69n55; voting ability of, 70–71
Jim Crow laws, 5–6, 9, 18; boxing after, 14; boxing influenced by, 12–13; desegregation and, 24; Negro boxers and, 125; poll tax and, 113–14; Supreme Court invalidation of, 126, 133; Wallace defending, 20; white supremacy and, 168. See also anti-Jim Crow

Johannesburg, 227, 242–43
Johansson, Ingemar, 164, 181–83
Johnson, Ellsworth ("Bumpy"), 114, 142, 178
Johnson, Harold, 182
Johnson, Jack, 8, 33, 36n37, 83, 251; bigotry fight of, 27–28; Black Militancy and, 207; Black Supremacy fears and, 13; boxing dangers and, 86; defensive strategy by, 44–45; with Euro-American women, 51; exile of, 57; German gym of, 85; Great White Hope and, 50–51; Jeffries brawl with, 74; as musician, 148n53; Negro boxers refused fight with, 74; political exile and, 24; press promotion of, 97; Willard defeating, 9
Johnson, John ("Mushmouth"), 47
Johnson, Lyndon Baines, 22
Johnson, Thomas ("Sarge"), 258
Johnston, James J., Jr., 89
Jolson, Al, 87, 126–27
Jones, Roy, 287
Jones, William ("Gorilla"), 99
Jordan, Don, 26, 169–70, 186, 188; battle for control of, 200; Cohen managing, 171–72, 187, 293; corrupt matched admitted by, 173; witness against Gibson, T., 171
journalists, 74–75
Jungle Boy, 235

Kabakoff, Harry, 188
Kahn, Irving, 181, 194
Kaplan, Hank, 76, 99, 152, 245
Kaplan, Harry, 65
Karpis, Alvin, 200
Katznelson, Abe, 276
Kearns, Jack ("Doc"), 120, 139, 143; Moore and, 199, 225; testimony of, 143n40
Kefauver, Estes, 139, 143, 145, 153, 201

Kelly, Jimmy, 15
Kennedy, Edward, 280
Kennedy, John F., 200
Kennedy, Robert F., 201
Kenny, Robert, 103
Kerkorian, Kerkor ("Kirk"), 18, 20, 186, 188, 292–93
Kerzner, Sol, 242
Kessler, Harry, 88, 96, 139, 166; career of, 19; as Millionaire Referee, 193; as newsboy, 69
Ketchel, Meyer, 34
Kid Chocolate, 109, 295, 304
Kid Norfolk, 78
Kilholm, F. J., 232
Kim, Phil, 127
Kimball, C. H., 62
King, Don, 14, 18, 97, 146; Ali, M., and, 210, 239–40; Arum, B., and, 151, 241–42; background of, 239–40; Birns clashes with, 255–56; boxing and, 250, 261; criminal investigations of, 288; Holmes and difficulties of, 246–47; imprisonment of, 240–41; Negro-phobia criticized by, 299; racially motivated, 241; revenue of, 247; scandal of, 262–63; threats to, 223; of World Boxing Council, 243
King, Martin Luther, Jr., 167, 225
King of the Beasts, 179
King's Cleveland, 19, 250
Kingsland, Bill, 118
Kiniski, Gene, 236
Klein, Allan, 171
Kleinman, Morris, 250
Klingman, ("Tropic") Kenny, 276
Klopper, H. W., 244
Knoetze, Kallie, 246
Korean war, 135
Koverly, George, 102
Kram, Mark, 288
Kuhlmann, Wolfgang, 245
Ku Klux Klan, 67, 91
Kushner, Cedric, 245

labor unions, 43–44, 199, 307; AAU, 128, 131; Motion Picture Operators Union, 61n25
Lamar, Henry, 296–97
La Motta, Jake, 142, 153, 203
Lanauze, Henry, 13n50
Lane, Franklin K., 58
Lane, Mills, 271–72, 279
Langford, Sam, 12, 40, 52, 74–75, 179
Lansky, Meyer, 150, 251, 254
Lardner, John, 8, 50, 74
Larkin, Tippy, 110
Las Vegas, 251, 290
law enforcement, 97
Layton, Reg, 243–44
LCN. *See* La Cosa Nostra
Lebrowitz, Barney, 66
Lederman, Harold, 248
Ledoux, Scott, 277
Lee, Bob, 18, 280, 283, 286
Lee, Canada, 100–101, 105
Lee, Curley, 270
Lee, Robert W., 267
Lefkowitz, Louis, 167
legal graft, 226
legislative bill, 131
Leo, Lorraine, 144
Leo, William, 144
Leonard, Benny, 7, 107, 108n3, 151; high esteem of, 94; as Jewish-American boxer, 25; Tendler bout with, 67
Leonard, Jack, 169–70, 186–87, 191–93, 196–97
Leonard, ("Sugar") Ray, 10, 293
Lepke, Louis, 154
Levene, Harry, 194
Levey, Dave, 148
Levey, Stan, 147
Levy, Robert, 78
Lewis, Butch, 280
Lewis, Joey, 176
Lewis, John Henry, 97, 119, 148
Lewis, Lennox, 271
Liberia, 100, 104
Licari, Andrew, 283, 289

lightweight championship, 41
lily-white affair, 131
Lindsay, Donell, 298
Lindsay, Gil, 104
Lindsay, John V., 305
Lippe, Al, 39
Liston, Sonny, 146, 191; Ali, M., battles with, 220; Ali regime and, 212–13; as Bad Negro, 202; bargaining power of, 195; boxing license denied, 306; conservatism and, 23–24; as King of Beasts, 179; Mann, A., comments on, 204; mobster ties to, 19–20, 178–80, 220; Palermo and, 193; Patterson, F., fight with, 203–4, 211n7; racketeers flocking to, 219; victory of, 205
Little Wolf (Chief), 236
loansharking, 279
Lockwood, Norman, 276
Logart, Isaac, 171
Lombardo, Carl, 250
London, Jack, 40–43
Lone Eagle (Chief), 237
Lopes, Louis, 103
Lopez, Danny ("Little Red"), 273
Lord, W. Leighton, III, 289
Losch, Steve, 173
Loubet, Nat, 261
Louis, Joe ("Brown Bomber"), 6, 13, 18, 114–16; Baer battle with, 85; Carnera boxing, 21–22, 91–92, 102; as folk-hero, 81–82, 111; as heavyweight champion, 81; Horne's leg broken by, 144; married well, 202; politics interest of, 23; retirement return of, 134; Schmeling knocked out by, 224; taxation of, 97–98, 202
Louis, Kenny, 291
Louis, Martha, 202
lower weight class, 156
Lucas, Frank, 115, 202, 257
Lucas, Van C., 11
Luciano, Charles ("Lucky"), 115
Lumumba, Patrice, 260

Lurie, Art, 220
Lynch Law, 37, 41

Machado, Victor, 269
Machen, Eddie, 270
Madagascar, 4
Madam Bey, 99–100
Madden, Owney, 99, 197
Madison Square Garden, 26, 135–36, 174; Jacobs, J., interest in, 185; revenue generated from, 228; violence at, 304
Mailer, Norman, 213, 240, 260
Malcolm X, 115n38, 213
Maldonado, G. G., 246
managerial contract, 87
Mandela, Nelson, 21
Mangho, Olivia, 234
Manila, 212, 257, 295
Mann, Arthur, 25, 63–64, 271; Liston fight comments of, 204; parasitical management and, 90; suburban fight clubs from, 163; win and loss records from, 173
Mann, Clyde, 45–46
Mantle, Mickey, 248
Mantor, Tom, 32
Mara, Tim, 65, 65n40, 93
Marciano, Rocky, 24, 73, 183; Moore bout with, 19, 166; plane crash killing, 15; Walcott fight with, 155
Margolis, Sam, 180
Marquess of Queensberry, 44
Marshall, Sammie, 265–66
Martin, Harry, 172
Martinez, Bob, 298
Marx, Karl, 240
Mascia, Pat, 305
masculinity, 10, 10n39, 47, 58, 194, 235
Masters, Viola, 174
Masterson, Bat, 45, 56
matchmaking, 14
Mathis, Buster, 270
Mathison, Charles, 39n51
Mauritius, 4

Maxim, Joey, 143, 199
Maxim, Moore-Joey, 19
Maxvill, Dal, 274
Mayweather, Floyd ("Money"), Jr., 18, 262
McBeth, Hugh, 104
McCain, John, 302
McCall, Oliver, 271
McCarthy, Joseph, 144, 203
McCarthy, Luther, 51
McCarthy, Raymond J., 168
McCoy, Babe, 182
McCoy, Jackie, 170
McDaniels, Jimmie, 126–27
McDevitt, Harry, 149
McGirt, Buddy, 288
McLaglen, Victor, 100
McTigue, Michael, 67
McVey, Sam, 74
Mead, Eddie, 88, 126–27
Meadows, Sammy ("Kid"), 86
Medina, Roberto, 291
Menendez, Gabe, 128
mental illness, 270–71
Meredith, Burgess, 273
Mexico, 9, 24, 25, 40, 52, 75, 76, 99, 110, 116, 122, 188, 198, 225, 234, 252, 267, 296
Mexico City Olympics, 225
Meyer, Eugene, 131
military conscription, 209
military facilities, 116
Miller, Doug ("Duggie"), 280
Miller, Loren, 104
Milligan, Bowman, 3
Millionaire Referee, 193
Ming, William, 26, 174, 189–90
mining camps, 42–43
Minnesota, 230–32, 265, 267, 298
Minuto, Lenny, 289
Miramontes, Felix, 122
Mirena, Cristofo, 72
miscegenation, 48
Mitchell, Arthur, 77
Mitchell, Frank, 179
Mitchell, L. R., 229

mobsters: in boxing, 5–6, 14–15, 14n53, 99, 145; Carbo, F., ties with, 198; Cohen as, 96–97, 154; fixed fights from, 148; Gibson, T., liaisons with, 91, 149, 159, 175–76; Hollywood Legion involving, 192; inner workings of, 154; Liston's ties to, 19–20, 178–80, 220; Mead in with, 126–27; Walcott, Jersey, used by, 155, 214; Williams, I, used by, 141–42
Mobutu, Joseph, 260
Mohr, Charlie, 305
Mokhtefi, Elaine, 205–7
Molineaux, Thomas, 30, 30n6
Mondale, Walter, 229
Montague, Victor, 57
Montreal Olympics, 264
Moolman, Eric, 281
Moore, Archie ("The Mongoose"), 22, 24, 114, 126, 203; boxing license for, 109; fixed fights agreement of, 225; Kearns and, 199, 225; as light heavyweight, 143; Marciano bout with, 19, 166; republicans praising, 227
Moran, Edmund, 170
Moriarty, John, 296
Morori, Anthony, 246
Moscow, 51, 52, 101, 130, 165, 166, 241, 258, 263, 264
Moscow Olympics, 263
Mosley, ("Sugar") Shane, 245
Motion Picture Operators Union, 61n25
Motley, Marion, 124
Moyer, Denny, 187
Mozambique, 281
Mugabi, John, 259
Muhammad, Elijah, 218, 221
Muhammad, Herbert, 221
Muhammad, Murad, 223
Muhammad Ali Boxing Reform Act (2000), 302
Muhammad Ali Professional Sports, Inc., 215

Mullins, Paddy, 76
murder charges, 270
musicians, 148n53
Muslim violence, 213

NAACP. *See* National Association for the Advancement of Colored People
Namibia, 259, 281
Napoli, James ("Jimmy Nap"), 214
Nash, Phileo, 144
National Association for the Advancement of Colored People (NAACP), 217
National Golden Gloves tournament, 128–29
Nation of Islam, 217, 256
Native Americans, 103, 114, 235–37
Navajo, 9, 248
Negro boxers, 245; all-Negro matchups in, 158; boxing licenses of, 103–4; boxing representation of, 124–25; box office draw and, 83–84; capital accumulated by, 77; Caucasian race and menace of, 8–9; Dempsey avoiding, 73; desegregation and, 158; discrimination experienced by, 12–13; Dundee, C., comment on, 84; Euro-Americans fighting, 49, 122; Golden Gloves representation of, 128–29; Jacobs, M., avoiding, 113; Jim Crow laws and, 125; Johnson, Jack, fight blocked to, 74; lower weight class opportunities of, 156; Overton objecting to, 128; parasitical management and, 90; political prices paid by, 23–24; racism influencing, 19; ring names changes of, 95–96; ruling race battered by, 133–34; success duplication for, 105; television revenue for, 133–34, 162; uncertain fates of, 101; weight class and, 81; white supremacy and, 37–38, 113; yellow streak and, 47, 84
Negro Communists, 130
Negro-phobia, 299
Negro Restoration, 165, 182–83
Nelson, Oscar ("Battling"), 40–43
neoliberalism, 16
Nesline, Joe, 222
Nesseth, Donald Paul, 187–88
Netro, Joe, 170
Neumann, Randy, 286
Nevada: African Americans in, 31–32; boxing in, 32–33; desperados attracted to, 46–47; prizefighting in, 42, 48, 55–56; prostitution in, 45–46; Roosevelt, T., sending troops to, 44
Nevis, 156
New Jersey, 26, 60, 66, 67, 75, 94, 100, 116, 129, 134, 151, 154, 155, 162, 168, 180, 188, 206, 214, 215, 221, 222, 247, 249, 254, 267, 275, 281, 283–87, 302
newspaper men, 15
New York, 60–61, 80
New York fight market, 112
New York State Athletic Commission (NYSAC), 15, 55–58, 75–76, 80, 86
Nicholas (Czar), 51
Nilon, Jack, 179
Nilon, John, 249
Nixon, Richard M., 22, 147, 207, 227
Nizer, Louis, 239
Non-Sectarian Anti-Nazi League, 93
Noriega, Manuel, 23
Norris, Jim, 14, 115, 137–39, 153, 169, 174–78
Norton, Ken, 277, 290
Notre Dame, 162–63, 166
Numbers King, 150
NYSAC. *See* New York State Athletic Commission

Oates, Joyce Carol, 24
O'Brien, Jack, 52

October Crisis (1962), 201
Oddie, Tasker, 49
O'Dwyer, Paul, 248
O'Hara, Jim, 292
oil embargo, 222
Olson, Culbert, 103
Olympic Auditorium, 126
Olympics, 164, 225, 256, 263–64
O'Neal, Ryan, 255
organized crime, 216, 262
O'Shea, Brian, 231–32
O'Toole, Jack, 96
Overton, John, 128

Pacheco, Ferdie ("Fight Doctor"), 146–47, 158, 203
Paige, Satchel, 198
Paiutes, 67
Palermo, Frank ("Blinky"), 14, 140–41, 146; aggravated assault sentence of, 149; Braverman disciple of, 255; bribery by, 192; Cristelli consulting with, 279; Gibson, T., and, 176–77; guilty verdict of, 186, 190; Liston and, 193; as Numbers King, 150; petty theft by, 197; trial of, 169
Palmer, Kenneth, 267
Palumbo, Frankie, 150
parasitical management, 90
Paret, Benny, 10, 205
Parker, Rick, 271–72
Parkinson disease, 265
Parkinsonian Syndrome, 25
Parsons, Louella, 172
Parsons, Russell, 200
partisan politics, 12
Patterson, Floyd, 24; Ali, M., fight with, 219; Chuvalo's fight with, 219; competitors to, 181; Gibson, T., impressed by, 180–81; as Good Negro, 201–2; Harris, R., bout with, 199; as heavyweight champion, 167; Johansson slugfest with, 182; legal graft and, 226; Liston's fight with, 203–4, 211n7; Negro Restoration from, 165
Patterson, William, 130
pay-perview television, 210, 248
Peacock, Billy ("Sweetpea"), 182
Pegler, Westbrook, 91
Pelkey, Arthur, 51
Pelton, Jerry, 117n47
Peltz, J. Russell, 269
Pension Plan for Fighters, 306
Pep, Willie, 157
Perez, Anthony, 265
Perlman, Clifford, 254
Perón, Juan, 24
petty theft, 197
Philadelphia, 6, 22, 52, 61, 63, 68, 71, 91, 96, 141, 142, 147–50, 168, 169, 173, 178, 214, 220, 225, 227, 228, 254–56, 269, 275, 278, 279, 284–86, 289
physical toll, 24–25, 27, 27n114, 269
Pickens, William, 85
Pinchot, Gifford, 62, 71
plantation slavery, 4
Podell, Leo, 27n114
Poitier, Sidney, 115n38, 260
Poland, 36, 70, 120, 153, 206, 294
Poland, Bill, 120
Polis, Bob, 304
Polis, Carol, 304
politics, 12, 20–24, 249
poll taxes, 113–14
Portnoff, Alex, 107
Powell, Adam Clayton, Jr., 79
press promotion, 97
Prince Maiva (Samoan Chief), 234
prizefighting: Ali, M., promotion of, 223–24; battle royals, 3, 3n1, 110–11; championships bought in, 112; in Europe, 39; interracial ban sought in, 37–38, 52, 55; Jewish Americans in professional, 68–69, 69n55; legalization of, 37, 73; in Nevada, 42, 48, 55–56; ring names changed in, 94–96
professional fighter, 187–88

profits, racism and, 72–73
prosecution witness, 191
prostitution, 45–46
Pryor, Aaron ("The Hawk"), 27, 273
Puerto Ricans, 211–12
Puerto Rico, 33, 211, 212, 241, 252, 295
punch drunk, from boxing, 25, 64–65, 270–71

Quarry, Jerry, 223, 249, 257
Quarry, Mike, 211, 252
queers, 205n108
Quihuis, Mike, 233

Rabb, Maurice, 217
race battle, 53
racism, 40, 253, 265, 281–82; African Americans protests against, 104; boxing between white men and, 48–49; championship for white race and, 84–85; Gibson, T., facing, 143–44; heavyweight bout not approved from, 76; Holmes, L., combating, 276–78; Motley facing, 124; Negro boxers influenced by, 19; profits and, 72–73; ruling race and, 133–34; war because of, 277–78. *See also* color line
racist socialism, 42–43
racketeers, 180, 201, 284–86; act against, 189; boxing and, 15, 97; Liston and, 219
Rademacher, Pete, 165
radio revenue, 84
Raft, George, 87, 127, 197
A Raisin in the Sun (play), 144
Ramos, Louis, 295
Raphael, Otto, 33
Ratner, Marc, 239
Ray, Terry, 299
Reagan, Ronald W., 22, 226, 261
Reagan Revolution, 274
Reed, Ishmael, 210, 215, 235
Reeves, Bass, 30–31

regulators, 111, 206, 210–11; anti-racists and, 90; revenues less for, 108; wagering and, 212; Walcott, Jersey, as, 285
Reich, John, 296
Reid, Harry, 21
Reisler, John, 53
religious war, 225
Resnick, Ash, 202
Resorts International, 254
revenue: of Arum, B., and King, D., 247; from boxing, 61, 72, 84, 210–11; film, 61; heavyweight champion increased, 83; Holmes, L., expanding, 247–48; of King, D., 247; Madison Square Garden generating, 228; Negro boxer's television, 133–34, 162; radio, 84; for regulators, 108; tax, 65, 82–83; television, 176
Riasco, Rigoberto, 272
Rice, Ricky, 292
Richards, Derwin, 287
Rickard, Tex, 26, 61, 74–76, 111, 142, 261
Rickover, Hyman, 35
The Ring (record book), 173, 212, 223, 261, 288
ring names, changes in, 94–96
riots, 102, 134
Rizzo, Frank, 22, 228, 257
Rizzuto, Phil, 248
Robeson, Paul, 23, 130, 143, 217
Robinson, Bill ("Bojangles"), 103
Robinson, Jackie, 202
Robinson, J. G., 71
Robinson, ("Sugar") Ray, 13, 108, 112; Armstrong, H., fighting, 127; Basilio fight with, 194; bribe offered to, 119; flying fear of, 145; Jacobs, J., lawsuit against, 177; Johannesburg fight of, 227; as musician, 148n53; as scrupulous boxer, 157; Turpin fighting, 134; white champion and, 164–65
Rockefeller, Nelson A., 226

Rockne, Knute, 162, 166
Rocky (film), 273
Rodel, ("Boer"), 243
Roderick, Ernie, 119
Rogers, Buddy, 236
Rogers, McKinley, Jr., 258
Rolvaag, Karl, 231
Rome Olympics, 164
Rommel, Sam, 197
Rooney, Art, 65n40
Roosevelt, Archie, 60
Roosevelt, Eleanor, 123
Roosevelt, Kermit, 60
Roosevelt, Theodore, 8, 20, 33, 44, 124
Root, Elihu, 60
rope-a-dope tactic, 5, 224, 260
Roselli, John, 180, 180n85
Rosen, ("Nigger"), 150, 153
Rosenbloom, ("Slapsie") Maxie, 79, 99
Rosensohn, Bill, 182
Ross, Barney, 35
Roth, Abe, 109
Rothstein, Arnold, 69
Roxborough, John, 92, 111, 114, 116
Rozallia, Larry, 272
ruling race, 133–34
rumble phrase, 213n16
Runyan, Damon, 101, 110
Russia, 24
Rutkin, ("Niggy"), 154
Ryan, Clarence, 206
Ryan, Tommy, 272

Saddler, Sandy, 156–57, 156n86
Salerno, ("Fat Tony"), 181
Salkeld, Alfred Tex, 125
Salow, Morris ("Mushky"), 223
Sandell, Al, 117
Sanders, Barefoot, 229
Saperstein, Abe, 152
Sarkis, Raymond, 179–80
Savold, Lee, 188
Sawyer, Grant, 20
Saxton, Johnny, 271

Scaraggio, Frank, 285
Scarfo, Nicodemo ("Nicky"), 254, 279, 283
Schacter, Harry, 139
schizophrenia, 270
Schmeling, Max, 92–94, 111, 111n21, 224
Schulberg, Budd, 162, 178
Schultz, Dutch, 69
Schwarzkopf, Norman, 296
Scionti, Mike, 299
Seales, ("Sugar") Ray, 297, 303
Segal, Harry ("Champ"), 34–35
segregation, in boxing, 37–38
Sekgapane, Norman ("Pangaman"), 246
Selective Service Act, 83
self-defense, of women, 4–5
Seligson, Lou, 104
Senegal, 78
Sennett, Gene, 78
settler colonialism, 243, 260
Shapiro, Barry, 283
Shavers, Ernie, 278–79
Shaw, Daniel, 103
Shenker, Morris, 171, 193
Sherman Antitrust Act, 186
Shub, Leon, 129
Sica, Joe, 186, 198–99
Sicilian Americans, 216
Siegel, Ben ("Bugsy"), 34, 69, 88, 96, 192; Carbo, F., selected by, 139; death of, 150
Siegel, Nate, 86
Sierra Leone, 200
Siki, ("Sweet Daddy"), 236
Silva, Albert Morales, 122
Silverman, Sam, 195, 195n59
Silverstein, Albert, 35
Simmons, Ernest, 121
Sims, William Sowden, 11, 58
Sinatra, Frank, 145, 172, 188, 196, 289
Singer, Izzy, 51
Singh, Jagat, 236
Sirica, John, 20, 59

Skelly, Jack, 37
Sklar, Irving, 193
slavery plantations, 4
Smith, ("Gunboat"), 50, 52
Smith, Billy, 116–17
Smith, Gerald L. K., 23, 123
Smith, Harold ('Rossfields'), 215, 265, 291
Smith, Herbert, 124
Smith, Johnny ("Ace"), 291–92
Smith, Phil, 210n4
Smith, Wendell, 5
Smith Act, 196
Snipes, Renaldo, 281, 287
Soto, Pedro, 252
South Africa, 206, 226, 243, 245, 264, 279–81
South African National Boxing Control Board, 244
Soviet Union, 101, 123, 263, 264
Sparks, John, 43
Spaw, Warren Wayland. *See* McCoy, Jackie
Spence, Jim, 288
Spilotro, Tony, 14, 15n56
Spinks, Leon, 280
Spinks, Michael, 280
Spoldi, Aldo, 164
spontaneous death, 268
Spoon, Maxie, 7
sports: antitrust rules in, 145–46; boxing abolishment in, 49–50; boxing as unsanitary, 25–26; corruption in, 36, 139–40; desegregation in, 164; Sherman Antitrust Act and, 186
Spota, Luis, 218
Stallone, Frank, 293
Stallone, Sylvester, 264, 273
Stanley, ("Sailor Joe"), 182
Stanley, Frank L., 217
Star of David, 67, 86, 94, 120, 216
State Athletic Commission, 12, 52, 72, 104–5, 125
Steele, Richard, 254
Stein, Andrew, 248

Steindler, Howie, 273
Stevens, Marvin A., 27n114
Steward, Emmanuel, 213, 291
Stillman, Lou, 68
St. Nicholas Arena, 26
Stolz, Allie, 110
Strenlinger, Seth, 105
stress tests, 302
Strong, William, 186
structural barriers, 114
suburban fight clubs, 163
Sudan, 200
Sugar, Bert, 25, 261, 263, 273
Sulaiman, Jose, 249, 290
Sullivan, Ed, 248
Sullivan, John L., 38, 47, 73
Supreme Court, 126, 133, 185
Supreme Life (Negro business), 189
Susman, Morton, 229, 230n97
Sussman, Jeffrey, 36
Sutton, Percy, 305
Swanson, Ryan, 33
Swaziland, 259
Swaziland exhibition, 259
systematic exclusion, 189

Taccetta, Martin, 284
Taft, William H., 8
Tallarita, Vito, 173, 276
taxation, of Louis, J., 97–98, 202
tax revenue, 65, 82–83
Taylor, ("Muggsy"), 150
Taylor, Bud, 56
Taylor, Guy, 232
Taylor, Meldrick, 291
Teamsters union, 199, 307
Technical Knockout (TKO), 194
television, 161; boxing on, 145; closed-circuit, 219, 266; Negro boxers revenue from, 133–34, 162; pay-perview via, 210, 248; revenues, 176; suburban fight clubs emptied by, 163; title match promoted for, 134
Tendler, Lew, 67, 96
Tennenbaum, Sam, 34

Tenny, Harry, 34
Terrell, Ernie, 213, 221, 221n56, 233
Testa, Philip, 254
theatrical aspect, 233
theft, petty, 197
Thembu, Theo, 246
Theseus (King of Athens), 29
Things Fall Apart (African novel), 21
Thomas, Buddy, 118
Thomas, George, 51
Thomas, Otis, 148
Thompson, Fred, 287
Thompson, George, 121
Thompson, Gloria, 4
Tiger, Dick, 211, 222, 259
Tillisch, Jan H., 231
TKO. *See* Technical Knockout
Tobias, George, 141
Tokyo Olympics (1964), 256
Tompkins, L. H., 116
Tonawanda, Jackie, 304
Topping, Dan, 176
Torres, José, 211, 241, 248
Torrijos, Omar, 294
tough man contests, 268
Tourine, ("Charlie the Blade"), 18, 222
Townsend, Alan, 17
trail, elongated, 191
Traitz, Steve, 284
transatlantic network, 245
Trump, Donald J., 17–18, 20
tuberculosis, 26–27
Tunney, Gene, 56, 61–66, 123–24, 180; heavyweight fighter desire of, 59; horizons expanding for, 101–2; Jacobs, M., observation by, 112; newspaper men and, 15; Smith, G., cooperation of, 23
Turner, Joe, 128
Turner, Leo, 125
Turpin, Randy, 122, 134
Tyson, Mike, 250, 290, 292, 299

Uganda, 259
Unger, Mike, 254–55
Unholz, Rudy ("Boer"), 243
United States (U.S.): anti-fascist activists in, 93; anti-Semitism in, 152; boxing fatalities in, 25n102; imperialism of, 81, 130, 247, 293; Silverman's relationship of, 195n59; slugger kayos in, 164
urban eruption, 228–29
U.S. *See* United States

Vacco, Dennis, 301
Vaillant, Doug, 147, 208
Valenzano, Frank, 262
Vanderbilt, William K., 60
Vann, Robert, 71
Vargas, Reuben, 128
Vega, Alex, 109
Verne, Joseph, 284
Vietnam, 208, 229, 257
violence, 97, 169, 304
violent dance (fagnorolahy), 3
Vitale, John, 178–80, 179n77
von Erich, Waldo, 236

Waddles, Tony, 287
wagering, regulators and, 212
Walcott, Joe (Barbados), 38, 113
Walcott, Joe (Jersey), 38, 236; Auletto fighting, 279; Charles battling, 65n40, 134, 158; disqualification of, 39; Marciano fight with, 155; mob using, 155, 214; as regulator, 285
Walker, Jimmy, 74, 141n31
Walker, Lacey, 267–68
Walker, Mickey, 143
Walker, Sidney. *See* Jack, Beau
Walker Law, 305
Wallace, Coley, 119n52
Wallace, George, 20, 23, 206
Wallace, Henry, 142, 217
Wallman, Hymie ("The Mink"), 140
Warner, Ralph, 164
Warren, Earl, 120, 126, 131
Watergate scandal, 208, 287
Watson, Everett, 111
Watson, V. P., 118

WBA. *See* World Boxing Association
Weeks, Freddie, 42
weight class, 81, 156, 267
Weill, Al, 144, 168, 249, 272
Weinstein, Theodore, 77
Weir, George, 232
Weisman, Max, 153
Weiss, Vic, 273
Weldon, Kenny, 262
Welensky, Roy, 206
Welles, Orson, 100
Wepner, Chuck ("The Bayonne Bleeder"), 214, 264–65, 281, 285
Werblin, Sonny, 262
Wergeles, Charles, 111
West, Mae, 98–99, 153
Westmoreland, Marvin, 231–32
Wharf Rats, 87
White, Byron ("Whizzer"), 196
White, Jimmy, 171
White, Tommy, 101
White, Tyree, 109
White, Walter, 128
White Hope Boxing Tournament, 114
White House, 229
whiteness, 77, 84–85
white slave traffic, 45, 51
white supremacy, 49, 81, 123, 131; against African Americans, 41, 110; anti-Jim Crow movement and, 168; Great White Hope sought by, 50–51; Negro boxers and, 37–38, 113
white *vs.* black matchup, 277–78
Whitfield, Mel, 263
Wilder, Deontay, 298
Wilkerson, ("Hollywood Godfather"), 98
Wilkins, Roy, 16, 218
Willard, Jess, 9, 45, 57, 59–60, 75
Williams, Cleveland, 19, 215, 270
Williams, Holman, 109
Williams, Ike, 141–42, 149, 191–92
Williams, James, 71

Wills, Harry, 12, 67, 74, 77
Wilson, Woodrow, 58
Winchell, Walter, 155
Winter, Robert, 231
Wipperman, Dick, 216
Wirtz, Arthur, 14, 115, 137–38, 174, 176
Wirtz, Norris, 174
Witherspoon, Tim, 250
The Wizard of Oz (film), 220
Womack, Ricky, 291
Womber, Danny ("Bang Bang"), 248
women: in boxing, 226, 304; Euro-American, 51; liberation of, 304; Marshall, S., planning show with, 266; self-defense of, 4–5; in wrestling, 226n85, 234
World Boxing Association (WBA), 218, 231, 240, 243–44
World Boxing Council, 240, 243
wrestling, 29, 102, 136, 236–37; battle royal, 83; professional, 232; tax collection from, 82–83; theatrical aspect of, 233; women in, 226n85, 234
Wright, ("Bearcat"), 236
Wright, ("Chalky"), 99, 101, 221
Wright, Bruce, 226
Wright, Ronald ("Winky"), 27
Wynn, Steve, 288

Yardley, Jonathan, 73
Yawitz, Eddie, 171, 273–74
yellow streak, 47, 84
Yom Dong Kyun, 272
Young, Andrew, 263
Young, Jimmy, 277–78, 285, 290

Zabala, Felix ("Tuto"), 276
Zambia, 259
Ziccardi, James, 168
Zimbabwe, 206, 259
Zulu Kid (boxer), 18–19
Zwillman, Abner ("Longie"), 107, 154